CONTROLLER'S GUIDE

TO PLANNING AND CONTROLLING OPERATIONS

CONTROLLER'S GUIDE

TO PLANNING AND CONTROLLING OPERATIONS

STEVEN M. BRAGG

WILEY

JOHN WILEY & SONS, INC.

Published by John Wiley & Sons, Inc., Hoboken, New Jersey

Published simultaneously in Canada

The chapters in this book first appeared in *Controllership: The Work of the Managerial Accountant, 7th edition,* Janice M. Roehl-Anderson and Steven M. Bragg, John Wiley & Sons, 2004.

For general information on our other products and services, or technical support, please contact our Customer Care Department within the United States at 800-762-2974, outside the United States at 317-572-3993 or fax 317-572-4002.

Wiley also publishes its books in a variety of electronic formats. Some content that appears in print may not be available in electronic books.

For more information about Wiley products, visit our web site at www.wiley.com.

Library of Congress Cataloging-in-Publication Data

Bragg, Steven M.
    Controller's guide to planning and controlling operations/Steven M. Bragg.
      p. cm.
    Includes index.
    ISBN 0-471-57680-8 (cloth)
     1. Controllership--Handbooks, manuals etc. 2. Business planning--Handbooks, manuals, etc. I. Title.
    HG4027.3.B7 2004
    658.4'013--dc22

                                                    2003063152

Printed in the United States of America

10 9 8 7 6 5 4 3 2 1

PREFACE

Though many companies can devise reasonable strategies, few are able to follow through on them due to a lack of ability in the areas of planning and control. If operations throughout a company are not run through a detailed planning and control process on a regular basis, it is quite likely that the corporate direction will eventually become less focused, resulting in reduced levels of profitability. Further, a missing planning and control function yields less attention to costs, so that expenses gradually increase out of proportion to sales levels, leading to reduced profits. This crucial area of corporate expertise falls squarely within the realm of the controller, who can make a major contribution to the well-being of the corporation by enhancing his or her level of skill in planning and controlling a variety of company functions. *A Controller's Guide to Planning and Controlling Operations* fills that need by describing key planning and control activities in every major area of the company, ranging from sales and manufacturing to the management of cash, receivables, and inventory.

The book places particular emphasis on the need for budgeting and the proper construction of budgeting models in every chapter, so one can devise a coherent framework of financial plans that can subsequently be used as the basis for ongoing corporate control systems. The book provides valuable information not just about the mechanics of budget creation, but also how to determine if the budget is reasonable, based on a variety of ratios, historical trends, capacity planning, staffing levels, and relationships with other parts of the budget model. This additional budgeting analysis typically is the difference between a usable budget model and one that has little basis in reality.

Each chapter also notes the types of controls needed that are unique to each functional area, and their impact on corporate results. This practical controls advice allows the controller to determine the appropriate mix of controls needed to ensure that operational results stay within expected boundaries, or at least that significant variations are promptly spotted.

Chapter One reveals the proper role of standards, how they may be set and by whom, and why they are so useful in controlling operations. Chapters Two and Three address the planning and control of the sales and marketing functions, including the analysis of sales, forecasting techniques, setting sales and marketing standards, and determining product pricing levels. Chapters Four and Five cover manufacturing—planning for direct material and direct labor costs and standard setting, as well as coverage of fixed and variable expenses, activity-based costing, and overhead allocation techniques. Chapter Six describes the unique characteristics of the research and development area, noting such points as budget formulation, project selection, and how this key area impacts corporate earnings. Chapter Seven completes the review of all key functional areas by addresses general and administrative expenses—its primary components, how to budget for them, and what control systems can be used thereafter.

The book then shifts to the planning and control of a number of key asset, liability and equity areas. Chapter Eight describes the extreme importance of cash management and the role of the case forecast in that effort, as well as how to control cash levels and invest them on a short-term basis. Chapter Nine describes how to create a budgeting model for accounts receivable, while also addressing the key control areas of granting customer credit and conducting collection activities. Chapter Ten describes a number of budgets that must be created for the proper planning of inventory, while also noting the impact on inventory of just-in-time and material requirements planning systems. Chapter Eleven describes the capital budgeting process, how to evaluate capital projects, the methods available for doing so, and how to monitor their progress. Chapter Twelve shows how to measure and control liabilities, determine the proper level of debt, and how to build a liabilities budget. Finally, Chapter Thirteen describes earnings per share, how to calculate the cost of capital, the considerations involved in issuing dividends, and how to plan for the correct equity level.

In short, this book improves the controller's toolkit of planning and control techniques with practical advise on the creation of usable budget models and in-depth discussions of the controls needed to ensure proper compliance with those budgets.

Steven M. Bragg
Centennial, Colorado
February 2004

ACKNOWLEDGMENTS

Creating new ideas for books is one of the hardest parts of writing, involving a good grasp of the marketplace, competing offerings, and emerging accounting practices. Every concept Sheck Cho has come up with has been a winner. Thank you, Sheck!

CONTENTS

1

GENERAL DISCUSSION OF ACCOUNTING/STATISTICAL STANDARDS: BENCHMARKING

MEANING OF ACCOUNTING/STATISTICAL CONTROL

Control by definition assumes that a plan of action or a standard has been established against which performance can be measured. To achieve the objectives that have been set forth for the business enterprise, controls must be developed so that decisions can be made in conformance with the plan.

In small plants or organizations, the manager or owner personally can observe and control all operations. The owner or manager normally knows all the factory workers and by daily observation of the work flow can determine the efficiency of operations. It is easy to observe the production effort of each employee as well as the level of raw materials and work-in-process inventory. In most cases, by the observation of the factory operation, inefficiencies or improper methods can be detected and corrected on the spot. The sales orders can be reviewed and determinations made about whether shipments are being made promptly. Through intimate knowledge of the total business and communicating on a daily basis with most employees and customers, the owner is able to discern the effectiveness of sales effort and customer satisfaction with the products.

However, as the organization grows, this close contact or direct supervision by the owner or manager is necessarily diminished. Other means of control are required to manage effectively, such as accounting controls and statistical reports. By the use of reports, management is enabled to plan, supervise, direct, evaluate, and coordinate the activities of the various functions, departments, and operating units. Accounting controls and reports of operations are part of a well-integrated plan to maintain efficiency and determine unfavorable variances or trends. The use of the accounting structure allows for the control of costs and expenses and comparison of such expenditures to some predetermined plan of action. Through the measurement of performance by means of accounting and statistical records and reports, management can provide appropriate guidance and direct the business activities. The effective application of accounting controls must be fully integrated into the company plans and provide a degree of before-the-fact control. The accounting/statistical control system must include records that establish accountability and responsibility to really be effective.

EXTENT OF ACCOUNTING/STATISTICAL CONTROL

Effective control extends to every operation of the business, including every unit, every function, every department, every territory or area, and every individual. Accounting control encompasses all aspects of financial transactions such as cash disbursements, cash receipts, funds flow, judicious investment of cash, and protection of the funds from unauthorized use. It includes control of receivables and avoidance of losses through inappropriate credit and collection procedures. Accounting control includes planning and controlling inventories, preventing disruption of production schedules and shipments or losses from scrap and obsolescence. It involves generating all the necessary facts on the performance of all functions such as manufacturing, research, engineering, marketing, and financial activities. It is mandatory that management be informed about the utilization of labor and material against a plan in producing the finished goods. The effectiveness of the sales effort in each territory or for each product must be subjected to review by management. Control relates to every classification in the balance sheet or statement of financial position and to each item in the statement of income and expense. In short, accounting/statistical control extends to all activities of the business. The accounting system that includes the accounting controls when integrated with the operating controls provides a powerful tool for management to plan and direct the performance of the business enterprise.

Statistical control also may relate to the nonfinancial quantitative measurement of any business functions and their effect, for example, customer satisfaction, development time for new products, cycle time from receipt of customer order to delivery of product.

NEED FOR STANDARDS

As industry has developed, grown, and become more complex, the need for increased efficiency and productivity has become more imperative. The successful executives developed more effective means of regulating and controlling the activities. It is no longer sufficient just to know the cost to manufacture or sell. There is a real need to know if we are using the most economical manufacturing techniques and processes. The distribution and selling costs must be evaluated and measured against some predetermined factors. Performance measurement should be applied to all activities. It is essential that a yardstick of desirable or planned results be established against which actual results may be compared if the performance measurement is to be effective. It is natural to compare current performance with historical performance such as last month, last quarter, or last year. Such a comparison points out trends, but it also serves to perpetuate inefficiencies. This comparison only serves a useful purpose if the measuring stick or past performance represents effective and efficient performance. Furthermore, changes in technologies, price levels, manufacturing processes, and the relative volume of production tend to limit the value of historical costs in determining what current costs should be.

There certainly is a compelling need for something other than historical costs for the standard of performance. For planning and pricing, management needs cost information that is not distorted by defective material, poor worker performance, or other unusual characteristics. Scientific management recognizes the value and need for some kind of engineering standards to plan manufacturing operations and evaluate the effectiveness with which the objectives are being accomplished. Engineering standards, expressed in financial terms, become cost standards; these standards, based on careful study and analysis about what it should cost to perform the operations by the best methods, become a much more reliable yardstick with which to measure and control costs.

Standards are the foundation and basis of effective accounting control. Standards provide the management tools with which to measure and judge performance. The use of standards is as adaptable to the control of income or expense as to the control of assets or liabilities. Standards are applicable to all phases of business and are an extremely important management tool.

DEFINITION OF STANDARDS

A standard of any type is a measuring stick or the means by which something else is judged. The standard method of doing anything can usually be described as the best method devised, as far as humanly possible, at the time the standard is set. It follows that the standard cost is the amount that should be expended under normal operating conditions. It is a predetermined cost scientifically determined in advance, in contrast to an actual or historical cost. It is not an actual or average cost, although past experience may be a factor in setting the standard.

Since a standard has been defined as a scientifically developed measure of performance, it follows that at least two conditions are implied in setting the standard:

1. *Standards are the result of careful investigation or analysis of past performance and take into consideration expected future conditions.* They are not mere guesses; they are the opinions, based on available facts, of the people best qualified to judge what performance should be.

2. *Standards may need review and revision from time to time.* A standard is set on the basis of certain conditions. As these conditions change, the standard must change; otherwise, it would not be a true measuring stick. Where there is really effective teamwork, and particularly, where standards are related to incentive payments, the probability of change is great.

Most of the foregoing comments on standards relate to that phase of the definition on which there is general agreement. There are, however, differences of opinion that seem to relate principally to the following points:

- Whether a standard should be (1) a *current standard,* that is, one that reflects what performance should be in the period for which the standard is to be used, or (2) a *basic standard,* which serves merely as a point of reference.

- The level at which a standard should be set—an *ideal* level of accomplishment, a *normal* level, or the *expected* level.

Where standard costs are carried into the formal records and financial statements, the current standard is generally the one used. Reference to the variances immediately indicates the extent to which actual costs departed from what they should have been in the period. A basic standard, however, does not indicate what performance should have been. Instead, it is somewhat like the base on which a price index is figured. Basic standards are usually based on prices and production levels prevailing when the standards are set. Once established, they are permanent and remain unchanged until the manufacturing processes change. They are a stationary basis of measurement. Improvement or lack of improvement involves the comparison of ratios or percentages of actual to the base standard.

The level at which standards should be set is discussed later in this chapter under the subject of standards for cost control.

ADVANTAGES OF STANDARDS

It has already been mentioned that standards arose, as part of the scientific management movement, from the necessity of better control of manufacturing costs. The relationship between this need and the advantages of standards is close. However, the benefits from the use of standards extend beyond the relationship with cost control to all the other applications, such as price setting or inventory valuation. Therefore, it may be well to summarize the principal advantages of standards, and the related scientific methods, by the four primary functions in which they are used:

1. *Controlling costs*

   o *Standards provide a better measuring stick of performance.* The use of standards sets out the area of excessive cost that otherwise might not be known or realized. Without scientifically set standards, cost comparison is limited to other periods that in themselves may contain inefficiencies.

   o *Use of the "principle of exception" is permitted, with the consequent saving of much time.* It is not necessary to review and report on all operations but only those that depart significantly from standard. The attention of management may be focused on those spots requiring corrective action.

   o *Economies in accounting costs are possible.* Clerical costs may be reduced because fewer records are necessary and simplified procedures may be adopted. Many of the detailed subsidiary records, such as production orders or time reports, are not necessary. Again, if inventories are carried as a standard value, there is no need to calculate actual costs each time new lots are made or received. Still further, much of the data for month-end closing can be set up in advance with a reduction in peak-load work.

   o *A prompter reporting of cost control information is possible.* Through the use of simplified records and procedures and the application of the exception principle, less time is required to secure the necessary information.

   o *Standards serve as incentives to personnel.* With a fair goal, an employee will tend to work more efficiently with the consequent reduction in cost. This applies to executives, supervisors, and workers alike.

2. *Setting selling prices*

   o *Better cost information is available as a basis for setting prices.* Through the use of predetermined standards, costs are secured that are free from abnormal distortions caused by excess spoilage and other unusual conditions. Furthermore, the use of standard overhead rates eliminates the influence of current activity. A means is provided to secure, over the long run, a full recovery of overhead expenses, including marketing, administrative, and research expense.

   o *Flexibility is added to selling price data.* Through the use of predetermined rates, changes in the product or processes can be quickly reflected in the cost. Furthermore, adjustments to material prices or labor rates are easily made. Again, the use of standards requires a distinction between fixed and variable costs. This cost information permits cost calculations on different bases. Since pricing is sometimes a matter of selection of alternatives, this flexibility is essential.

   o *Prompter pricing data can be furnished.* Again, the use of predetermined rates permits the securing of information more quickly.

3. *Valuing inventories*

   ○ *A "better" cost is secured.* Here, too, as in pricing applications, a more reliable cost is secured. The effect of idle capacity, or of abnormal wastes or inefficiencies, is eliminated.

   ○ *Simplicity in valuing inventories is obtained.* All like products are valued at the same cost. This not only assists in the recurring monthly closings but also is an added advantage in pricing the annual physical inventory.

4. *Budgetary planning*

   ○ *Determination of total standard costs is facilitated.* The standard unit costs provide the basic data for converting the sales and production schedules into total costs. The unit costs can readily be translated into total costs for any volume or mixture of product by simple multiplication. Without standards, extensive analysis is necessary to secure the required information because of the inclusion of nonrecurring costs.

   ○ *The means is provided for setting out anticipated substandard performance.* A history of the variances is available, together with the causes. Since actual costs cannot be kept exactly in line with standard costs, this record provides the basis for forecasting the variances that can reasonably be expected in the budget period under discussion. This segregation permits a determination of realistic operating results without losing sight of unfavorable expected costs.

RELATIONSHIP OF ENTITY GOALS TO PERFORMANCE STANDARDS

Much of the discussion in this chapter relates to detailed performance measures or standards. However, prior to any review of such standards, a key relationship to certain company goals or broad financial standards should be emphasized.

Some of the overall *financial* goals for a business include (1) measures of *profitability,* such as return on shareholder equity, return on assets, return on sales; (2) measures of *growth,* such as increase in sales, increase in net income, and increase in earnings per share; and (3) *cash flow* measures, including aggregate operating cash flow or free cash flow. But is there, or should there be, any relationship between such overall goals, which are a type of standard, and more specific performance measures, such as the direct labor hour standard in cost center 21 for manufacturing product A? A business usually has goals or objectives as well as strategies for reaching them. It is only logical, therefore, that the goals or standards of a cost center, or factory, or function or division, support the entity goals. The hierarchy of goals, or performance measures or standards, may be pictured as a pyramid. (See Exhibit 1.1.)

In examining performance measures, beginning at the top of the pyramid (company goals) and moving down the structure, these characteristics exist (although not all are identified):

- Performance measures usually become narrower and more specific.

- The planning horizon becomes shorter.

- In the lower levels, cost factors tend to dominate more; and the measurement or activity period shortens considerably from years to months, days, or even hours.

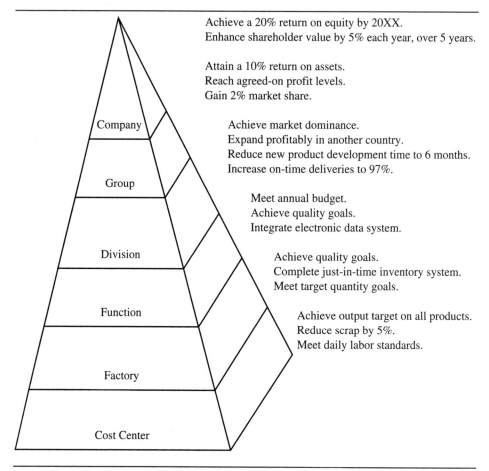

Achieve a 20% return on equity by 20XX.
Enhance shareholder value by 5% each year, over 5 years.

Attain a 10% return on assets.
Reach agreed-on profit levels.
Gain 2% market share.

Achieve market dominance.
Expand profitably in another country.
Reduce new product development time to 6 months.
Increase on-time deliveries to 97%.

Meet annual budget.
Achieve quality goals.
Integrate electronic data system.

Achieve quality goals.
Complete just-in-time inventory system.
Meet target quantity goals.

Achieve output target on all products.
Reduce scrap by 5%.
Meet daily labor standards.

EXHIBIT 1.1   HIERARCHY OF PERFORMANCE MEASURES

Performance measures at the lower levels should be expressed in terms of what an individual employee can do. For example, an accounts payable clerk might have as a standard the number of invoices processed per day or the number of cash discounts taken (or lost). This activity level performance cannot be directly measured against a percent return on assets goal.

As the standards are expressed in terms of smaller, specific tasks, the time span between assigning the task, accomplishing the task, and rewarding the employee should grow shorter.

Care should be taken that objectives at the lower levels are not contradictory. For example, encouraging higher throughput should not be at the expense of causing excess inventories in another department. A given individual, cost center, or department should not be overpowered by having to meet too many different standards. Standards should be current; that is, they should relate to the processes or methods in use—not obsolete ones. They should be updated minimally each year, ideally, each quarter.

Formulating consistent standards that move the company objective forward takes a great deal of thought and time and is a management task of great importance.

TYPES OF STANDARDS NEEDED

Standards for All Business Activity

Managerial control extends to all business functions including selling, production, finance, and research. It would appear highly desirable, therefore, to have available standards for measuring effort and results in all these activities. The word *standard* in much of the accounting literature applies to manufacturing costs. But the fact remains that the principles underlying the development of standards can and should be applied to many nonmanufacturing functions. Business executives generally do not question the need or desirability of standards for the control of administrative, distribution, and financial activities; they do, however, recognize the difficulties involved. Some activities are more susceptible to measurement than others, but application of some standard is generally possible. Moreover, as business processes change, some performance standards will increase in importance, while others will decrease, for example, the use of a labor standard in which "direct" labor is less crucial and will be combined with related service support labor standards such as inspection or quality control.

Standards for Individual Performance

Costs are controlled by people. It is through the action of an individual or group of individuals that costs are corrected or reduced to an acceptable level. It is by the efforts of the individual salesperson that the necessary sales volume is secured. It is largely through the operational control of the departmental foreperson that labor efficiency is maintained. As a result, any standards, to be most effective, must relate to specific phases of performance rather than merely general results. In a manufacturing operation, for example, standards should relate to the quantity of labor, material, or overhead in the execution of a particular operation rather than the complete product cost standard. In the selling field, a sales quota must be set for the individual salesperson, perhaps by product, and not just for the branch or territory.

Thus the setting of standards and measurement of performance against such yardsticks fit into the scheme of "responsibility accounting."

Keeping in mind these general comments, specific types of standards can now be examined. In addition to the remarks in this chapter, further observations are made in some of the chapters in which the relevant function is reviewed.

Material Quantity Standards

In producing an article, one of the most obvious cost factors is the quantity of material used. Quantitative standards, based on engineering specifications, outline the kind and quantity of material that should be used to make the product. This measuring stick is the primary basis for material cost control. This quantity standard, when multiplied by the unit material price standard, results in the cost standard. When more than one type of material is involved, the sum of the individual material cost standards equals the total standard material cost of the product.

Material Price Standards

To isolate cost variances arising out of excess material usage from those arising because of price changes, it is necessary to establish a material price standard. Usually, this price standard represents the expected cost instead of a desired or "efficient" cost. In many companies, this price is set for a period of a year, and, although actual cost may fluctuate, these changes are not reflected in the standard unit cost of material used. In other words, every piece of material used is charged with this predetermined cost.

Labor Quantity Standards

The labor content of many products is the most costly element. But whether it is the most costly or not, it is usually important. Because we are dealing with the human element, the labor cost is one of the most variable. It is indeed a fertile field for cost reduction and cost control.

For these reasons, it is necessary to know the amount of labor needed to produce the article. The technique, determining the time needed to complete each operation when working under standard conditions, involves time and motion study.

Labor Rate Standards

The price of labor is generally determined by factors outside the complete control of the individual business, perhaps as a result of union negotiations or the prevailing rate in the area. In any event, it is desirable to have a fixed labor rate on each operation to be able to isolate high costs resulting from the use of an excess quantity of labor. Also, the utilization of labor within a plant is within the control of management, and some rate variances arise due to actions controllable by management. Examples are the assignment of the wrong people (too high a rate) to the job or the use of overtime.

The standard time required, when multiplied by the standard rate, gives the standard labor cost of the operation.

Manufacturing Overhead Expense Standards

One of the many problems most controllers must resolve is that of determining standards for the control of manufacturing overhead as well as absorption into inventory. The determination of these standards is somewhat more complicated than in the material or labor standards. Several conditions complicate their determination:

- Manufacturing overhead consists of a great variety of expenses, each of which reacts in a different fashion at varying levels of plant activity. Some costs, such as depreciation, remain largely independent of plant activity; others vary with changes in production, but not in direct proportion. Examples are supervisory labor, maintenance, and clerical expense. Still other overhead expense varies directly with, and proportionately to, plant volume. This may include certain supplies, indirect labor, and fuel expense.
- Control of overhead expenses rests with a large number of individuals in the organization. For example, the chief maintenance engineer may be responsible for maintenance costs, the factory accountant for factory clerical costs, and foremen in productive departments for indirect labor.

- The proper estimate of the rate and amount of production must be made to serve as the basis of setting standard rates. An improper level of activity not only affects the statement of income and expense, but also gives management an erroneous picture of the cost of an insufficient volume of business and distorts inventory values.

Overhead expenses are best controlled through the use of a flexible budget. It requires a segregation of fixed and variable expenses. Proper analysis and control permit a realistic look at overhead variances in terms of cause: (1) volume, (2) rate of expenditure, and (3) efficiency.

Standards for manufacturing overhead can be expressed in the total amount budgeted by each type of expense as well as unit standards for each item, such as power cost per operating hour or supplies per employee-hour. Such standards should reflect the impact of just-in-time (JIT) production techniques as well as the "cost drivers."

Sales Standards

Sales standards may be set for the purpose of controlling and measuring the effectiveness of the sales or marketing operations. They also may be used for incentive awards, stimulating sales efforts, or the reallocation of sales resources. The most common form of standard for a territory, branch, or salesperson is the sales quota, usually expressed as a dollar of physical volume. Other types of standards found useful in managing and directing sales effort are:

- Number of total customers to be retained
- Number of new customers to be secured
- Number of personal calls to be made per period
- Number of telephone contacts to be made per period
- Average size of order to be secured
- Amount of gross profit to be obtained

Distribution Cost Standards

Just as production standards have been found useful in controlling manufacturing costs, so an increasing number of companies are finding that distribution cost standards are a valuable aid in properly directing the selling effort. The extent of application and degree of completeness of distribution cost standards will differ from production standards, but the potential benefits from the use of such standards are equally important.

Some general standards can be used in measuring the distribution effort and results. However, more effective standards are those measuring individual performance. Some illustrative standards are:

- Selling expense per unit sold
- Selling expense as a percentage of net sales
- Cost per account sold
- Cost per call
- Cost per day
- Cost per mile of travel
- Cost per sales order

In addition to individual performance standards, another type of control relates to budgets for selling expenses. The procedure for setting budgets is similar to that used for manufacturing operations.

Administrative Expense Standards

As business expands and volume increases, there is a tendency for administrative expenses to increase proportionately and get out of line. The same need for control exists for these types of expenses as for manufacturing or production costs. Control can be exercised through departmental or responsibility budgets as well as through unit or individual performance standards. The general approach to control administrative expenses is essentially the same as for control of selling and manufacturing expenses. It is necessary to develop an appropriate standard for each function or operation to be measured.

Examples of types of standards to be considered are:

Function	Standard Unit of Measurement
Purchasing	Cost per purchase order
Billing	Cost per invoice rendered
Personnel	Cost per employee hired
Traffic	Cost per shipment
Payroll	Cost per employee
Clerical	Cost per item handled (filed)

Financial Ratios

The types of standards discussed to this point relate primarily to human performance associated with elements of the statement of income and expense—sales revenues, cost factors, and expense categories of several types. Yet another category of standards deals with the utilization of assets or shareholders' equity, or the liquidity of the entity. These measures relating to financial condition and profitability rates are of special interest to the financial executives in testing business plans and the financial health of the enterprise.

A short list of some of the more important financial and operating ratios includes:

- Current ratio
- Quick ratio
- Ratio of net sales to receivables
- Turnover of inventory
- Turnover of current assets
- Ratio of net sales to working capital
- Ratio of net sales to assets
- Return on assets
- Return on shareholders' equity
- Other profitability ratios:
  - Ratio of net income to sales
  - Gross margin percentage

Generally speaking, the standards for these financial ratios may be developed from several sources:

- Ratios accepted by the industry of which the company is a member, perhaps developed by the industry association
- Ratios ascertained from the published financial statements of the principal competitors of the entity, or industry leaders
- Ratios developed by computer modeling
- Ratios based on the past (and best) experience of the company or on the opinions of its officers

TREND TO MORE COMPREHENSIVE PERFORMANCE MEASURES

The majority of the standards described relate to very specific activities and are largely *cost* standards (labor cost per unit). Additionally, some relate to number or size of functions performed (number of sales calls made), or financial relationships. It is common practice in U.S. companies to compare hourly, daily, weekly, or monthly actual performance with such a standard, or a budget, or prior experience. Such comparisons with the relevant internal activity of a prior period or calculated proper measure are useful.

Managements are discovering that other types of measures may be helpful for a number of reasons:

- Some *non–cost-related* measures can highlight functional areas that need improvement, for example, number of new customers, number of customer complaints, product development time.
- For some activities, comparisons with an *external* standard, such as industry average or performance of a principal competitor, may provide useful guidelines. Examples include inventory turnover and research and development expenditures.
- Quantified standards may cause supervisors to focus attention on the wrong objective. For instance, attention to the average size of sales orders may take attention away from the need for a profitable product mix.
- On occasion, emphasis on output can create problems in, or transfer problems to, other departments (defects, excessive inventory, or wrong mix of parts).
- Some standards may conflict with other management efforts, such as attempting to reduce indirect manufacturing expense as related to direct labor, when the overall trend is to automation.

In the search for a broader base than accounting or financial standards to check or measure company performance, the controller, perhaps in collaboration with other functional executives, could take these actions:

- Discuss with management members the critical success factors of the company, suspected areas of weaker performance, and what changes might be examined.
- Review existing performance measures and try to ascertain whether they are relevant to the newer techniques or processes (JIT purchasing, delivery and manufacturing).
- Seek to determine if the measures relate to the true cost drivers of the function under review.

- Update practices, using the current literature or periodicals for possible leads to examine.
- Talk with controllers, line managers, or workers, in other companies about the performance measures and other guides they use.
- Consider hiring outside consultants to review areas of suspected weaknesses and to make recommendations. Such a review might lead to a starting list of (1) cost measures and (2) noncost performance measures for important internal activity checking (based on trends and relative *internal* importance, and relative cost and noncost measures when examined or compared to *external* factors). A sample outline of what could be measured is:

1. Internal Factors

    (a) *Cost Measures*
        Direct labor costs
        Direct material costs
        Manufacturing expense
        Marketing expense
        Research and development (R&D) costs
        Delivery costs
        Inventory carrying costs
        Accounts receivable carrying costs

    (b) *Noncost Measures*
        Length of design cycle
        Number of engineering changes
        Number of new products
        Manufacturing cycle time
        Number of parts/raw material deliveries
        Number of on-time customer deliveries
        Number of suppliers
        Number of parts

2. External Factors (Relative Measurement)

    (a) *Cost Measures*
        Relative R&D expense
        Relative material content cost
        Relative labor cost content
        Relative delivery expense
        Relative selling expenses

Time-Based Standards

One group of standards receiving attention are time-based measures. Management which uses these diagnostic tools believes that time analysis is more useful than simple cost analysis because activity review identifies exactly what occurs every hour of the working day. It seems to encourage such time-oriented questions as: Why are the two tasks done serially and not in parallel? Why is the process speeded up in some departments only to then let the product lie idle? When points of time are identified, then related cost reduction possibilities can be examined.

Examples of time-based standards that have been found useful in four key functions include:

1. *Decision-making process:* Time lost in waiting for a decision
   o Product development
   o Manufacturing
   o Marketing
   o Finance (accounting)

2. *New product development*
   o Total time required from inception of idea to marketing of product
   o Number of times (or percent) company has beat a competitor to market
   o Number of new products marketed in a given time period

3. *Manufacturing or processing*
   o Cycle time from commencement of manufacture through billing process
   o Inventory turnover
   o Total elapsed time from product development to first time acceptable output
   o Value added per factory hour
   o Credit approval time
   o Billing cycle time—from receipt of shipping notice to completion of invoice preparation
   o Collection time—from mailing of invoice to receipt of payment

4. *Customer service*
   o Number (or percent) of on-time deliveries
   o Response time to customer questions
   o Quoted lead time for shipment of spare parts, repairs, and product delivery
   o Delivery response time

BENCHMARKING

The practice by a company of measuring products, services, and business practices against the toughest competitor or those companies best in its class, or against other measures, has been named "benchmarking." Technically, those who consult about the process differentiate between three kinds, depending on the consultant. Distinctions are made about these three types:

1. Competitive benchmarking
2. Noncompetitive benchmarking
3. Internal benchmarking

Competitive benchmarking studies compare a company's performance with respect to customer-determined notions of quality against direct competitors.

Noncompetitive benchmarking refers to studying the *"best-in-class"* in a specific business function. For example, it might encompass the billing practices of a company in a completely different industry.

Internal benchmarking can refer to comparisons between plants, departments, or product lines within the same organization. The benchmarking studies involve steps such as:

1. Determining which functions within the company to benchmark
2. Selecting or identifying the key performance variables that should be measured
3. Determining which companies are the best-in-class for the function under review
4. Measuring the performance of the best-in-class companies
5. Measuring the performance of the company as to the function under study
6. Determining those actions necessary to meet and surpass the best-in-class company
7. Implementing and monitoring the improvement program

Although benchmarking has produced some legendary corporate successes, it often has not produced an improvement on the net income line. In part, this reflects the fact that it is a complicated process and does not consist merely of some random observations of different methods used by some businesses, or some short field trips. A successful benchmarking effort must be undertaken in a clearly defined and systematic manner. A benchmarking study wherein the only product or result is a report to management, with no modification of a substandard activity, could be regarded as a failure.

To put the topic of benchmarking in the proper perspective, it should be recognized that successful benchmarking efforts have addressed a wide variety of issues, including:

- Increased market share
- Improved corporate strategy
- Increased profitability
- Streamlined processes
- Reduced costs
- More effective R&D activities
- Improved quality
- Higher levels of customer satisfaction

In those instances when benchmarking activity has not met expectations, some of the reasons include:

- Top management did not comprehend the full potential of the proposed changes and consequently did not push aggressively for their adoption.
- The functions or activities selected for improvement may in fact have been improved, but the greater efficiency was too small to have a meaningful impact on overall business performance.
- The study team made observations but failed to develop an actionable plan.
- In some instances, the analysis was incomplete: the study team learned *what* the best-in-class companies were doing, but it did not learn *how* the actions were implemented.

Another facet of benchmarking that should be noted is the makeup of the study team. It should include people in the company who have been performing the function. Those selected should be highly knowledgeable about the function, should be good communicators, and should be curious and highly analytical. It probably is preferable to have consultants, not company employees, make contacts with competitors. In some circumstances, the presence of a member of the board of directors might be the means of better communicating to the board the complexities and potential impact of the study. In summary, benchmarking is a complicated process, and full preparation should be made.

BALANCED SYSTEM OF PERFORMANCE MEASURES

Performance measures range from broad company standards to *detailed* functional standards applied to a daily departmental manufacturing activity. Moreover, many of these standards are used for both planning and control purposes. Then, too, some are cost-related and others are noncost measures; some address the important subject of customer satisfaction, and others simple efficiency; and finally, some deal with innovation while others emphasize routine operations.

Many years ago, the use of one type of standard (generally cost type) for control purposes was the point of emphasis. Since that time, management has recognized that it cannot rely on one set of measures to the exclusion of all others. Rather, a combination of measures are necessary that must properly relate to each other and take into account the critical success factors of the enterprise. This is to say that management needs a balanced set of performance measures.

The article by Kaplan and Norton mentions a company that grouped its performance measures into four types, each with separate measures of performance, and each critical to the future success of the entity.[1]

The four measurement groups discussed, together with some added goals and measures of individual performance mentioned earlier in this chapter follow.

Financial Perspective		Customer Perspective	
Goals	**Measures**	**Goals**	**Measures**
Survive	Cash flow	New products	Percentage of sales from new products
Succeed	Sales and income growth	Customer supply	Number of on-time deliveries
Prosper	Return on equity	Preferred supplier	Share of key account purchases
Internal Business Perspective		**Innovation Perspective**	
Goals	**Measures**	**Goals**	**Measures**
Manufacturing excellence	Unit cost cycle time	Time to market	Versus competition
New product introduction	Actual vs. planned introduction schedule	Technology leadership	Time to develop new process

---

1. Kaplan, Robert S., and David P. Norton, "The Balanced Scorecard—Measures That Drive Performance," *Harvard Business Review*, Jan.–Feb. 1992, pp. 71–79.

SETTING THE STANDARDS

Who Should Set the Standards?

Standards should be set by those who are best qualified by training and experience to judge what good performance should be. It is often a joint process requiring cooperation between the staffs of two or more divisions of the business. Fundamentally, the setting of standards requires careful study and analysis. The controller and staff, trained in analysis and possessing essential records on the various activities, are in an excellent position to play an important part in the establishment of yardsticks of performance.

Since standards are yardsticks of performance, they should not be set by those whose performance is to be measured. Sufficient independence of thought should exist. The standards should be reviewed with those who will be judged by them and any suggestions considered. However, final authority in establishing the standard should be placed in other hands.

Exactly which staff members cooperate in setting standards depends on the standards under consideration. Material quantity standards, for example, are generally determined by the engineers who are familiar with the operation methods employed as well as the product design. Assisting the engineers may be the production staff and the accounting staff. The production people can make valuable contributions because of their knowledge of the process. Furthermore, permitting the production staff to assist usually enlists their cooperation in making the standards effective. The accounting department assists by providing necessary information on past experience.

The determination of material price standards is usually the responsibility of both the purchasing and accounting departments. The purchasing department may indicate what expected prices are. These should then be challenged by the accounting department, taking into account current prices and reasonably expected changes. In other instances, the accounting department sets the standards, based again on current prices, but takes into consideration the opinion of the purchasing department about future trends.

Quantitative labor standards are usually set by industrial engineers through the use of time and motion study. This is properly an engineering function in that a thorough background of the processes is necessary. On occasion, the accounting department furnishes information of past performance as a guide. Standard labor rates are set by the department that has available the detailed job rates and other necessary information, typically the cost department. The cost department must also translate the physical standards into cost standards.

Manufacturing overhead standards, too, are often a matter of cooperation between the accounting and engineering departments. Engineers may be called on to furnish technical data, such as power consumption in a particular department, or maintenance required, or type of supplies necessary. However, this data is then costed by the accounting staff. In other instances, the unit standards or budgets may be set in large part on past experience. The role played by the accountant tends to be much greater in the establishment of overhead standards due to the familiarity with the techniques of organizing the data into their most useful form for cost and budget reporting. Setting the standards for distribution activities is best done through the cooperation of sales, sales research, and accounting executives. Reliance is placed on the sales staff for supplying information pertaining to market potentials and sales methods. The accountant contributes the analysis and interpretation of past performance, trends, and relationships. The sales and accounting executives jointly must interpret the available data as applied to future activity.

Unit standards for the measurement of administrative expenses are usually determined on the basis of time and motion study by industrial engineers, observation of the functions, or a detailed analysis of past performance to ensure that standards reflect the norm. In many instances, the accountant is involved in either costing the data or analyzing past experience.

Financial and operating ratios should be set by the controller based on the objectives for the company, experience in the particular company or industry, and special analysis or consideration of factors that have a significant influence on the ratio or external sources.

In many instances, it may be desirable to have the assistance of independent consultants. For example, when sources outside the company are to be contacted, as in "benchmarking," these noncompany personnel may be especially helpful.

Method of Setting Standards

Those aspects of setting standards that are beyond the sphere of accounting responsibility are adequately covered in various management and engineering literature. Only the general steps taken in the establishment of standards will be considered here. Any outline of procedure regarding standards is basically only the application of logic and prudent judgment to the problem. The eight phases involved in the setting of standards are summarized below:

1. *Recognition of the need for a standard in the particular application.* Obviously, before action is taken, the need should exist. This need must be acknowledged so that the problem can be attacked.

2. *Preliminary observation and analysis.* This involves "getting the feel" of the subject, recognizing the scope of the problem, and securing a general understanding of the factors involved.

3. *Segregation of the function, or activity, and/or costs in terms of individual responsibility.* Since standards are to control individual actions, the outer limits of the responsibility of each individual must be ascertained in the particular application.

4. *Determination of the unit of measurement in which the standard should be expressed.* To arrive at the quotient, the divisor is necessary. And in many applications, the base selected can be one of many.

5. *Determination of the best method.* This may involve time and motion study, a thorough review of possible materials, or an analysis of past experience. It must also involve consideration of possible changes in conditions.

6. *Statement or expression of the standard.* When the best method and the unit of measurement have been determined, the tentative standard can be set.

7. *Testing of the standard.* After analysis and synthesis and preliminary determination, the standard must be tested to see that it meets the requirements.

8. *Final application of the standard.* The testing of a standard will often result in certain compromises or changes. When this has been effected, when the best judgment of all the executives concerned has been secured, then and only then can the standard be considered set and ready to be applied.

USE OF STANDARDS FOR CONTROL

The fact that management has set standards for cost control by no means assures control of costs. It takes positive action by individuals to keep costs within some predetermined limits. It is a management challenge to communicate the value of standards to all concerned and convince them how the yardsticks can be utilized in accomplishing the goals and objectives. To be effective it must be demonstrated that the standards are fair and reasonable.

The controller must have sufficient facts to illustrate the reasonableness of the standards when questions arise or the yardsticks are considered unfair.

When standards are shown clearly to be unreasonable, the controller must be prepared to gather new data and make appropriate adjustments.

Technique of Cost Control

In the final analysis, the objective of cost control is to secure the greatest amount of production or results of a desired quality from a given amount of material, manpower, effort, or facilities. It is the securing of the best result at the lowest possible cost under existing conditions. In this control of performance, the first step is the setting of standards of comparison; the next step is the recording of actual performance, and the third step is the comparing of actual and standard costs as the work progresses. This last step involves:

- Determining the variance between standard and actual
- Analyzing the cause of the variance
- Taking remedial action to bring unfavorable actual costs in line with the predetermined standards

Control is established through prompt follow-up, before the unfavorable trends or tendencies develop into large losses. It is important that any variances be determined quickly, and it is equally important that the unfavorable variance be stated in terms that those responsible will understand. The speed and method of presentation have a profound bearing on the corrective action that will be taken and, hence, on the effectiveness of control.

Role of Statistical Process Control

One approach to cost control is to determine the variance between a standard and actual performance, seek out the cause of the variance, and take remedial action. Yet global competition is causing management to adopt more sophisticated strategies to remain or become competitive. Among these devices are automatic JIT, total quality management (TQM), and statistical process control (SPC). This latter technique can assist in properly setting standards and in better evaluating or interpreting variances. SPC is based on the assumption that process performance is dynamic, that variation is the rule. Consequently, proper assessment of performance requires correct interpretation of the variation over a period of time. Charts or graphic aids are used in SPC to understand and reduce the fluctuations in processes until they are considered stable (under control). A stable process would have only the normal variances. On the other hand, an unstable process is subject to uncommon fluctuations resulting from special causes. The performance of a stable process can be improved only by making fundamental changes in the process itself, while an unstable production process can be stabilized only by locating and eliminating the special causes. The statistical approach assists in identifying the character of the variance. An incorrect decision that a process is operating in an unstable manner may result in costs from searching for special causes of process variation that do not exist. An incorrect decision that a process is operating in a stable manner will result in failure to search for special causes that do exist.

Suffice it to say that SPC is a complex subject that seeks to provide long-term solutions. Someone with a high level of statistical knowledge ordinarily will be needed to assist in implementing the strategy. Management accountants should understand the SPC approach.

Who Should Control Costs?

Costs must be controlled by individuals, and the question is raised about who should control costs, the controller representing accounting personnel or the operating executive in charge of the activity (manufacturing sales or research) to be cost controlled. It has already been explained that operational control preceded accounting control. In many thousands of small businesses, operating control is the only type used. Cost control is not primarily an accounting process, although accounting plays an important part. Control of costs is an operating function. The controller, in the capacity of an operating executive, may control costs within the accounting department. Beyond this, the function of the controller is to report the facts on other activities of the business so that corrective action may be taken and to inform management of its effectiveness in cost control. The part played by the controller is advisory or facilitative in nature.

In many instances, the development of the standards to be used in measuring performance is largely the work of nonaccountants, whether product specifications, operational methods, time requirements, or other standards. Likewise, decision about the corrective action to be taken is generally up to the operating personnel. However, the controller is in an excellent position to stimulate and guide the interest of management in the control of costs through the means of reports analyzing unusual conditions. The controller's work is usually confined to summarizing basic information, analyzing results, and preparing intelligently conceived reports. It follows that the controller must produce reports that a non–accounting-trained executive or operator can understand and will act on. To do this requires being thoroughly conversant with the operating problems and viewpoints. The effectiveness of any cost control system depends on the degree of coordination between the accounting control personnel and the operating personnel. One presents the facts in an understandable manner; the other takes the remedial action.

Cooperation at *all* levels is essential in the control of costs. Cooperation is secured, in part, through the application of correct management policies. The use of standards, when fully understood, should be of great assistance in securing this cooperation, for the measuring stick is based on careful analysis and not preconceived ideas or rule-of-thumb methods.

Level of the Standard

Because one of the primary purposes of a standard is as a control tool—to see that performance is held to what it should be—it is necessary to determine at what level the standard should be set. Just how "tight" should a standard be? Although there is no clear-cut line of demarcation among them, the three following levels may be distinguished:

1. The ideal standard
2. The average of past performance
3. The attainable good performance standard

The ideal standard is the one representing the best performance that can be attained under the most favorable conditions possible. It is not a standard that is expected to be attained but rather a goal toward which to strive in an attempt to improve efficiency. Hence variances are always unfavorable and represent the inability to reach the ideal level of efficiency. The use of an unattainably tight standard confuses the objectives of cost reduction and cost control. Cost reduction involves the finding of ways and means to achieve a given result through improved design, better methods, new layouts, new equipment, better plant layout, and so forth, and therefore results in the establishment of new standards. If the standards set are more restrictive than currently attainable performance, the lower cost will not necessarily be achieved until cost reduction has found the means by which the standard may be attained. Ideal standards, then, are not highly desirable as a means of cost control.

Standards are frequently set on the basis of what was done in the past, without adjustments to reflect improved methods or elimination of wastes. A standard set on this basis is likewise a poor measuring stick in that it can be met by poor performance. Hence the very inefficiencies that standards should disclose are obscured by the loose standard.

A third level at which a standard may be set is the attainable level of good performance. This standard includes waste or spoilage, lost time, and other inefficiencies only to the extent that they are considered impractical of elimination. This type of standard can be met or bettered by efficient performance. It is a standard set at a high level but is attainable with reasonably diligent effort. Such a standard would seem to be the most effective for cost control purposes.

Point of Control

Costs are controlled by individuals, so it follows that the accounting classifications must reflect both standard and actual performance in such a manner that individual performance can be measured. As stated previously, "responsibility accounting" must be adopted. Provision must be made for the accumulation of costs, by cost centers, cost pools, or departments, that follows organizational structure. Furthermore, this cost accumulation must initially reflect only those costs that are direct as to the specific function being measured. Allocations and reallocations may be made for product cost *determination* and for certain other *planning* applications, but this is not desirable for cost *control*. If a great many prorations are made, it is often difficult to determine where the inefficiency exists or the extent of it. Therefore, it is desirable from a cost control standpoint to collect the costs at the point of incurrence.

If, as in some companies, allocated costs are reflected in control reports, it is desirable to separate them from direct expenses or costs. Some companies show allocated costs so that the department manager will be aware of the cost of the facilities or services they use.

Discussion of the point of control of costs involves, in addition to placement of responsibility, the matter of timing. Costs must be controlled not only at the point of incurrence but also, preferably, at or before the time of incurrence. Thus, if a department on a budget basis processes a purchase requisition and is advised at that time of the excess cost over budget, perhaps action can be taken then—either delaying the expenditure until the following month or getting a less expensive yet satisfactory substitute. Again, material control is best exercised at the point of issuance. Only the standard quantity should be issued. In the case of purchases, the price and type are best controlled at the time of purchase.

What Costs Should Have Standards?

From the viewpoint of standards for cost control, a question may be raised about the extent to which attempts should be made to set standards. Factors to be considered include the relative amount of cost and the degree of control possible over the cost.

It may be stated that standards should be set for all cost items of a significant or material amount. In many cases, the more important the cost, the greater is the opportunity or need for cost control. With such items as overhead, it may be necessary to combine certain elements but, so far as practicable, a standard should be set to measure performance.

Another factor to be considered is the degree of control possible, needed, or desired over the cost. At first, it might appear that little control can be exercised over some types of cost, such as depreciation, salaries of key personnel, or personal property taxes. However, the fact is that most costs can be controlled by someone. The time and place and method of control of costs generally considered as "fixed" may differ from the control of material, direct labor, or variable overhead expense, but a certain degree of control is possible. Control of the fixed charges may be exercised in at least two ways:

1. *By limiting the expenditure to a predetermined amount.* For example, depreciation charges are controlled through the acquisition of plant and equipment. Any control must be exercised at the time of purchase or construction of the asset. This is usually done by means of an appropriation budget, which is a type of standard. A similar plan can be applied to the group of salaried personnel generally considered as a part of the fixed charges. In many instances, control of this type of expense or expenditure is a top-management decision. It may be observed, however, that control at this high level does exist.

2. *By securing the proper utilization of the facilities and organization represented by the fixed charges.* The controller can assist in this task by properly isolating the volume costs or cost of idle equipment. An acceptable standard might be the percent of plant utilization as related to "normal." In the monthly statement of income and expense, the lack of volume costs should be set out as part of the effort to direct management's attention to the excess costs and to a consideration of ways and means of reducing personnel, if necessary, or increasing volume through other products, intensified sales activity, and so on.

PROCEDURE FOR REVISING STANDARDS

Revision of Standards

Whether standards are used for cost control or the related function of budgetary planning or whether standards are for the purpose of price setting or inventory valuation, they must be kept up to date to be most useful. From a manufacturing operations viewpoint, revision appears desirable when important changes are made in material specifications or prices, methods of production, or labor efficiency or price. Changes in the methods or channels of distribution and basic organizational or functional changes would necessitate standard changes in the selling, research, or administrative activities. Stated in other terms, current standards must be revised when conditions have changed to such an extent that the standard no longer represents a realistic or fair measure of performance.

It is obvious that standard revisions should not be made for every change, only the important ones. However, the constant search for better methods and for better measurements of performance subjects every standard to possible revision. The controller constantly must be on the alert about the desirability of adjusting standards to prevent the furnishing of misleading information to management.

Program for Standard Revision

The changing of standards is time consuming and may be expensive. For this reason, it should not be treated in a haphazard manner. It is desirable to plan in advance the steps to be taken in revising standards. Through the use of an orderly program for constant review and revision of standards, the time and money spent on standard changes can be less and the effort more productive.

In planning the program of standard revision, the ramifications of any changes should be considered. For example, changes in manufacturing standards usually necessitate changes in inventory values. Accordingly, it may appear desirable to review the standards at the end of each fiscal year and make the necessary changes. A chemical plant may review material price standards every quarter because the selling price of the finished product is sympathetic to changes in commodity prices. This frequent revision would result in cost information that is more useful to the sales department. In some companies, a general practice is to change standards whenever basic selling price changes occur. This results in a more constant standard gross profit figure by which to judge sales performance. In considering frequent changes, however, the expense should be weighed against the benefits. In this connection, the value for cost control should be matched against the lessened degree of comparability of the variances from period to period.

Judgment should be exercised about the necessity for, and extent of, changes in the records. For example, general changes in labor rates, raw material costs, standard overhead rates, or product design may dictate a complete revision of product and departmental costs, extending through every stage of manufacture. However, a change in one department, or in one part, or in a small assembly might necessitate the change of only one standard for control purposes. The difference between old and new, with respect to other stages of manufacture, or the finished product cost, could be temporarily written off as a variance until the time is ripe for a complete product standard revision.

RECORDING STANDARDS
Importance of Adequate Records

If the controller is to serve management most effectively and if the business is to have the advantage of accurate, reliable, and prompt cost information, then an adequate recording of the facts is necessary. This principle is as applicable to recording standards and standard costs as it is to actual costs—perhaps even more so. The degree of intelligence applied to the form and method of recording determines in large measure that:

- The data underlying the development and revision of standards will be available as needed.
- The facts relating to operating efficiency will be ascertainable and accurately analyzed.
- The information will be made available on an economical basis.
- The records will have the necessary flexibility to meet promptly the needs of the various applications of the standards.

Types of Records Necessary

In the manufacturing function, the records incident to the establishment and use of standards may be classified into four basic groups:

1. Physical specifications that outline the required material and the sequence of manufacturing operations that must be performed
2. Details of standard or budgeted overhead based on normal capacity
3. Standard cost sheets for each product and component part, which indicate standard cost by elements
4. Variance accounts that indicate the type of departure from standard

The extent and form of these records depend on the size and characteristics of the business. In an assembly type operation, for example, there would be a product specification for each part. These, in turn, would form the basis for cost sheets on subassemblies and assemblies. In most cases this data would be recorded, accumulated, stored, and reported through the integrated computer processing system. This would include information from the production order, standard labor hours for each operation, and the ability to calculate the standard cost of each part and assembly. With the details of standards available, changes are easily made for substitution of parts in determining the standard cost of modifications of a basic product. Standards are equally applicable to processing operations like the chemical industry—the key is setting fair and reasonable standards for each operation or process and making adjustments for changed conditions.

Administrative Controls

Although the use of standards is not as well developed for administrative functions as for manufacturing operations, yardsticks can be established for such usage in most cases. Some companies collect and analyze statistical data from which some performance measurements can be made. The controller should continue to evaluate these functions to determine the best method or standard against which actual performance can be compared.

Incorporation of Standard Costs in Accounts

Historically, some companies use standard costs for statistical comparisons only and do not incorporate them into the accounting record system. This is probably more true for administrative-type expenses than for direct manufacturing costs. With the data storage and processing capabilities of computers, it appears essential that the standard cost records be integrated into the accounting system. This will result in better cost control, inventory valuation, budgeting, and pricing.

APPLICATION OF STANDARD COSTS

Even though standard costs are incorporated in the accounts, there is considerable difference about the period in the accounting cycle when the standards should be recorded. Whereas there are several variations in accounting treatment, the distinction may be twofold:

1. Recognition of the standard cost at the time of cost incurrence
2. Recognition of the standard cost at the time of cost completion

The first method charges work in progress at standard cost, whereas the second method develops the standard cost at the time of transfer to the finished goods account. Recognition of costs at incurrence would imply a recording of material price variance at the time of purchase and material usage variance at the time of usage or transfer to work in process. However, many firms record material at actual cost and recognize price variances only as the material is used. This practice permits a write-off of excess costs proportionate to usage so that unit costs tend to approximate the actual cost each month.

MANAGEMENT USE OF STANDARD COSTS

Extensive use of standard cost data can be made by management in directing the activities of the company. Some areas to be considered are:

- Planning and forecasting
- Motivation of employees

- Rewarding employees
- Performance measurement
- Analyzing alternative courses of action—new products
- Pricing decisions
- Inventory valuation
- Make or buy decisions
- Control and cost reduction

2

PLANNING AND CONTROL OF SALES

INTRODUCTION

Primary responsibility for the planning and control of sales, of course, rests with the chief sales or marketing executive of the company or the business segment. However, the chief accounting officer, with the knowledge of costs and cost behavior as well as the familiarity with sales accounting and analysis, is in a position to use these skills to assist the various marketing executives. Some of the areas where the controller might be helpful include:

- Selection and application of mathematical/statistical methods to develop or verify sales level trends and relationships
- Analysis of internal sales data to reveal trends and relationships
- Analysis and assembling of the proposed sales plan/budget
- Development and application of sales standards for use by the marketing executive, if applicable
- Application of the relevant costs as a factor in setting product sales prices

While the controller has a supporting role to the chief sales executive with respect to sales planning and control, there are also some basic independent responsibilities, as a member of the financial staff, to see that adequate procedures are followed and that the sales planning and control is sound from a financial or economic viewpoint.

These subjects and others are discussed in this chapter. First, however, to provide background for the controller or for other readers, a brief review is made of the sales management function and some of its concerns.

SALES MANAGEMENT CONCERNS

The tasks of any management function are many, varied and complex. Sales management is certainly confronted with a broad range of problems. It is a dynamic area, with changing conditions, constantly resulting in new and different problems. The controller can be an important influence on the resolution of these problems and decisions. An extensive and objective analysis of sales and distribution costs can assist sales executives in making prudent decisions consistent with the short- and long-range goals of the company.

One problem area that has a significant impact on the planning process of the company is sales forecasting. The accuracy of the sales forecast is essential to good planning. The controller can work with sales management to realistically evaluate the degree to which the

25

actual sales will relate to sales budget or forecast. There are many mathematical techniques available to establish standard deviations or variations that can be expected.

Significant progress has been made in developing more sophisticated management tools for sales executives. With the utilization of personal computers, management can have available summarized information on sales activity allowing it to make effective decisions in a timely manner. The controller should be an active participant in the development of these information systems and reports.

Although there are many types of problems encountered in the sales management function, there may be some that are found in most companies. The following is representative of some of the fundamental questions that are constantly raised:

- *Product.* What product is to be sold and in what quantity? Is it to be the highest quality in its field or lower? Is the product to be a specialty or a staple?
- *Pricing.* At what price is the article to be sold? Shall the company follow a policy of meeting any and all price competition? What are the terms of sale to be granted?
- *Distribution.* To whom shall the product be sold; that is, shall the firm sell directly to the ultimate consumer or through others, such as wholesalers? What channels of distribution should be used?
- *Method of sale.* How shall the goods be sold? Is it to be by personal solicitation, advertising, or direct mail? What sales promotion means shall be used?
- *Organization.* How shall salespersons be selected, and how shall they be trained? What is to be the basic organizational setup? Are there to be branch offices? Will sales supervisors handle all lines of product, or will each specialize? Into what departments shall the sales organization be divided? How many salespersons should be employed?
- *Planning and control.* How are sales territories to be set up? Shall sales standards be used as measuring sticks of performance? How will salespersons be compensated— salary, commission, bonus? What controls will be employed?

Questions relating to these six categories are found in every company, regardless of size. The answers to many depend, in large part, on the facts available within each organization.

CONTROLLER'S ASSISTIVE ROLE IN SALES MANAGEMENT PROBLEMS

As stated earlier, the final solution to sales management concerns must, of course, rest largely with the chief sales executive. However, an intelligent executive will always seek any assistance available. The controller can help by bringing to bear a scientific, analytical approach, using judgment as well as imagination. It should be realized that the solution in one firm may not be the solution in another and that the answers to today's problems may not be the answer tomorrow. The controller is of value primarily in getting the facts. In presenting the facts, though, it is necessary to merchandise or sell the product; the controller's approach must be one that invites reception.

The degree of assistance the controller can render in solving the previously mentioned sales problems is indicated in the following outline:

1. *Problems of product.* The initial selection of the product or consideration of changes in the line, sizes, and colors should generally be based on the collective judgment of the marketing considerations by the sales manager, of production problems by the manufacturing executive, and of cost considerations by the controller. Costs are not

the only factor in the decision, but they are an important factor. The chief accounting official should be able to indicate the probable margin on the product, as well as the margins on alternative choices. The controller should also be able to indicate the probable effect of volume on the margin or the effect of changes in quality, composition, and manufacturing processes on the cost to make or sell.

In the continuous reviews of sales trends, the controller may be able to identify unfavorable trends that might call for redirection of the sales effort or a change in product.

2. *Problems of price.* In many companies, pricing procedures are not reviewed on a periodic or methodical basis. The pricing procedure may not be responsive to increased costs. Although cost is not the only determining factor, it must be considered in maximizing the return on investment. The controller must be able to provide all the available information. Total costs, marginal or differential costs, out-of-pocket costs, or cost differences must be considered in developing the price structure. This is true for competitive bids or establishing price lists for the usual type of sale.

In an analysis of sales volume and related prices, it may be revealed that unfavorable variances often have resulted from salespersons or sales managers having too much authority in setting a selling price. As production costs change, the information should be communicated to the sales executives for consideration of appropriate price changes. Also, assistance should be provided in setting volume price breaks for different sizes of orders.

3. *Problems of Distribution.* The controller contributes the cost analysis necessary, as well as a review of statistics for unfavorable trends in distribution. Being able to provide indications of the selling cost through the various channels of distribution, the controller should be on the alert for major changes in sales trends through particular channels or margins thereon. Frequently, there are chances to show ingenuity in analysis regarding types and sizes of accounts and orders to be sought. Questions of policy may relate to:

(a) The minimum order to be accepted

(b) Restriction of the sales effort on large volume accounts that purchase only low-margin products or are unprofitable because of special laboratory service

(c) Desirability of servicing particular types of accounts through jobbers, telephone, mail order, and so forth

(d) Discontinuance of aggressive sales effort on accounts where annual sales volume is too low

(e) Best location for branch warehouses

4. *Problems relating to the method of sale.* Many factors will determine the method of sale, and the sales management must make this determination in view of the long-term goals and objectives. The controller can assist by providing information on historical costs and preparing alternative cost estimates for various methods. For example, analyses could be made related to the distribution of samples and the impact on costs and sales trends. Cost data related to advertising programs are useful in making decisions for future media communications. Special cost structures can be developed for market-test situations to determine the cost effectiveness. In the long run, of course, the best method should result in achieving the greatest sales volume with the best return on investment.

5. *Problems of organization.* Because the sales management function is dynamic, organizational changes are necessary to satisfy the new requirements. In making these

changes, information related to potential sales by product or territory may assist in reassigning or hiring new salespersons. Also, comparative cost data on different organizational structures are useful in determining the change.

6. *Problems of planning and control.* So numerous are the applications where the controller can be of assistance in planning and controlling the sales effort that only a few can be indicated. The controller is able to aid the sales executive in solving some of the previously mentioned problems through special studies, yet in the planning and control fields many of the controller's functions are repetitive. The accounting official may contribute in the following ways:

(a) *Sales budgets and quotas.* Detailed records and knowledge about the distribution of sales by territory, product, and customer, coupled with the knowledge of the sales manager on product changes and trends, provide basic information necessary in an intelligent setting of sales budgets, quotas, and standards. The controller also may provide services in connection with forecasting and market studies.

(b) *Distribution expense budgets and standards.* A history of past expenses as recorded in the accounting department provides much needed data in setting budgets and standards for the measurement and control of selling effort.

(c) *Monthly or periodic income and expense statements:*
   (i) By territories
   (ii) By commodities
   (iii) By methods of sale
   (iv) By customers
   (v) By salespersons
   (vi) By organization or operating divisions

   These and other analytical statements can provide a vast amount of useful information. The disclosure of the contribution to the net profit of each territory or some other factor analyzed, over and above the direct expense, may reveal spots of weakness.

(d) *Special analyses to reveal conditions needing correction or as an audit of performance:*
   (i) *Sales incentive plans.* The probable cost of various plans as applied to the business and degree to which they are mutually profitable for the company and salesperson. A determination about whether they direct salespeople's efforts toward the most profitable products.
   (ii) *Branch office and warehouse expense.* Periodic reviews of expense, in relationship to sales, growth, and earnings of the activity.
   (iii) *Customer development expense.* Analysis of entertainment expense or other business development expense by customer, salesman, or territory, with emphasis on necessity and possible alternatives—all with reference to the related margin or profit.
   (iv) *Salespersons' compensation and expenses.* Review and analysis of salespersons' salaries, bonuses, and expenses related to budgets, salary structure, and industry.

CONTROLLER'S INDEPENDENT ROLE IN
THE PLANNING AND CONTROL OF SALES

As previously stated, the primary responsibility for the development of the sales plan and its subsequent implementation is that of the chief sales executive. But, as just commented on in the preceding section, the controller can be of substantial assistance to the sales executive in supplying analytical and historical data for use in planning and control decisions. However, it should not be assumed that the controller will provide only the data the sales executive wants and that the controllership role is by and large a passive one as to sales activity. Given the analytical background of controllers and their knowledge of the financial data concerning the company, they have a series of independent functions to perform in furtherance of a sound business plan and prudent control procedures. Some of their conclusions might not be in agreement with the initial thinking of the sales executive; and some of the procedures they develop might appear redundant to some salespersons. Yet to one sensitive to the need for financially sound policies and procedures, and the desirability of proper checks and balances, the role of the controller is indispensable. For most companies, the responsibility of the controller and staff extends to the following outline of functions in the development of a sound annual sales plan (as well as the entire annual business plan) and the related implementation:

1. *The planning phase*

    (a) Development, and revision when required, of a practical set of systems and procedures for arriving at a suitable sales plan (and the entire financial aspects of the annual plan). This would include:

        (i) Outlining the steps in the planning procedure

        (ii) Assigning responsibility for each specific procedure to specific executive positions (with the concurrence of executive management)

        (iii) Providing the format in which the sales plan (quantified data) must be presented

        (iv) Examining the economic justification for certain decisions

        (v) Providing the schedule when the data are to be submitted

    (b) Ensuring that the cognizant sales executives have the necessary statistical and historical internal sales data required to develop a sound sales plan

    (c) Supplying the relevant analyses of past sales performance, including the significant trends and relationships, for the appropriate executives sales management.

    (d) Providing for an in-depth financial analysis and evaluation of the tentative sales plan, when completed by the marketing executives. The analysis should bring to the attention of the appropriate executive any inconsistencies, questionable assumptions, reasonableness tests, or other matters that warrant discussion. These could include adequacy of margins, comparisons with competitive prices, questions about market growth, economic comparisons of different product sales mixes, etc.

    (e) When the iteration is complete, preparing the consolidated sales plan with related supplemental adjustments for such matters as returns, allowances, and other sales deductions.

    (f) Incorporating the sales plan into the total business plan for the period involved, including comparative profit data.

2. *The control phase*

    (a) Develop and revise (when necessary) appropriate financial control systems for the use of the cognizant executive.

    (b) Provide the useful and timely comparisons of budget and actual sales performance for the sales executive, by appropriate segment, and in an understandable form (by product, by territory, by salesperson, etc.).

    (c) Provide useful supplemental analytical data such as sales trends, gross margin trends, and relationships, market share information, sales effectiveness, and other control type information. These data can be furnished on a regular basis or when an observed unfavorable condition seems to be arising.

These are some of the basic functions performed by many controllers. In each situation, accounting executives will find ways in which their analytical capability and business acumen may be put to use.

CONTROL OF SALES

Sales must be controlled to achieve the best or expected return on investment. The optimum net income is realized only when a proper relationship exists among these four factors: (1) investment in working capital and facilities, (2) volume of sales, (3) operating expenses, and (4) gross margins. The accounting control of sales, therefore, relates to the reports analyzing sales activity that bring to light undesirable trends and relationships or departures from goals, budgets, or standards in the manner best calculated to secure corrective action.

SALES ANALYSIS

Getting at the Facts

The stress sometimes placed on sales volume can be misleading. If a business were to ignore the profit factor, it could probably secure any desired volume. Through the cutting of prices or through the spending of huge amounts on direct selling expense or sales promotion or advertising, volume itself could be secured. Yet what good would result? It is obvious that the implied factor is *profitable* sales volume.

If business is to achieve profitable sales, it must know where the areas of greatest profit are. This means both sales analysis and cost analysis. There is little doubt that the analysis of sales has reached different peaks of achievement in different firms and industries. Many large companies devote a great deal of time to this phase of marketing control and have well-developed programs. A large number of medium-sized or small firms have little or none. It is also probably true that the sales executive in consumer goods lines has many more facts than the industrial marketing executive.

The evidence is unmistakably clear in any business that overall or average figures are not sufficient. Such general information is of little value in making key marketing decisions and directing sales efforts. The data must be specific and related directly to the problem on which a resolution must be achieved.

Types of Sales Analyses Needed

What is needed, then, is detailed analysis to guide sales effort. Some required analysis relates solely to past sales performance as such. Other studies involve the determination of trends by comparison with previous periods. Still other reviews show the relationship to budget or standard, to gross profit, selling expense, or net profit. Analyses may be expressed in physical units, or dollar volume, or both.

The types of analyses frequently used are:

- *Product*—type of product sold, colors, sizes, price lines, style, quality (reclaimed material, odd lot, first quality)
- *Territory* —area used for sales direction—states, cities, counties, other marketing areas
- *Channel of distribution*—wholesalers, retailers, brokers, agents
- *Method of sale*—direct mail, house call, ad or coupon, delivered vs. nondelivered
- *Customer*—domestic vs. foreign, industrial vs. ultimate consumer, private vs. governmental, tabulated according to volume of purchases
- *Size of order*—average size of individual purchase
- *Terms of sale*—cash, cash on delivery (C.O.D.), regular charge account, installment, lay-away
- *Organization*—branches, departments
- *Salesperson*—either individual or groups

These analyses may be developed, not merely with regard to sales but through gross profit to profit after direct selling expense or ultimately to the net profit of the segment being measured.

Other analyses relating to unrealized sales may also be useful, for example:

- Orders received
- Unfilled orders
- Cancellations
- Lost sales

These studies may be used as an integral part of sales planning or to eliminate reasons for ineffective effort. Analysis of orders may be important where production is made to order. For example, all sales of a given size or type may be summarized to necessitate only one production run in the period.

Many subanalyses can be prepared. Thus, management may want to know not merely the overall sales by product but the product sales in each territory.

The controller may find that the sales manager can use certain of these analyses monthly or periodically—for example, sales by territory, by product lines, or by salesperson. Other analyses may be made only as a special investigation, when it is expected the tabulation will reveal out-of-line conditions. In any event, it is the controller's responsibility to design and install procedures and records in such a fashion that the maximum information is made available with the minimum of time and effort, both clerical and analytical. It is axiomatic that in many situations the company getting the information most quickly is in a better competitive position.

This information will answer the typical questions of an analytical sales executive: What was sold? Where was it sold? Who sold it? What was the profit?

Deductions from Sales

In any analysis of sales the importance of sales deductions should not be overlooked. Although reviews may relate to net sales, the clue to substandard profits may lie in the deductions—high freight cost, special allowances, or discounts. These factors may reveal why unit prices appear low.

Useful analyses and reports on sales deductions can be prepared. For example, an informative summary may be compiled to indicate the general types and amounts of sales deductions, namely, returns, freight allowances, price adjustments, or customer sales policy adjustments. It may be helpful, also, to prepare an analysis of deductions by responsibility—the manufacturing division for defective product, the traffic department for erroneous freight allowances, the sales division for allowances to retain customer goodwill.

Typical Conditions Found by Sales Analysis

In many businesses, a large proportion of the sales volume is done in a small share of the product line. Likewise, a relatively small proportion of customers will provide the bulk of the volume. Such conditions reflect the fact that only a very small part of the selling effort is responsible for most of the business. This information should prove useful to the sales executive. It might permit the concentration of sales effort and the consequent reduction in selling expense. Again, it might mean a change in territorial assignments of sales staff. Where product analysis reveals unsatisfactory conditions, a simplification of the product line may be indicated. Although the line may not be limited to only volume items, many sales managers are beginning to realize that not all sizes, all colors, and all varieties need be carried. Smart executives will let their competitors have the odd sizes or odd colors and concentrate on the more profitable articles. After all, the economies of production also must be considered in developing the product line.

Illustrative Use of Sales Analysis: Control Application

Some examples will help in illustrating certain benefits to be gained from sales analysis. Assume a case where the sales executive has just been advised by the accountant that sales for the month then ended total $125,000. Assume further that this is $15,000 lower than the preceding month and that the aggregate volume failed by $25,000 to meet the commitment to the chief executive. What can the sales manager do with merely the information that sales were $125,000? The answer, of course, is not very much. It is the position of a hunter who has a shotgun but needs a high-powered rifle. This sales manager's controller has done a poor job.

Now assume that an analysis of sales by territories is made available. The results might be as shown in Exhibit 2.1. This analysis gives the sales executive some useful information. Instead of prodding the managers of all territories, the sales manager can concentrate on the poor performers—B, D, and C, probably in just that order.

If more than one salesperson is assigned to a territory, a further analysis of the substandard territories could prove useful. Although territory B, for example, was badly under budget, it could well be that some of the salespersons did a good job. The picture might appear as in Exhibit 2.2.

It is evident that something went wrong in the areas covered by Smith, Jones, and Black. Where did they fall down? A subanalysis of the sales by Smith might reveal the data in Exhibit 2.3.

Now we are beginning to get at the root of the trouble! Smith has done much better than expected on hard resins and glue, getting what sales management feels is the maximum share of hard resin sales in the territory. While there is still an unrealized share of the potential

Territory	Total Sales		Over (or Under) Budget	
	Actual	Budget	Value	%
A	$ 15,000	$ 12,500	$ 2,500	20.00
B	50,000	70,000	(20,000)	(28. 56)
C	10,000	12,500	(2,500)	(20.00)
D	25,000	37,500	(12,500)	(33.33)
E	13,000	8,500	4,500	52.94
F	12,000	9,000	3,000	33.33
Total	$125,000	$150,000	$(25,000)	(16.67)

EXHIBIT 2.1 ANALYSIS OF SALES BY TERRITORIES

	TERRITORY B—ANALYSIS BY SALESPERSON			
	Total Sales		Over (or Under) Budget	
Salesperson	Actual	Budget	Value	%
Knight	$17,000	$14,000	$ 3,000	21.43
Black	11,500	15,000	(3,500)	(23.33)
Smith	8,500	20,500	(12,000)	(58.54)
Jones	8,000	16,000	(8,000)	(50.00)
Nesser	5,000	4,500	500	11.11
Total	$50,000	$70,000	$(20,000)	(28.56)

EXHIBIT 2.2 ANALYSIS OF SALES BY SALESPERSON

	Sales			Over (or Under) Budget	
Product	Potential	Actual	Budget	Value	%
Urea molding compound	$20,000	$2,500	$12,000	$ (9,500)	(79.17)
Alkyd molding compound	4,000	500	3,600	(3,100)	(86.11)
Hard resins	1,000	1,000	900	100	11.11
Powdered glue	6,000	4,500	4,000	500	12.50
Total	$31,000	$8,500	$20,500	$(12,000)	(58.54)

EXHIBIT 2.3 SUBANALYSIS OF SALESPERSON BY PRODUCT

sales, Smith exceeded the budget. However, Smith has performed very poorly on molding-compound. A review of Smith's call reports indicates that important users of molding compound have not been called. For example, Smith is completely overlooking the molders of electrical fixtures, yet this is where the greatest potential lies. The sales, as an analysis by customers shows, have been only to molders of bottle caps and the like. Now the sales manager has the facts and can take corrective action, and the controller can feel that the analysis has been useful.

Other Uses of Sales Analysis

In many businesses, particularly small concerns, budget applications are neither well developed nor applied. Budget information by product or by salesperson is not available. In some instances, the cost of maintaining an elaborate budget system is not cost effective. Sales analyses may be made that are useful but not related to a budget. An analysis by customer by commodity class, indicating sales this month, sales same month last year, sales year to date, and sales last year to date will provide some comparative data as well as trends. If the sales executive has detailed knowledge of each territory and general level of activity by customer, the report can be of use in directing the sales effort. Observations can be made about which customers are growing or declining in sales volume. With knowledge of the margin by commodity class, it can be determined if growth is in the profitable lines or on the low margin products; this may indicate that prices should be reviewed.

There are many simple analyses that can be made to guide the sales effort. The controller should continuously work with sales executives to develop those reports that are most useful, like special or one-time reports. The information developed should be interpreted and the important trends or measures should be highlighted.

Other uses of sales analyses that may be considered are:

- *For sales planning and setting of quotas.* Past experience is a factor.
- *For inventory control.* To properly plan inventories, a business should be familiar with past sales and probable future trends in terms of seasonal fluctuations and type of product.
- *For the setting of certain sales standards.* Here, also, past experience is a factor.
- *For the better distribution of sales effort in territories.* It may well prove that the business is concentrating its effort in too restrictive an area. Consideration of potential sales, competitive conditions, and cost factors may dictate a wider coverage. Again, analysis might reveal that the territory is not being fully covered.
- *For better direction of sales effort on products.* A study of sales and the potentials may reveal the restriction of sales effort to certain products to the neglect of other and more profitable ones. Also, a comparison of sales by product with previous periods will reveal trends. If the trends are away from the more profitable lines, corrective action may be necessary.
- *For better direction of sales effort in terms of customers.* Analysis by customers should reveal trends about the types of merchandise purchased by each customer. Also, comparison with the sales of a similar period for the previous year will reveal facts on whether the company is making headway in securing the maximum amount of profitable business from the customer. Analysis by customer account, coupled with other information and discussions with the sales manager, will show certain accounts that cannot possibly provide a profitable volume, even if developed. This, too, may permit greater utilization of sales effort elsewhere.

Sales and Gross Profit Analysis

Sales efforts, as previously stated, should be directed and focused on *profitable* volume. To accomplish this, sales executives must be provided with all the facts related to profit. Therefore, analysis of sales must include a detailed analysis of contribution margin and/or gross profit. For example, a sales report by a salesperson should indicate the comparative gross profit by periods as well as sales. Although high gross profit does not necessarily signify a high net profit, since the selling costs may be excessive, it is an indicator. It certainly serves as a guide, however, in determining areas for concentration of the sales effort.

One other aspect of gross profit deserves comment. Variations in gross profit may result from changes in the selling price, product sales mixture, returns, or volume (largely controlled by the sales executive) or from changes in manufacturing efficiency (controlled by the production executive). These facts should be recognized when reviewing changes in gross profit. The causes should be isolated. If a standard cost system is in operation, this process is simplified somewhat. In this case, the best measure of sales performance will be standard gross profit. When the standard eliminates the manufacturing efficiency factor, then the sales department is generally responsible for the result, as well as the volume variance.

Limitations of Sales Analysis

Sales analysis is only one management tool used by the sales executive. Such analysis, however, is no substitute for the professional leadership needed to properly direct and manage the sales function. It is obvious that analysis of the actual sales volume must be used in conjunction with other factors like sales potential, plans, budgets, standards, historical performance, industry comparisons, manufacturing costs, and operating expenses. Most important, the sales executive must use the data to make effective decisions.

Although sales volume analyses can be used extensively in measuring or studying sales performance, those using the data must recognize that high volume does not mean high profits. Profits will certainly vary, and a business does not earn the same rate of profit on all products. An analysis of sales volume alone will not provide sufficient information to maximize the return on investment on any given product. Many other factors must be considered. Even with some limitations, the analysis of sales is an integral part of any well-managed sales function.

SALES PLANNING: BASIS OF ALL BUSINESS PLANS

Sales analysis is a useful function. As mentioned in the prior section, it may be applied to better direct and control sales effort, and for other related sales *control* activities. Yet, one of the other principal applications is to sales *planning;* that is, in helping to determine a proper sales level (by product or territory or salesperson, etc.) for the next year or two of the annual business plan. The application to sales planning is also used in selecting the more profitable sales potential areas for the strategic, or long-range, plan.

It will bear mentioning that the sales plan is the foundation for the entire system of plans including: the production plan, the marketing plan, the research and development plan, the administrative expense plan, the facilities plan, the working capital plan, and the financing plan. Thus, the sales plan is so pervasive and fundamental that it is in the interest of the company to develop the best possible plan, using all fairly available information (both internal and external).

A reasonable amount of time will be spent in developing the short-term sales plan or budget for the next year in considerable detail. But the chief sales executive has to keep in perspective the relationship of the immediate short-term or tactical plan to the strategic longer-term plan. The flow of products and services in these two plans may be as illustrated in Exhibit 2.4. As a practical matter, the sales manager often will view the marketing task as threefold:

1. Sales of existing products and/or services to existing customers
2. Sales of existing products/services to new customer

3. Sales of new products to existing, as well as new customers

Sales often may be estimated by these segments.

    These facets of the near- and long-term sales plans, as well as the increase in sales from acquisitions (newly acquired companies or products), are shown in Exhibit 2.4. All these sales targets may be necessary to avoid the natural decline in sales over a period of time and to reach the long-term corporate sales objective.

STEPS IN DEVELOPING THE NEAR-TERM SALES PLAN/BUDGET

Each company has its own way of developing the sales plan or budget, and providing such information to those executives, who, in turn, use it for developing their segment of the total business plan.

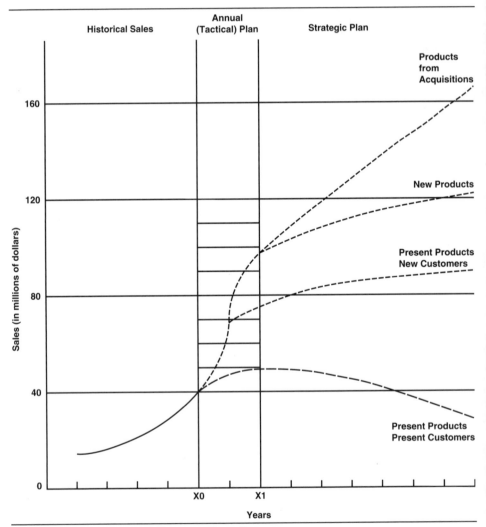

EXHIBIT 2.4   STRATEGIC AND TACTICAL SALES PLAN

The planning steps outlined next are somewhat typical when industry estimates of future sales levels are available, or when some useful external data may be secure, and when the involved executives are accustomed to being provided with relevant sales and gross profit analyses.

1. The chief sales executive who is responsible for preparing the sales plan, also called the sales budget, and meeting it, is given some or all of the following data:

    (a) Computer sheets or other worksheets in proper format for providing the sales estimate, by month, and by product or salesperson, for the planning year

    (b) Sales performance for the last year (estimated for the balance of current year) or two by salesperson, and perhaps subanalyzed by territory or customer—in monetary or physical units

    (c) Industry data on expected next-year total sales

    (d) Any other analyses based on external information, developed by the market research department or economist or perhaps the controller, giving a clue as to expected sales (correlation techniques, etc.; U.S. government statistics) or business conditions for the coming plan year

    (e) Any other data the sales manager or salespersons reasonably request as helpful in developing sales estimates

    (f) Analyses, if available, giving the estimated sales impact of planned sales promotions, and reasons for the cause or precise location of below-plan performance in the sales area (current year)

    (g) Any guidance, or expected sales levels that the CEO or other influential executives (e.g., manufacturing executives as to new production capacity) may wish to provide

2. The sales executive provides an estimate of sales for the planning year in appropriate detail (by product, salesperson, or territory). While the sales executive may prepare such an estimate unaided, it is preferable to ask each salesperson (through appropriate organization channels) to make an estimate of sales for that person's assigned area or product, in appropriate detail, by month or other time period, for the coming year. The chief sales executive, directly or acting through territorial or product sales managers, will provide guidance to the sales staff on such subjects as:

    ○ Percent sales increase expected

    ○ Estimated impact of planned promotional programs

    ○ Competitive actions and the like

    Assuming each salesperson prepares their own estimate (by customer, product, etc.), as the plan is forwarded up the organization structure to the chief sales executive, it may be modified by the intervening sales executives—each giving reasons for the changes.

3. Finally, at the top executive level, the estimates are consolidated (probably by the controller's staff) and company totals determined.

    The summarized sales plan, following the territorial organization structure is illustrated in Exhibit 2.5. Supporting territorial budgets for each territory sales manager, by salesperson, would be available from the database. Other analyses, such as by product, could be prepared.

4. Each proposed sales level is discussed by executive management as to acceptability, reasonableness, etc.

5. When the sales budget is tentatively approved (an iterative process) then other functional executives who need the data are provided with it so they can develop their segments of

THE ILLUSTRATIVE COMPANY
SALES PLAN BY TERRITORY
FOR THE YEAR 20XX
(DOLLARS IN THOUSANDS)

		Plan				
			Quarter			
	Sales					
Territory	This Year	Total	1	2	3	4
West	$212,400	$230,000	$ 46,000	$ 63,720	$ 79,040	$ 41,240
Rockies	75,000	78,750	15,750	23,620	31,500	7,880
Southwest	134,600	150,750	37,690	45,200	45,200	22,660
Central Plains	53,400	56,100	14,000	16,900	16,900	8,300
Midwest	171,300	186,700	33,600	65,300	50,000	37,800
Southeast	91,400	95,100	19,000	28,500	21,000	26,600
Total	$738,100	$797,400	$166,040	$243,240	$243,640	$144,480

EXHIBIT 2.5 SALES PLAN BY TERRITORY

the annual plan (the marketing plan, production plan, research and development plan). Several iterations can take place (adjusting for capacity, competitive actions, probable lack of raw material, etc.) until an operating plan is agreed upon.

6. The operating budget and capital budget, together with the related financial statements, are consolidated and tested for financial acceptability, and so on. Through iteration a final plan is arrived at.

7. When the board of directors approves the plan, each segment becomes a commitment for the plan period by the relevant or responsible executive.

CONTROL PHASE

In the context of the budgeting process (a two-pronged device consisting of the planning phase and the control phase) the steps discussed in Section Section "Steps in Developing the Near-Term Sales Plan/Budget" complete the *planning* phase when the sales plan is approved by the board of directors. Then, the task consists of, among other things, monitoring actual sales results and directing the sales effort so that the plan is achieved. This is generally identified as the *control* phase. The implementing steps are essentially as:

- Actual performance is compared with plan (or quota), for each salesperson involved in the sales effort, for the appropriate time period, which may be the day (cumulative), week, or month.
- The data are analyzed, much as described earlier, to determine the cause of the subperformance.
- Corrective action, if needed, is taken by the sales executive to get sales "on plan." This might include special sales promotion, etc., especially if the cause of under-plan sales is a general condition, that is, not one induced by the lack of effort of a salesperson.
- Aside from analysis of actual and planned sales, a review of some selected statistical performance measures may provide clues on how sales could be improved (e.g., conversion rate of prospects to customers). See the sections on standards and benchmarking.

METHODS OF DETERMINING THE SALES LEVEL

The development of a sound sales plan, together with the program for directing the sales effort, ultimately must rest largely on the judgment of the cognizant sales executive. The means used to arrive at a decision obviously may influence its quality. Ordinarily, weight must be given to both external and internal factors. External factors (including such elements as general economic conditions, industry trends, total market potential, and competitive actions or reactions) are beyond the control of the individual company, but nevertheless may largely prescribe the sales potential. Internal factors relate to conditions within the entity and are composed of matters such as production capacity, product quality, sales experience, history, special advertising and sales promotion programs, pricing policy, and sales method changes.

In this section, some of the more commonly used methods of estimating sales levels, to help the sales executive reach decisions or judgments, are discussed. What system will be used may depend on several related attributes:

- *Time.* The time span available, the frequency of the data
- *Resources needed or available.* Manpower, computers, financial sophistication, cost
- *Data input.* What is needed, consistency, availability, variability
- *Output.* Reliability, extent of detail, capability of detecting trend changes, capability of revealing direction changes that have taken place

For the knowledge of the controller, the more or less proven techniques of forecasting sales demand may be categorized in these three groups:

1. *Mathematical/statistical methods*
   ○ Time series analysis
   ○ Correlation

2. *Judgmental methods (nonstatistical)*
   ○ Estimates of salespersons
   ○ Customer surveys
   ○ Executive opinion composites

3. *Other methods*
   ○ Share of market
   ○ End-use analysis
   ○ Product line analysis
   ○ Market simulation
   ○ Combinations of methods

Mathematical/Statistical Methods

The various mathematical/statistical methods usually require the services of a person or persons skilled in the techniques (statisticians, economists, and perhaps accountants). Basically, a statistical technique is applied to a series of relevant numbers to arrive at a *forecast* of sales for the industry or company. Then, this *forecast* is modified by the expected impact of sales efforts, promotional campaigns, and so forth, to arrive at a sales *plan* for the company. Two types of mathematical applications are addressed here.

Time Series Analysis.   With the use of a model already programmed in the computer, or by the application of the well-known least squares method, an existing series of values is converted into a trend, and extrapolated for a future time period. Basically, the existing series of values is isolated into its statistical components:

- Secular or long-term trend
- Cyclical movements
- Seasonal patterns
- The remaining random fluctuations

The long-term trend is projected to estimate the future sales for the planning periods.

Correlation Analysis.   As the name implies, a series is located with which the company sales, or sales of a particular product line, seem to correlate or move sympathetically. Presumably, the data are readily and timely available, are reliable, and are those that lead the company sales. The annual product sales are plotted against the index and, based on the leading factor, calculated for the planning period. Some illustrative correlation bases could be the U.S. Department of Commerce composite index of leading indicators (discussed later) or Series No. 20, contracts and orders for plant and equipment, also issued by the U.S. Department of Commerce, or the Federal Reserve Index of Industrial Production.

Other statistical methods, such as the Box-Jenkins computer-based iterative procedure, or use of moving averages, can be employed.

Judgmental Methods

Another popular method is the gathering of opinions or estimates from several groups. Some common variations of this method are discussed.

Estimates of Salespersons.   In using the estimates of salespeople, one method involves securing the estimates of the sales staff itself. Each salesperson is provided with a record of his or her sales, by month, for the past year or two. With this data and that person's knowledge of the sales territory and customer, an estimate by product and/or customer is obtained from the person who will be responsible for securing the sale.

A variation of this procedure is to have the sales manager to whom the salesperson reports and the salesperson jointly arrive at a sales estimate.

Another procedure involving the sales department personnel is to secure the opinions of the various sales managers—the product sales managers, division sales managers, or territory sales managers, together with the general sales manager. Through discussions and cross-checking, and considering the impact of sales programs, many believe a reliable estimate can be secured. Of course, the extent of knowledge of the sales manager level must be considered. Hopefully, they are close enough to the firing line to know the sales conditions, products, and customers.

The use of only sales department personnel has both advantages and disadvantages:

- *Advantages*
  - The knowledge of the persons closest to the sales picture is used.
  - Those who must meet plan have a voice in setting it.
- *Disadvantages*
  - The level may be biased in that sales personnel often tend to provide optimistic estimates when the business level is high, and too low estimates when the level is poor.

○ The participants may not give proper weight to broad economic trends that the sales force or managers either do not recognize or fail to properly evaluate.

○ If compensation levels depend on meeting the sales plan, a deliberate effort might be made to keep the estimate on the low side so that enhanced remuneration is more likely.

Care must be taken (by the CEO, other top executives, or the controller) in weighing the sales personnel opinions.

Customer Surveys.   The practice of asking customers for their estimate of purchases for the coming year often is used when there is no other source of reliable and specific data to make a sales estimate. It may be employed when there is a good relationship between the salesperson and the customer, and when the customers tend to be very large and limited in number. An example is the glass companies who make the windshields and glass windows used by automobile manufacturers.

The disadvantages include the facts that:

• The user may be ill-informed or uncooperative in such sensitive matters.

• It is time consuming if many customers must be contacted.

The possible advantages are:

• It may be the only suitable manner of preparing a sales plan.

• It gives the questioner an opportunity to delve into the thinking of the customers about the business outlook.

• It is an opportunity to secure information directly from those who will be using the product.

Executive Opinion Composites.   Another commonly used and convenient method of estimating future sales volume is by securing opinions from a group of top and middle management executives who have reason to be familiar with the industry and company sales picture. The method involves simply securing the estimates from a group of executives, perhaps weighting them, and then combining the opinions. Thus, the CEO and sales, production, research, and financial executives may be contacted, and weightings given to their opinions, depending on their knowledge of the market and perhaps on the accuracy of their past estimates. Each executive may determine his expectation based on his own methods; and the groups may meet to discuss the levels and the basis for the opinion.

While this method may provide a broader base than from sales personnel only, and be more convenient, if the executives don't really know the market, then the opinion may be one big guess, based on few facts.

Other Methods

There are numerous other methods for developing sales forecasts or plans, some of which may be used alone or in combination with other procedures. A few brief comments follow.

Share of Market.   For some types of products the total market is well known. In addition to the industry total unit volume and/or dollar volume, the rate of growth has been calculated, and often the estimated sales for the next year or two have been determined— perhaps by the industry association. In any event, the planner knows what share of the market the company has secured in the past. This market share, say 27 percent, adjusted for the estimated impact of special sales promotions, or guessed competitive activity is applied to the projected total market to arrive at the company segment of, for example, 29 percent of the estimated industry sales for the coming year.

End-Use Analysis. This technique depends on having a sound estimate of the total end-use market for which products the company's articles serve as component parts or elements. Again, to use the automotive industry as an example, if the expected unit sales of automobiles are known or have been estimated, then the supplier company can estimate its probable sales for the planning period for its product, the new car business. This market, plus the estimated replacement business, or other business, can be combined to arrive at sales expectations. This method bears a close relationship, in some cases, to the customer survey procedure.

Product Line Analysis. Quite often major products are sold through different channels of distribution or methods of sales than other products, and the sales and sales effort may be managed by product line. Under these circumstances, a company's internal sales (and gross profit) analyses by product, subanalyzed by territory, and so on (as discussed earlier in Section "Relationship of Entity Goals to Performance Standards") may be the starting point of determining the sales estimate, supplemented by some of the other techniques to arrive at the sales plan.

Market Simulation. This technique ordinarily involves the use of a computer, and the construction of a mathematical model of the market. Modifying input for the different factors that influence the market permits the calculation of various sales estimates. This is another helpful tool, often developed by the market research organization, that can assist in arriving at a realistic sales plan.

It should be understood that, whatever estimating technique is used:

- Even a good forecast reduces only *some* of the risk that confronts sales management.
- It is often helpful to compare the results of several forecasting methods.
- Some of the simplest methods work best, because they are more easily understood; the heart of good forecasting probably often is intelligently based intuition on the part of sales management.

USEFUL SOURCES OF FORECASTING INFORMATION

Business executives long have been intrigued by the promise of a practical indicator of business trends that could be useful in their business forecasting. Some have found broad economic measures helpful, such as gross national product (GNP), new car sales in a given territory, etc. But for many, no practical guide has been located either for the business as a whole or for major lines. Many of the broad indicators have suffered from late availability, significant revisions, inaccuracies in compilation, and components out of touch with the market, to name a few. These executives, therefore, have encouraged their staffs to develop in-house models, perhaps based on some readily available indicators. Sometimes these models have been built from data furnished by commercial banks, or in other instances developed from a factor, such as regional car sales, that an executive has noticed appears to correlate quite closely with the company's sales experience on certain products.

Given the conflicting or indecisive signals put out by some indicators and the inability to find a suitable one, sometimes the intuition of the chief executive or chief sales executive is one of the best guides.

The controller should be aware of external sources of sales forecasting data just in case the present sales estimating techniques could stand some testing or improvement.

Some Specific Sources

There are numerous sources, ranging from the federal government to selected financial services, such as Standard & Poor's (S&P) and Moody's, that supply information which may be useful in sales forecasting. Market planners, market research analysts, and many financial executives often are familiar with them. Of course, libraries may provide assistance on this subject. The secret is to find an index or economic data useful in a particular business. A partial outline of some sources follows:

1. *U.S. government Department of Commerce*
   (a) Bureau of Economic Analysis (BEA)
       Includes cyclical indicators and economic measures published in the *Survey of Current Business*
   (b) Department of Labor
       Bureau of Labor Statistics
   (c) Department of Agriculture
   (d) Bureau of Mines
   (e) U.S. Government Printing Office
2. *Commercial banks*[1]
3. *Other sources*
   (a) Trade associations
   (b) State governments
   (c) Federal Reserve Board
   (d) Universities (economics departments and schools of business, etc.)
   (e) Financial services providing economic data for pay
   (f) Numerous business magazines, such as:
       (i) *Survey of Current Business*
       (ii) *Business Week,* with its weekly "Business Week Leading Index"
       (iii) *Fortune* magazine (its "Forecast")
   (g) Libraries

Validity of Economic Indicators

While the wealth of economic data provided by Washington is useful, the data need careful interpretation by those who know what to look for.

---

1. The controller can check through the appropriate company channel or directly from its commercial bankers as to data available.

FORECASTING THE BUSINESS CYCLE[2]

Nature of the Business Cycle

A business cycle is a recurring series of expansions and contractions, involving and driven by a vast number of economic variables, that manifests itself as changes in the level of income, production, and employment. As will be described in the next section, these swings can have a profound impact on a company. A business cycle tends to be long-term in nature, and is very difficult to predict in terms of length or intensity. It is driven by so many variables, most of which interact with each other, that it is excruciatingly difficult to determine the exact causes of previous cycles and the timing of the next one based on those variables.

Though the exact causes of the business cycle are difficult to discern, there are essentially two types of variables that cause business cycle changes to occur. The first is an *exogenous variable*. This is a variable that impacts the economic system, though it is not an integral component of the system. For example, a bad rainy season will impact the crop yields in the farming community, which in turn reduces the amount of purchases by farmers for the next season's crop, which in turn impacts the activity of the suppliers of those purchases, and so on. Another exogenous variable is a war, which can wreak enough destruction to entirely shatter an economy. These types of variables can, to some extent, be called "acts of God." The other type of variable is the *endogenous variable*. This is a variable that impacts an economic system from within. For example, overcapacity in the resin-production industry causes suppliers to reduce their resin prices to plastic molding companies, which in turn can now reduce the prices of their products, which creates an increase in sales, and contributes to an increase in the level of economic activity. Other examples of this type include the demand for products, and pricing changes.

The typical company operates within a single sector of the economy, where a single major shock, either of the endogenous or exogenous variety, can cause immediate and massive changes, since individual sectors are much smaller than the national economy, and so can be severely impacted by smaller events. For example, an increase in the price of aviation jet fuel will cause the airlines to increase their prices, which reduces the number of seats filled, which drives down airline profits and forces them to postpone orders for new jets, which in turn harms the airline manufacturing companies and *their* supporting groups of suppliers— all due to an increase in the price of jet fuel, which is just a single variable.

Consequently, a controller may not be overwhelmingly concerned with the operations of the entire national or international economy, since the typical economic contraction corresponds to a drop in GNP of only a few percentage points. However, industry-specific changes within that larger economy can be truly catastrophic, and it is within this smaller economic environment that a company operates and must make management changes. This leads us to the next section, which covers the specific problems a company faces as a result of changes in the business cycle.

Impact of the Business Cycle on the Corporation

What happens to a company when the business cycle changes to a new phase, either upward or downward? We will begin with the impact of an economic contraction.

When management realizes that sales have declined, it must contract the business. One of the first steps taken is to reduce inventories, so that the company is not stuck with a large

---

2. Section "Forecasting the Business Cycle" adapted with permission from Steven M. Bragg, *Financial Analysis: A Controller's Guide* (Hoboken: Wiley, 2000 Chapter 9.)

investment of products that will be at risk of becoming obsolete before they can be sold. One way to reduce inventories is to sell them off at reduced prices, but this cuts into gross margins and also fills the distribution pipeline, so that no additional sales can be made until the pipeline clears. The more common approach is to reduce the production staff and all related overhead staff with a layoff, the extent of which will be driven by management's perception of the depth of the upcoming cyclical decline. Management will also likely curtail capital expenditures and increase controls over incidental expenses. Further, the controller will be called on to tighten credit to customers and heighten collection activities to ensure that accounts receivable do not include any bad debts, and that collections are made as soon as possible. If there are excess funds available, management will likely use them to pay down debt, so that fixed costs are reduced to the bare minimum in anticipation of poor sales conditions at the bottom of the economic cycle.

Also during business downturns, there will be a few adventurous companies that will buck the industry trend and *expand*. They do this because they anticipate a short downturn in the economy, and they want to pick up new business, either by undercutting competitors or (more commonly) by waiting until financially weaker companies begin to fail, and then buying them. They may also take advantage of lower real estate and equipment costs during these periods to add to their capacity with inexpensive new production facilities. This strategy is possible only if a company has substantial cash reserves or available debt, and has an aggressive management team that is willing to take chances.

When the economy begins to turn in an upward direction, management must make several contrary decisions. The first one is to ramp up existing production capacity, which may have been shuttered, and now requires refurbishment before production can begin. Then management must determine the extent to which it wants to rebuild its inventory levels to anticipate renewed sales. This is a critical decision, for overproduction in a weakly rebounding economy will create more inventory than is needed, whereas producing too little in the midst of a strong economic rebound will result in sales being lost to more aggressive competitors. If the rebound is sudden, the company must spend more money on staff overtime and rush equipment deliveries to bring production back up to speed as soon as possible. Credit policies likely will be loosened in order to bring in new business, and management must decide on how much new capital equipment to purchase, and the most appropriate time for when to acquire it.

All of the changes noted here, for either an increase or decrease in the business cycle, call for changes in a company's operations that will certainly have some impact on profits, but even more so on the level of working capital and fixed assets. For example, waiting too long to cut back production will result in an excess investment in inventory, as well as any new capital projects that were not curtailed in time. The reverse problem arises during an economic upswing, when reacting too slowly will result in a cash inflow from the sale of all inventory, followed by the loss of additional profits because *all* of the inventory has been sold, and there is none left to sell. Thus proper management of working capital and fixed assets lies at the heart of management's decisions regarding how to deal with changes in the business cycle.

Elements of Business Cycle Forecasting

In this section, we will review who does forecasting, what information they forecast, and the methods they use for doing so.

Forecasting is conducted not only by various branches of the federal government, such as the Department of Commerce and the Federal Reserve Board, but also by a number of universities and private institutions. The governments and schools do so as a public service, but the private groups do so for an entirely different reason—they create tailored forecasts that churn out estimates on very specific items, such as stock prices or exchange rates, that are requested by top-paying clients. These forecasts commonly cover a series of quarterly periods, which, due to the short time frames involved, are much more difficult to predict with any degree of reliability than the annual forecasts that were more common in the last few decades. The governments and universities focus on such macro issues as the Gross National Product or the rate of inflation. The trade group to which most of these organizations belong is the National Association of Business Economists.

There are four primary methods used to arrive at forecasts. Since each one is based on different information and may arrive at somewhat different results, it is common for forecasters to blend the results of two or more methods to arrive at their estimates of future conditions. The methods are:

- *Anticipation surveys.* These are surveys of key people in the business community. The purpose of these surveys is to collect information about the intentions of the survey participants to engage in capital purchases, acquisitions, changes in headcount, or any other steps that may impact the economy, and then aggregate this information to arrive at general estimates of trends.

- *Time series models.* These are trend lines that are based on historical information. For a forecast, one finds the trend line that fits a similar set of previous conditions, and fits it to the current conditions to arrive at a trend line of future expectations. These can be relatively accurate in the short run, but do not generate good results very far into the future.

- *Econometric models.* These are highly complex and iterative models that simulate the real economy, and are frequently composed of hundreds of variables that interact with each other. These can yield good results over periods longer than those predicted by time series models. However, changes in the results of the models are difficult to explain, given the complexity of the underlying formulas.

- *Cyclical indicators.* These are the leading, coincident, and lagging indicators that foretell changes in the economy. This method is a good way to confirm the existence of business cycle changes that have been predicted by other forecasting methods. A leading indicator is something that changes in advance of an alteration in a business cycle, such as the number of new business formations, new capital expenditure requests, construction contracts, the length of the average work week, layoff rate, unemployment insurance claims, profit margins, new orders, investments in residential structures, capacity utilization, and new bond or equity issues. These can change anywhere from a few months to over a year in advance of a related change in the phase of the business cycle. A lagging indicator is something that changes after an alteration in the business cycle has occurred, and is used by forecasters to confirm the business cycle change that was indicated by leading indicators. Examples of lagging indicators are investments in nonresidential structures, unit labor costs, and the amount of consumer credit outstanding.

The exact forecasting method used depends on the person doing the forecasting, and is largely influenced by judgment. The reason why judgment is such a necessary factor in forecasting is that all of the forecasting methods, with the exception of anticipation surveys, are based on the interpretation of historical economic data, which may no longer impact the economy in the same manner as it did when the various models were constructed. Thus, having an in-depth knowledge of the current economic situation, and using their information to adjust the results of quantitatively derived forecasts is the key difference between a quantitative analyst who does nothing but tweak the numbers, and a great forecaster who consistently outperforms the outcomes predicted by the various models.

In addition to judgment, forecasters will use numeric weighting schemes, where they give greater value to the results of certain forecasting models or specific variables, depending on their experience of past forecasting results, or their guesses regarding changes in the economy for the period being predicted. Some forecasters will even combine and average out the predictions of groups of other forecasters, on the grounds that this will create a consensus opinion that has a better chance of being accurate. However, there may be a wide dispersion in the various forecasts being predicted, which makes it difficult to arrive at a time period for forecasted changes in the business cycle based on this approach.

Once the forecasters make their predictions, they also compare their forecasts to the actual results as that information arrives. They will then spend a great deal of time modifying their forecasting methods to make their next set of forecasts more closely match the future results. This is an ongoing process that never ends, because the underlying variables that drive business cycles are constantly altering the degrees of force with which they impact the economy. Also, old variables may eventually have so little impact on business cycles that they are dropped entirely from the forecasting systems, while new variables must be researched and inserted into the models. Thus, the after-the-fact review of forecasting models and their component parts is a major forecasting task.

When reviewing the effectiveness of the variables that comprise a forecast, there are several factors to consider. One is that a small pool of variables may result in an incorrect forecast, because each of them may be adversely impacted by exogenous variables that yield results not truly representing their impact on the business cycle as a whole. However, by using a large number of variables in a forecasting model, one can tolerate a minority of variables that yield incorrect results, while still arriving at an overall forecast that is made accurate by the sheer volume of variables included in the model. Another item to review is the number of months by which leading indicators presage a change in the business cycle. Though there may be historical justification for using a certain number of months in a forecasting model, these periods can change, sometimes to the extent of having a leading indicator turn into a lagging indicator. Also, the selection process for variables needs to be very in-depth before they are added to a forecasting model. For example, a new variable should be thoroughly researched to determine the extent of its linkage to a business cycle, how well it predicts business cycle behavior, how consistently it does so, and also how frequently information about the variable is reported (so that it can be included in the forecast in a timely manner). Only if all these questions receive favorable answers should a new variable be included in a forecasting model.

Having briefly described who creates forecasts, what information they issue, and how they arrive at these forecasts, we now turn to the role of the controller in creating forecasts that are tailored for the use of company management.

Business Cycle Forecasting at the Corporate Level

What can a controller do in his or her role as a financial analyst to provide business cycle predictions to the management team? There are several possible routes to take.

The main factor a controller must decide on is balancing the time needed for forecasting against the perceived value of the information. For example, if a company has a stable sales base that rarely varies, irrespective of what stage the business cycle is currently in, then there is no reason to track cycles very carefully. Also, if the accounting function is understaffed, the needs of day-to-day activities will probably supersede any demands for forecasting. However, if a controller can prove that the deleterious effects of *not* tracking business cycle conditions will lead to company losses that significantly exceed the cost of having extra staff on hand to perform the analysis, then this second factor disappears.

Let us assume that there is some time available for forecasting work, and that business cycles have a sufficient impact on company conditions to be worthy of review. If so, here are some possible actions to take to obtain, analyze, and report on business cycle forecasts. They are listed in ascending order of difficulty:

- *Report on published forecasts.* There are forecasts published by nearly every major business magazine for the economy at large, which can be easily extracted, reformatted into an internal report, and presented to management, perhaps as part of the monthly financial statements. Several key advantages are that the information is fairly accurate for the entire economy, it is prepared by professional forecasters, and it is essentially free. The problem is that each company operates in a smaller industry within the national economy, and as such is subject to mini-business cycles that may not move in lockstep with that of the national economy. For this reason, the reported information may be only generally relevant to a company's specific situation.

- *Subscribe to a forecasting service.* A company can pay a significant fee, probably in the five-to six-figure range, to a forecasting service for more specific reports that relate to the industry in which it operates. This is a good approach for those organizations that do not have the resources to gather, summarize, and interpret economic data by themselves. However, some industries are too small to be serviced by a specialized forecasting service, or the fee charged is considered too high in comparison to the value of the information received.

- *Develop an in-house forecasting model.* In cases where a company either wants to run its own forecasting model, or there are no forecasting services available that can provide the information, and it is deemed relevant, it is time to try some in-house forecasting. This effort can range from a minimalist approach to a comprehensive one, with each level of effort yielding better results. The first step is to go through the steps noted in the preceding section to find the right kinds of data to accumulate, followed by implementing a data-gathering method that yields reliable data in a timely manner. Then, one must work with management to determine what resulting information is desired (usually a sales estimate). Then the controller must arrive at a methodology for translating the underlying data into a forecast. Then the controller should develop a standard reporting format that imparts the results to management. This report should include the underlying assumptions and data used to arrive at the forecast, so that any changes in the assumptions are clearly laid out. Finally, there should be a methodology for comparing the results against actual data, and adjusting the forecasting methodology based on that information. Though this approach is a time-consuming one, it can yield the best results if a carefully developed forecasting system is used.

For example, let us assume that a controller of a sport rack company has elected to use the last of the above options for creating forecasting information. Sport racks is a very small niche market that creates and sells racks for skis, snowboards, bicycles, and kayaks that can be attached to the tops of most kinds of automobiles. The controller wants to derive a forecasting system that will give management an estimate of the amount by which projected sales can be expected to vary. She decides to subdivide the market into four categories, one each for skis, snowboards, bicycles, and kayaks. Based on a historical analysis, she finds that 25 percent of ski purchasers, 35 percent of snowboard purchasers, 75 percent of bicycle purchasers, and 30 percent of kayak purchasers will purchase a car-top rack system to hold their new equipment. The typical delay in these purchases from the time when they bought their sports equipment to the time they bought sport racks was six months. The controller finds that she can obtain new sports equipment sales data from industry trade groups every three months. Given the lag time before users purchase car-top racks, this means that she can accumulate the underlying data that predict sport rack sales and disseminate them to management with three months to go before the resulting sport rack sales will occur. Thus, she concludes that these are usable data.

The next task is to determine the company's share of the sport rack market, which is readily obtainable from the industry trade group for sport racks, though this information is at least one year old. Given the stability of sales within the industry, she feels that this information is still accurate. She then prepares the report shown in Exhibit 2.6. It shows total sports equipment sales for the last quarter, uses historical percentages to arrive at the amount of resulting sport rack sales, and then factors in the company's market share percentage to determine the forecasted sales of each type of sport rack. By comparing this information to the previously forecasted sales information, the report reveals that the company should significantly ramp up its production of snowboard sport racks as soon as possible.

The example used was for an extremely limited niche market, but it does point out that a modest amount of forecasting work can yield excellent results that are much more company-specific than would be the case if a company relied solely on the forecasts of experts who were concerned only with general national trends. For most companies, there will be a number of additional underlying indicators that should be factored into the forecasting model; however, the work associated with tracking these added data must be compared to the benefit of more accurate results, so that a controller arrives at a reasonable cost-benefit compromise.

SALES STANDARDS

Definition of Sales Standards

A *standard* has been defined as a scientifically developed measure of performance. It was further noted that standards can be adapted to the measurement of sales performance in somewhat the same way they have been used to judge performance in the factory. The primary requirements in developing tools for the sales executive are threefold:

1. *Sales standards are the result of careful investigation and analysis of past performance, taking into consideration expected future conditions.* Sales standards represent the opinion of those best qualified to judge what constitutes satisfactory performance. Judgment about detailed operations must rest largely with the sales executives. Opinions about expected general business conditions and market potentials should represent the combined judgment of the executive staff, including the chief executive, the sales manager, and the controller.

Description	Sports Equipment Unit Sales	% Buying Sport Racks	Company Market Share	Forecasted Company Unit Sales	Original Company Forecast	Variance
Ski	3,200,000	25%	40%	320,000	300,000	+20,000
Snowboard	2,700,000	35%	40%	378,000	300,000	+78,000
Bicycle	2,500,000	75%	30%	562,500	550,000	+16,500
Kayak	450,000	30%	30%	40,500	45,000	−4,500

EXHIBIT 2.6 INDUSTRY-SPECIFIC FORECASTING MODEL

   2. *Sales standards must be fair and reasonable measures of performance.* Nothing will be so destructive of morale as a sales quota, or any other standard, set much too high. Experience shows that such standards will be ignored. The standards must be attainable by the caliber of salesman the company expects to be representative of its selling staff.

   3. *Sales standards will need review and revision from time to time.* As sales conditions change frequently, so the measuring stick must change.

Purpose of Sales Standards

Sales managers are sometimes of the opinion that sales standards are not welcome. Some sales executives feel that sales standards are an attempt to substitute impersonal statistics for sales leadership. There is no substitute for dynamic and farsighted sales executives; there is no intent that sales standards in any way replace personal guidance. But sales standards do provide management with an important tool of sales control, a basis for fairly rewarding merit, and a stimulating device under many circumstances, but not all. As a tool of control they reveal weaknesses in performance that, if properly analyzed in terms of causes, open the way for correction and strengthening. As a basis for rewarding merit they result in a fairer and more accurate relationship between compensation and performance. As a stimulating device they provide each salesperson and executive with a goal of accomplishment and with assurance of fair reward.

Nature of Sales Standards

The sales standards may be expressed in terms of effort, results, or the relation of effort to result. For example, a salesperson may be required to make three calls a day or fifteen calls per week. Making this number of calls meets this particular standard of effort. As a result of these calls, the expectations may be to secure ten orders for every fifteen calls or a certain dollar volume per call. Doing this meets this particular relationship standard. Securing a certain dollar volume from a given territory, regardless of the number of calls made or the orders and sales per call, meets another particular standard of results.

   Again, the standards may involve a relationship between selling cost and sales results. For example, in a retail furniture store, the standard may require that one prospective customer be attracted to the store for every $2 expended in advertising or that $1 of sales be secured for every $0.07 expended for advertising. If these goals are achieved, those responsible for the advertising expenditures are meeting the standards of advertising results.

Illustrations of Sales Standards

Although the applicability of sales standards to various industries and types of trading concerns may differ, suggestive standards the controller may consider discussing with the sales manager are:

   1. *Standards of effort*
- Number of calls to be made per period
- Number of calls to be made on prospective customers
- Number of dealers and agencies to be established
- Number of units of sales promotional effort to be used (e.g., demonstrations or pieces of direct mail sent)

2. *Standards of results*

  ○ Percentage of prospects to whom sales are to be made

  ○ Number of customers to whom new articles are to be introduced or sold

  ○ Number of new customers to be secured

  ○ Amount of dollar volume to be secured

  ○ Number of physical units to be sold

  ○ Amount of gross profit to be secured

  ○ Amount of profit to be secured (here profit is frequently considered as the excess of gross profit over the expenses that are subject to the control of the salesperson or executive to whom the standard is to apply)

  ○ Amounts to be sold to individual customers (especially larger customers)

  ○ Dollar or physical volume of individual products or product classes to be sold

  ○ Percentage of gross profit to be returned (where there is a varied line or where the salesperson has price latitude)

  ○ Average size of order to be secured

  ○ Relation of sales deductions to gross sales

3. *Standards expressing relationship of effort and result*

  ○ Number of orders to be received per call made

  ○ Number of new customers to be secured per call made on prospects

  ○ Number of inquiries or orders to be received per unit or per dollar of sales promotional effort expended

  ○ Relation of individual direct selling expense items to volume or gross profit

  ○ Relation of sales administration or supervision costs to volume or gross profit

Developing Sales Standards: Benchmarking

Now that sales standards have been defined, their purpose and nature explained, and illustrations provided, the question arises as to how sales standards are and should be developed.

To be effective, the standards must be accepted by those who use them as fair and reasonable, not the product of the whim of some overzealous bean counter. Benchmarking is used by a company to measure its products, services, and business practices against the toughest competitor, or those companies best in its class, or other comparisons. Brief commentary on this process and results are presented in the "Benchmarking" section of Chapter 1.

Revision of Sales Standards

Some standards of sales performance can be set with a high degree of exactness. The number of calls a salesperson should make, the percentage of prospects to whom sales should be made, and the physical units that should be sold to each customer are illustrative of performances that frequently lend themselves to accurate measurements. On the other hand, there are many factors in sales performance that are so governed by conditions beyond the control of the salespeople that the standards must be promptly revised to meet important changes in such conditions. Where a salesperson is given some latitude in price setting, the gross profit percentage may vary with competitive conditions beyond the salesperson's control. Strikes, droughts, and floods may suddenly affect the sales possibilities in a particular territory. If the sales standards are to be effective measures of sales performance, they must be promptly revised as conditions change. Careless measurement of performance soon leads to discouragement, resentment, and disinterest in the task.

Use of Sales Standards

As stated previously, the purposes of sales standards are to control sales operations, to reward merit, and to stimulate sales effort. The standards in themselves are of limited value, except as they are made effective in the accomplishment of such purposes. To make the standards effective requires the following be done:

- The variations between actual and standard performance be promptly determined
- The causes of such variations be investigated and explained
- The responsibility for the variations be definitely fixed
- The individuals held responsible be given full opportunity to present their explanations
- Prompt action be taken to correct any weaknesses revealed
- The method of compensation shall provide a fair and accurate reward for performance

Sales Quotas as Standards

The most widely used sales standard is the sales quota. As usually constituted, the sales quota is the dollar amount of physical volume of sales assigned to a particular salesperson, department, branch, territory, or other division as a measure of satisfactory performance. The quota may, however, involve other considerations, such as gross profit, new customers, collections, or traveling expense, thereby representing something of a composite or collective standard of performance.

The quota does not differ in its purpose and use from other sales standards as discussed earlier. The applicability of the quota to various types of concerns depends largely on the extent to which sales and other results are actually affected by the direct efforts of the salespeople involved and the extent to which such results are affected by other factors, such as expenditures for advertising, special sales promotion, styles, and acceptability of products. Where the former is the dominant factor, sales quotas constitute a valuable type of sales standard.

Basis of Sales Quotas

Generally speaking, sales quotas are of value only to the extent that they are based on known facts relative to sales possibilities. They must not be based on the greed of the company or fanciful ideas of what might be done but on actual facts relating to past sales, sales in allied industries, population, buying power, or territorial conditions. The sales representative should be thoroughly informed about the method of arriving at the quota and convinced that the amount of sales assigned is entirely justified according to the existing conditions. Then, and only then, will the salesperson exert full effort in meeting the quota.

The quota should not be thought of primarily as a basis for contests. The salesperson should consider the quota as representing a careful measurement of the task rather than a temporary target at which to shoot.

Actual experience with sales quotas, as with all standards, will reveal that sales representatives react to them somewhat differently, particularly at first. Some are stimulated to their highest efficiency, whereas others are discouraged. Some sales executives place considerable emphasis on this human element in setting their quotas. In general, however, good salespeople will, in the long run, respond favorably to intelligently devised quotas, particularly when compensation is fairly adjusted to performance.

The objection sometimes raised, that efforts are lessened after quotas are reached, is seldom valid if performance is properly rewarded. The chief difficulty arises when quotas are exceeded as a result of some fortuitous circumstance in which the sales representative has had no part or for which the share of the credit is uncertain. The solution here usually rests with extreme fairness in handling individual cases and with the development of confidence in the knowledge and integrity of sales executives.

The method of establishing sales quotas is still unsatisfactory in many concerns. The matter is frequently given insufficient study, and the results are ineffective. There has, however, been a vast improvement in such methods in recent years, and alert controllers have made a substantial contribution to this improvement.

Past performance is greatly influenced by conditions beyond the control of the individual salesperson. Hence a quota set when business is poor is likely to result in undue reward to the salesperson. Conversely, one set when business is good is likely to prove too high to serve as an effective incentive, or even provide fair compensation.

Method of Expressing Quotas

Insofar as practicable, quotas should be broken down into their detailed elements. This helps to show the sales representative where, how, and to whom the goods should be sold. To illustrate, a certain company gives each of its sales representatives the following details relative to the sales quota:

- The proportion of the quota assigned to each product line
- The part of the quota that represents an expected increase in business from new customers
- The part of the quota that represents an expected increase in business among old customers
- The part of the quota to be secured in cities of various sizes
- The part of the quota assigned to particular kinds of outlets or classes of customers
- The part of the quota to be secured from special or exceptional sources
- The distribution of the quota by months

Although such a plan entails considerable work, it tends to balance the sales effort and to assist the sales representative in directing work most effectively.

It should be realized that such details require the necessary detailed analysis of past performance by the controller's staff. Furthermore, such detail is indicative of a well-developed program. Many firms, particularly the small and medium sized, will express quotas in general terms only—so many dollars of sales or so many overall units. Where quotas are relatively new, the controller should proceed cautiously and develop the details gradually so that the sales executives can be guided step by step. Only when the data are available and the sales staff realizes the advantages of detailed planning can the quota type of standard serve most usefully.

It frequently happens that the quota cannot be fairly expressed directly in money or physical volume. For example, a sale of $100 of class A goods may deserve more credit than a like amount of class B goods, or a sale to a new customer may deserve more credit than a similar sale to an old customer. In such cases, the quota may be expressed in points that give effect to a weighting for different types of sales performance. Thus a sale of $100 class A goods may be counted as 10 points, whereas $100 of class B goods would be counted as only 5 points. The "point" system may likewise be extended to include other types of service, such as calls on new prospects, demonstrations, or collections.

The final requirement for effective standards is an adequate method of compensation as a reward for good performance.

SALES REPORTS

Effecting Sales Control

Fundamentally, control is the prompt follow-up of unfavorable trends or conditions before they develop into large losses. In the small business, the owner or manager can exercise current control of sales through a review of orders received and so forth. In the larger businesses, however, such personal contact must be supplemented by reports that indicate current conditions and trends as well as current performance.

It is the function of the controller, of course, to furnish the sales executives with the sales facts. However, it is one thing to furnish the information; it is quite another thing to see that it is understood and acted on. To assure the necessary understanding, the controller must adapt the report to the reader. Information for the needs of the chief executive will be different from that for the sales manager, and reports for subordinate sales executives will differ even more. The extent of the information required and the form of presentation will depend on the capabilities of the individual, the type of organization, the responsibilities of the vender, and the philosophy of sales management.

Nature of Sales Reports

Sales executives have many management styles and backgrounds. Some sales managers can effectively use vast amounts of statistical data, whereas others prefer summarizations. Accordingly, the controller should offer to develop reports to meet the requirement. The use of charts, graphs, and summaries will greatly enhance the communication of the sales data to sales management. In many instances, a narrative report citing the significant issues or problems is the most effective tool. Depending on the seriousness of the problem, or where major actions are being recommended, a meeting may be in order. It is up to the controller to ensure that the information provided is understood and can be properly used.

Content of Sales Reports

The matters that may be included in a sales report cover a broad front. Such reports might contain:

- Actual sales performance, with month- or year-to-date figures
- Budgeted sales for both the period and year to date
- Comparison of actual sales by firm with industry figures, including percentages of total
- Analysis of variances between budgeted and actual sales and reasons for differences
- Sale–cost relationships, such as cost per order received
- Sales standards—comparison of actual and quota sales by salesperson
- Unit sales price data
- Gross profit data

These data often may be expressed in physical units or in dollars. Aside from actual or standard sales performance, some may relate to orders, cancellations, returns or allowances, or lost sales.

Illustrative Features in Sales Reports

As stated previously, the content of sales reports must be varied to suit the needs and personality of the user. Reports to the chief executive and top sales executive, for example, should present the overall view in summary fashion. A simple comparison of actual and planned sales by major product line or territory, as shown in Exhibit 2.7, summarizes the sales in a brief but informative manner. Summary information is also presented comparing the company performance against industry by months (or years) in Exhibit 2.8. A graphic comparison of actual with planned sales as illustrated in Exhibit 2.9 is also useful.

Sales executives also find trend reports on product lines to be of value. A percentage bar chart, illustrated in Exhibit 2.10, would be particularly significant if the profit by product group is greatly different. Trends in sales volume are easily shown by vertical bar charts similar to that pictured in Exhibit 2.10. Sales managers typically need information on the probable future course of sales. For this purpose, timely reports summarizing the orders-on-hand picture are helpful. Such a report, which may be desired daily, weekly, or monthly, is illustrated in Exhibit 2.11.

The graphs and reports presented thus far have been rather simple in nature. Whereas reports always should be understood, in many cases, particularly in larger companies, they must be more analytical or detailed in nature. Moreover, for control purposes and adopting the concept of "responsibility reporting," the performance of each segment of the sales organization should be made known to the supervisor responsible. It follows, therefore, that reporting must be available for each division, district, area, branch, or salesperson. A typical branch report is illustrated in Exhibit 2.12 and is very brief. However, as reports relate to increasingly lower levels of management, such information can become massive in extent. Therefore, although data may be periodically prepared on each segment of the organization, it has been found practical to apply the "exceptional principle" in a great many cases. This method eliminates data where performance was satisfactory and details only that which did not reach acceptable levels. An example is Exhibit 2.13, indicating only those salespersons who were 5 percent or more under budget. Another report prepared on only out-of-line performance is that shown in Exhibit 2.14. Only customers on which a loss was realized are listed. It is to be noted that two profit or loss computations are made:

1. Actual out-of-pocket losses, using the direct costing concept
2. Gross loss, wherein all fixed and allocated charges are considered

Frequency of Reports

The frequency of any report will depend on the individual requirements of each executive or staff member and may be daily, weekly, monthly, or quarterly. For example, the top executive and general sales manager may want a daily report on sales, orders received, and orders on hand; a weekly report may suffice; or a report may be wanted daily during a critical period and less frequently thereafter.

In those cases where sales data are collected by use of data input devices from remote locations and stored in the computer, reports and data can be provided on a visual display unit on a real-time basis.

PRODUCT PRICING: POLICY AND PROCEDURE

Prices in a Competitive Economy

From the economic viewpoint, prices are the regulator of our economy in that they determine the distribution of goods and services. Over the long run, when prices in a given industry are insufficient to provide an adequate return, capital and labor tend to shift to more attractive fields. In the individual business, also, skill in setting prices has a tremendous impact on the profitability of the operation and therefore on its economic life.

ABC MANUFACTURING COMPANY
COMPARATIVE STATEMENT OF SALES
MONTH OF _____ 200X

Product or Territory	Month			Year to Date				Total Year		
	Actual	Plan	Over (under) Plan	Last Year Actual	Actual	Plan	Over (under) Plan	Last Year Actual	Indicated Final	Plan	Over (under) Plan
Product line "A"										
Item 1										
Item 2										
Item 3										
Item 4										
Total										
Product line "B"										
Item 1										
Item 2										
Item 3										
Item 4										
Total										
Total										

Comments (to be coded to figures)

* Significance variance.

(1) Action assigned to.

(2) Strike.

(3) Other—(explain).

EXHIBIT 2.7 COMPARISON OF ACTUAL TO PLANNED SALES

ABC MANUFACTURING COMPANY
COMPARISON OF COMPANY AND INDUSTRY SALES

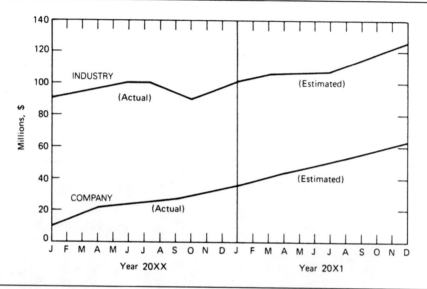

EXHIBIT 2.8   GRAPHIC COMPARISON OF COMPANY VS. INDUSTRY SALES

Product pricing is a difficult area in which to make decisions because of the many forces at play. It is so complex a subject that it is not ordinarily a one-man job or one-activity job. Rather the combined talents of marketer, accountant, engineer, and economist may be needed. It might be said that pricing is one-third computation and two-thirds judgment. From the accounting viewpoint, however, the one-third computation is an essential aid to the judgment factor. Factors that influence prices include market conditions, costs of manufacturing and distribution, plant capacity, competitive activity, capital investments, financial liquidity, government pressures, and a multitude of others. It is therefore understandable that there exists a diversity of approaches to the problem. But this situation presents an equally valid reason to attempt to set out some guiding principles.

Prices and the Controller

The accountant's contribution to the accounting control of sales is in most cases largely after the fact. That is, comparisons of actual performance are made with budget, forecast, or standard; or sales data are analyzed to reveal unfavorable trends and relationships. In the field of product pricing, however, the controller may be able to exert "preventive" accounting control before the occurrence by bringing facts to bear on the problem before unwise decisions are made. This activity is closely related to profit planning as well as control. The influence of prices on company profits is obvious, and the finest controls on costs and expenses will not succeed in producing a profit if selling prices are incorrectly set. If the controller is charged with a responsibility for protecting the assets of the company, or of exercising the control function on costs and expenses or capital expenditures, then an important role should also be played in price determination.

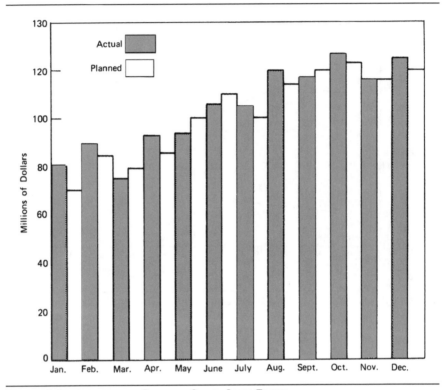

ABC Manufacturing Company
Product A Sales

Exhibit 2.9   Actual and Planned Sales; Sales Trend

And just what should the function be in price determination and related accounting control? It is hoped that it will not be merely as a source of information, providing data only when requested, and even then in the form and of the content specified. In many companies, it is questionable whether the pricing officials are fully aware of the kinds of facts required. Therefore, the controller should be expected to show some initiative and supply intelligent information from the legitimate sphere of activity. More specifically, the chief accounting official ordinarily can be of assistance by performing the following functions:

- Help establish a pricing policy that will be consistent with the corporate objectives— for example, earning the desired return on investment.
- Provide unit cost analysis, in proper form, as one factor in price setting.
- Project the effect on earnings of proposed price changes and alternatives.
- To the extent necessary or practicable, gather pertinent information on competitive price activity (this may be the function of the market research group or economics department in some companies).
- Analyze the historical data on prices and volumes to substantiate probable trends as they may influence proposed price changes.

ABC Manufacturing Company
Sales of Product Lines, by Months

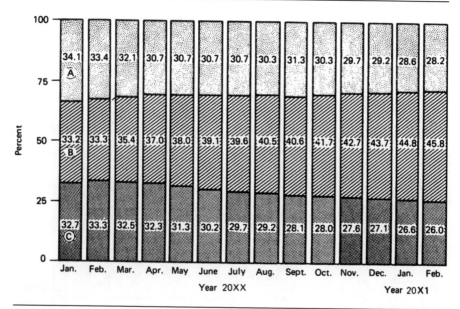

Exhibit 2.10   Percentage of Sales by Product Lines

ABC Manufacturing Company
Summary of Orders on Hand

Description	Orders on Hand June 30, 20XX	Orders Received	Orders Canceled	Orders Delivered	Orders on Hand July 31, 20XX	
					Units	Sales Value ($ in thousands)
Vehicles						
Type A	50	25	5	10	60	120.0
Type B	100	—	5	20	75	262.5
Type C	150	50	—	5	195	838.5
Type D	60	10	—	5	65	97.5

Exhibit 2.11   Report on Sales Order Activity

• Determine for management, on a regular basis (such as the monthly operations report) the influence on profit of changes in price, product mix, sales volume, etc.; in other words, focus attention on the price problem where such action may bring about intelligent direction.

Some of these procedures are reviewed in the sections that follow.

GENERAL MANUFACTURING COMPANY

COMPARISON OF BUDGETED AND ACTUAL SALES BY BRANCH

REPORT No. 7

DATE December

DESCRIPTION	BRANCH NUMBER	NET SALES THIS MONTH	SALES BUDGET THIS MONTH	VARIANCE THIS MONTH	NET SALES YEAR TO DATE	SALES BUDGET YEAR TO DATE	VARIANCE YEAR TO DATE
BOSTON	1	1443564	1500000	56436 CR	19056325	18000000	1056325
CHICAGO	4	2348217	2000000	348217	25637940	24000000	1637940
CLEVELAND	7	2607686	2500000	107686	32642950	30000000	2642950
DETROIT	10	1112667	1000000	112667 CR	10912624	12000000	1087376CR
BALTIMORE	12	425835	500000	74165 CR	7316940	6000000	1316940
HOUSTON	13	495133	500000	4867 CR	6923423	6000000	923423
LOS ANGELES	16	592329	500000	92329	5730916	6000000	269084 CR
NEW ORLEANS	19	442174	500000	57826 CR	6612213	6000000	612213
NEW YORK	22	4094685	4000000	94685	50364912	48000000	2364912
PHILADELPHIA	25	1007489	1000000	7489	13064175	12000000	1064175
PITTSBURGH	28	935731	1000000	64269 CR	10316942	12000000	1683058CR
SAN FRANCISCO	31	913875	1000000	86125 CR	12316431	12000000	316431
ST. LOUIS	34	662284	500000	162284	6014314	6000000	14314
FACTORY	58	279504		279504	1210640		1210640
		17361173	16500000	861173	208120745		10120745

EXHIBIT 2.12 COMPARISON OF BUDGETED AND ACTUAL SALES BY BRANCH

ABC MANUFACTURING COMPANY
SALES ANALYSIS BY SALESPERSON—UNDER BUDGET 5% OR MORE—YEAR TO DATE
DISTRICT PITTSBURGH
APRIL 20XX AND YEAR TO DATE

Description	Salesperson No.	Current Month			Year to Date			"Lost Gross"
		Actual Sales	Under Budget Amount	%	Actual Sales	Under Budget Amount	%	
Performance Satisfactory:		$ 827,432	$112,610*	15.8*	$4,623,096	$497,830*	12.1*	
Under Budget Performance:								
Abernathy	2609	32,016	1,760	5.2	102,600	6,300	5.8	$ 1,520
Bristol	2671	17,433	1,390	7.4	61,080	4,270	6.5	1,080
Caldwell	2685	19,811	1,320	6.2	70,100	4,600	6.2	1,150
Fischer	2716	24,033	1,470	5.8	84,390	5,090	5.7	1,270
Gorder	2804	8,995	480	5.1	31,600	1,810	5.4	450
Inch	2827	27,666	1,820	6.2	97,010	5,930	5.8	1,480
Long	2982	4,277	600	12.3	15,020	900	5.7	230
Mather	3007	39,474	3,800	8.8	138,400	8,540	5.8	2,150
Owens	5066	43,189	4,400	9.6	151,800	9,080	5.6	2,270
Subtotal		216,894	17,040	7.3	752,000	46,520	5.8	11,600
District Total		$1,044,326	$ 95,570*	10.1*	$5,375,096	$451,310*	9.2*	$11,600

* Better than budget.

EXHIBIT 2.13 EXCEPTION REPORTING—SALESPERSON PERFORMANCE

ABC MANUFACTURING COMPANY
Sales Analysis by Customer—Gross Losses Only
District California
Year to Date through June 30, 20XX
(DOLLARS IN THOUSANDS)

Customer	Customer No.	Net Sales	Direct Costs	Gain or Loss over Direct Costs		Gross Margin or Loss	
				Amount	% Net Sales	Amount	% Net Sales
Margins satisfactory		$224,390	$156,430	$67,960	30.3	$37,301	16.6
Gross losses year to date:							
American Steel Co.	839	127	94	33	25.9	13	10.2
Barrett Machine Corp.	876	243	246	3	1.2	62	25.5
Benson Mfg. Co.	11314	182	189	7	3.8	23	12.6
Central Heating Co.	207	24	20	4	16.7	12	50.0
Fagan Steel, Inc.	436	281	307	26	9.3	56	19.9
Jones Iron Co.	920	19	22	3	15.8	9	47.4
Luckey Bridge Corp.	800	76	70	6	7.9	6	7.9
Oppowa Metals Co.	392	32	43	11	34.4	20	62.5
Subtotal		984	991	7	.7	201	20.4
District total		$225,374	$157,421	$67,953	30.2	$37,100	16.5

EXHIBIT 2.14 Sales Analysis by Customers—Exception Basis

Cost Basis for Pricing

There is a great tendency to either underrate or overrate costs as a factor in setting prices. Frequently, the statement is heard that "prices are based on competition." Less often, the statement is made that "prices are based on costs." There are certainly circumstances where these comments apply. Rarely, however, can costs be ignored entirely.

Over any extended period, no business can consistently sell all or most products at less than cost, cost that results from production and distribution functions and the related service activities. It is further recognized as a highly desirable condition that a profit be made on every product, in every territory, with every customer. Although this may not always be practicable, the closer such conditions are approached, the more certain or assured is the net profit. Hence, it is apparent that adequate cost information is absolutely indispensable.

In summary, costs may be viewed as the point of departure or starting place in product pricing. And the role to be played by the cost factor depends on the circumstances. If the product is built to customer order, and is not a stock item, costs will be more important. Further, if competition is weak or if the company is a price leader, cost information will play a larger part than if the opposite situations exist. Also, elasticity of demand influences the weighting of costs in that an inelastic demand probably will cause costs to be a greater factor and costs at various volume levels must be studied to maximize earnings.

The question then arises, "What kinds of costs are required?" For different purposes, different types of costs may be desirable. One type of cost may be suitable for a short-range decision and quite another type for longer-term purposes. Moreover, for pricing, the usual historical cost approach may not meet the requirement. In summary, then, the controller is expected to be aware of the several costing methods and the limitations of each and to select that concept most suited to the purpose at hand.

Before reviewing several alternative costing techniques, some general observations are desirable. First, prices relate to the future. Therefore, costs to be used in determining prices must be prospective. Recognition should be given to cost levels expected to prevail in the period under review. Probable raw material and labor costs should be considered. Prospective changes in process ought to be reflected in the cost estimates.

Inflation must be considered, and the best available information should be obtained to recognize what future rates of inflation can be expected. In this forecasting or projecting, the modern scientific tools should be utilized to the extent practicable, such as statistical sampling, sound economic principles, simulation methods, decision analysis techniques, price level analysis. Consideration should also be given to replacement cost of the productive capacity or capital assets. Prices must provide for the future replacement of these productive assets at the projected costs.

Finally, it should be obvious that *all* costs related to a product should be considered and not merely the cost to manufacture. It defeats the purpose if manufacturing costs are carefully calculated but selling or other expenses are applied as an overall percent without regard to the direct expense and effort specifically applicable to the product.

Although many costing methods or variations are in use, there are three basic approaches that warrant discussion:

1. Total cost method
2. Marginal or direct cost method
3. Return on assets method

As a prelude to reviewing costing methods, it seems desirable first to review an example of the influence of costs on profit at differing volume levels. Further, the role of competitive conditions and demand in relation to costs needs to be understood.

Elasticity of Demand

In exercising judgment on prices, elasticity of demand should be given proper weighting in any cost–profit–volume calculations. Normally, the pricing executives will have some general knowledge of the extent to which demand will react to changes in price. However, to provide supplemental assurance, perhaps controlled experimentation will be helpful in gauging this factor. If demand is relatively inelastic, and competitive conditions permit, then it may be possible to pass cost increases on to the customers. Under such circumstances, the controller can show the effect of cost changes on profits and the desirability of effecting price changes. If demand is highly elastic, and the market is somewhat noncompetitive, unit costs can be employed to determine the optimum price with which to produce the optimum profit.

Under such circumstances, it is desirable to determine the sales price that will produce the greatest net profit over a long period of time. Too high a profit over a short term might invite competition or governmental regulation.

Where conditions approach monopoly, it is perhaps of interest to review a typical procedure in setting selling prices. Basically, an estimate is secured from the sales manager about the probable number of units that can be sold at various price levels. Then the unit cost and total cost at the corresponding production level are calculated. That volume at which the greatest total profit is secured can then be determined.

Exhibit 2.15 illustrates the application of this procedure. Here, it is suggested that the unit selling price may be set at $12, $10, $8, $6, $4, or $2. Estimates are then made about the number of units that can be sold at each price. These are indicated by the *sales* line. Thus it is estimated that 1,600 units can be sold at a price of $10 per unit, whereas 4,000 units can be sold at a price of $4. Likewise, the *cost* line shows the estimated total unit cost (including interest on investment) at each volume level. Thus it is estimated that the unit cost will be $5 when volume reaches 2,400 units. The spread between selling price and costs constitutes the unit profit that, multiplied by the number of units, gives the total profit at various price levels. At a price of $10, the profit will be $2 per unit, the volume 1,600 units, and the total profit $3,200. At a price of $8, the total profit will be $7,200. At a price of $6, the total profit will be $6,400. It is apparent here that the greatest profit will be made at a unit price of $8.

Total Cost Method

Now let us consider the three important costing techniques, the first of which is the "total cost" or "full cost" method. Under this concept, the cost of the individual product is determined, and to this figure is added the desired profit margin. Such a margin is usually expressed as a percentage of either cost or the selling price. As an example, the proposed selling price might be calculated as shown in Exhibit 2.16.

In Exhibit 2.16, costs were used as the basis for determination of the markup, as well as the charge for each of the nonmanufacturing expense levels. As an alternative, each cost element could have been calculated in relation to the proposed selling price. Thus the profit margin might have been expressed in the formulas as 20 percent of the selling price, and expenses might have been treated in the same manner.

Such a method has at least two advantages: (1) it is simple in application, and (2) it bases selling prices on all costs expected to be incurred—thus tending to assure full cost recovery, if the product sells and if the costs are generally as estimated. Over the longer run, all costs must be recovered.

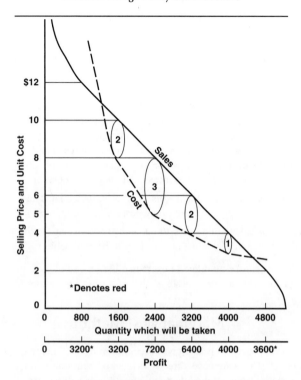

EXHIBIT 2.15 METHODS OF SETTING SELLING PRICE IN A CONTROLLED MARKET

	Unit Cost and Selling Price	
	Product A	**Product B**
Cost and expenses		
Raw material (quantity × expected purchase cost)	$10.00	$ 3.00
Direct labor (hours × expected hourly rate)	4.00	8.00
Manufacturing overhead (150% of direct labor)	6.00	12.00
Total manufacturing cost	20.00	23.00
Research and development expense (10% of manufacturing cost)	2.00	2.30
Selling and advertising expense (20% of manufacturing cost)	4.00	4.60
General and administrative expense (10% of manufacturing overhead)	.60	1.20
Total cost	26.60	31.10
Desired profit margin (25% of total cost)	6.65	7.78
Proposed selling price	$33.25	$38.88

EXHIBIT 2.16 TOTAL COST METHOD

From the cost viewpoint, at least four disadvantages exist in using such a method exclusively:

1. It fails to distinguish between out-of-pocket costs and total costs. In the short run and with available plant capacity, there will be circumstances when business should be accepted on something less than a total cost basis.

2. It does not recognize the inability of all products to return the same rate of profit. Moreover, it fails to distinguish the elements of cost creating the profit, some of which cannot be expected logically to generate the same rate of income. For example, a product that is largely purchased materials may not reasonably return the same percentage of profit on total cost as one constituted mainly of labor and a consequent higher relative share of factory overhead and management talent.

3. The method does not recognize the optimum profit potential. The effect of elasticity in demand and the consequent point of greatest return are ignored.

4. This method of calculating tends to encourage a constant overhead application percent to the exclusion of volume factor likely to be applicable.

The cost calculations can be modified to overcome the second objection. Then, too, several computations can be made to compensate partially for differing volumes.

Marginal Cost Method

The marginal cost approach to prices gives recognition to the "incremental" or "marginal" costs of the product. These are costs directly associated with the product that would not be incurred if the product were not manufactured or sold. Any selling price received above this floor represents a contribution to fixed expenses and/or profit.

The application of this principle to products A and B described in the full cost method might produce a picture as shown in Exhibit 2.17.

In Exhibit 2.17, incremental costs have been segregated from direct expenses of a fixed nature applicable to the product, and these direct costs have been identified separately from the allocated costs of a fixed nature.

If the product must be sold for the incremental costs or less, then the company would earn no less a profit, or possibly even a higher profit, by *not* manufacturing and selling such

	Unit Cost	
	Product A	Product B
Raw materials	$10.00	$ 3.00
Direct labor	4.00	8.00
Variable manufacturing expense	1.50	2.00
Variable selling expense	1.50	1.90
Variable administrative expense	.30	.40
Total variable or incremental cost	17.30	15.30
Fixed expense directly applicable to product	2.50	3.10
Total direct costs	$19.80	$18.40

Exhibit 2.17 Marginal Cost Method

product. Full consideration must be given, of course, to related profit results, namely, sales of other products to the customers, and so on, if the withdrawal of a given product would in fact cause loss of the other business. From the longer-range viewpoint, the minimum price to be charged would be that covering all direct costs, and for the company to continue in business over the longer term, all costs must be recouped.

It can be appreciated that marginal and direct cost data—before allocated continuing costs—are of value in any one of several situations:

- Where additional sales may be made at reduced prices, over and above direct costs, to another class of customer, namely, private brand business, or under another trade name and so forth.
- Where idle plant capacity can be utilized only at reduced prices and in other than regular sales outlets
- Under circumstances where these added sales at reduced prices do not create problems in the regular marketplace

The use of marginal costs is for short-term decisions only. The great danger is the tendency to secure a larger and larger volume of sales on an incremental basis, with an ultimate deteriorating effect in the market and a large share of business that does not return its full and proper share of all costs. Furthermore, under such conditions there is no return on assets employed from the products priced at not more than total costs.

Return-on-Assets-Employed Method

From the profit viewpoint, the most desirable costing method is that which maximizes the return on total assets employed. This is the approach that has been given more attention in recent years. It is to be noted that under the two costing procedures just reviewed, no consideration has been given, for example, to the capital invested in manufacturing or sales facilities or in working capital. Yet the real test of business efficiency is the rate of return on total assets employed. Growth generally takes place only when the product yields a reasonable return on the funds devoted to it. If the business objective is to maximize return on capital, then, as a starting point at least, the price of each product required to achieve the desired rate of return should be known.

This method of determining markup over total costs for the desired percent return on assets rather than markup for a percent return on costs (or percent of net sales) has considerable merit in the opinion of the authors. Some of the assets employed are fixed in nature, such as plant and equipment. But a share of the investment—primarily current assets—is a variable of volume and prices. For example, accounts receivable will be higher as sales volume and sales prices are higher. Investment in inventory will increase or decrease as volume changes and as manufacturing costs and raw material prices fluctuate. In view of the variables, a formula may be employed to calculate the sales price required to produce a planned return on assets employed:

$$\text{Unit price} = \frac{\dfrac{\text{Cost} + (\text{Desired \% return} \times \text{fixed assets})}{\text{Annual sales volume in units}}}{1 - \left(\dfrac{\text{Desired \%}}{\text{return}}\right)\left(\dfrac{\text{Variable assets expressed}}{\text{as \% of sales volume}}\right)}$$

In the formula:

Cost represents total cost of manufacturing, selling, administrative, research, etc.

% return represents that rate desired on assets employed (before income taxes).

The fixed assets represent plant and equipment, although some of the current assets might be placed in this category.

The variable assets represent the current assets that are a function of volume and prices.

Applying some assumptions, a unit price on product A may be calculated as:

$$= \frac{\dfrac{\$2,660,000 + (.20 \times \$300,000)}{100,000}}{1 - (.20 \times .30)}$$

$$= \frac{\$2,720,000/100,000 \text{ units}}{1 - .06}$$

$$= \left(\frac{27.20}{.94} = \$28.936 \right)$$

The proof is computed in this manner:

Income and costs	
Sales (100,000 units at $28.936)	$2,893,600
Costs	2,660,000
Income before taxes	$ 233,600
Assets employed	
Variable (30% of $2,893,600)	$ 868,080
Fixed	300,000
Total assets employed	$1,168,080
20% Return on assets employed of $1,168,080 (fractions ignored)	$ 233,600

The foregoing is intended to show the method of determining unit sales prices to provide a target or planned return on investment. Although applied to a single product, the percentages used were those of the product class or group of which product A is one segment.

Applying the Return-on-Assets-Employed Concept

The simple example just cited purposely avoided some of the controversial or problem areas in using the return-on-assets-employed concept. Some brief observations on the subject may prove helpful.

Under this procedure, total assets employed is considered to include all assets used in manufacturing and selling the product (including related services). It is immaterial how the funds were provided—whether by debt or equity. The management of a company should effectively use all assets, whether owner supplied or creditor supplied.

Another question often raised is the basis of valuation of assets. Should replacement value be considered? Should fixed assets be included on a gross or depreciated basis?

Essentially, policies of valuation will have no appreciable effect on price determination. Recognition can be provided directly or indirectly in the rate of return objective. Consistency is the important consideration.

In a multiproduct company, a problem to be solved is the allocation of capital employed to the various product lines. On reflection, this need not be a major stumbling block. Just as controllers have been allocating costs to products for years, so also they can allocate assets on a reasonable basis consistent with the facts of the particular business. Some suggested methods of prorating assets to product lines are:

Item	Possible Bases
Cash	In ratio to total product cost
Accounts receivable	In ratio to sales, adjusted for significant differences in terms of sale
Raw material	In ratio to actual or expected usage
Work in process	In ratio to actual or expected usage
Finished goods	In ratio to cost of manufacture
Fixed assets	In ratio to conversion costs (labor and variable manufacturing overhead) or labor hours—either actual, normal, or standard

Conversion Costs for Pricing Purposes

Still another economic concept useful in pricing is termed the "conversion cost theory of value." In essence, this view holds that profits are, or should be, earned commensurate with the effort and risk inherent in converting raw materials into finished products. This approach has merit, particularly in situations where relative material content varies widely by product. For example, if one product is largely an assembly of purchased parts and another requires extensive processing in expensive facilities, application of the same markup to each probably would result in a price too high on the assembly item and too low on the fabricated product. Differences in types of costs may therefore need to be recognized. A combined use of the return-on-assets concept and direct costs may be illustrative.

Assume the following is a typical pricing and profit-planning problem:

- A given product line R is made up of products of varying material content.
- $24,000,000 are the gross assets employed for the line.
- Management desires a 20% return (before taxes) on the assets employed.
- The pertinent profit data are:
  - Period (fixed or continuing) expenses are $6,000,000.
  - The profit to volume or contribution margin (P/V) ratio is 30%.
  - Direct materials and conversion expenses are, on the average, in a 4 to 3 ratio.
  - Material turnover is twice a year.

With these premises, it is necessary to calculate the following:

- The sales volume needed to produce the desired rate of return
- The markup to be applied on each of the direct cost factors in the product line

Net sales and aggregate costs by element may be determined in this manner:

Required operating profit (20% of $24,000,000)		$ 4,800,000
Add: Continuing or period expenses		6,000,000
Required margin over direct costs		10,800,000
Required sales [$10,800,000 + 30% (P/V ratio)]		36,000,000
Deduct: Margin		10,800,000
Direct costs		25,200,000
Segregated on a 4 to 3 ratio as:		
Direct material	$14,400,000	
Conversion	10,800,000	$25,200,000

Inasmuch as the material turnover is two times per year, the investment is $7,200,000 ($14,400,000 ÷ 2). Twenty percent of this figure is $1,440,000. Consequently, the additive factor is 10% ($1,440,000 ÷ $14,400,000), and the portion of sales revenue needed to provide a 20% return is $15,840,000 ($14,400,000 + $1,440,000).

The additive factor on conversion costs may be determined by the difference method as:

Total required income (sales)	$36,000,000
Less: Direct material and related profit additive	15,840,000
Balance attributable to conversion factor	$20,160,000

Thus, the conversion markup is 1.867 ($20,160,000 ÷ $10,800,000).

If the direct costs of product R162 in the line are known, the target or "ideal" selling price is then determined in this fashion:

	Unit Direct Cost	Factor	Unit Selling Price
Direct material	$16.10	1.100	$17.71
Conversion	20.30	2.867	58.20
Total	$36.40		$75.91

Such proposed prices are only a starting point—they must be considered in relationship to competitive prices.

The setting of product prices is complex and includes the evaluation of many variables. It is the task of the controller to provide for management's judgment all pertinent facts. The various costing methods must be considered and the most appropriate applied in the particular company set of circumstances. In addition to the applicable costs, other factors in setting product prices to be summarized for management's review are:

- Return on invested capital or assets employed
- Assets employed and turnover
- Percentage of plant capacity utilized
- Percentage of product line for each product
- Percentage of market

- Competition pricing and percentage of market
- Margin over direct costs

Recognizing the numerous "what-if" situations in setting prices, the controller should be familiar with the many computer models available for evaluating such business decision as price formulation. The variable inputs can be provided to the system, and when combined with the stored data, the alternatives can be quickly and easily evaluated. From a control viewpoint, a key responsibility for the controller is to participate actively in the costing and pricing function.

3

PLANNING AND CONTROL
OF MARKETING EXPENSES

INTRODUCTION

The planning and control of sales are discussed in the preceding chapter. But the relationship between sales and the effort (the marketing effort) to achieve the sales plan is so close, that it is practical to now review the planning and control of marketing expenses.

DEFINITION

In a broad sense, *marketing expenses* may be defined as the costs relative to all activities from the time goods are produced/manufactured or from the time of purchase in a nonmanufacturing company until the products reach the customer—the cost of marketing or selling. This would include the applicable portion of all costs, including general, administrative, and financial expenses. For our purposes here, however, the discussion is limited to those expenses, exclusive of general, administrative, and financial expenses, that are normally under the control of the marketing or sales executive. They may include, but are not limited to, the following general classifications:

- *Direct selling expense.* All the direct expense of order-getting costs, including direct expenses of salespersons, sales management and supervision, branch sales offices, and sales service (the expenses generally incident to the solicitation of orders).
- *Advertising and sales promotion expense.* All media advertising expenditures, expenses relating to various types of sales promotions, market development, and publicity.
- *Transportation expense.* All transportation charges on outbound goods to customers and returned sales and costs of managing and maintaining the operation of outbound transportation facilities.
- *Warehousing and storage expense.* Includes all costs of warehousing, storing, inventory handling, order-filling, packaging, and preparation for shipment.
- *Market research expense.* The expenses of the various project studies, including the expenses of administering the department activity, undertaken to test or obtain information on the various products, markets, channels of distribution, or other distribution segments.
- *General distribution expense.* All other expenses related to distribution functions under sales management that are not included in the foregoing items. They may include general

sales management expenses, recruitment and training, and staff functions such as accounting, if applicable.

SIGNIFICANCE

The costs of getting the manufactured products to the customer, consumer, or user have become increasingly more significant in recent years. In fact, for many companies the total costs of distribution of the products are in excess of the production or procurement costs. In general, it may be stated that the manufacturing costs have been decreasing, whereas the costs of selling and distributing the product have been increasing. To some degree, the increase in selling expense that results in increased sales volume has enabled companies to achieve greater efficiency in the manufacturing process.

In most companies, more effort has been directed toward analysis and control of production costs, and the costs of marketing have either not been available in usable form or not communicated to responsible marketing management for decision making. Executives responsible for the selling and distribution of the products must be made aware of the cost components to effectively plan and carry out a proper distribution system effort. The controller must develop the control mechanisms, secure the facts and interpret them, and communicate the information to the marketing executives. To be effective, the marketing executive must understand the accounting control information and use it in developing his marketing plans and resolving any problems that may develop. The increasing costs of marketing can be effectively controlled and even reduced if the controller works with the sales and marketing management to develop the necessary control techniques and thus obviously have a positive impact on the bottom line—net profit.

FACTORS INCREASING THE DIFFICULTY OF COST CONTROL

Any controller who tackles the matter of marketing expenses control will find that the problems usually are much more complex than those relating to production costs. First, the psychological factors require more consideration. In selling, the attitude of the buyer as well as the salesman is variable, and competitive reaction cannot be overlooked. This is in sharp contrast to production where the worker is generally the only human element. Moreover, in marketing activities the methods are more flexible and more numerous than in production, and several agencies or channels of distribution may be used. Such conditions make the activities more difficult to standardize than production activities. Also, the constant changes or switches in method of sale or channel of distribution are factors that make it harder to secure basic information. Even when the information is secured, great care must be used in interpretation. Finally, the nature of the activities requires different types of costs than might be needed in production. Where the indirect or allocated costs are significant, the analyses may require a more relative marginal or incremental cost approach under various circumstances.

Such conditions create problems that may test the ingenuity of the controller.

SALES MANAGER AND MARKETING EXPENSES

The sales manager is responsible for two primary functions in a business: (1) the requisite sales volume of the right products, and (2) the planning and control of marketing expenses. These may seem like two diametrically opposed objectives. However, the situation may be described as a problem of balance: If more money is spent for the distribution effort, what does the business receive in return? Usually, the sales manager will be under continuous pressure to increase sales and yet reduce selling expenses. It is obvious, then, that the sales manager must be in a position to know whether marketing expenses really are too high, and if they are too high, just where—what salesperson? what territory? what expense? The sales effort must be wisely guided, and if this is to be done the controller must provide the necessary financial facts. The sales manager must have an intelligent analysis of distribution costs as a basis on which to work. Marketing decisions must be based on adequate knowledge.

BASIC APPROACH IN THE PLANNING AND CONTROL OF MARKETING EXPENSES

The many variables already mentioned in connection with marketing costs should make it fairly obvious that the problem of control is complex and difficult. In production cost control, a usual procedure is to compare actual and standard or budgeted expenses and exert continuous pressure on actual expenses until they are brought in line with the standard or budget. To an extent this can be done with respect to marketing costs, particularly those of a routine, repetitive, and nonselling nature, such as order handling or warehousing. But by and large, a more positive approach is necessary to avoid an injurious curtailment of necessary distribution services. That approach consists in securing the greatest possible effectiveness in the selling or marketing operations.

As a matter of experience, any controller will find many occasions when suggestions that selling costs be reduced will arouse resentment on the part of the sales force. But almost any sales manager will listen when the approach is that of getting more distribution effort and results for the same money. Unit selling costs can be effectively reduced by getting greater volume from the same sales force, whether by securing larger orders, more customers, or otherwise. This does not obviate the fact that there will be many instances where costs must and will be reduced, but it does emphasize the consideration necessary about the effect on sales volume of reduced marketing expenses.

Since emphasis in the marketing operations is in large measure directed to securing more effective results (more earnings per dollar of distribution cost) it can be seen that much of the study and effort will be applied in a preventive way. Comparative margins and distribution costs may be used in setting *future* action, in changing plans to secure improved results.

MARKETING EXPENSE ANALYSIS

Marketing costs are analyzed for three primary purposes:

1. Cost determination
2. Cost control
3. Planning and direction of the selling and distribution effort

Perhaps the least important of these is cost determination. Yet costs must be ascertained to establish selling prices, formulate distribution policies, and prepare various operating statements. However, the most important purpose is to supply the marketing executives with the necessary information in the planning, direction, and control of the marketing effort. Sales plans must be developed on the basis of those programs or projects that seem to offer a reasonable return. The sales effort must be directed along the most profitable channels, and inefficiencies eliminated. The what, when, and where questions of sales direction must be answered. An analysis of marketing expenses will not provide all the answers to all the sales manager's problems, but it can play an important part in making decisions. Therefore, since marketing cost analysis is useful in the early stages of both the planning and control of costs, it seems logical to review this function before proceeding to the detailed planning and control procedures.

TYPES OF ANALYSES

There are three basic methods of analyzing marketing expenses:

1. By nature of the expense or object of expenditure
2. By functions or functional operations performed
3. By the manner of application of the distribution effort

The effective direction and control of sales effort usually require all these various types of analyses if the sales manager is to be furnished with the necessary information.

Analysis by Nature of Expense

Generally, the ledger accounts in even the smallest companies provide for a recording of marketing expenses by nature of expense or object of expenditure. For example, salaries, payroll taxes, supplies, rent, traveling expense, and advertising space are usually set out in separate accounts. This is often the first, and sometimes the only, analysis made of marketing expenses.

Such an analysis does provide some information for cost control purposes, general though it may be. With the type of expense segregated month by month, it is possible to follow trends and compare the expense with the previous month and with the same month last year. The ratio of the expense to net sales can also be determined. But a comparison with other periods serves to perpetuate inefficiency, and weaknesses will be revealed only in extreme instances.

It should be clear that an analysis by nature of the expense is of limited value. The cost of marketing *generally* is known. Yet the controller cannot tell the sales manager the traveling expense is too high or that too much is being spent on advertising. It must be known whose selling expenses are too high and how it is known they are too high. The points of high cost must be clearly defined and responsibility placed, and possibly even the solution suggested. The controller cannot expect cooperation from the sales manager or chief executive on the basis of generalities. The excess cost of specific operations or the excess cost of securing particular results must be set out if an intelligent effort is to be made in reducing the cost or improving the effectiveness of the effort.

The limitation of analysis by the nature of the expense, from a control standpoint, is obvious. And since the information provided is very general, it serves little useful purpose for the direction of the sales effort.

Analysis by Functional Operations

An analysis that has been found useful, particularly for the *control* of marketing expenses, is that by functions or functional operations. It is of assistance in measuring the performance by individual responsibility, especially in those applications where the organization is complex or large.

The approach is substantially similar to that used in analyzing production costs and may be outlined as:

1. Establish the functional operations to be measured, taking care to see that the functions are properly segregated in terms of individual responsibility. Some illustrative functional operations are:

    (a) Salesperson's calls on prospects or customers

    (b) Shipments from warehouse

    (c) Circular mailing

2. Provide for a cost segregation of these functions. In this connection the classification should provide for those costs that are direct in regard to the function. For *cost determination,* perhaps cost allocations should be made. Generally, however, for *cost control,* emphasis must be on the direct expenses only. Thus in a small branch warehouse such expenses as the indirect labor, supervisory salaries, and fuel should be known, but these costs should be distinct from the allocated share of the regional sales office expense.

3. Establish units of measurement of functional service to the extent practicable. For example, the pounds of shipments might be the measure of the shipping expense, or the number of salesperson's calls might serve as one measurement of direct field selling expense.

4. Calculate a unit cost of operation by dividing the total controllable functional cost by the number of units.

5. Take corrective action if out-of-line conditions appear. This situation may become more readily apparent if standards are established and actual performance is measured against them.

It will be appreciated that this method cannot be applied to all marketing costs, but it may extend to a considerable portion.

The functional approach is useful in control and also in analysis by manner of application. For example, if an analysis is being made by territories, it is necessary to record the number of functional units of the particular activity used in that territory and then simply multiply this number by the unit cost to arrive at a fair cost of the function for each territory.

A specific application of the functional analysis in controlling costs is discussed in the "Marketing Expense Standards" Section.

Analysis by Manner of Application

It is one thing to have an efficient organization from the standpoint of performance of the individual functions and quite another thing to see that the performance is so directed and coordinated that it is productive of the most fruitful results. For example, the controller might well show the sales manager that the cost per call is very reasonable or that the cost per hundredweight of handling material in the New York warehouse is below standard. Yet the controller must go much further in his analysis. It is as important, perhaps even more important, that the controller provide information about income or results achieved in relation to the effort or cost expended. Sales effort must relate to sales possibilities, and these factors must be brought into proper balance. Analysis by manner of application is primarily for the purpose of providing information in the direction of sales effort. The income from a particular factor is being measured against the cost applied against that factor. This type of analysis indicates the distribution cost of different territories, products, customers, channels of distribution, methods of sale, or salespeople. Depending on the problem, the controller must counsel with the sales manager and decide which ones are most useful. These analyses probably will extend to various subanalyses. For example, the breakdown of territorial costs among different products distributed or expected to be distributed might be necessary.

In making any analysis by manner of application, an important consideration is the proper segregation of costs. The value of the cost study will depend in large part on this factor. For this type of analysis, marketing expenses may be divided into three main groups: direct costs, semidirect costs, and indirect costs. As the name implies, direct costs are those immediately identified with a segment and need no allocation. For example, in an analysis by salesperson, the field expense of salary, traveling expense, and entertainment incurred by that salesperson is direct. However, in an analysis by product these expenses might be semidirect or indirect. Expenses that are direct in one application are usually not in another. Ordinarily, the classification of accounts is such that one application is direct for many of the expenses.

Semidirect costs are those related in some measurable way with the particular segments under study. The variability factor responsible for the amount of the expense is known and recorded quantitatively, and the costs may be distributed in accordance with the service required. Thus, the cost factor of the warehousing function might be pounds handled. The order-handling costs might relate to the number of item lines. Stated in other terms, the basis of allocation is less arbitrary than a basis selected at random, such as net sales; and the cost results are therefore of more significance. This might be said to be the distinction between the semidirect costs and those other common or joint costs here designated as indirect.

Indirect expenses are a general charge against the business and must be allocated on a more or less arbitrary basis. No simple measure is available to identify the expense with one territory or product, as distinguished from any other. In practice this may be found to be due as much to records kept as to the nature of the expense. Common examples are institutional advertising or the salaries of general sales executives. There perhaps is little relationship between institutional advertising and the sales in the Western territory as contrasted with the Middle Atlantic territory. There might be little relationship between the costs of general sales administration and sales of product X as compared with product Y. Where it is practical for the general sales executive to keep a time record, the allocation of the expense may be less arbitrary and of more significance.

For marketing expense analysis, as for any intelligent analysis, the type of costs most suitable will depend on the purpose of the study. For long-term decisions, total costs should be known; hence allocated costs need to be identified. If, however, decisions are of limited scope and for a short period, such as the sale to a private brand customer for the next year, then perhaps only direct expenses ought to be considered. The advisability of making arbitrary allocations of indirect costs may be questioned. It is most important, however, that those who use the figures are knowledgeable about limitations.

Contribution Margin Approach

In making a choice between alternative business decisions, usually some costs are unaffected regardless of the conclusions reached. For this reason, among others, it has been found practical to isolate and identify those costs that do change to the exclusion of those costs that do not. The contribution margin approach adopts this concept, although such a segregation may be made in a total cost study as well.

The "contribution margin" is calculated by deducting from sales income those costs incurred in obtaining that segment of the sales income being analyzed. It may be the sales and costs of a given territory or product or customer and need not relate to the company's entire sales of the period. These costs may be described as costs that would not be incurred if the segment being reported on were not present. Such costs are sometimes known also as "variable costs" or as "direct costs." As costs are defined in the preceding section, the costs deducted would include all direct costs, plus, in some instances, the semidirect costs. The inclusion of the latter would depend on the extent to which some of the content is fixed or continuing in nature. As an example, if the bulk of warehousing expense is variable, the period expense content, such as the foreman's salary, might be ignored. In such a case, the entire semidirect costs for the warehousing function might be included. (As a practical matter, the authors assume in all illustrations of semidirect costs that such costs relate basically to an activity factor and would be reduced generally in proportion to volume.)

The costs and expenses not deducted from sales income in computing contribution margins are those not changed in the total amount by the decision under review. The contribution margin, therefore, is the contribution that the activity under question makes toward meeting the fixed or continuing expenses and profit. The use of such an approach does not ignore the period costs. Rather it recognizes that the separation of the common expenses in relation to the business decision at hand serves little useful purpose and emphasis should be placed on the "contribution" or provision made by the segment toward the joint expenses and profit.

The contribution margin approach and the related "direct costing" have these advantages:

- Measurement of the immediate gain to the company's overall profit by the transaction or segment under review.
- Facilitation of management's decision because those costs to be changed are already separated from costs not affected.
- Avoidance of errors and controversy that arise by reason of cost allocations and allocation methods.
- Simplicity of application, since direct costs usually are identifiable more readily than total costs, including the necessary allocations.
- Data can be secured much more quickly and with less effort.

In practice, marginal costs are used for short-term tactical decisions and their value can be appreciated. However, over the longer term, a business must recover total costs and a reasonable profit if it is to survive. Under the circumstances, there is no good reason why the total cost method and contribution margin approach cannot be used jointly. Such a statement would indicate the immediate profit effect of the business decision and, by inclusion of the joint or pooled costs, can reveal the operating income picture.

Management's needs and the judgment of the controller will ordinarily dictate the type of costing most adaptable. For reasons of prudence, sometimes distribution costs will be segregated on a contribution basis, whereas manufacturing costs will be shown in total. An example of such a situation would be in circumstances where top management adopts the viewpoint that a sale must always recoup all manufacturing expenses, plus, at a minimum, the direct selling expenses.

Technique of Analysis by Manner of Application

There has been sufficient experience with marketing expense analysis by manner of application to prove the value of the technique. Although the degree of refinement may vary in different companies, the general approach may be outlined as:

1. Determine which analysis (or analyses) needs to be made. Determine which might be required in a particular application, such as an analysis by method of delivery.

Again, some may be recurring and others may be made only as weaknesses are indicated.

2. Classify marketing expense according to those that are direct, semidirect, and indirect.

3. Select and apply the allocation bases to the semidirect and indirect expenses. This includes a segregation and proper treatment of variable, as contrasted with fixed, costs where such a segregation is a factor.

4. Prepare the analysis and commentary for the use of the proper executive. This will involve the following steps in arriving at significant cost and profit relationships:

   (a) Determine the gross profit by segment (e.g., territory, product, size of order).

   (b) Accumulate the direct expense by segment, and deduct this from gross profit to arrive at *profit after direct expense.*

   (c) Distribute the semidirect expenses, and deduct these to arrive at *profit after semi-direct expense.*

   (d) Prorate the indirect expense to arrive at the final net profit (in some instances steps c and d will be combined).

   (e) Prepare the necessary subanalyses to pinpoint the conditions needing correction.

These comments should indicate the principles and technique involved so that any controller can proceed to prepare the facts necessary in his particular situation.

Comments on the need and use of certain analyses by manner of application are made hereafter.

Analysis by Territory

A *territory* may be defined, for this purpose, as any geographical area, whether city, trading area, county, state, or sales district, used by a company for sales planning, direction, or analysis. Where, or in which territory, goods are sold has a great effect on the net profit. There are striking variations between territories in terms of sales potentials, net profit, and gross margins. If goods are sold free on board (F.O.B.) a central point and at the same price, the gross profit, of course, is unchanged. But if the product is sold on a delivered price basis, the gross margin is different because of transportation charges. In different areas the consumers' wants and needs are different, and this factor affects the total gross margins. Even aside from these considerations, experience has shown that the costs to sell and distribute are different in different territories. The cost to sell in densely populated New York is much different from the cost to sell in Western Texas. Because of all these dissimilar conditions, executives must have an analysis of distribution costs by territory. Such information permits the sales manager to rearrange sales effort where necessary and direct sales effort into the most profitable areas. Control of marketing costs is facilitated through this same analysis, perhaps with the aid of cost standards. Sales planning, of course, with respect to new territories and new markets is affected by distribution cost considerations.

Not every concern will find analysis by territory necessary. Such an analysis applies largely in those instances where a large geographical area is covered. Thus a manufacturer covering a national market would greatly benefit from such an analysis, whereas a retail store probably would not. Exactly what type of territorial analysis needs to be made depends on the problem and type of organization. If a territorial sales executive is largely responsible for costs and results, a complete analysis by this responsibility area is desirable. Or if the problem is one of costs to sell in small towns versus cities, such a segregation is to be made.

A statement of income and expense by territory is shown in Exhibit 3.1.

THE P COMPANY
STATEMENT OF INCOME AND EXPENSE BY TERRITORY
FOR THE MONTH ENDED JANUARY 31, 20XX

	Total		West		Territory Middle West		Middle Atlantic		New England	
Description	Amount	% of Net Sales	Amount	% of Net Sales	Amount	% of Net Sales	Amount	% of Net Sales	Amount	% of Net Sales
Gross sales	$840,000		$50,000		$390,000		$240,000		$160,000	
Less:										
Freight	35,359		4,200		13,500		10,750		6,909	
Returns	5,000		750		1,050		1,840		1,360	
Allowances	10,650		670		3,890		3,750		2,340	
Total sales deductions	51,009		5,620		18,440		16,340		10,609	
Net sales	788,991	100.00	44,380	100.00	371,560	100.00	223,660	100.00	149,391	100.00
Cost of sales	550,127	69.73	31,066	70.00	241,514	65.00	167,745	75.00	109,802	73.50
Gross profit	238,864	30.27	13,314	30.00	130,046	35.00	55,915	25.00	39,589	26.50
Direct selling expenses	45,568	5.78	2,219	5.00	16,720	4.50	20,129	9.00	6,500	4.35
Profit after direct selling expenses	193,296	24.49	11,095	25.00	113,326	30.50	35,786	16.00	33,089	22.15
Semidirect expenses	17,854	2.26	1,000	2.25	7,800	2.10	6,330	2.83	2,724	1.82
Profit after semidirect expenses	175,442	22.23	10,095	22.75	105,526	28.40	29,456	13.17	30,365	20.33
Allocated share of general expenses	15,780	2.00	888	2.00	7,431	2.00	4,473	2.00	2,988	2.00
Profit before income taxes	$159,662	20.23	$ 9,207	20.75	$ 98,095	26.40	$ 24,983	11.17	$ 27,377	18.33
Other Data										
Units sold	36,692		2,000		17,333		10,550		6,809	
Sales potential	$850,000		$85,000		$400,000		$225,000		$140,000	
% of potential	92.8		52.2		92.9		99.4		106.7	

EXHIBIT 3.1 STATEMENT OF INCOME AND EXPENSE BY TERRITORY

Once the points of weakness are discovered through analysis, corrective action needs to be taken. Some of the possibilities for such are:

- Reorganization of territories to permit effort more nearly in line with potentials
- Rearrangement of territorial boundaries to reduce selling expense, secure better coverage, and so forth
- Shifting of salespersons
- Increased emphasis on neglected lines or customers in territory
- Change in method of sale or channel of distribution (shift from salesperson to agent, etc.)
- Changes in physical facilities (warehouses, etc.) in territory
- Elimination of unprofitable territories (potentials of area and out-of-pocket costs vs. allocated costs considered)
- Change in advertising policy or expenditure in territory

Analysis by Product

In our dynamic and competitive economy, the design or style or type of product a firm sells may change constantly. The tremendous strides of research, among other factors, are repeatedly bringing new products into the market. Hence, every company is sooner or later faced with the problem of what products it should sell. Will the firm sell the best or the cheapest line? Will it promote the use of a new plastic? Should it introduce a silent airplane motor? The answer to questions like these are twofold. First, through market analysis a determination must be made about what the consumers want and what price they will pay. Then, through cost analysis it must be determined whether the company can make and sell the article at a profit. Therefore, an analysis by products is desirable.

Many firms, in their urge to increase sales volume to better utilize facilities and personnel, often add new products to the line. Sometimes these new products "fit" into the line and permit certain economies. Often, however, the different products require services in varying degree. For this reason, too, an analysis by product is necessary to determine the cost to sell, as well as the net profit.

Generally speaking, sales effort should be directed toward those products with the greatest net profit possibilities, and cost analysis is necessary to know just which products these are. This is not to say that a company should drop a low-margin item; it may be contributing more than out-of-pocket costs, or it may be necessary for customer convenience. Furthermore, there may be little possibility of selling a high-margin item to a customer. For example, there may be no chance of selling to a paint manufacturer any quantity of a high-profit glue instead of a low-margin paint vehicle. There are more factors than merely cost considerations in selling. But such conditions must be watched and held within reasonable limits. Marketing expense analyses by commodity, then, are of use in the direction of the sales effort.

Many controllers may find, in making product cost analyses, that the net profit on an entire line of products is not great enough or even that losses are being sustained. When such conditions are revealed, steps are usually taken to increase that margin because the firm may not be in a position to drop an entire line. This is but another way of saying that analysis is a means of controlling costs, because the manufacturing costs or marketing costs may be too high.

Finally, product cost analyses are helpful in setting selling prices when the company is in a position to use costs as a major guide. Such analyses are desirable in conjunction with determining maximum price differentials to particular customers.

It is probably self-evident to most controllers or accountants that a product analysis of distribution costs should be made when the characteristics of the commodity or their methods of marketing are such that a uniform basis of allocation is not indicative of the effort or cost to sell. Thus, pounds or units of sale or sales dollars may be a fair measure of selling expense. There are numerous circumstances when such an apportionment is inaccurate or misleading:

- *If there are differences in the time or amount of sales effort required.* Thus product A that sells at $0.60 each may require about three times the effort of product V which sells at $0.30 each. Neither sales dollar nor units would be a fair basis. Perhaps one product would require a high degree of technical assistance with frequent callbacks as compared with another. Again, specialty salespeople may merchandise one product, and a general-line salesperson may handle another. All such circumstances result in different costs to sell, and should be so reflected in the analyses.
- *If there are differences in the method of sale.* Obviously, if one product is sold exclusively by mail order and another by salespeople, the selling cost cannot be prorated on a sales dollar or unit basis.
- *If there are differences in the size of the order.* When one product is sold in 10-pound lots and another is sold in tank cars, many of the distribution costs can be different.
- *If there are differences in channels of distribution.* One product may be sold directly to retailers, whereas another is distributed through wholesalers. Here, also, there is a difference in distribution cost.

The analysis by product ordinarily will reveal areas of weakness about which corrective action can be taken in some degree, such as:

- Shifting emphasis of the sales effort to more profitable lines or bringing effort in line with sales potential
- Adjusting sales prices
- Eliminating certain unprofitable lines, package sizes, colors, and so forth
- Adding product lines related to the "family," with consequent sharing of fixed distribution expense
- Changing the method of sale or channel of distribution
- Changing the type, amount, and emphasis of advertising
- Revising packages, design, quality, and the like

A statement of income and expense that incorporates the contribution margin concept by products is shown in Exhibit 3.2.

Analysis by Customer

It is no secret that many manufacturers or distributors carry unprofitable accounts or customers. Such a condition may result from a philosophy of "get the volume," or from insufficient effort to do something about the status quo, or probably because the sales executive just does not have sufficient knowledge about marketing costs.

Yet it costs more to sell to some types of customers than to others and more to one customer within a type than another. Some customers require more services than others, such as warehousing, delivery, or financing. Some customers insist on different prices, particularly where different size orders or annual purchases are factors. Again, the types of products sold to some classes differ from others. All these are reasons why analyses by customers are necessary to measure the difference in net profit. Aside from use in the direction of sales effort, these analyses serve in setting prices and controlling distribution costs.

THE BEST COMPANY
STATEMENT OF INCOME AND EXPENSE BY PRODUCT
FOR THE MONTH ENDED JUNE 30, 20XX

Description	All Products Amount	% of Net Sales	A Amount	A Per Cwt.	B Amount	B Per Cwt	C Amount	C Per Cwt.	D Amount	D Per Cwt.
Gross Sales	$27,890		$14,600	$14.60	$ 620	$12.40	$11,040	$13.80	$1,630	$16.30
Less: Sales Deductions	1,295		600	.60	25	.50	640	.80	30	.30
Net Sales	26,595	100.0	14,000	14.00	595	11.90	10,400	13.00	1,600	16.00
Variable Cost of Sales	8,100	30.5	5,000	5.00	300	6.00	2,400	3.00	400	4.00
Profit After Direct Mfg. Costs	18,495	69.5	9,000	9.00	295	5.90	8,000	10.00	1,200	12.00
Direct Marketing Expense	1,255	4.7	500	.50	25	.50	640	.80	90	.90
Semidirect Distribution Expense (Variable)	3,355	12.6	800	.80	185	3.70	1,840	2.30	530	5.30
Contribution Margin	13,885	52.2	7,700	7.70	85	1.70	5,520	6.90	580	5.80
Fixed Expenses										
Manufacturing	4,900	18.4	3,000	3.00	100	2.00	1,600	2.00	200	2.00
Marketing	1,170	4.4	600	.60	30	.60	480	.60	60	.60
Total	6,070	22.8	3,600	3.60	130	2.60	2,090	2.60	260	2.60
Profit (or Loss) Before Income Tax	$ 7,815	29.4	$ 4,100	$ 4.10	$ (45)	$(.90)	$ 3,440	$ 4.30	$ 320	$ 3.20
Other Data										
Hundredweight Sold	1,950		1,000		50		800		100	
Average Sale per Call (when sold)	$348.63		$486.67		$124.00		$736.00		$54.33	
Number of "No Sale" Calls	20		10		3		4		3	
Lack of Volume Manufacturing Costs	$ 2,800		$ 600		$ 500		$ 1,400		$ 300	

EXHIBIT 3.2 STATEMENT OF INCOME AND EXPENSE BY PRODUCT

83

In most firms, the analyses by customers will not be continuous. Perhaps the sales manager will be interested in whether money is being made on a particular account, or changes may be contemplated only on certain groups of accounts. On these occasions special analyses can be made.

Although analyses may be made by individual customers, particularly when there are a few high-volume accounts, by and large the analyses will relate to certain groups or categories. The two basic factors in selecting the classification to be used are the amount of marketing services required, for this is the primary reason for differences in marketing costs, and the practicability of segregating the marketing costs. Classifications that have proved useful are:

- Amount of annual purchases
- Size of orders
- Location
- Frequency of salespersons' calls
- Type of agent (retailer, wholesaler, or jobber)
- Credit rating of customers

In making an analysis by classification of customer, one approach is to segregate all customers in the applicable group and determine total costs for each group. This may often be time consuming. Another method involves a sampling procedure, wherein representative customers in each category are selected and the cost of servicing them is determined. A modification of this approach is to make a thoroughly detailed analysis in some areas and a sample run in other areas.

It will be appreciated that relatively few marketing expense items can be charged directly to customers and that allocations must be made. Statistical data from various reports will be found necessary, namely, the number of calls made to customers or customer classes and the time spent with customers or the number of orders.

Presentation of the analysis by customers may take the form of an income and expense statement as shown in Exhibit 3.3. This example classifies customers according to type, but a similar analysis could be made by annual volume of sales.

Occasions will arise when a decision must be made about whether the business with a specific customer should be continued or whether the method of sale ought to be changed. The use of unit analysis of individual customers, the contribution margin concept, and an alternative method of sale for small customers are illustrated in Exhibit 3.4. In this instance, changing the selling method from field calls to a phone basis resulted in the retention of valuable business and securing a contribution margin in line with normal operating requirements. Other data may be presented in graphic form, as in Exhibit 3.5.

An analysis by customers will provide information of great value to the sales manager. It will give a clear view of the number of accounts in various volume brackets and the average value of orders. In using this information for corrective action, consideration must be given to potential volume and the absorption of fixed production costs. But it will furnish facts for executive discussion regarding:

- Discontinuance of certain customer groups
- Price adjustments
- The need for higher margin for certain groups
- Change in method of sale

THE BEST COMPANY
STATEMENT OF INCOME AND EXPENSE BY CUSTOMER CLASS
FOR THE MONTH ENDED APRIL 30, 20XX

Description	Total		Retailers		Jobbers		Mail Order Houses	
	Amount	% of Net Sales	Amount	% of Net Sales	Amount	% of Net Sales	Amount	% of Net Sales
Gross Sales	$1,220,000		$690,000		$220,000		$310,000	
Less: Sales deductions	33,000		20,000		3,000		10,000	
Net sales	1,187,000	100.0	670,000	100.0	217,000	100.0	300,000	100.0
Cost of goods sold	957,600	80.7	503,800	75.2	187,700	86.5	266,100	88.7
Gross profit	229,400	19.3	166,200	24.8	29,300	13.5	33,900	11.3
Direct customer marketing costs	108,300	9.1	82,400	12.3	20,800	9.6	5,100	1.7
Profit remaining after direct costs	121,100	10.2	83,800	12.5	8,500	3.9	28,800	9.6
Indirect customer marketing costs	53,400	4.5	40,900	6.1	8,900	4.1	3,600	1.2
Profit (or loss) after marketing costs (and before income taxes)	$ 67,700	5.7	$ 42,900	6.4	$(400)	(.2)	$ 25,200	8.4

EXHIBIT 3.3 STATEMENT OF INCOME AND EXPENSE BY CUSTOMER CLASS

THE ROTH COMPANY
SELECTED CUSTOMER ANALYSIS ON A SALES UNIT BASIS
FOR THE SIX MONTHS ENDED JUNE 30, 20XX

	By Calls of Field Force				Proposed Centralized Phone Order Desk
	Customer W	Customer X	Customer Y	Customer Z	Customer Z
Net sales	$10.09	$10.16	$10.13	$10.21	$10.21
Direct costs					
Manufacturing	8.07	8.09	8.08	8.08	8.08
Transportation	.11	.12	.14	.18	.18
Warehousing	.02	.02	.02	.04	.04
Selling	.09	.10	.09	.22	.09
Total	8.29	8.33	8.33	8.52	8.39
Contribution margin	$ 1.80	$ 1.83	$ 1.80	$ 1.69	$ 1.82
Units sold	1,200	1,090	800	390	390
Aggregate contribution	$2,160	$1,995	$1,440	$ 559	$ 710

EXHIBIT 3.4   CUSTOMER ANALYSIS ON CONTRIBUTION MARGIN BASIS

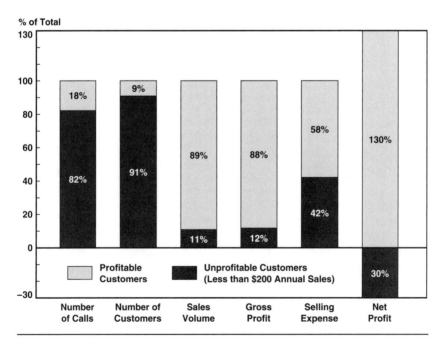

COMPARISON OF PROFITABLE AND UNPROFITABLE CUSTOMERS
NUMBER OF CASES, NUMBER OF CUSTOMERS, SALES VOLUME,
GROSS MARGIN AND SELLING EXPENSE
BASED ON ANNUAL SALES VOLUME

EXHIBIT 3.5   COMPARATIVE DATA ON PROFITABLE AND UNPROFITABLE ACCOUNTS

Analysis by Size of Order

Another analysis that may be made advantageously in many business concerns is that by size of orders. It has been recognized for some time that one of the causes of both high marketing expense and unprofitable sales is the small order—generally not because it is small in itself but because the prices are not high enough to cover the costs and leave a profit. There are many instances where small orders cannot be discontinued. But again, the problem can be solved. Corrective action can be taken; it can be brought under control. Obviously, the first step a controller must take is to get the facts through an analysis of marketing costs by size of order.

The problem is naturally more important in some concerns than in others, particularly where the order-handling costs are relatively large or fixed.

By and large, the procedure for analyzing marketing expense by size of order is similar to that for other analyses. It involves segregating costs by factor of variability and applying the factors. In this case, certain costs will be recognized as fixed for all sizes or orders, others will vary with the money volume, and still others will vary with physical volume. By way of general suggestion, the steps to be followed might be:

1. Determine the size of the order groups to be studied (e.g., below $25, $25 to $50).
2. Classify the costs according to (a) those that vary with the size of the order (e.g., packing); (b) those uniform for orders of all sizes (e.g., accounts receivable bookkeeping); and (c) those that must be considered as general overhead with no direct relation to orders (e.g., certain advertising and supervision costs).
3. Identify the factors that appear to govern the amount of the variable expense (expense that varies with the size of the order) applicable to orders of different sizes (e.g., dollar value, weight, or handling time).
4. Apply the factors of variability to the variable expenses and add the uniform costs, thereby arriving at a direct cost of orders by sizes.
5. Apply the overhead costs by some suitable factor, such as hundredweight or dollar value, to arrive at the total order cost.

Other Analyses

There are other analyses that may prove useful in a particular concern, for example:

- *By channel of distribution.* Useful where a choice in channel of distribution may be made in order to direct sales into the most profitable channel. The analysis needs to be made from time to time as cost trends change.
- *By method of sale.* The same comments are applicable as in the case of analysis by channels of distribution.
- *By salesperson.* For the purpose of measuring the salesperson's performance in terms of profit and to better direct salespeople in their activity.
- *By organization or operating division.* Useful where there are separate and distinct selling divisions. Such an analysis is used to measure performance of the divisional executive. Examples are analyses by departments in a department store, by stores in a retail chain store company, or by branches in a manufacturing organization.

Using Mathematical Techniques

The analyses indicated herein are only illustrative. The many variables and alternatives in the distribution or marketing function can indeed make the task of analyzing seem overwhelming. Problems to be solved include warehouse locations, transportation routes, most economical

shipment patterns, and a host of others. To perform the needed review, and to effect economies in these functions, use of mathematical formulas or "models" in conjunction with a personal computer can be most helpful. By using mathematical symbolization and techniques,
the many relationships and quantities can be expressed and dealt with.

Interpreting the Results of Analysis

It has already been stated that the primary purpose of distribution cost analysis is to supply
the marketing executives with the necessary information for the planning, direction, and
control of marketing effort. The preceding section has suggested the technique and purpose
or use of various analyses. It is clear, however, that these methods and studies will be varied
as the controller finds necessary.

The controller must be alert to the pitfalls or limitations of any figures prepared. Perhaps
the problem will be attacked from several sides. In some cases only the variable marketing
expenses (or even production costs) will be used, whereas in others both the fixed and variable
will be included. Again, in making recommendations based on the marketing expense analysis, the decisions reached must consider every possible effect on every activity of the business. For example, the conclusion that a certain territory must be dropped must consider the
net effect on profit—the change in factory volume with the same fixed expense and resulting differences in unit costs.

PLANNING MARKETING EXPENSES

Just as sales must be planned in attempting to reach the annual profit objective, so also must
marketing expenses. It is usually the task of the controller or the budget director to develop
the procedures for estimating the expense levels, and to provide the proper format and supporting data so that the chief marketing executive can furnish the financial data for consolidating the annual business plan.

But marketing costs differ in nature especially as to how the costs vary, or should vary,
with volume and how they are best planned and controlled. Depending on industry practice
and company experience, budgetary control of distribution costs may be achieved through
one of these types of budgets:

- Administrative
- Project
- Volume—variable
- Competitive service

Administrative-Type Budget

Probably the most commonly used budget for planning and controlling marketing expenses
is what is described here as an "administrative-type" budget. The circumstances when this
kind of planning and control device is most applicable include:

- The expense level is not, and should not be, influenced by the day-to-day variations in
  the sales level. To be sure, expenses must bear a certain relationship to sales, but this is
  accomplished over a longer time span, say from year to year.
- The output is not necessarily or easily quantified over very short periods, but rather
  over months—if then. Moreover, often the function is subjective in nature and relates
  to planning and controlling sales or to some other distribution effort.
- The number of routine and recurring functions is limited.

- Most of the expense is in the form of "people costs," represented largely by the expense of salaries, fringe benefits, occupancy, and travel and entertainment.
- The function is such that it cannot be planned and controlled on a project or program basis (as discussed in the next section).

Typical departments whose expenses usually are managed by an administrative budget include direct selling, field sales offices, general and territorial or product sales management units, and possibly the order department.

A typical procedure for developing an administrative-type planning budget is (see also Chapter 7):

1. The controller or budget administrator provides each marketing department manager (who will use this kind of budget) with last year's budget, and with the current head count and year-to-date expenses (by type of expense). This may be furnished through computer access or by worksheet.

2. The department manager estimates expenses for the remaining period of the current year (as in Exhibit 3.6), thus having two years of cost experience as a guide.

3. The sales executive estimates the departmental expenses by type of expenses and by month or quarter for the coming year. The sales executive takes into account the activity level expected, special tasks to be performed, general pay increases, and any other expected change in the function. Of course, the controller provides the sales executive with appropriate guidelines, such as fringe benefit rates, and other needed data. If traveling expenses are applicable, the marketing executive must estimate them, based on the number and types of trips to be made, etc.

4. The completed estimate is forwarded by the marketing manager through organization channels for review and approval, before reaching the financial representative.

THE ILLUSTRATIVE COMPANY
ANNUAL BUDGET
SALES ADMINISTRATION DEPARTMENT
(DOLLARS IN THOUSANDS)

Item	Prior Year	Current Year Actual (9 mos)	Current Year Estimated (3 mos)	Total	Plan Year Total	Increase (Decrease)
No. of staff	6	8	8	8	10	2
Expenses						
Salaries and wages	$209	$194	$ 65	$259	$306	$47
Fringe benefit costs (40%)	84	78	26	104	123	19
Travel	110	90	32	122	133	11
Entertainment	49	40	13	53	60	7
Communication	8	7	2	9	10	1
Occupancy	25	19	7	26	28	2
Supplies	12	12	2	14	16	2
Depreciation	8	6	2	8	8	—
Insurance	6	6	1	7	8	1
Dues and subscriptions	5	5	—	5	6	1
Miscellaneous	1	1	—	1	1	—
Total	$517	$458	$150	$608	$699	$91

EXHIBIT 3.6 ADMINISTRATIVE-TYPE BUDGET

5. The controller or budget officer reviews the departmental estimates for completeness and reasonableness. When the data seem in order, they are summarized for the marketing function. An administrative-type departmental marketing budget might appear as in Exhibit 3.6.

6. When the business plan is completed and approved, the departmental executive is so informed. (Of course, there may be iterative changes.)

7. After the planning period has commenced, the marketing executive is provided periodically (usually monthly) a comparison of actual and budgeted expenses for information and for corrective action, if warranted. (See Exhibit 3.7.)

Project-Type Budget

Probably the second most widely used budget in the planning and control of marketing expenses is the project type. This is so designated because many of the cost elements are best planned on a project basis; that is, certain tasks or programs or projects are planned, then executed, and then the results are measured sometime in the future. The level of planned expense is not directly related to the *immediate* sales, but rather future sales over perhaps a year or two. The project is completed and the expense largely stops until another project is undertaken. The expense level bears a necessary relationship to sales, but only indirectly and over a period of time. Emphasis is on getting a certain task done within a certain time and within cost constraints. Typical activities handled largely on a project basis are advertising and sales promotion expense or market research.

THE ILLUSTRATIVE COMPANY
BUDGET REPORT
SALES ADMINISTRATION DEPARTMENT
MONTH: JUNE   (DOLLARS IN THOUSANDS)

	Current Month			Year to Date		
Item	Actual	Budget	(Over) Under Budget	Actual	Budget	(Over) Under Budget
No. of staff	9	10	1 (a)	9	10	1
Expenses						
Salaries and wages	$23	$25	$ 2	$138	$150	$12.
Fringe benefit costs (40%)	10	10	—	55.2	60.0	4.8
Travel	14	11	(3)(b)	75	67	(8.0)(b)
Entertainment	4	5	1	29	30	1
Communications	1	1	—	5	5	—
Occupancy	3	3		14	14	—
Supplies	2	1	(1)	8	8	—
Depreciation	.5	.5	—	4	4	—
Insurance	.7	.7	—	4	4	—
Dues and subscriptions	.5	.5	—	3	3	—
Miscellaneous	.1	.1	—	.5	.5	—
Total	$58.8	$57.8	$(1)	$335.7	$345.5	$9.8

Notes: (a) Market analyst not yet located.
       (b) No provision made for London trips.

EXHIBIT 3.7   BUDGET REPORT—A SALES DEPARTMENT

The budgetary procedure for a project type budget is essentially:

1. The marketing executives agree or decide what projects of a given departmental type are necessary to attain the planned sales objective or are otherwise desirable.

2. The department manager (e.g., advertising or market research) estimates the cost for each project by type of expense, if applicable—usually in a format suggested by the controller. In some instances, budget limits are set based on estimated unit sales, or as related to prior year expenses (e.g., advertising).

3. The various projects are summarized and included in the departmental budget for the planning period. (See Exhibit 3.8.)

THE ILLUSTRATIVE COMPANY, INC.
ADVERTISING AND SALES PROMOTION BUDGET
(DOLLARS IN THOUSANDS)

Category	Current Year Project Budget	Plan Year Requested Budget	(Increase) Decrease over Current Year	Comments
Broadcast media				
Radio—local	$ 500	$ 525	$(25)	Price increase
Television				
Regional	1,300	1,400	(100)	Price increase ($65,000) Expanded coverage
Local spots	2,500	2,625	(125)	5% price increase
Total	3,800	4,025	(225)	
Total broadcast media	4,300	4,550	(250)	
Print media				
Local newspapers	400	420	(20)	Price increase
Business publications	700	700	—	
General public magazines	1,200	1,100	100	Elimination of Oregon
Subtotal	2,300	2,220	80	
Catalogs	900	900	—	
Newspaper stuffers	350	300	50	
Direct mail	1,900	2,000	(100)	
Total print media	5,450	5,420	30	
Total media	9,750	9,970	(220)	
Advertising administration				
Salaries and wages	400	420	(20)	General wage increase of 5%
Fringe benefits	160	168	(8)	
Travel	140	120	20	No foreign trips
Communications	100	90	10	Negotiation Pac Bell and AT&T
All other	90	90	—	
Total administration	890	888	2	
Grand total	$10,640	$10,858	$(218)	
Percentage of sales	8.0%	7.4%		

EXHIBIT 3.8 ADVERTISING AND SALES PROMOTION BUDGET

4. After appropriate review and change, if necessary, the budget is approved as part of the annual plan. (In many companies the advertising budget is approved by the board of directors as a special budget.)

5. Periodically, perhaps monthly, the actual expenses and commitments are updated and compared with the project budget and corrective action taken if necessary or possible. (See Exhibit 3.9.)

Variable Volume Budget

A limited number of distribution activities are high-volume repetitive tasks that probably can be directly related to the immediate physical volume handled. The loading and unloading of trucks, freight cars, or packaging products are examples. Giving recognition to the need to have an adequate number of workers available, even when the volume fluctuates greatly, these activities can be planned, measured, and controlled much like some factory operations.

The steps involved in this type of variable budget are (see also Chapter 5):

1. For each department or activity grouping, expenses are identified by type (salaries and wages, fringe benefits, supplies, etc.).

2. Such expenses are segregated into their fixed and variable components for the planning period. Recognition must be given to the true cost drivers, as in activity-based costing. (See Chapter 5.)

3. For the *planning* budget, the estimated expenses are determined for each applicable time period (monthly or quarterly) by applying the estimated units to be handled to the unit variable expense rate, and adding the fixed components. (See Exhibit 3.10, which is expanded to show budget structure.) This planning budget is approved by the supervisor, when in order, and consolidated with the other distribution cost budgets to arrive at the total marketing department budget.

4. When approved, and when the year is underway, actual costs are measured monthly against the budgeted expense (fixed costs plus unit variable expense multiplied by the units handled) and corrective action taken if necessary. (See Exhibit 3.11.)

Competitive Service Budget

In a limited number of cases, the competitive service-type budget, or profit or loss-type budget, may be useful. Basically, it can be applied when the costs of a distribution operation can be readily compared with an independent and similar service activity. Examples include building maintenance or warehousing activities.

The procedure is closely related to the variable budget system just reviewed, combined with an in-house billing rate based on competitive prices. Steps in the process are:

1. The competitive price to be charged for each type of service is determined based on the area prevailing practice.

2. Expenses are accumulated on a responsibility accounting basis for the department.

3. Expenses are analyzed or identified into their fixed and variable components.

4. For the planning budget, the expected unit volumes are estimated and applied to the budget structure of fixed and variable elements:

   (a) To the competitive unit service prices to arrive at the net billings. (See Exhibit 3.12.)

THE ILLUSTRATIVE COMPANY, INC.
ADVERTISING AND SALES PROMOTION BUDGET
STATUS REPORT AS AT JUNE 30, 20XX
(DOLLARS IN THOUSANDS)

Category	Project Budget	Actual to 6/30/XX			Estimated Cost to Complete	Indicated Total Cost	(Over) Under Budget
		Expenditures	Commitments	Total			
Broadcast media							
Radio—local	$ 525	$ 220	$ 60	$ 280	$ 245	$ 525	$ —
Television							
Regional	1,400	600	700	1,300	200	1,500	(100)
Local spots	2,625	1,125	500	1,625	800	2,425	200
Total	4,025	1,725	1,200	2,925	1,000	3,925	100
Total broadcast media	4,550	1,945	1,260	3,205	1,245	4,450	100
Print media							
Local newspapers	420	140	60	200	200	400	20
Business publications	700	450	150	600	150	750	(50)
General public magazines	1,100	510	400	910	200	1,110	(10)
Subtotal	2,220	1,100	610	1,710	550	2,260	(40)
Catalogs	900	400	300	700	200	900	—
Newspaper stuffers	300	100	50	150	150	300	—
Direct mail	2,000	1,300	900	2,200	—	2,200	(200)
Total print media	5,420	2,900	1,860	4,760	900	5,660	(240)
Total media	9,970	4,845	3,120	7,965	2,145	10,110	(140)
Advertising administration							
Salaries and wages	420	210	—	210	210	420	—
Fringe benefits	168	84	—	84	84	168	—
Travel	120	50	—	50	60	110	10
Communications	90	40	—	40	50	90	—
All other costs	90	50	—	50	40	90	—
Total administration	888	434	—	434	444	878	10
Grand total	$10,858	$5,279	$3,120	$8,399	$2,589	$10,988	$(130)
Percentage of sales	7.4%					7.5%	

EXHIBIT 3.9 ADVERTISING BUDGET—STATUS REPORT

THE ILLUSTRATIVE COMPANY
LOS ANGELES TERMINAL
ANNUAL PLANNING BUDGET FOR THE YEAR 200X

Estimated Units—200W 360,000
200X 420,000

Item	Mo. Budget Structure		Est. Budget—Current Year 200X			Estimated Budget—200X		
	Fixed	Variable	Fixed	Variable	Total	Fixed	Variable	Total
Salaries	$15,000	—	$180,000	—	$ 180,000	$189,000	—	$ 189,000
Hourly wages	6,000	.70	72,000	$252,000	324,000	75,600	$323,400	399,000
Incentive pay—M	1,500	—	18,000	—	18,000	18,900	—	18,900
—H	600	.07	7,200	25,200	32,400	7,560	30,870	38,430
Subtotal	23,100		277,200	277,200	554,400	291,060	354,270	645,330
Fringe benefits	9,240		110,880	110,880	221,760	116,424	141,708	258,132
Supplies	1,000	.10	12,000	36,000	48,000	12,000	42,000	54,000
Gas and oil	1,000	.30	12,000	108,000	120,000	12,000	126,000	138,000
Repairs—regular	400	.10	4,800	36,000	40,800	4,800	42,000	46,800
—special	500	.20	6,000	72,000	78,000	6,000	84,000	90,000
Communications	1,000	.03	12,000	10,800	22,800	12,000	12,600	24,600
Occupancy	3,000	—	36,000	—	36,000	36,000	—	36,000
Utilities	650	.15	7,800	54,000	61,800	7,800	63,000	70,800
Property taxes and insurance	700	—	8,400	—	8,400	8,400	—	8,400
Depreciation	2,500	—	30,000	—	30,000	30,000	—	30,000
Miscellaneous	100	.05	1,200	18,000	17,200	1,200	21,000	22,200
Total	$43,190		$518,280	$722,880	$1,241,160	$537,684	$886,578	$1,424,262

Notes: Increases requested: 5% on all salaries and wages and incentive pay.
No other changes.

EXHIBIT 3.10 VARIABLE VOLUME BUDGET

THE ILLUSTRATIVE COMPANY
LOS ANGELES TERMINAL
BUDGET—REPORT—MONTH OF MARCH

Supervisor: Johnsen
Units Handled: 36,000

Item	March Budget Fixed	March Budget Variable	March Budget Total	March Actual	March (Over) Under Budget	Year to Date Budget	Year to Date Actual	Year to Date (Over) Under Budget
Salaries	$15,750	—	$ 15,750	$ 15,750	—	$ 47,250	$ 47,250	$ —
Hourly wages	6,300	$26,460	32,760	32,500	$ 260	98,280	98,000	280
Incentive pay—M	1,575	—	1,575	1,575	—	4,725	4,725	—
—H	630	2,646	3,276	3,250	26	9,828	9,800	28
Subtotal	24,255	29,106	53,361	53,075	286	160,083	159,775	308
Fringe benefits (40%)	9,702	11,642	21,344	21,230	114	64,032	63,910	122
Supplies	1,000	3,600	4,600	4,300	300	13,800	13,900	(100)
Gas and oil	1,000	10,800	11,800	12,120	(320)	35,400	35,000	400
Repairs—regular	400	3,600	4,000	4,600	(600)	12,000	12,000	—
—special	500	7,200	7,700	7,200	500	23,100	21,100	2,000
Communications	1,000	1,080	2,080	2,000	80	6,240	6,040	200
Occupancy	3,000	—	3,000	3,000	—	9,000	9,000	—
Utilities	650	5,400	6,050	5,950	100	18,150	18,000	150
Property taxes and insurance	700	—	700	700	—	2,100	2,100	—
Depreciation	2,500	—	2,500	2,500	—	7,500	7,500	—
Miscellaneous	100	1,800	1,900	1,300	600	5,700	5,900	(200)
Total	$44,807	$74,228	$119,035	$117,975	$1,060	$357,105	$354,225	$2,880

Notes: Telephone companies have announced an 8% increase in the tariff. Since no budget was provided for such an increase, Johnsen is requesting a budget adjustment.

EXHIBIT 3.11 VARIABLE BUDGET CONTROL REPORT

THE ILLUSTRATIVE COMPANY
OREGON DISTRIBUTION CENTER
BUDGET REPORT

Month of __January__
Units handled __200,000__

Item	Budget	Actual	Favorable (Unfavorable) Variance
Net billings to using activities	$242,330	$201,100	$(41,230)
Operating Expenses			
Salaries and wages	162,500	164,100	(1,600)
Supplies	4,900	4,810	90
Vehicle maintenance	18,760	16,440	2,320
Repairs	5,800	5,900	(100)
Occupancy charges	25,000	25,000	—
Depreciation	10,000	10,000	—
Property taxes	3,000	3,000	—
Miscellaneous	300	310	(10)
Total	$230,260	$229,560	$ 700
Operating profit (or loss)	$ 12,070	$(28.460)	$(40,530)

EXHIBIT 3.12 COMPETITIVE SERVICE BUDGET REPORT

(b) To unit variable cost rates to arrive at the variable budget. This is added to the fixed expense budget, by type of expense, to arrive at the budget level for each type of expense.

(c) As to "billings," these should be properly handled in the distribution budget consolidation (i.e., eliminated in most cases).

5. For control purposes, the unit budget times the actual volume handled, plus the budgeted fixed costs, is compared to actual expense to determine budget performance. (See Exhibit 3.12.)

6. Corrective action is taken as required.

Summarized Marketing Expense Budget

When the individual department planning budgets are approved, they are summarized by the controller's staff to arrive at the tentative marketing expense budget as in Exhibit 3.13. For illustrative purposes only, this summary budget identifies the supporting types of budgets in the marketing function. When the complete annual plan is approved, the chief sales executive is advised by the chief executive officer (CEO) of the approved budget. This becomes a commitment by the CEO as to expense levels for the year.

SPECIAL COMMENTS ON ADVERTISING AND SALES PROMOTION EXPENSE

In discussing marketing expenses, the example selected for a project-type budget (see Exhibit 3.8) was advertising and sales promotion expense. This expense, as well as market research expense, often is planned and controlled on a project basis. Planning and controlling

THE JOHNSON COMPANY, INC.
SUMMARY MARKETING DIVISION BUDGET
FOR THE PLAN YEAR ENDING DECEMBER 31, 20XX
(DOLLARS IN THOUSANDS)

| Department | Type of Budget | Prior Year Actual | Total | Plan Year Quarter | | | | Annual Budget (Increase) Decrease |
				1	2	3	4	
General and administrative								
V.P. sales	Administrative	$ 3,840	$ 3,910	$ 950	$ 990	$ 1,010	$ 960	$ 70
Customer relations	Administrative	780	820	205	205	205	205	40
Market research	Project	1,120	1,140	280	290	285	285	20
Total		5,740	5,870	1,435	1,485	1,500	1,450	130
Branch offices								
San Francisco	Administrative	410	415	104	103	105	103	5
Chicago	Administrative	620	630	158	157	159	156	10
New Orleans	Administrative	360	365	91	91	92	91	5
Total		1,390	1,410	353	351	356	350	20
Direct selling								
West	Administrative	8,310	9,120	2,270	2,290	2,310	2,250	810
Rocky Mountains	Administrative	6,120	6,230	1,550	1,570	1,590	1,520	110
Great Plains	Administrative	5,870	6,040	1,510	1,510	1,530	1,490	170
Southwest	Administrative	7,960	8,170	2,020	2,050	2,070	2,030	210
Middle West	Administrative	9,540	9,980	2,470	2,510	2,500	2,500	440
Total		37,800	39,540	9,820	9,930	10,000	9,790	1,740
Advertising and sales promotion	Project	10,470	10,560	2,220	2,610	2,140	3,590	90
Warehousing								
Portland	Variable	2,960	3,170	790	780	810	790	210
Denver	Variable	1,840	1,990	480	500	510	500	150
Chicago	Variable	3,480	3,495	860	870	865	900	15
New Orleans	Variable	1,710	1,725	420	430	460	415	15
Total		9,990	10,380	2,550	2,580	2,645	2,605	390
Grand total—division		$65,390	$67,760	$16,378	$16,956	$16,641	$17,785	$2,370

EXHIBIT 3.13 SUMMARY MARKETING EXPENSE BUDGET

advertising and sales promotion expense is the responsibility of the chief sales executive, and such expenses are included in the marketing expense budget for internal administration purposes. However, the approval process at the board-of-director level often considers this kind of expense in a separate budget review. For this reason, among others, some special comments appear appropriate.

First, it may be well to define advertising as any paid form of nonpersonal presentation and promotion of ideas, goods, and services by an identified sponsor. Inherent in this and similar definitions is the fact that presentations are nonpersonal, that is, there is no face-to-face personal selling to the customer. It is a controlled, paid-for service, not free publicity. Sales promotion ims more difficult to describe. It may be supplementary to either advertising or personal selling. Typically, it takes the form of a special effort, usually for a limited time only, of inducements such as price reductions, cents-off coupons, cash refunds, or contests or prizes, to induce the purchase of the goods or service. The campaign may be directed to consumers, or salespeople, or other intermediaries.

Second, the reasons for often separate consideration or approval by a board of directors (or internal management) include these factors:

- For many companies, such as retail stores or consumer goods producers (e.g., Procter & Gamble, Kimberly-Clark, or Coca-Cola, Inc.), it is a major expenditure.
- It is difficult to measure the effectiveness of advertising or sales promotion programs.
- Closely related to the difficulty of measurement is the fact that the results of the program may be less immediate and less direct than some other type of marketing effort, such as direct selling.
- Finally, advertising and sales promotion effort is usually organized as a separate department or as an outside agency, as compared with other selling efforts.

All of these factors are among the reasons for separate budgetary treatment.

Third, the type of expenses involved here differ somewhat from other marketing expenses. A large portion will represent media costs, whether for television or radio broadcasts, for printed media (such as newspapers and/or magazines), or for direct mail costs, or other public media costs (such as outdoor advertising). Associated with the media costs are the usual administrative expenses: salaries and wages, fringe benefits, travel, occupancy costs, automobile maintenance, and so on.

Fourth, the purpose of advertising will vary in differing circumstances. While the general purpose is to support the broad marketing objectives, more specific goals may include:

- Educate consumers in the use of the product or service.
- Reduce the cost of other selling effort.
- Increase sales.
- Establish or maintain trademarks or brand names.
- Develop new markets.
- Meet or outdo competition.
- Maintain prices.
- Introduce new products or services.
- Create favorable public opinion.
- Avoid unfavorable legislation.

Fifth, two basic ways are currently in use of establishing an advertising and sales promotion budget: the lump-sum appropriation method estimating the amount required to attain certain objectives. Comments on each follow.

The simple lump-sum appropriation method consists of authorizing the expenditure for advertising and sales promotions related to some factor. Under this plan the total amount to be spent could be based on:

- A percentage of planned or budgeted sales
- A percentage of the prior year sales or perhaps of an average of several past years
- A fixed amount per unit of product expected to be sold (the units are obtained from the sales plan)
- An arbitrary percentage increase over the prior year's expenditure
- A percent of gross profit on the product for the prior year or the planning year
- A percentage of net income of the prior year or the planning year

The advantage of the lump-sum appropriation method is sheer simplicity. Basically it seems to lack any scientific basis, although there may be a perceived long-term relationship between advertising expenditures and level of sales.

The estimated "cost of attaining the objective" procedure seems a more logical process: Objectives are set; the detailed steps to reach the objective are decided upon; the relevant costs for each such program are estimated and are summarized to arrive at the total cost for the planning year. This estimating process may be performed by the advertising department, perhaps assisted by an outside advertising agency, or sometimes it is done by the agency itself. Obviously, a skilled financial analyst should review such costs for any evidence of waste. Moreover, in some cases the marginal or gross profit from the additional units estimated to be sold can be compared with the advertising expense to determine if the project seems to make financial sense. This can be done on an incremental advertising expense and quantity basis to ascertain at which point, if any, the incremental unit advertising cost exceeds the incremental marginal profit all direct expenses.

A simple example is shown in the matrix illustrated in Exhibit 3.14. If these estimates are valid, then not more than $100,000 (incremental block 5) should be spent in advertising Product 10. Financial analysis would sometimes identify some possibly uneconomic programs.

Incremental Block	Incremental Advertising Expense	Additional Units Estimated to Be Sold	Estimated Marginal Unit Income*	Incremental Unit Advertising Cost	Unit Increment or (Decrement) Margin	Total Margin
1	$ –0–	20,000	$1.00	$ —	(1.00)	$ 20,000
2	25,000	30,000	1.20	.83	.37	11,100
3	25,000	70,000	1.30	.36	.94	65,800
4	25,000	50,000	.90	.50	.40	20,000
5	25,000	50,000	.80	.50	.30	15,000
6	25,000	30,000	.70	.83	(.13)	(3,900)
7	25,000	30,000	.60	.83	(.23)	(6,900)
8	25,000	20,000	.50	1.25	(.75)	(15,000)
9	25,000	10,000	.40	2.50	(2.10)	(21,000)

* After all direct costs and before advertising cost.

EXHIBIT 3.14 INCREMENTAL ADVERTISING EXPENSE COMPARED TO INCREMENTAL PROFIT MARGIN

It is beyond the scope of this section to review the many facets of advertising and sales promotion that might interest the controller or staff in attempting to financially appraise the advertising and sales promotion budget. Books on advertising and sales promotion are worth perusing for more detailed information.

CONTROL OF MARKETING EXPENSES

As already explained, the budgetary control process involves comparing the actual expenses with the budgeted expenses (or the budgeted rates time the actual volume handled for variable expenses) and taking corrective action.

Where budgets are not used, actual expenses may be compared with the unit standards and actual unit volumes, as reviewed in the next section.

MARKETING EXPENSE STANDARDS

Standards and Control

The very foundation of marketing cost control lies in the correlation of sales effort with the potential and the use of analysis to avoid misdirection. Although this may be done, and although the income and expense statement may reveal a satisfactory result for a time, still this is not enough. It must be known that the business is being operated efficiently, and this requires measuring sticks—standards.

A complete analysis of past operations must be taken as a starting point. By this it may be determined that 1,000 calls have been made by salespeople in a given territory, at a cost of $5 per call, and with certain sales results. But the questions are left unanswered about how many calls should have been made by the salespeople and what the cost per call should have been. These also must be ascertained if effective control of sales effort is to be exercised. It may be known that 1,000 orders have been handled at a clerical cost of $0.50 per order, but it needs to be known also what the cost would have been if the clerical work had been efficiently directed. In brief, standards are needed by which to judge the distribution performance and signal its weaknesses. Knowing in detail what it has been is not enough; it needs also to be known in detail what it should be in the immediate future.

Can Standards Be Established for Marketing Activity?

It would be foolish to contend that all distribution activity can be highly standardized. In fact, it is never possible completely to standardize production activities. The answer to just exactly what results should be obtained from a dollar expended for advertising or direct sales effort when developing a new territory or a new product or just what costs will be necessary to accomplish certain definite ends pertaining to customer goodwill is frequently problematic. But it would be equally foolish, and a fatal management error, to evade the fact that standards can be successfully applied to a vast amount of the distribution activity. If no one is competent to judge what distribution effort is necessary to secure certain results and what it will cost to do it, then management must indeed be in a helpless position.

Although a new venture may be undertaken here and there on something of an experimental basis, the entire distribution effort will scarcely be directed along such lines continuously. It is hardly to be expected that an intelligent executive will direct $1 million into the distribution effort in the vain hope that profit will result at the end of the year. Rather the executive may be expected to provide for the continuous measurement of individual and group performance as expressed in costs and results. Knowledge is needed of when billing clerks are wasting time, when automotive equipment is too costly, when direct mail prices fail to "pull," when bad debt losses are excessive, when warehouse labor hours are too high, when long-distance telephone costs are exorbitant, and when salespeople produce insufficient orders. If these costs and performance factors are not under constant control, the executive's profit goal is almost certain to be unmet. But such control implies standards and depends entirely on the establishment and use of standards. Warehouse labor hours never appear too high in the absolute. They become too high only when measured against what they should be under the circumstances—only when a standard is applied.

Although it must be admitted that it is difficult to establish standards for some marketing activities; that psychological factors are relatively more, and physical and mechanical factors relatively less, influential than in production; that relatively more depends on the judgment of executives and relatively less on objective measurements; and that a somewhat greater tolerance must be allowed in the consideration of variances, it should be understood that this applies only to a part of the marketing activity. Much of the marketing activity is fully as measurable as production. There is no important difference, for example, between the method of establishing standards for order handling, warehousing, shipping, delivery, and clerical work and the methods employed in production. Even those distribution activities that are largely affected by psychological factors, such as advertising and personal selling, are usually capable of reasonably accurate measurement when the activities are continuous or repetitive.

The types of standards needed, as well as the techniques used for their establishment, change as circumstances change, such as increased globalization. Whereas at one time much attention was focused on internal unit cost standards and unit revenue standards, now other facets are involved. While internal comparisons of internal trends and relationships are still made, there is a movement to measure against *external* standards. Moreover, some standards are now time related, such as the time required to develop a new product. Standards might relate to customer satisfaction, such as number of prospects converted to customer status. Some of the newer standards, some of which are applicable to marketing efforts, are reviewed in Chapter 1.

Types of Marketing Expense Standards

Marketing expense standards may be either (1) of a very general nature, and applicable to distribution functions as a whole, or by major divisions, or (2) units that measure individual performance. Illustrative of the former are:

- Selling cost as a percentage of net sales
- Cost per dollar of gross profit
- Cost per unit sold
- Cost per sales transaction
- Cost per order received
- Cost per customer account

Standards such as these are useful indicators of trends for the entire distribution effort. Furthermore, such standards can be applied to individual products, territories, branches, or departments.

However, these general standards do not necessarily indicate points of weaknesses in terms of individual responsibility. If costs are to be controlled, the performance of the individual must be measured. Hence it is necessary to set standards for controllable costs of individual cost items or functions. In warehousing, for example, standards might be set for direct labor as:

- Cost per item handled
- Cost per pound handled
- Cost per shipment
- Cost per order filled

Similar standards might be set for shipping supplies or delivery and truck expense. In the direct sales field, standards might be set for a salesperson's automobile expense in terms of the following:

- Cost per mile traveled
- Cost per day
- Cost per month

Again, entertainment expense standards might relate to cost per customer or cost per dollar of net sales.

Other Considerations in Setting Marketing expense Standards

The controller has a joint responsibility with the sales executives in setting marketing expense standards. In fulfilling this responsibility, it is well to keep in mind the complications. For example, in manufacturing there is usually only one standard cost for the product. There are, however, many standard costs for distribution of the same article. Thus, the cost per call may be different in every territory or sales district. Even in the same territory the standard cost to sell to different classes of customers may vary.

By and large, the same principles applicable to manufacturing expense standards apply to distribution costs. Thus, standards will require revision when operating conditions change materially. Also, where fixed elements of cost are included in the standards, the effect of volume must be recognized.

How to Set Marketing Expense Standards: Benchmarking

The methods of establishing standards vary depending on whether external or only internal standards are the objective. A procedure of measuring products, or services, or business practice against the toughest competitor, or the companies best in their class, or other measures—benchmarking—is discussed in the "Benchmarking" Section in Chapter 1.

Another method that may be somewhat more internally oriented, but also involves an analytical approach is reviewed next.

When the need for standards has been agreed to with the sales executive, the detailed work of setting standards can proceed.

The first step in setting the marketing expense standards is to classify the costs according to functions and activities expressive of individual responsibility. How far such classification can and should be carried depends, of course, on the nature of the business, its size, methods of operation, and internal organization. The cost of such major functions as direct selling, advertising, transportation, warehousing, credit and collection, and financing can be separated in most businesses and subjected to individual study and control. Even such a general classification as this is not universal. For example, in a concern doing a house-to-house business, the functions of direct selling and credit and collection are merged, since the work is done by the same people under the same supervision.

The costs of the major functions should be further classified by individual activities that make up the functional service. For example, the credit and collection costs may be separated into credit approvals, posting charges, posting credits, preparing customers' monthly statements, writing collection letters, and so on.

The second step is to select units or bases of measurement through which the standards can be expressed. Such units or bases will vary with the type of measurement to be applied; thus the measurement may apply to effort used, to cost, to results achieved, or to the relationship of these factors. To illustrate, a salesperson may be expected to make a given number of calls per day. This constitutes a measure of effort used and the unit of measure is the call. The cost of writing orders in the order department may be measured in terms of the number of orders or order lines[1] written. This is a measure of costs, and the unit of measurement is the order or order line. Salespeople may each be expected to produce a certain number of orders or to secure a certain number of new accounts. This is a measure of results, and the units of measurement are orders and new accounts. Finally, salespeople may be required to hold their direct costs within 8 percent of their sales volume. Here, the measurement is in terms of the relationship of particular costs to the results in the sales volumes and the basis of measurement is the ratio of one to the other.

Although such specific units of measurement are not available for all distribution activities, some basis must be selected before the standards can be applied. Where specific units are not available, more inclusive or composite bases must be used. For example, the entire credit and collection cost may be measured by the number of accounts carried, or the entire advertising cost may be measured by its ratio to dollar sales volume.

The third step is to analyze past experience relative to the cost of the functions and specific activities involved with a view to selecting the best experience and indications about the best procedure. This may involve intensive study of individual methods of procedure and operation similar to that employed in the development of production standards.

The fourth step is to consider the effect on costs of expected changes in external conditions and of the sales program as planned. If increased sales resistance is expected, an estimate must be made about its effect on such costs as advertising and direct selling. If the program calls for a lengthening of the installment credit period, the effect on the financing cost must be estimated.

The final step is to summarize the judgment of those executives, division heads, department heads, and salespersons whose experience and training qualify them to judge the measures of satisfactory performance. The standards set must be the final expression of such judgment, based on an intelligent study of past experience and future outlook.

Standards as finally set will result in much overlapping. Thus a standard cost may be applied to the warehousing function as a whole. Within this general function, many individual cost standards may be applied that relate to specific activities such as clerical costs of order handling and physical assembling.

Finally, different standards must frequently be set for different territories, products, channels of distribution, classes of customers, departments, and so forth, wherein different conditions prevail.

Additional Information Needed

To establish and use marketing expense standards successfully, a concern must accumulate and have available a considerable amount of information relative to marketing activities and

---

1. *Order line* here means the writing of one line on a sales order (e.g., "200 1/2" Malleable Iron Nipples No. 682 at $8.00 = $16.00).

the cost factors pertaining to such activities. This includes a considerable body of information not available in the regular accounting records. Permanent records must be designed for regularly recording and accumulating these data in readily usable form. Just as it is now the custom to record regularly such production factors as labor hours, chargeable hours, idle hours, machine hours, power loads, and number of operations, records must likewise be made of the marketing factors.

Illustrative of such data are:

- Analyses of sales in physical units
- Number of sales transactions classified in terms of size, hour of day, and so on
- Number of quotations made
- Number of orders classified in terms of size, period in which received, and the like
- Number of order lines written
- Average number of salespersons
- Number of salesperson days
- Number of calls on old and new customers
- Number of days of salespersons' travel
- Number of miles of salespersons' travel
- Average number of customers classified with regard to location, annual volume, and so forth
- Number of labor hours of salespeople advertising and display people, warehouse workers, truck drivers, delivery people, maintenance workers, clerical workers, and so on
- Number of returns and allowances classified in terms of cause
- Number of units of advertising space or time used in the various advertising media
- Number of advertising pieces mailed: letters, circulars, folders, calendars, and so on
- Number of pieces of advertising material distributed: window cards, store displays, inserts, and the like
- Number of samples distributed
- Number of demonstrations made
- Number of inquiries received
- Number of new customers secured
- Number of shipments
- Analyses of shipments in physical units
- Dollar value of shipments
- Number of ton-mile units of shipping
- Number of deliveries
- Number of parcels delivered
- Number of miles of truck operation
- Number of shipping claims handled
- Physical volume of goods handled in warehouses
- Average size of physical inventory carried
- Rates of turnover in dollars and physical units
- Average number of accounts carried
- Number of invoices
- Number of invoice lines

- Number of remittances received
- Number of credit letters sent
- Average number of days accounts are outstanding
- Average amount of receivables carried
- Number of mail pieces handled
- Number of postings
- Number of letters written—distribution sections
- Number of units filed
- Percentage of sales from new products
- Percentage of on-time customer deliveries
- Number of customers for which company is sole supplier

Many of the foregoing items must be further classified by territories, commodities, and departments to supply the full information needed.

Such information will be found useful for many purposes in the direction of distribution activity but is essential to a program of standards. Many concerns have in the past neglected to accumulate and use such information. It is not uncommon to find a concern that has the most exacting records of a production machine (the date of its purchase, full detail about its cost, working hours, number and cause of idle hours, and cost of maintenance) almost to the point of a complete diary of the machine's daily routine over a long period of years. During the same time, the concern may have been employing a salesperson whose total cost through the years has greatly exceeded the cost and maintenance of the machine, but little detailed record of activities has been kept. How the salesperson has spent time, the number of calls made, the number of prospects interviewed, orders received, gross profit, and even the type of goods sold has not always been recorded. The salesperson's activity report can provide some of these data.

With many concerns the distribution information is entirely too meager. More information must be collected if the distribution program is to be wisely directed.

Use of Standards for Control

The essence of control is the prompt follow-up of unfavorable trends before they develop into large losses. Once the standards are determined, the stage is set for action. The controller compares actual and standard performance and reports the results to the sales executive.

4

PLANNING AND CONTROL
OF MANUFACTURING COSTS:
DIRECT MATERIAL AND DIRECT LABOR

GENERAL ASPECTS OF MANUFACTURING

Responsibilities of the Manufacturing Executive

To those not familiar with the intricacies of the modern manufacturing processes, it might seem that once a determination has been made of the products to be manufactured and sold, and of the quantities required, then the remaining task is simple: proceed to manufacture the articles. As compared with the task of the sales executive, many of the variables in manufacturing are more subject to the control of the executive than they are in selling, many are more easily measured, and the psychological factors may be less pronounced. But the job is by no means an easy one, and many difficulties plague the manufacturing manager who is attempting to deliver a quality product, within cost, and on schedule.

Consider some of the numerous decisions the manufacturing executive is called upon to make—in many of which the controller is not involved at all, others with which he may be only tangentially concerned, and yet others where he may be, or should be, of assistance to the production executive. While any number of classifications may be used, these groupings of the duties seem practical:

- *Physical Facilities*
    - Acquisition of plant and equipment
    - Proper layout of machinery and equipment, storage facilities, and so on
    - Adequate maintenance of plant and equipment
    - Proper safeguarding of the physical assets (security)

- *Product and Production Planning*
    - Product design
    - Decisions on product specifications
    - Determination of material requirements—specifications and quantities
    - Selection of manufacturing processes
    - Planning the production schedule

○ Decisions on manufacturing or purchasing the components—"make-or-buy" decisions

○ Material purchases

○ Labor-requirements—skill needs, employment, training, and job assignment and transfer

○ Inventory levels required

○ Preparing the production and manufacturing plans—short and long term

- *Manufacturing Process*

  ○ Planning and controlling labor

  ○ Receiving, handling, routing, and processing raw materials and work-in-process in an economical manner

  ○ Controlling quality

  ○ Coordinating manufacturing with sales

  ○ Planning and controlling all manufacturing costs—direct and indirect

And the list could go on.

For some phases, the controller may coordinate procedures and see that adequate internal controls exist, that needed economic analysis is made, as in acquisition of plant and equipment or as part of the annual planning process. But perhaps the biggest contribution of the controller is the development and maintenance of a general accounting and cost system that will assist the manufacturing executive, and that will provide the necessary information for the planning and control of the business.

Objectives of Manufacturing Cost Accounting

A manufacturing cost accounting system is an integral part of the total management information system. In analyzing costing systems for control, the controller must recognize the purpose of the manufacturing cost accounting system and relate it to the production or operating management problems. The objectives must be clearly defined if the system is to be effectively utilized. There are four fundamental purposes of a cost system that may vary in importance from one organization to another:

1. Control of costs
2. Planning and performance measurement
3. Inventory valuation
4. Deriving anticipated prices

Control of costs is a primary function of manufacturing cost accounting and cost analysis. The major elements of costs—labor, material, and manufacturing expenses—must be segregated by product, by type of cost, and by responsibility. For example, the actual number of parts used in the assembly of an airplane section, such as a wing, may be compared to the bill of materials and corrective action taken when appropriate.

Closely related to cost control is the use of cost data for effective planning and performance measurement. Some of the same information used for cost control purposes may be used for the planning of manufacturing operations. For example, the standards used for cost control of manufacturing expenses can be used to plan these expenses for future periods with due consideration to past experience relative to the established standards. Cost analysis can be utilized, as part of the planning process, to determine the probable effect of different courses of action. Again, a comparison of manufacturing costs versus purchasing a particular part or component can be made in making the determination in make-or-buy decisions. The use of costs and analysis would extend to many facets of the total planning process.

One of the key objectives of a costing system is the determination of product unit cost and the valuation of inventories. This is also a prerequisite to an accurate determination of the cost of goods sold in the statement of income and expense. The manufacturing cost system should recognize this fact and include sufficient cost details, such as layering part costs and quantities for items in inventory, to accomplish this purpose.

A critical purpose of cost data is for establishing selling prices. The manufactured cost of a product is not necessarily the sole determinant in setting prices, since the desired gross margin and the price acceptable to the market are also significant factors. As more companies realize that direct labor and materials are relatively fixed costs, management will concentrate on designing the product to fit a specific price, cost, and gross margin; the controller should be included in this process to advise management about indirect and direct costs.

Controller and Manufacturing Management Problems

A fundamental responsibility of the controller is to ensure that the manufacturing cost systems have been established to serve the needs and requirements of production executives. The controller is the fact finder regarding costs and is responsible for furnishing factory management with sufficient cost information on a timely basis and in a proper format to effect proper control and planning. Unfortunately, under a just-in-time (JIT) system, manufacturing managers need feedback regarding costs far more frequently than on a monthly basis. JIT products are manufactured with little or no wait time, and consequently can be produced in periods far less than was the case under the line manufacturing concept. Therefore, if a cost problem occurred, such as too many direct labor hours required to finish a part, the formal accounting system would not tell the line managers until well after the problem had happened.

Fortunately, JIT principles stress the need to shrink inventories and streamline processes, thereby making manufacturing problems highly visible *without* any product costing reports. A subset of JIT is cellular (i.e., group) manufacturing, in which equipment is generally arranged in a horseshoe shape, and one employee uses those machines to make one part, taking the piece from machine to machine. Consequently, there is little or no work-in-process (WIP) to track, and any scrapped parts are immediately visible to management. Based on this kind of manufacturing concept, line managers can do without reports, with the exception of daily production quantities versus budgeted quantities that meet quality standards.

Just-in-time manufacturing places the controller in the unique position of looking for something to report on. Since direct labor and materials costs are now largely fixed, the controller's time emphasis should switch to planning the costs of new products, and tracking planned costs versus actual costs. Because the JIT manufacturing environment tends to have small cost variances, the controller should seriously question the amount of effort to be invested in tracking direct labor and materials variances versus the benefit of collecting the data.

Another area in which the controller can profitably invest time tracking information is the number of items that increase a product's cycle time or the non–value-added cost of producing a product. Management can then work to reduce the frequency of these items, thereby reducing the costs associated with them. Here is a partial list of such items:

- Number of material moves
- Number of part numbers used by the company

- Number of setups required to build a product
- Number of products sold by the company, including the number of options offered
- Number of product distribution locations used
- Number of engineering change notices
- Number of parts reworked

If a process is value-added, the controller can initiate an operational audit to find any bottlenecks in the process, thereby improving the capacity of the process. For example, engineering a custom product is clearly value-added; internal auditors could recommend new hardware or software for designing the product to allow the engineering department to design twice as many products with the same number of staff.

Under JIT, there are several traditional performance measures that the controller should be careful *not* to report:

- If the report is on machine efficiency, then line managers will have an incentive to create an excessive amount of WIP in order to keep their machines running at maximum utilization.
- If the report is on purchase price variances, the materials staff will have an incentive to purchase large quantities of raw materials in order to get volume discounts.
- If the report is on headcount, the manufacturing manager will have an incentive to hire untrained contract workers, who may produce more scrap than full-time, better-trained employees.
- If you include a scrap factor into a product's standard cost, then line managers will take no corrective action unless scrap exceeds the budgeted level, thereby incorporating scrap into the production process.
- If the report is on labor variances, then the accountants will expend considerable labor in an area that has relatively fixed costs and not put time into areas that require more analysis.
- If the report is on standard cost overhead absorption, then management will have an incentive to overproduce to absorb more overhead than was actually expended, thereby increasing profits, increasing inventory, and reducing available cash.

Types of Manufacturing Cost Analyses

The question will arise often about what type of cost data should be presented. Just how should production costs be analyzed? This will depend on the purpose for which the costs are to be used, as well as the cost experience of those who use the information.

Unit costs or total costs may be accumulated in an infinite variety of ways. The primary segregation may be by any one of the following:

Product or class of product	Process
Operation	Customer order
Department	Worker responsible
Machine or machine center	Cost element

Each of the primary segregations may be subdivided a number of ways. For example, the out-of-pocket costs may be separated from the "continuing costs," those that would be incurred whether a particular order or run was made. Again, production costs might be segregated between those which are direct or indirect; that is, those attributable directly to the operation and those prorated. Thus the material used to fashion a cup might be direct, whereas the power used to operate the press would be indirect. Sometimes the analysis of costs will differentiate between those that vary with production volume and those which are constant within the range of production usually experienced. For example, the direct labor consumed may relate directly to volume, whereas depreciation remains unchanged. The controller must use judgment and experience in deciding what type of analysis is necessary to present the essential facts.

The mix of product-cost components has shifted away from direct labor and material dominance to overhead (such as depreciation, materials management, and engineering time). Overhead takes up a greater proportion of a typical product's cost. Because of this change in mix, the controller will find that product cost analyses will depend heavily on how to assign overhead costs to a product. Activity-based costing (ABC) is of considerable use in this area. For more information about ABC, refer to Chapter 5.

Types of Cost Systems

Experience in cost determination in various industries and specific companies has given rise to several types of cost systems that best suit the kinds of manufacturing activities. A traditional costing system known as a "job order cost system" is normally used for manufacturing products to a specific customer order or unique product. For example, the assembly or fabrication operations of a particular job or contract are collected in a separate job order number. Another widely used costing system is known as a "process cost system." This system assigns costs to a cost center rather than to a particular job. All the production costs of a department are collected, and the departmental cost per unit is determined by dividing the total departmental costs by the number of units processed through the department. Process cost systems are more commonly used in food processing, oil refining, flour milling, paint manufacturing, and so forth. No two cost accounting systems are identical. There are many factors that determine the kind of system to use, such as product mix, plant location, product diversity, number of specific customer orders, and complexity of the manufacturing process. It may be advisable to combine certain characteristics of both types of systems in certain situations. For example, in a steel mill the primary system may be a process cost system; however, minor activities such as maintenance may be on a job cost basis. The controller should thoroughly analyze all operations to determine the system that best satisfies all needs.

There are two issues currently affecting the job order and process costing systems of which the controller should be aware:

1. JIT manufacturing systems allow the controller to reduce or eliminate the recordkeeping needed for job cost reporting. Since JIT tends to eliminate variances on the shop floor by eliminating the WIP that used to mask problems, there are few cost variances for the cost accountant to accumulate in a job cost report. Therefore, the time needed to accumulate information for job costing may no longer be worth the increase in accuracy derived from it, and the controller should consider using the initial planned job cost as the actual job cost.

2. One of the primary differences between process and job-shop costing systems is the presence (job shop) or absence (process flow) of WIP. Since installing a JIT manufacturing system inherently implies reducing or eliminating WIP, a JIT job-shop costing system may not vary that much from a process costing system.

Factory Accounts and General Accounts

The selection of the manufacturing cost accounting system should recognize the relationship of the factory cost accounts to the general accounts. Normally, the factory accounts should be tied into the general accounts for control purposes. It should enhance the accuracy of the cost information included in the top-level manufacturing cost reports as well as the profit or loss statements and balance sheet. Periodic review and reconciliation of the accounts will also minimize unexpected or year-end adjustments. This integration of the cost accounts is extremely important as the company expands and the operations are more complex.

Although there are situations where the factory and general accounts are not coordinated, it is not recommended. If such a system is used additional effort is required to ensure the accuracy and preclude misstatement of cost information. Such a procedure requires extreme care in cutoffs for liabilities and the taking of physical inventories as well as analyzing inventory differences.

DIRECT MATERIAL COSTS: PLANNING AND CONTROL

Scope of Direct Material Involvement

Direct material, as the term is used by cost accountants, refers to material that can be definitely or specifically charged to a particular product, process, or job, and that becomes a component part of the finished product. The definition must be applied in a practical way, for if the material cannot be conveniently charged as direct or if it is an insignificant item of cost, then it would probably be classified as *indirect material* and allocated with other manufacturing expenses to the product on some logical basis. Although this section deals primarily with direct material, certain of the phases relate also to indirect material.

In its broadest phase, material planning and control is simply the providing of the required quantity and quality of material at the required time and place in the manufacturing process. By implication, the material secured must not be excessive in amount, *and* it must be fully accounted for and used as intended. The extent of material planning and control is broad and should cover many phases or areas, such as plans and specifications; purchasing; receiving and handling; inventories; usage; and scrap, waste, and salvage. In each of these phases, the controller has certain responsibilities and can make contributions toward an efficient operation.

Benefits from Proper Material Planning and Control

Because material is such a large cost item in most manufacturing concerns, effective utilization is an important factor in the financial success or failure of the business. Proper planning and control of materials with the related adequate accounting has the following ten advantages:

1. Reduces inefficient use or waste of materials
2. Reduces or prevents production delays by reason of lack of materials
3. Reduces the risk from theft or fraud
4. Reduces the investment in inventories
5. May reduce the required investment in storage facilities
6. Provides more accurate interim financial statements
7. Assists buyers through a better coordinated buying program
8. Provides a basis for proper product pricing

9. Provides more accurate inventory values
10. Reduces the cost of insurance for inventory

Defining and Measuring Direct Material Costs

There is some confusion regarding what costs can be itemized as direct materials. This section defines the various cost elements and explains why some costs are categorized as direct materials and others are not.

It is common to charge any material that is listed on a product's bill of materials (BOM) to that product as a direct material cost. If there is no BOM, then it may be necessary to physically break down a product to determine the types and quantities of its component parts. Though this definition seems simple enough, there are a variety of peripheral costs to consider:

- *Discounts.* It is reasonable to deduct discounts from suppliers from the cost of direct materials, because there is a direct and clearly identifiable relationship between the discount and the payment for the materials.

- *Estimates.* It is reasonable to credit or debit material costs if the estimates are based on calculations that can be easily proved through an audit. For example, it may be easier to allocated purchase discounts to specific materials than to credit them individually; if so, there should be a calculation that bases the estimated credit on past discounts for specific materials.

- *Freight.* It is reasonable to include the freight cost of bringing materials to the production facility, because this cost is directly related to the materials themselves. However, outbound freight costs should not be included in direct materials, because this cost is more directly related to sales or logistics than to manufacturing.

- *Packaging costs.* It is reasonable to include packaging costs in direct materials if the packaging is a major component of the final product. For example, perfume requires a glass container before it is sold, so the glass container should be included in the direct materials cost. This should also include packing supplies.

- *Samples and tests.* It is reasonable to include the cost of routine samples and tests in direct materials. For example, the quality assurance staff may pull a specific number of products from the production line for destructive testing; this is a standard part of the production process, so the materials lost should still be recorded as direct materials.

- *Scrap.* It is reasonable to include the cost of scrap in direct materials if it is an ongoing and fairly predictable expense. For example, there is a standard amount of liquid evaporation to be expected during the processing of some products, while other products will require a percentage of scrap when raw materials are used to create the finished product. However, an inordinate level of scrap that is above usual expectations should be expensed off separately and immediately as scrap, since it is not an ongoing part of the production process. If there is some salvage value to scrapped materials, this amount should be an offset to the direct materials cost.

- *Indirect materials costs.* There are a number of costs that are somewhat related to materials costs, but which cannot be charged straight to direct materials because of accounting rules. These costs include the cost of warehousing, purchasing, and distribution. Instead, these costs can be combined into one or more cost pools and allocated to products based on the proportion of usage of the expenses in those cost pools.

Planning for Direct Material

The planning aspect of direct material relates to four phases, budgets, or plans:

1. *Material usage budget.* This budget involves determining the quantities and related cost of the raw materials and purchased parts needed to meet the production budget (quantities of product to be manufactured) on a time-phased basis. Basically it is a matter of multiplying the volume of finished articles to be produced times the number of individual components needed for its manufacture. This determination is the responsibility of the manufacturing executive. However, the aggregate costs must be provided to the controller in an appropriate format. In most instances, it will be under the direction of the controller that the planning procedure and format of exhibits required will be established. The controller requires the total cost, by time period, to provide for the charge to work-in-process inventory and for relief of raw materials and purchased parts inventory in the financial planning process of preparing the business plan for the year or for other planning periods. Obviously, the material usage budget must be known so that the required purchases can be made and the required inventory level maintained.

   The determination of the material usage budget is described in more detail in Chapter 10 on inventory planning and control.

   The material usage budget generally will be summarized by physical quantities of significant items for use by manufacturing personnel. A cost summary is needed by the controller for preparing the plan in monetary terms. The usage budget may be presented in any one of several ways. A time-phased summary by major category of raw material for a small aircraft manufacturer is illustrated in Exhibit 4.1.

THE AIRCRAFT COMPANY
SUMMARIZED MATERIAL USAGE BUDGET
FOR THE PLAN YEAR 20XX
(DOLLARS IN THOUSANDS)

Material Category

Month	Engine	Aluminum	Electrical	Purchased Assemblies	All Other	Total
January	$ 7,500	$ 1,500	$ 990	$ 790	$ 200	$ 10,980
February	5,500	1,000	660	530	130	7,820
March	8,000	1,600	1,050	840	210	11,700
April	8,500	1,800	1,200	960	240	12,700
May	9,000	1,800	1,200	960	240	13,200
June	10,000	2,000	1,320	1,060	260	14,640
July	9,000	1,800	1,200	960	240	13,200
August	8,000	1,600	1,050	840	210	11,700
September	7,000	1,400	920	740	190	10,250
October	6,000	1,200	790	630	160	8,780
November	5,000	1,000	660	530	130	7,320
December	6,000	1,200	790	630	160	8,780
Total	$89,500	$17,900	$11,830	$9,470	$2,370	$131,070

EXHIBIT 4.1   SUMMARIZED MATERIAL USAGE BUDGET

2. *Material purchases budget.* When the material usage budget is known, the purchases budget can be determined (by the purchasing department), taking into account the required inventory levels.

    The time-phased material purchases budget is provided by the purchasing director (usually reporting to the manufacturing executive) to the controller for use in planning cash disbursements, and additions to the raw materials and purchased parts inventories—as part of the annual planning process (or planning for any other period). A highly condensed raw material purchases budget for the annual plan is illustrated in Exhibit 4.2.

3. *Finished production budget.* This represents the quantities of finished product to be manufactured in the planning period. Such estimates are provided by the manufacturing executive to the controller for determining the additions to the finished goods inventory and the relief to the work-in-process inventory.

    The quantities of production usually are costed by the cost department under the supervision of the controller.

4. *Inventories budgets.* The three preceding budgets, plus the cost-of-goods-sold budget, determine the inventory budgets for the planning period. In the annual planning process, the inventory costs usually are determined monthly.

Inventory budgets, together with the related purchases, usage, and completed product, are shown in Chapter 10 on planning and control of inventories.

While the raw materials, purchased parts, and work-in-process budgets usually are the responsibility of the manufacturing executive, and the finished goods budget is the responsibility of either the manufacturing executive or the sales executive, the controller has certain reporting functions (see Chapter 10) as to planned versus actual inventory levels and turnover rates, as well as responsibility for the adequacy of the internal control system.

To summarize, any *planning* responsibilities for direct materials rest with other line executives, although the controller will use these related data in the financial planning process—

THE ILLUSTRATIVE COMPANY
SUMMARIZED RAW MATERIAL PURCHASES BUDGET
FOR THE PLAN YEAR 20XX
(DOLLARS IN HUNDREDS)

Quarter/	Material Category				
Month	A	B	C	D	Total
Quarter 1					
January	$ 40,000	$ 20,000	$ 50,000	$ 10,000	$ 120,000
February	35,000	17,000	45,000	8,000	105,000
March	50,000	25,000	60,000	12,000	147,000
Subtotal	125,000	62,000	155,000	30,000	372,000
Quarter 2	150,000	70,000	165,000	40,000	425,000
Quarter 3	116,000	60,000	150,000	20,000	346,000
Quarter 4	103,000	50,000	160,000	25,000	358,000
Total	$514,000	$242,000	$630,000	$115,000	$1,501,000

Note: A 5% price increase is assumed for the last two quarters.

EXHIBIT 4.2   SUMMARIZED RAW MATERIAL PURCHASE BUDGET

in preparing the statement of estimated income and expense, the statement of estimated financial condition, and statement of estimated cash flows. Also, the controller will often test-check or audit the information furnished by the manufacturing executive for completeness, reasonableness, and compatibility with other plans. On occasion, the chief manufacturing executive will request the controller and staff to assemble the needed figures, with the help of the production staff.

The various budgets related to materials generally will be developed following a procedure and format coordinated (and sometimes developed by) the controller.

Those interested in a more detailed explanation of developing the plans or budgets for raw material usage and purchases may wish to check some of the current literature.

Basic Approach to Direct Material Cost Control

With an overview of the *planning* function behind us, we can now review the *control* function. With respect to materials, as with other costs, control in its simplest form involves the comparison of actual performance with a measuring stick—standard performance—and the prompt follow-up of adverse trends. However, it is not simply a matter of saying "350 yards of material were used, and the standard quantity is only 325" or "The standard price is $10.25 but the actual cost to the company was $13.60 each." Many other refinements or applications are involved. The standards must be reviewed and better methods found. Or checks and controls must be exercised before the cost is incurred. The central theme, however, is still the use of a standard as a point of measurement.

Although the applications will vary in different concerns, some of the problems or considerations that must be handled by the controller are:

- *Purchasing and receiving*

  - Establishment and maintenance of internal checks to assure that materials paid for are received and used for the purpose intended. Since some purchases are now received on a just-in-time basis, the controller may find that materials are now paid for based on the amount of product manufactured by the company in a given period, instead of on a large quantity of paperwork associated with a large number of small-quantity receipts.

  - Audit of purchasing procedures to ascertain that bids are received where applicable. A JIT manufacturing system uses a small number of long-term suppliers, however, so the controller may find that bids are restricted to providers of services such as janitorial duties and maintenance activities.

  - Comparative studies of prices paid for commodities with industry prices or indexes.

  - Measurement of price trends on raw materials. Many JIT supplier contracts call for price decreases by suppliers at set intervals; the controller should be aware of the terms of these contracts and audit the timing and amount of the changes.

  - Determination of price variance on current purchases through comparison of actual and standard costs. This may relate to purchases at the time of ordering or at time of receipt. The same approach may be used in a review of current purchase orders to advise management in advance about the effect on standard costs. In a JIT environment, most part costs would be contractually set with a small number of suppliers, so the controller would examine prices charged for any variations from the agreed-upon rates.

- *Usage*
  - ○ Comparison of actual and standard quantities used in production. A variance may indicate an incorrect quantity on the product's bill of materials, misplaced parts, pilferage, or incorrect part quantities recorded in inventory.
  - ○ Preparation of standard cost formulas (to emphasize major cost items and as part of a cost reduction program).
  - ○ Preparation of reports on spoilage, scrap, and waste as compared with standard. In a JIT environment, no scrap is allowed for and therefore is not included in the budget as a standard.
  - ○ Calculation of costs to make versus costs to buy.

This list suggests only some of the methods available to the controller in dealing with material cost control.

Setting Material Quantity Standards

Because an important phase of material control is the comparison of actual usage with standard, the controller is interested in the method of setting these quantitative standards. First, assistance can be rendered by contributing information about past experience. Second, the controller should act as a check in seeing that the standards are not so loose that they bury poor performance, on the one hand, and represent realistic but attainable performance, on the other.

Standards of material usage may be established by at least three procedures:

1. By engineering studies to determine the best kind and quality of material, taking into account the product design requirements and production methods
2. By an analysis of past experience for the same or similar operations
3. By making test runs under controlled conditions

Although a combination of these methods may be used, best practice usually dictates that engineering studies be made. To the theoretical loss must be added a provision for those other unavoidable losses that it is impractical to eliminate. In this decision, past experience will play a part. Past performance alone, of course, is not desirable in that certain known wastes may be perpetuated. This engineering study, combined with a few test runs, should give fairly reliable standards.

Revision of Material Quantity Standards

Standards are based on certain production methods and product specifications. It would be expected, therefore, that these standards should be modified as these other factors change, if such changes affect material usage. For the measuring stick to be an effective control tool, it must relate to the function being measured. However, the adjustment need not be carried through as a change in inventory value, unless it is significant.

Using Quantity Standards for Cost Control

The key to material quantity control is to know in advance how much material should be used on the job, frequently to secure information about how actual performance compares with standard during the progress of the work, and to take corrective action where necessary.

The supervisor responsible for the use of materials, as well as the superior, should be aware of these facts. At the lowest supervisory level, details of each operation and process should be in the hands of those who can control usage. At higher levels, only overall results need be known.

The method to be used in comparing the actual and standard usage will differ in each company, depending on several conditions. Some of the more important factors that will influence the controller in applying control procedures about material usage are:

- The production method in use
- The type and value of the materials
- The degree to which cost reports are utilized by management for cost control purposes

A simple excess material report that is issued daily is shown in Exhibit 4.3. It shows not only the type of material involved as excess usage, but also the cause of the condition. This report could be available on a real-time basis, with the use of a computer, and could be summarized daily for the plant manager.

One of the most important considerations is the nature of the production process. In a job order or lot system, such as an assembly operation in an aircraft plant, where a definite quantity is to be produced, the procedure is quite simple. A production order is issued, and a bill of material or "standard requisition" states the exact quantity of material needed to complete the order. If parts are spoiled or lost, it then becomes necessary to secure replacements by means of a nonstandard or excess usage requisition. Usually, the foreman must approve this request, and, consequently, the excess usage can be identified immediately. A special color (red) requisition may be used, and a summary report issued at certain intervals for the use of the production executives responsible.

If production is on a continuous process basis, then periodically a comparison can be made of material used in relation to the finished product. Corrective action may not be as quick here, but measures can be taken to avoid future losses.

			THE COMPUTER CHIP COMPANY		Dept. No.		42	
			DAILY EXCESS MATERIAL USAGE		Foreperson:		Magraudy	
			(DATE)					

Material Used	Amount of Finished Product	Standard Usage (Units)	Actual Usage (Units)	Excess Usage (Units)	Unit Cost	Total Excess Cost	Comments
A	3,960	3,960	4,110	150	$ 4.75	$ 712.50	(a)
B	7,920	15,840	15,960	120	2.00	240.00	(b)
C	1,980	3,960	4,000	40	21.50	860.00	(c)
D	3,960	3,960	3,970	10	65.40	654.00	(d)
E	15,840	15,840	15,920	80	3.25	260.00	(e)
Total						$2,726.50	

Comments:
(a) Parts defective (Vendor Bush).
(b) Careless workmanship.
(c) Power down.
(d) Wrong speed drilling.
(e) Maintenance technician dropped case.

EXHIBIT 4.3 DAILY EXCESS MATERIAL USAGE REPORT

Just as the production process is a vital factor in determining the cost accounting plan, so also it is a consideration in the method of detecting material losses. If losses are to be localized, then inspections must be made at selected points in the process of manufacture. At these various stations, the rejected material can be counted or weighed and costed if necessary. When there are several distinct steps in the manufacturing process, the controller may have to persuade the production group of the need and desirability of establishing count stations for control purposes. Once these stations are established, the chief contribution of the accountant is to summarize and report the losses over standard. The process can be adopted to the use of personal computers and provision of control information on a real-time basis.

Another obvious factor in the method of reporting material usage is the type and value of the item itself. A cardinal principle in cost control is to place primary emphasis on high-value items. Hence, valuable airplane motors, for example, would be identified by serial number and otherwise accurately accounted for. Items with less unit value, or not readily segregated, might be controlled through less accurate periodic reporting. An example might be lumber. The nature and value of the materials determine whether the *time* factor or the *unit* factor would be predominant in usage reporting.

Management is often not directly interested in *dollar cost* for control purposes but rather only in *units*. There is no difference in the principle involved but merely in the application. Under these conditions, the controller should see that management is informed of losses in terms of physical units—something it understands. In this case, the cost report would be merely a summary of the losses. Experience will often show, however, that as the controller gives an accounting in dollars, the other members of management will become more cost conscious.

The essence of any control program, regardless of the method of reporting, however, is to follow up on substandard performance and take corrective action.

A variation on using quantity standards and materials variation reporting is JIT variance reporting. One of the cornerstones of the JIT concept is that you order only what you need. That means you won't waste what you use and that there should be no materials variances. Of course, even at world-class JIT practitioners such as Motorola and Toyota, there is scrap; however, there is much less than will be found at a non-JIT company. Consequently, the controller must examine the cost of collecting the variance information against its value in correcting the amount of scrap accumulation. The conclusion may be that JIT does not require much materials variance reporting, if any.

Limited Usefulness of Material Price Standards

In comparing actual and standard material costs, the use of price standards permits the segregation of variances as a result of excess usage from those incurred by reason of price changes. By and large, however, the material price standards used for inventory valuation cannot be considered as a satisfactory guide in measuring the performance of the purchasing department. Prices of materials are affected by so many factors outside the business that the standards represent merely a measure of what prices are being paid as compared with what was expected to be paid.

A review of price variances may, however, reveal some informative data. Exceedingly high prices may reveal special purchases for quick delivery because someone had not properly scheduled purchases. Or higher prices may reveal shipment via express when freight shipments would have been satisfactory. Again, the lowest cost supplier may not be utilized because of the advantages of excellent quality control methods in place at a competitive shop. The total cost of production and impact on the marketplace needs to be considered—not merely the purchase price of the specific item. To generalize, the exact cause for any price variance must be ascertained before valid conclusions can be drawn. Some companies have found it advisable to establish two standards—one for inventory valuation and quite another to be used by the purchasing department as a goal to be attained. One negative result of recording a purchase price variance is that the purchasing department may give up close supplier relationships in order to get the lowest part cost through the bidding process. Part bidding is the nemesis of close supplier parings (a cornerstone of JIT), since suppliers know they will be kicked off the supplier list, no matter how good their delivery or quality, unless they bid the lowest cost.

Setting Material Price Standards

Practice varies somewhat about the responsibility for setting price standards. Sometimes the cost department assumes this responsibility on the basis of a review of past prices. In other cases, the purchasing staff gives its estimate of expected prices that is subject to a thorough and analytical check by the accounting staff. Probably, the most satisfactory setup is through the combined effort of these two departments.

Other Applications of Material Control

By using a little imagination, every controller will be able to devise simple reports that will be of great value in material control—whether in merely making the production staff aware of the high-cost items of the product or in stimulating a program of cost reduction. For example, in a chemical processing plant, a simple report detailing the material components cost of a formulation could be used to advantage. Another report is illustrated in Exhibit 4.4, wherein the standard material cost of an assembly-type operation, in this case a self-guided small plane, is given

Where the products are costly, and relatively few in number, it may be useful to provide management periodically with the changes in contracted prices, as well as an indication about the effect of price changes on the planned cost of the product. Such statements may stimulate thinking about material substitutions or changes in processes or specifications.

LABOR COSTS: PLANNING AND CONTROL

Labor Accounting under Private Enterprise

One of the most important factors in the success of a business is the maintenance of a satisfactory relationship between management and employees. Controllers as well as their staff can do much to encourage and promote such a relationship, whether it is such a simple matter as seeing that the payroll checks are ready on time or whether it extends to the development of a wage system that rewards meritorious performance.

Aside from this fact, labor accounting and control are important. As automation and the use of robots and computers become even more prevalent, what was once called direct labor may not any longer increase in relative importance. But labor is still a significant cost. Likewise, those costs usually closely related to labor costs have grown by leaps and bounds—costs for longer vacations, more adequate health and welfare plans, pension plans, and increased Social Security taxes. These fringe benefit costs are 50% or more of many payrolls. For all these reasons, the cost of labor is an important cost factor.

THE SMALL PLANE MANUFACTURING COMPANY
STATEMENT ON UNIT STANDARD MATERIAL COSTS
FOR THE MONTH OF JUNE 20XX

Description	Standard Cost 5/31/XX	Changes Increases	Changes Decreases	Standard Cost 6/30/XX	Remarks
Power unit	$ 820.00	$ 30.00	$ —	$ 850.00	Price increased by manufacturer
Raw stock aluminum	277.40	—	—	277.40	
Fabric	142.60	—	—	142.60	
Paint	127.54	—	22.54	105.00	Installation of electric equipment
Steel tubing	117.50	—	—	117.50	
Stabilizer	106.22	—	—	106.22	
Instruments	93.14	—	1.14	92.00	New altimeter
Hardware	92.20	—	—	92.20	
Radio equipment	91.20	—	—	91.20	
Exhaust stock	34.17	—	—	34.17	
Steel small parts	76.16	—	—	76.16	
Synthetic small parts	14.20	—	—	14.20	
Plastic	19.06	—	.06	19.00	
Rubber	12.00	—	—	12.00	
Aluminum forging	32.14	—	2.00	30.14	Substitute "R" forging
Raw stock steel	43.15	—	—	43.15	
Directional control component	39.15	—	—	39.15	
Battery	18.00	—	—	18.00	
Cushion	14.70	—	—	14.70	
Miscellaneous trim parts	22.13	—	—	22.13	
Total	$ 2,192.66	$ 30.00	$ 25.74	$ 2,196.92	

EXHIBIT 4.4 DETAIL OF, AND CHANGES IN, STANDARD MATERIAL COSTS

The three objectives of labor accounting are outlined as:

1. A prompt and accurate determination of the amount of wages due the employee.
2. The analysis and determination of labor costs in such a manner as may be needed by management (e.g., by product, operation, department, or category of labor) for planning and control purposes.
3. The advent of JIT manufacturing systems has called into question the need for reporting the direct labor utilization variance. This variance revolves around the amount of a product that is produced with a given amount of labor; thus, a positive labor utilization variance can be achieved by producing more product than may be needed. An underlying principle of JIT is to produce only as much as is needed to produce, so JIT and labor utilization variance reporting are inherently at odds with each other. If JIT has been installed, then the controller should consider eliminating this type of variance reporting.

Classification of Labor Costs

With the increasing trends to automation, to continuous process type of manufacturing, and to integrated machine operations under which individual hand operations are replaced, the traditional accounting definition of *direct labor* must be modernized. As a practical matter, where labor is charged to a cost center and is directly related to the main function of that center, whether it is direct or indirect labor is of no consequence. Rather, attention must be directed to *labor* costs. Perhaps the primary considerations are measurability and materiality rather than physical association with the product. For planning and control purposes, any factory wages or salaries that are identifiable with a directly productive department as contrasted with a service department and are of significance in that department are defined as *manufacturing labor.*

All other labor will be defined as *indirect labor,* treated as overhead expense, and discussed under manufacturing expenses.

Expanded Definition of Direct Labor

Direct labor is that labor which is traceable to the manufacturing of products or the provision of services for consumption by a customer. This cost includes incidental time that is part of a typical working day, such as break time, but does not include protracted down time for nonrecurring activities, such as training or downtime caused by machine failures. Direct labor should also include those benefits costs that are "part and parcel" of the direct labor worker, such as medical and dental insurance costs, production-related bonuses, FICA, cost of living allowances, workers' compensation insurance, vacation and holiday pay, unemployment compensation insurance, and pension costs. Overtime bonuses should also be included in direct labor costs. It is also acceptable to track labor costs as standard costs, as long as one periodically writes off the difference between standard and actual direct labor costs, so that there is no long-term difference between the two types of labor costs. These are the components of direct labor.

Direct labor is only that labor that adds value to the product or service. However, there are many activities in the manufacturing or service areas, not all of which add value to the final product, so one must be careful to segregate costs into the direct labor and indirect labor categories. Direct labor is typically incurred during the fabrication, processing, assembly, or packaging of a product or service. Alternatively, any labor incurred to maintain or supervise the production or service facility is categorized as indirect labor.

There are several costs that should not be included in direct labor. These are excluded because they do not directly trace back to work on products or services, nor are they a standard part of a direct labor worker's benefits package. These costs include the maintenance of recreational facilities for employees, any company-sponsored meal plans, membership dues in outside organizations, separation allowances, and safety-related expenses. These costs are typically either charged off to current expenses, or else rolled into overhead costs.

Planning of Labor Costs

Planning labor costs might be described as planning or estimating the required manpower and costs associated with direct manufacturing departments (not indirect) for the annual plan or some other relevant planning period. It consists of determining the labor planning budget.

The process, which is essentially the responsibility of the manufacturing executive, consists of extrapolating the planned production of units times the standard labor content, plus an allowance for variances, to arrive at the labor hours required. This is a tedious job, but the computer as applied to the standard labor hour content of expected production makes it much easier. Essentially, this process has several purposes, such as:

- Ascertaining by department, by skill, and by time period the number and type of workers needed to carry out the production program for the planning horizon
- Determining the labor cost for the production program, including: labor input, labor content of completed product, and labor content of work-in-process. These data may then be used by the controller for determining the transfers to/from work- in-process and finished goods—in the same manner material costs were accounted for.
- Determining the estimated cost (payroll) requirements of the time-phased manufacturing labor budget for the planning period
- Determining the unit labor content of each product so that the inventory values, cost of manufacturer, and cost of sales can be calculated for use in the statements of planned income and expense, planned financial condition, and planned cash flows
- Seeing that the planned funds are available to meet the payroll

A summarized direct labor budget for annual planning purposes, based on the underlying required labor hours by department, by product, and time-phased, might appear as in Exhibit 4.5.

A JIT manufacturing environment creates significant changes in direct labor costs that the controller should be aware of. When a manufacturing facility changes from an assembly line to manufacturing cells, the labor efficiency level drops, because machine setups become more frequent. A major JIT technique is to reduce setup times to minimal levels, but nonetheless, even the small setup times required for cellular manufacturing require more labor time than the zero setup times used in long assembly line production runs. Consequently, if management is contemplating switching to cellular manufacturing, the controller should expect an increase in the labor hours budget. Also, if the labor cost does not increase, the controller should see if the engineering staff has changed the labor routings to increase the number of expected setup times.

To the extent more information is desired on the planning aspects of direct labor, the reader may wish to consult some of the books on the subject.[1]

---

1. See, for example, James D. Willson, *Budgeting and Profit Planning Manual,* 3rd ed. (Boston: Warren, Gorham & Lamont, 1994). Chap. B3.

THE GIDGET COMPANY
SUMMARIZED DIRECT LABOR BUDGET
FOR PLAN YEAR 20XX

	Direct Labor Hours			Gross Cost		
Month/Quarter	Standard	Provision for Variances	Total	Standard	Provision for Variances	Total
First Quarter						
January	222,500	4,450	226,950	$ 3,337,500	$ 66,750	$ 3,404,250
February	204,300	4,100	208,400	3,064,500	61,500	3,126,000
March	223,400	4,500	227,900	3,351,000	67,500	3,418,500
Total	650,200	13,050	663,250	9,753,000	195,750	9,948,750
Second Quarter	712,000	14,240	726,240	10,680,000	213,600	10,893,600
Third Quarter	725,700	10,890	736,590	11,429,775	171,518	11,601,293
Fourth Quarter	719,300	11,510	730,810	11,328,975	181,283	11,510,258
Total	2,807,200	49,690	2,856,890	$43,191,750	$762,151	$43,953,901

Note: Present wage rates used through second quarter. Balance of year assumes a 5% wage increase.

EXHIBIT 4.5 SUMMARIZED DIRECT LABOR BUDGET

Controller's Contribution to Control

In controlling direct labor costs, as with most manufacturing costs, the ultimate responsibility must rest with the line supervision. Yet this group must be given assistance in measuring performance, and certain other policing or restraining functions must be exercised. Herein lie the primary duties of the controller's organization. Among the means at the disposal of the chief accounting executive for labor control are the following seven:[2]

1. Institute procedures to limit the number of employees placed on the payroll to that called for by the production plan.
2. Provide preplanning information for use in determining standard labor crews by calculating required standard labor-hours for the production program.
3. Report hourly, daily, or weekly standard and actual labor performance.
4. Institute procedures for accurate distribution of actual labor costs, including significant labor classifications to provide informative labor cost analyses.
5. Provide data on past experience with respect to the establishment of standards.
6. Keep adequate records on labor standards and be on the alert for necessary revisions.
7. Furnish other supplementary labor data reports, such as:

    (a) Hours and cost of overtime premium, for control of overtime
    (b) Cost of call-in pay for time not worked to measure efficiency of those responsible for call-in by union seniority
    (c) Comparative contract costs, that is, old and new union contracts

---

2. In a JIT environment, this reporting would not be necessary in items 3, 4, 5, and 7e.

(d) Average hours worked per week, average take-home pay, and similar data for labor negotiations

(e) Detailed analysis of labor costs over or under standard

(f) Statistical data on labor turnover, length of service, training costs

(g) Union time—cost of time spent on union business

Setting Labor Performance Standards

The improvement of labor performance and the parallel reduction and control of costs require labor standards—operating time standards and the related cost standards. Setting labor performance standards is a highly analytical job that requires a technical background of the production processes as well as a knowledge of time study methods. This may be the responsibility of a standards department, industrial engineering department, or cost control department. Occasionally, although rarely, it is under the jurisdiction of the controller. Establishment of the standard operation time requires a determination of the time needed to complete each operation when working under standard conditions. Hence this study embodies working conditions, including the material control plan, the production planning and scheduling procedure, and layout of equipment and facilities. After all these factors are considered, a standard can be set by the engineers.

In using time standards for measuring labor performance the accounting staff must work closely with the industrial engineers or those responsible for setting the standards. The related cost standards must be consistent; the accumulation of cost information must consider how the standards were set and how the variances are analyzed.

The following discussion on labor standards does not apply to a JIT manufacturing environment, especially one that uses cellular (i.e., group) manufacturing layouts. Labor utilization standards can be improved by increasing the amount of production for a set level of labor, and this is considered to be good in an assembly line environment. Under JIT, however, producing large quantities of parts is not considered acceptable; under JIT, good performance is producing the exact quantity of parts that are needed, and doing so with quality that is within preset tolerance levels. Once the correct quantity of parts are produced, the direct labor staff stops production; this creates unfavorable labor utilization variances. Therefore, measuring a JIT production facility with a labor utilization variance would work against the intent of JIT, since the production manager would have an incentive to produce more parts than needed, and would not be mindful of the part quality.

Revision of Labor Performance Standards

Generally, performance standards are not revised until a change of method or process occurs. Since standards serve as the basis of control, the accounting staff should be on the alert for changes put into effect in the factory but not reported for standard revision. If the revised process requires more time, the production staff will usually make quite certain that their measuring stick is modified. However, if the new process requires less time, it is understandable that the change might not be reported promptly. Each supervisor naturally desires to make the best possible showing. The prompt reporting of time reductions might be stimulated through periodic review of changes in standard labor hours or costs. In other words, the current labor performance of actual hours compared to standard should be but one measure of performance; another is standard time reductions, also measured against a goal for the year.

It should be the responsibility of the controller to see that the standards are changed as the process changes to report true performance. If a wage incentive system is related to these standards, the need for adjusting process changes is emphasized. An analysis of variances, whether favorable or unfavorable, will often serve to indicate revisions not yet reported.

Although standard revisions will often be made for control purposes, it may not be practical or desirable to change product cost standards. The differences may be treated as cost variances until they are of sufficient magnitude to warrant a cost revision.

Operating under Performance Standards

Effective labor control through the use of standards requires *frequent* reporting of actual and standard performance. Furthermore, the variance report must be by *responsibility*. For this reason the report on performance is prepared for each foreman as well as the plant superintendent. The report may or may not be expressed in terms of dollars. It may compare labor-hours or units of production instead of monetary units. But it does compare actual and standard performance.

Some operations lend themselves to daily reporting. Through the use of computer equipment or other means, daily production may be evaluated and promptly reported on. A simple form of daily report, available to the plant superintendent by 8:00 A.M. for the preceding day's operations, is shown in Exhibit 4.6. With the use of computers, this data can be made available, essentially on a real-time basis.

If required, the detail of this summary report can be made available to indicate on what classification and shift the substandard operations were performed. Another report, issued weekly, that details the general reason for excess labor hours is illustrated in Exhibit 4.7.

In a JIT environment, the manufacturing departments are tightly interlocked with minimal WIP between each department to cover for reduced staff problems. In other words, if an area is understaffed, then downstream work stations will quickly run short of work. Consequently, the most critical direct labor measure in a JIT environment is a report of absent personnel, delivered promptly to the production managers at the start of the work day, so they can reshuffle the staff to cover all departments, and contact the missing personnel.

	PLANT		
	DAILY LABOR REPORT		
	FOR DAY ENDING AT 4:00 P.M. ON (DATE)		
	Man-Hours		% Standard to Actual
Department	Actual	Standard	
51 Fabricating	2,322	2,360	101.6
52 Subassembly	1,846	1,821	98.6
53 Painting	492	500	101.6
54 Assembly	3,960	4,110	103.8
55 Polishing	2,120	2,060	97.2
56 Packing	970	1,320	136.1
Total	11,170	12,171	103.9

EXHIBIT 4.6 SAMPLE DAILY REPORT

JOHNSON MANUFACTURING COMPANY
WEEKLY LABOR REPORT
WEEK ENDED DECEMBER 28, 20XX

Department	Units Reported (a)	Actual Hours	Standard Hours	(Over) or Under Standard	(Over) or Under Standard Due to			
					Training	Lack of Material	Machine Breakdown	Low Production
25 Stamping (b)	16,320	153	194	41	—	—	—	41
26 Foundry (b)	4,390	56	103	47	—	—	—	47
27 Paint	12,800	30	25	(5)	—	—	(5)	—
41 Subassembly A	18,920	366	384	18	(5)	(2)	—	25
42 Final assembly	17,777	106	120	14	—	(6)	—	20
44 Receiving and shipping	44,310	323	271	(52)	(16)	—	—	(36)
Total		1,034	1,097	63	(21)	(8)	(5)	97
Percentage (Over) or under standard				5.7	(1.9)	(.7)	(.5)	8.8

Distribution: J.R.M.
J.A.M. (2)
L.L.B. (6)
R.E.H.
File

Notes:
(a) Equivalent units per 6/12/XX letter.
(b) Standards for Departments 25 and 26 are in process of review.

Issued by Cost Department—December 29, 20XX

EXHIBIT 4.7 WEEKLY LABOR REPORT

Use of Labor Rate Standards

Generally speaking, labor rates paid by a company are determined by external factors. The rate standard used is usually that normally paid for the job or classification as set by collective bargaining. If standards are set under this policy, no significant variances should develop because of base rates paid. There are, however, some rate variances that may be created and are controllable by management. Some of these reasons, which should be set out for corrective action, include:

- Overtime in excess of that provided in the standard
- Use of higher-rated classifications on the job
- Failure to place staff on incentive
- Use of crew mixture different from standard (more higher classifications and fewer of the lower)

The application of the standard labor rate to the job poses no great problem. Usually, this is performed by the accounting department after securing the rates from the personnel department. Where overtime is contemplated in the standard, it is necessary, of course, to consult with production to determine the probable extent of overtime for the capacity at which the standard is set.

It should be mentioned that the basic design of the product will play a part in control of costs by establishing the skill necessary and therefore the job classification required to do the work.

Control through Preplanning

The use of the control tools previously discussed serves to point out labor inefficiencies *after* they have happened. Another type of control requires a determination about what should happen and makes plans to assure, to the extent possible, that it does happen. It is forward looking and preventive. This approach embodies budgetary control and can be applied to the control of labor costs. For example, if the staff requirements for the production program one month hence can be determined, then steps can be taken to make certain that excess labor costs do not arise because too many people are on the payroll. This factor can be controlled; thus the remaining factors are rate and quality of production and overtime. Overtime costs can be held within limits through the use of authorization slips.

The degree to which this preplanning can take place depends on the industry and particular conditions within the individual business firm. Are business conditions sufficiently stable so that some reasonably accurate planning can be done? Can the sales department indicate with reasonable accuracy what the requirements will be over the short run? An application might be in a machine shop where thousands of parts are made. If production requirements are known, the standard labor hours necessary can be calculated and converted to staff hours. The standard labor hours may be stored in a computer by skills required and by department. After evaluating the particular production job, an experienced efficiency factor may be determined. Thus, if 12,320 standard labor hours are needed for the planned production but an efficiency rate of only 80% is expected, then 15,400 actual labor hours must be scheduled. This requires a crew of 385 people (40 hours per week). This can be further refined by skills or an analysis made of the economics of some overtime. Steps should be taken to assure that only the required number is authorized on the payroll for this production. As the requirements change, the standard labor hours should be reevaluated.

In an Manufacturing Resource Planning II environment, labor routings must be at least 95% accurate, and the firm must strictly adhere to a master production schedule. If the controller works in such an environment, then labor requirements can easily be predicted by multiplying the related labor routings by the unit types and quantities shown on the master schedule.

There are many computer-based labor control systems available for adoption to particular or specific needs. The controller or accounting staff should be familiar with the various systems so that labor costs are controlled and performance reported in a timely and accurate manner.

Labor Accounting and Statutory Requirements

One of the functions of a controller is to ensure that the company maintains the various payroll and other records required by various federal and state government agencies, including the IRS. It is mandatory that the employee's earning records be properly and accurately maintained, including all deductions from gross pay. The required reports must be submitted, and withheld amounts transmitted to the appropriate agencies. It is not the purpose of this book to discuss in detail these reporting requirements, since many publications are available to the controller on this subject.

Wage Incentive Plans: Relationship to Cost Standards

In an effort to increase efficiency, a number of companies have introduced wage incentive plans—with good results. The controller is involved through the payroll department, which must calculate the amount. The controller's responsibilities for the system are best left to authorities on the subject. One facet, however, is germane to the costing process and should be discussed. When an incentive wage plan is introduced into an operation already on a standard cost basis, a problem arises about the relationship between the standard level at which incentive earnings commence and the standard level used for costing purposes. Moreover, what effect should the wage incentive plan have on the standard labor cost and standard manufacturing expense of the product? To cite a specific situation, a company may be willing to pay an incentive to labor for performance that is lower than that assumed in the cost standard (but much higher than actual experience). If such a bonus is excluded from the cost standard, the labor cost at the cost standard level will be *understated*. Further, there may be no offsetting savings in manufacturing expenses since the costs are incurred to secure performance at a *lower* level than the cost standard. These statements assume that the existing cost standard represents efficient performance even under incentive conditions. However, if the effect of the incentive plan is to increase sustained production levels well above those contemplated in the cost standards, it may be that the product will be *over-costed* by using present cost standards and that these standards are no longer applicable. How should the cost standards be set in relation to the incentive plan?

In reviewing the problem, several generalizations may be made. First, there is no necessary relationship between standards for incentive purposes and standards for costing purposes. The former are intended to stimulate effort, whereas the latter are used to determine what the labor cost of the product should be. One is a problem in personnel management, whereas the other is strictly an accounting problem. With such dissimilar objectives, the levels of performance could logically be quite different.

Then, too, the matter of labor costing for statement purposes should be differentiated from labor control. As we have seen, labor control may involve nonfinancial terms—pieces per hour, pounds per labor hour, and so on. Labor control can be accomplished through the use of quantitative standards. Even if costs are used, the measuring stick for control need not be the same as for product costing. Control is centered on variations from performance standards and not on product cost variations.

A thorough consideration of the problem results in the conclusion that labor standards for costing purposes should be based on normal expectations from the operation of a wage incentive system under standard operating conditions. The expected earnings under the bonus plan should be reflected in the standard unit cost of the product. It does not necessarily follow that the *product* standard cost will be higher than that used before introduction of the incentive plan. It may mean, however, that the direct labor cost will be higher by reason of bonus payments. Yet, because of increased production and material savings, the *total* unit standard manufacturing cost should be lower.

5

PLANNING AND CONTROL OF MANUFACTURING COSTS: MANUFACTURING EXPENSES

NATURE OF MANUFACTURING EXPENSES

The indirect manufacturing expenses or overhead costs of a manufacturing operation have increased significantly as business has become more complex, and the utilization of more sophisticated machinery and equipment is more prevalent. As the investment in computer-controlled machinery has increased, improving productivity and reducing direct labor hours, the control of depreciation expense, power costs, machinery repairs and maintenance, and similar items has received a greater emphasis by management.

Manufacturing overhead has several distinguishing characteristics as compared with the direct manufacturing costs of material and labor. It includes a wide variety of expenses, such as depreciation, property taxes, insurance, fringe benefit costs, indirect labor, supplies, power and other utilities, clerical costs, maintenance and repairs, and other costs that cannot be directly identified to a product, process, or job. These types of costs behave differently from direct costs, as the volume of production varies. Some will fluctuate proportionately as production increases or decreases, and some will remain constant or fixed and will not be sensitive to the change in the number of units produced. Some costs are semivariable and for a particular volume level are fixed; however, they may vary with volume but less proportionately and probably can be segregated into their fixed and variable components.

The control of overhead costs rests with many individuals involved in the manufacturing process. Certain costs such as repairs and maintenance are controlled by the head of the maintenance department. Manufacturing supplies may be controlled by each department head who uses the supplies in carrying out his function. Other costs may be decided by management and assigned to a particular manager for control—for example, depreciation, taxes, insurance. Accounting planning and control of manufacturing indirect expenses is diverse and a challenging opportunity for the controller.

RESPONSIBILITY FOR PLANNING AND CONTROL OF MANUFACTURING EXPENSES

Responsibility for the planning and control of manufacturing expenses is clearly that of the manufacturing or production executive. However, this executive will be working through a financial information system largely designed by the chief accounting official or his staff—although there should be full participation by the production staff on many aspects of the system development.

In formulating the expense account structure under which expenses will be planned and actual expenses matched against the budget or other standards, the controller should heed these common sense suggestions to make the reports more useful to the manufacturing executive:

- The budget (or other standard) should be based on technical data that are sound from a manufacturing viewpoint.

  Among other things, this will call for cooperation with the industrial engineers or process engineers who will supply the technical data required in developing the budget and/or standards. As manufacturing processes change, the standards must change. Adoption of just-in- time (JIT) techniques may require, for example, a different alignment of cost centers. Further, with the increased use of robots or other types of mechanization, direct labor will play a less important role, while manufacturing expense (through higher depreciation charges, perhaps more indirect labor, higher repairs and maintenance, and power) will become relatively more significant.

- The manufacturing department supervisors, who will do the actual planning and control of expenses, must be given the opportunity to fully understand the system, including the manner in which the budget expense structure is developed, and to generally concur in the fairness of the system.

- The account classifications must be practical, the cost departments should follow the manufacturing organization structure (responsibility accounting and reporting), and the allocation methods must permit the proper valuation of inventories (usually under general accepted accounting principles), as well as proper control of expense.

- The manufacturing costs must be allocated as accurately as possible, so the manufacturing executive can determine the expense of various products and processes. This topic is covered in more detail later in this chapter, under activity-based costing.

Also, industrial engineers will provide the technical data required for the development of standards, such as manpower needs, power requirements, expected downtime, and maintenance requirements. Finally, if an activity-based costing (ABC) system is in place, then the manufacturing executive should work with the controller to develop information collection procedures for resource drivers.

APPROACH IN CONTROL OF MANUFACTURING EXPENSES

The diverse types of expenses in overhead and the divided responsibility may contribute to the incurrence of excessive costs. Furthermore, the fact that many cost elements seem to be quite small and insignificant in terms of consumption or cost per unit often encourages neglect of proper control. For example, it is natural to increase clerical help as required when volume increases to higher levels, but there is a reluctance and usually a delay from a timing viewpoint in eliminating such help when no longer needed. The reduced requirement must be forecasted and anticipated and appropriate actions taken in a timely manner. There are numerous expenses of small unit-cost items that may be insignificant but in the aggregate can make the company less competitive. Some examples are excessive labor hours for maintenance, use of special forms or supplies when standard items would be sufficient, personal use of supplies, and indiscriminate use of communication and reproduction facilities.

All types of overhead expenses must be evaluated and controls established to achieve cost reduction wherever possible.

Although these factors may complicate somewhat the control of manufacturing overhead, the basic approach to this control is fundamentally the same as that applying to direct costs: the setting of budgets or standards, the measurement of actual performance against these standards, and the taking of corrective action when those responsible for meeting budgets or standards repeatedly fail to reach the goal. Standards may change at different volume levels; or stated in other terms, they must have sufficient flexibility to adjust to the level of operations under which the supervisor is working. To this extent the setting and application of overhead standards may differ from the procedure used in the control of direct material and direct labor. The degree of refinement and extent of application will vary with the cost involved. The controller should make every attempt to apply fair and meaningful standards, not thinking that little is needed or that nothing can be accomplished.

Also, the controller can use ABC to assign costs to products (or other entities, such as production departments or customers). This approach is better than the traditional method of assigning a uniform overhead rate to all production, since it assigns overhead costs to specific products based on their use of various activities, resulting in more accurate product costs.

PROPER DEPARTMENTALIZATION OF EXPENSES

One of the most essential requirements for either adequate cost control or accurate cost determination is the proper classification of accounts. Control must be exercised at the source, and since costs are controlled by individuals, the primary classification of accounts must be by individual responsibility—"responsibility accounting." This generally requires a breakdown of expenses by factory departments that may be either productive departments or service departments, such as maintenance, power, or tool crib. Sometimes, however, it becomes necessary to divide the expense classification more finely to secure a proper control or costing of products—to determine actual expenses and expense standards by cost center. This decision about the degree of refinement will depend largely on whether improved product costs result or whether better expense control can be achieved.

A cost center, which is ordinarily the most minute division of costs, is determined on one of the following bases:

- One or more similar or identical machines
- The performance of a single operation or group of similar or related operations in the manufacturing process

The separation of operations or functions is essential because a foreman may have more than one type of machine or operation in his department—all of which affect costs. One product may require the use of expensive machinery in a department, and another may need only some simple hand operations. The segregation by cost center will reveal this cost difference. Different overhead rates are needed to reflect differences in services or machines required.

If the controller chooses to install an ABC system, a very different kind of cost breakdown will be required. The ABC method collects costs by activities, rather than by department; for example, information might be collected about the costs associated with engineering change orders, rather than the cost of the entire engineering department. If management decides that it wants both ABC and departmental cost information, then the controller must record the information twice—once by department and again by activity.

VARIATIONS IN COST BASED ON FIXED AND VARIABLE COSTS[1]

One factor that can cause costs to vary is that they contain both variable and fixed elements. The cost of most products is itemized in a bill of materials (BOM) that itemizes all the components that are assembled into it. An example of a bill of materials for a desk light is shown in Exhibit 5.1. Each of the line items in this BOM are variable costs, for each one will be incurred only if a desk light is created—that is, the costs vary directly with unit volume.

In its current format, the BOM is very simple; we see a quantity for each component, a cost per component, and a total cost for each component that is derived by multiplying the number of units by the cost per unit. The only line item in this BOM that does not include a cost per unit or number of units is the overhead cost, which is situated near the bottom. This line item represents a variety of costs that are being allocated to each desk lamp produced. The costs included in this line item represent the fixed costs associated with lamp production. For example, there may be a legal cost associated with a patent that covers some feature of the desk lamp, the cost of a production supervisor who runs the desk lamp assembly line, a buyer who purchases components, the depreciation on any equipment used in the production process—the list of possible costs is lengthy. The key factor that brings together these fixed costs is that they are associated with the production of desk lamps, but they do not vary directly with the production of each incremental lamp. For example, if one more desk lamp is produced, there will be no corresponding increase in the legal fees needed to apply for or protect the patent that applies to the lamp.

This splitting of costs between variable and fixed costs can occupy the extremes of entirely fixed costs or entirely variable ones, with the most likely case being a mix of the two. For example, a software company that downloads its products over the Internet has entirely fixed costs; it incurs substantial costs to develop the software and set up a web site for downloading purposes, but then incurs zero costs when a customer downloads the software from the web site (though even in this case, there will be a small credit card processing fee charged on each transaction). Alternatively, a custom programming company will

Component Description	Quantity	Cost/Each	Total Cost
Base	1	$17.00	$17.00
Switch	1	.75	.75
Spring	4	.25	1.00
Extension arm, lower	1	3.75	3.75
Extension arm, upper	1	4.25	4.25
Adjustment knob	2	.75	1.50
Bulb holder	1	.30	.30
Bulb	1	2.15	2.15
Bulb lens	1	1.50	1.50
Overhead costs	—	6.20	6.20
Total cost	—	—	$ 38.40

EXHIBIT 5.1 BILL OF MATERIALS

---

1. Summarized with permission from Chapter 29 of Steven M. Bragg, *Cost Accounting* (Wiley, Hoboken, NJ: 2001).

charge customers directly for every hour of time its programmers spend on software development, so that all programming costs are variable (though any administrative costs still will be fixed). To use a variation on the software example, a software developer that sells its products by storing the information on CDs or diskettes, printing instruction manuals, and mailing the resulting packages to customers will incur variable costs associated with the mailed packages, and fixed costs associated with the initial software development. All three variations on the variable-fixed cost mix are shown in Exhibit 5.2. In the exhibit, the first graph shows a straight horizontal line, indicating that there is no incremental cost associated with each additional unit sold. The second graph shows a steeply sloped line that begins at the X-Y intercept, which indicates that all costs are incurred as the result of incremental unit increases in sales. Finally, the third graph shows the sloped line beginning partway up the left side of the graph, which indicates that some (fixed) costs will be incurred even if no sales occur.

To return to the BOM listed earlier in Exhibit 5.1, the format does a good job of itemizing the variable costs associated with the desk lamp, but a poor one of describing the fixed costs associated with the product; there is only a single line item for $6.20 that does not indicate what costs are included in the overhead charge, nor how it was calculated. In most cases, the number was derived by summarizing all overhead into a single massive overhead cost pool for the entire production facility, which is then allocated out to the various products based on the proportion of direct labor that was charged to each product. However, many of the costs in the overhead pool may not be related in any way to the production of desk lamps, nor may the use of direct labor hours be an appropriate way in which to allocate the fixed costs.

This is a key area in which the costing information provided by controllers can result in incorrect management decisions of various kinds. For example, if the purpose of a costing inquiry by management is to add a standard margin to a cost and use the result as a product's new price, then the addition of a fixed cost that includes nonrelevant costs will result in a price that is too high. Similarly, using the same information but without any fixed cost may result in a price that is too low to ever cover all related fixed costs unless enormous sales volumes can be achieved. One of the best ways to avoid this problem with the proper reporting of fixed costs is to split the variable and fixed cost portions of a product's cost into two separate pieces, and then report them as two separate line items to the person requesting the information. The variable cost element is reported as the cost per unit, while the fixed cost element is reported as the entire fixed cost pool, as well as the assumed number of units over which the cost pool is being spread. To use the desk lamp example, the report could look like this:

> In response to your inquiry regarding the cost of a desk lamp, the variable cost per unit is $32.20, and the fixed cost is $6.20. The fixed cost pool upon which the fixed cost per unit is based is $186,000, and is divided by an assumed annual sales volume of 30,000 desk lamps to arrive at the fixed cost of $6.20 per unit. I would be happy to assist you in discussing this information further.

We do not know the precise use to which our costing information will be put by the person requesting the preceding information, so we are giving her the key details regarding the fixed and variable cost elements of the desk lamp, from which she can make better decisions than would be the case if she received only the total cost of the desk lamp. This approach yields better management information, but, as we will see in the following sections, there are many other issues that can also impact a product's cost and that a controller should be aware of before issuing costing information to the rest of the organization.

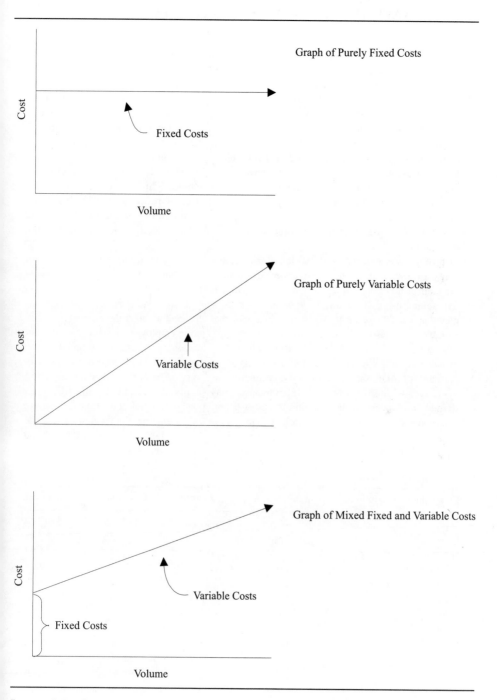

EXHIBIT 5.2 GRAPHS OF FIXED COSTS, VARIABLE COSTS, AND MIXED COSTS

VARIATIONS IN COST BASED ON DIRECT LABOR

One of the larger variable costs noted in a product's bill of materials is direct labor. This is the cost of all labor that is directly associated with the manufacture of a product. For example, it includes the cost of an assembly person who creates a product, or the machine operator whose equipment stamps out the parts that are later used in a product. However, it does not include a wide range of supporting activities, such as machine maintenance, janitorial services, production scheduling, or management, for these activities cannot be quite so obviously associated with a particular product. Consequently, direct labor is itemized separately on the BOM (as noted in Exhibit 5.3), while all other indirect labor elements are lumped into the fixed cost line item. In the exhibit, we have now switched from just one type of unit-based cost, as was noted in Exhibit 5.1, to two types of costs; one is still based on a cost per unit, but now we have included direct labor, which is based on a cost per hour. Accordingly, there is now a "unit of measure" column in the BOM that identifies each type of cost. The two types of direct labor itemized in the BOM are listed as a cost per hour, along with the fraction of an hour that is required to manufacture the desk lamp.

The trouble with listing direct labor as a separate variable product cost is that it is not really a variable cost in many situations. Companies are not normally in the habit of laying off their production workers when there is a modest reduction in production volume, and will sometimes retain many key employees even when there is no production to be completed at all. This is hardly the sort of behavior that will lead a controller to treat a cost as variable. The reason why companies retain their production employees, irrespective of manufacturing volume, is that the skills needed to operate machinery or assembly products are so valuable that a well-trained production person can achieve much higher levels of productivity than an untrained one. Accordingly, companies are very reluctant to release production employees with proven skills. While this issue may simply result in the layoff of the least trained employees, while retaining the most experienced personnel at all times, the more common result is a strong reluctance by managers to lay off anyone; the level of experience that is lost with even a junior employee is too difficult to replace, especially in a tight job market where the pool of applicants does not contain a high level of quality.

Component Description	Unit of Measure	Quantity	Cost/Each	Total Cost
Base	Ea	1	$17.00	$ 17.00
Switch	Ea	1	.75	.75
Spring	Ea	4	.25	1.00
Extension arm, lower	Ea	1	3.75	3.75
Extension arm, upper	Ea	1	4.25	4.25
Adjustment knob	Ea	2	.75	1.50
Bulb holder	Ea	1	.30	.30
Bulb	Ea	1	2.15	2.15
Bulb lens	Ea	1	1.50	1.50
Fabrication labor	Hr	2.5	18.00	45.00
Assembly labor	Hr	2.0	12.50	25.00
Overhead costs	—	—	6.20	6.20
Total cost		—	—	$ 108.40

EXHIBIT 5.3   BILL OF MATERIALS WITH DIRECT LABOR COMPONENT

Direct labor also can be forced into the fixed cost category if there is a collective bargaining agreement that severely restricts the ability of management to lay off workers or shut down production facilities. This issue is exacerbated by some national laws, such as those of Germany, that lay significant restrictions on the closure of production facilities.

Managers are also forced by the unemployment tax system to avoid layoffs. The unemployment tax is based on the number of employees from a specific company who applied to the government for unemployment benefits in the preceding year. If there was a large layoff, then the unemployment tax will rise. Managers who are cognizant of this problem will do their best to avoid layoffs in order to avoid the unemployment tax increase, though layoffs are still the most rational approach for a company that faces massive overstaffing with no near-term increase in production foreseen. In this instance, the cost of the unemployment insurance increase is still cheaper than the cost of keeping extra workers on the payroll.

The primary impact of these issues on the bill of materials is that the BOM identifies direct labor as a variable cost, when in reality it is a fixed one in many situations. Accordingly, it may be best for a controller to itemize this cost as fixed if there is no evidence of change in staffing levels as production volumes vary.

VARIATIONS IN COST BASED ON BATCH SIZE

A major issue that can significantly affect a product's cost is the size of the batches in which parts are purchased, as well as manufactured. For example, if the purchasing department buys a trailer-load of switches for the desk lamp in our ongoing example, then the per-unit cost will be very low, since the switch manufacturer can produce a lengthy production run of switches, with minimal setup costs. The per-unit cost will also be lowered due to the reduced cost of packaging and transportation, given the benefits of bulk shipping. However, if the purchasing staff buys only one switch, then the manufacturer will charge a premium amount for it, either because a single production run must be set up for the single unit of output, or (if the item is already stored in the manufacturer's warehouse) because the switch must be pulled from stock, individually packaged, and shipped. All of these manufacturing, shipping, and handling costs cannot be spread over many switches, since only one unit has been ordered. Accordingly, the per-unit cost is much higher when ordering in smaller volumes.

This is a particular problem when a company orders in odd-lot volumes. When this happens, the manufacturer of the part must repackage the items ordered into a new shipping configuration, possibly having to recreate the correct-size shipping containers, just to satisfy the company's order size.

Another way of looking at the volume-related cost issue is that the proportion of fixed costs to variable costs within a product increases as the production volume drops. For example, if a product has $10 of variable costs and a onetime machinery setup cost of $4,500, then the proportion of variable to fixed costs will change with production volumes as noted in Exhibit 5.4.

Volume	Total Variable Cost	Total Fixed Cost	Percentage of Fixed Cost
2,000 units	$20,000	$4,500	18%
1,000 units	$10,000	$4,500	31%
500 units	$ 5,000	$4,500	47%

EXHIBIT 5.4 PROPORTION OF FIXED TO TOTAL COSTS AS VOLUME CHANGES

A controller must be cognizant of the proportional increase in fixed cost as volume drops, since this means that the full cost per unit will increase as volume declines. To use the example in Exhibit 5.4, at the volume level of 2,000 units produced, the full cost per unit is $12.25, but this cost per unit increases to $19.00 as volume drops to 500 units.

To ensure that the most accurate possible information is assembled regarding order sizes, it is best to specify a volume range in the BOM within which the per-unit costs are accurate. An example of this format is shown in Exhibit 5.5, where we have included an extra column denoting the batch range for each line item. This range is also useful for labor, since there is a learning curve (covered in a later section) associated with longer production runs that results in greater labor efficiency.

The controller may need to supply a copy of the BOM with any reports that itemize batch sizes, since the reader may need to know the specific volumes within which the costs of certain line items will be valid.

An additional problem related to batch size is sudden jumps in costs that are incurred when production volumes surpass a specific level; these are known as step costs. An example of a step cost is the purchase of a new machine to relieve a production bottleneck. If the machine were not obtained, there would be no way to increase production capacity. The machine must be purchased in order to increase production volume by just one additional unit, so this constitutes a considerable incremental cost if the unit volume is to be increased by only a small amount. This concept is particularly important if a company is operating at production levels that are close to the maximum possible with existing equipment and personnel, for nearly any subsequent decision to increase production may result in the incurrence of a step cost. Other types of step costs are the addition of a supervisor if a new shift is opened up, or a new building if a production line must be built elsewhere, or a new warehouse to store the additional volumes of material needed for a new production line. A controller must be particularly cognizant of this volume-driven issue, since the costing information he issues may be relied upon to increase production to levels where new step costs will take effect, thereby rendering the initial cost report irrelevant. A good way to ensure that a cost report is used correctly is to list on it the volume range within which the stated costs are accurate, and to further note that the controller should be consulted if volumes are expected to vary beyond this range.

Component Description	Unit of Measure	Batch Range	Quantity	Cost/Each	Total Cost
Base	Ea	500–1,000	1	$17.00	$ 17.00
Switch	Ea	1,000–2,000	1	.75	.75
Spring	Ea	5,000–8,000	4	.25	1.00
Extension arm, lower	Ea	250–500	1	3.75	3.75
Extension arm, upper	Ea	250–500	1	4.25	4.25
Adjustment knob	Ea	400–800	2	.75	1.50
Bulb holder	Ea	1,000–5,000	1	.30	.30
Bulb	Ea	2,000–2,500	1	2.15	2.15
Bulb lens	Ea	500–1,000	1	1.50	1.50
Fabrication labor	Hr	250–500 Units	2.5	18.00	45.00
Assembly labor	Hr	250–500 Units	2.0	12.50	25.00
Overhead costs	—	—	—	6.20	6.20
Total cost		—	—	$ 108.40

EXHIBIT 5.5   BILL OF MATERIALS WITH BATCH RANGE

An excellent competitive tool for companies that want to adjust their prices to match different production volumes is to maintain a separate database of unit costs for a wide range of production and purchasing volumes. The marketing staff can use this information to conduct what-if analyses for a specific level of sales volume, so that it can estimate, with a fair degree of precision, the profits to be expected at each volume level. Unfortunately, such a database is usually custom-designed, and requires a great deal of research to assemble the data for all relevant volume ranges. Some Japanese companies have taken over a decade to create such systems.

VARIATIONS IN COST BASED ON OVERHEAD

The line item in a BOM that continually raises the most questions from the recipients of cost reports is for overhead cost. They ask if this cost is relevant, what makes up the number, and how it is allocated.

The relevance of overhead costs is entirely dependent on the use to which the cost information will be put. If the report recipient is concerned only with pricing a product to a level near its variable cost, then there is certainly no need for the overhead cost, which can be ignored. However, if the issue is what price to set over the long term in order to cover all fixed costs, then the overhead figure must be included in the calculation.

If the latter reasoning is used, then the controller must delve deeper into the manner in which overhead costs are calculated and allocated, to ensure that only relevant overhead costs are charged on the BOM. There are two factors that go into the production of the overhead number. One is the compilation of the overhead pool, which yields the grand total of all overhead costs that subsequently will be allocated to each product. The second factor is the allocation method that is used to determine how much of the fixed cost is allocated to each unit.

The overhead cost pool can contain a wide array of costs that are related to the production of a specific product in varying degrees. For example, there may be machine-specific costs, such as setup, depreciation, maintenance, and repairs, that have some reasonably traceable connection to a specific product at the batch level. Other overhead costs, such as building maintenance or insurance, are related more closely to the building in which the production operation is housed, and have a much looser connection to a specific product. The overhead cost pool may also contain costs for the management or production scheduling of an entire production line, as well as the costs of distributing product to customers. Given the wide-ranging nature of these costs, it is evident that a hodgepodge of costs are being accumulated into a single cost pool, which almost certainly will result in very inaccurate allocations to individual products.

The allocation method is the other factor that impacts the cost of overhead. Far and away the most common method of allocation is based on the amount of direct labor dollars used to create a product. This method can cause considerable cost misallocations, because the amount of labor in a product may be so much smaller than the quantity of overhead cost to be allocated that anywhere from $1 to $4 may be allocated to a product for every $1 of direct labor cost in it. Given the high ratio of overhead to direct labor, it is very easy for the amount of overhead charged to a product to swing drastically in response to a relatively minor shift in direct labor costs. A classic example of this problem is what happens when a company decides to automate a product line. When it does so, it incurs extra costs associated with new machinery, which adds to the overhead cost pool. Meanwhile, the amount of direct labor in the product plummets, due to the increased level of automation. Consequently, the increased amount of overhead—which is directly associated with the newly automated production line—is allocated to other products whose production has not yet been automated. This means that a product that is created by an automated production line does not have enough overhead cost allocated to it, while the overhead costs assigned to more labor-intensive products is too high.

There are solutions to the problems of excessively congregated cost pools, as well as allocations based on direct labor. One is to split the single overhead allocation pool into a small number of overhead cost pools. Each of these pools should contain costs that are closely related to each other. For example, there may be an assembly overhead cost pool (as noted in Exhibit 5.6) that contains only those overhead costs associated with the assembly operation, such as janitorial costs, the depreciation and maintenance on assembly equipment, and the supervision costs of that area. Similarly, there can be another cost pool (as also noted in Exhibit 5.6) that summarizes all fabrication costs. This pool may contain all costs associated with the manufacture and procurement of all component parts, which includes the costs of machinery setup, depreciation, and maintenance, as well as purchasing salaries. Finally, there can be an overall plant overhead cost pool that includes the costs of building maintenance, supervision, taxes, and insurance. It may not be useful to exceed this relatively limited number of cost pools, for the complexity of cost tracking can become excessive. The result of this process is a much better summarization of costs.

Each of the newly created cost pools then can be assigned a separate cost allocation method that has a direct relationship between the cost pool and the product being created. For example, the principal activity in the assembly operation is direct labor, so this time-honored allocation method can be retained when allocating the costs of the assembly overhead cost pool to products. However, the principle activity in the fabrication area is machine hours, so this becomes the basis of allocation for fabrication overhead costs. Finally, all building-related costs are best apportioned through the total square footage of all machinery, inventory, and related operations used by each product, so square footage becomes the basis of allocation for this cost pool.

Component Description	Unit of Measure	Batch Range	Scrap Percentage	Quantity	Cost/Each	Total Cost
Base	Ea	500–1,000	—	1	$17.00	$ 17.00
Switch	Ea	1,000–2,000	—	1	.75	.75
Spring	Ea	5,000–8,000	—	4	.25	1.00
Extension arm, lower	Ea	250–500	8%	1	3.75	4.05
Extension arm, upper	Ea	250–500	8%	1	4.25	4.59
Adjustment knob	Ea	400–800	5%	2	.75	1.58
Bulb holder	Ea	1,000–5,000	—	1	.30	.30
Bulb	Ea	2,000–2,500	1%	1	2.15	2.17
Bulb lens	Ea	500–1,000	2%	1	1.50	1.53
Fabrication labor	Hr	250–500 units	—	2.5	18.00	45.00
Assembly labor	Hr	250–500 units	—	2.0	12.50	25.00
Assembly overhead	Assembly labor hour	500–1,000 hours	—	2.0	3.25	6.50
Fabrication overhead	Fabrication machine hour	625–1,250 hours	—	2.5	1.20	3.00
Plant overhead	Square footage	5,000 square feet	—	1	1.75	1.75
Total cost			—		—	$ 114.22

EXHIBIT 5.6   BILL OF MATERIALS WITH MULTIPLE OVERHEAD COSTS

The result of these changes, as noted in Exhibit 5.6, is an altered BOM that replaces a single overhead cost line item with three different overhead costs, each one being allocated based on the most logical allocation measure.

A final issue related to overhead is the frequency with which the overhead cost per unit is calculated. When the controller adds the overhead cost to a BOM, the typical process is to calculate the overhead cost pool, apply an allocation formula, and enter the cost—and not update the resulting figure again for a long time. The updating process can be as laborious as manually accessing each BOM to make an update, or else entering a dollar cost for each unit of allocation (such as per dollar of direct labor, hour of machine time, etc.) into a central computer screen, which the computer system then uses to automatically update all BOMs. In either case, the overhead cost in each BOM will not be updated unless specific action is taken by the controller to update the overhead figures. Consequently, the overhead cost in a BOM must be regularly updated to ensure its accuracy.

By using this more refined set of overhead allocation methods, the accuracy of cost reports can be increased. In particular, it tells managers which cost pools are responsible for the bulk of overhead costs being assigned to specific products. This is information they can use to target reductions in these cost pools, thereby reducing overhead charges.

VARIATIONS IN COST BASED ON TIME

The old adage points out that in the long run, nothing is certain except for death and taxes. This is not precisely true. Also, virtually all costs are variable in the long run. Accountants are good at classifying costs as fixed or variable, but they must remember that *any* cost can be eliminated if enough time goes by in which to effect a change. For example, a production facility can be eliminated, as can the taxes being paid on it, as well as all of the machinery in it and the people employed there. Though these items may all seem immovable and utterly fixed in the short run, a determined manager with a long-term view of changing an organization can eliminate or alter them all.

Some fixed costs can be converted into variable costs more easily than others. There are three main categories into which fixed costs can fall:

1. *Programmable costs.* These are costs that are generally considered to be fixed but that can be eliminated relatively easily and without the passage of much time, while also not having an immediate impact on a company's daily operations. An example of such a cost is machine maintenance. If a manager needs to hold down costs for a short period, such as a few weeks, eliminating machine maintenance should not have much of an impact on operations (unless the equipment is subject to continual breakdown!).

2. *Discretionary costs.* These are costs that are not considered to vary with production volume and that frequently are itemized as administrative overhead costs. Again, these are costs that can be eliminated in the short run without causing a significant impact on operational efficiencies. Examples of discretionary costs are advertising costs and training expenses.

3. *Committed costs.* These are costs to which a company is committed over a relatively long period, such as major capital projects. Due to the amount of funding involved, the amount of sunk costs, and the impact on production capabilities, these are costs that can be quite difficult to eliminate.

A manager who is looking into a short-term reduction in costs will focus his or her attention most profitably on the reduction of programmable and discretionary costs, since they are relatively easy to cut. If the intention is a long-term reduction, and especially if the size of reduction contemplated is large, then the best type of fixed cost to target is committed costs.

If the manager requesting costing information is undertaking a long-term cost-reduction effort, the controller should go to great lengths to identify the exact nature of all fixed costs in the costing analysis, so that the recipient can determine whether these costs can be converted to variable costs over the long term, or even completely eliminate them.

COST ESTIMATION METHODS

We have covered a number of issues that impact cost. After reviewing the preceding list, one might wonder how anyone ever estimates a cost with any degree of accuracy, given the number of issues that can impact it. In this section, we cover a number of methods, with varying degrees of accuracy and difficulty of use, that can be used to derive costs at different levels of unit volume. These methods are of most use in situations where the costs listed in a BOM are not reliable, due to the impact of outside variables (as noted in the preceding sections) that have caused costs to vary to an excessive degree.

The first and most popular method by far is to have very experienced employees make a judgment call regarding whether or not a cost is fixed or variable, and how much it will change under certain circumstances. For example, a plant manager may decide that the cost of utilities is half fixed and half based on the number of hours that machines are operated in the facility, with this number becoming totally fixed when the facility is not running at all. This approach is heavily used because it is easy to make a determination, and because in many situations the result is reasonably accurate—after all, there is something to be said for lengthy experience! However, costs may be much more or less variable than an expert estimates, resulting in inaccurate costs. Also, experts tend to assign costs to either the fixed or variable categories, without considering that they really might be mixed costs (as in the last example) that have both fixed and variable portions. The problem can be resolved to some degree by pooling the estimates of a number of experts, or by combining this method with the results obtained from one of the more quantitative approaches to be covered shortly in this section.

A more scientific approach is the engineering method. This involves having a qualified industrial engineer team with a controller to conduct exact measurements of how costs relate to specific measurements. For example, this approach may use time-and-motion studies to determine the exact amount of direct labor that is required to produce one unit of finished goods. The result is precise information about the relationship between a cost and a specific activity measure. However, this approach is extremely time consuming, and so is difficult to conduct when there are many costs and activities to compare. Also, the cost levels examined will be accurate only for the specific volume range being used at the time of the engineering study. If the study were to be conducted at a different volume of production, the original costing information per unit produced may no longer be accurate. However, since many businesses operate only within relatively narrow bands of production capacity, this latter issue may not be a problem. A final issue with the engineering method is that it cannot be used to determine the per-unit cost of many costs for which there is no direct relationship to a given activity. For example, there is only a tenuous linkage in the short run between the amount of money spent on advertising and the number of units sold, so the engineering method will be of little use in uncovering per-unit advertising costs. Despite these problems, the engineering method can be a reasonable alternative if confined to those costs that bear a clear relationship to specific activities, and for which there are not significant changes in the level of activity from period to period.

An alternative approach that avoids an intensive engineering review is the scattergraph method. Under this approach, the cost accounting staff compiles activity data for a given period, and then plots it on a chart in relation to the costs that were incurred in the same period. An example of a scattergraph is shown in Exhibit 5.7. In the exhibit, we plot the relationship between the number of units produced and the total variable material cost for the period. The total material cost is noted on the Y axis and the number of units on the X axis. Though there is some variability in the positioning of costs per unit at different volume levels, it is clear that there is a significant relationship between the number of units produced and the total variable material cost. After completing the scattergraph, the controller then manually fits a line to the data (as also noted in the exhibit). Then, by measuring the slope of the line and the point where the line intercepts the Y axis, one can determine not only the variable cost per unit of production, but also the amount of fixed costs that will be incurred, irrespective of the level of production. This is a good quantitative way to assemble relevant data into a coherent structure from which costing information can be derived, but suffers from the possible inaccuracy of the user's interpretation of where the average slope and placement of the line should be within the graph. If the user creates an incorrect Y intercept or slope angle, then the resulting information pertaining to fixed and variable costs will be inaccurate. However, this approach gives the user an immediate visual overview of any data items that are clearly far outside the normal cluster of data, which allows her to investigate and correct these outlying data points, or to at least exclude them from any further calculations on the grounds that they are extraneous. Further, the scattergraph method may result in a shapeless blob of data elements that clearly contain no linearities, which tells the controller that there is no relationship between the costs and activity measures being reviewed, which means that some other relationship must be found. There are two ways to create a more precise determination of the linearity of this information—the high/low method and the regression calculation.

Since the manual plotting of a "best-fit" line through a scattergraph can be quite inaccurate, a better approach is to use a mathematical formula that derives the best-fit line without the risk of operator error. One such method is the high/low method. To conduct this calculation, take only the highest and lowest values from the data used in the scattergram

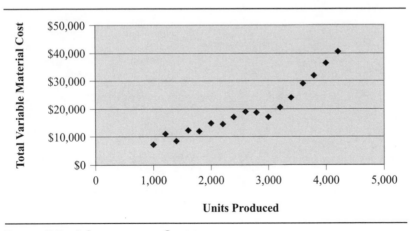

EXHIBIT 5.7 A SCATTERGRAPH CHART

and determine the difference between them. If we use the same data noted in the scatter-graph in Exhibit 5.7, the calculation of the differential would be:

	Total Variable Material Cost	Units Produced
Highest value in data set	$40,000	4,250
Lowest value in data set	$ 8,000	1,000
Difference	$32,000	3,250

The calculation of the cost per unit produced is $32,000 divided by 3,250, which is the net change in cost divided by the net change in activity. The result is $9.85 in material costs per unit produced.

There may also be a fixed cost component to the trend line, indicating the existence of costs that will be present even if no activities occur. This is not the case in the example, since we are focusing on variable material costs. However, it may very well be the case in many other situations. For example, if the preceding trend line were the result of an analysis of machine costs to units produced, we would intuitively know that some machine costs will still occur even if there are no units produced. These costs can include the depreciation on equipment, preventive maintenance, and personal property taxes. We can still use the high/low method to determine the amount of these fixed costs. To do so, we will continue to use the $9.85 per unit in variable costs that we derived in the last example, but we will increase the cost for the lowest data value observed to $11,000. We then multiply the variable cost per unit of $9.85 times the total number of units produced at the lowest observed level, which is 1,000 units, which gives us a total variable cost of $9,850. However, the total cost at the lowest observed activity level is $11,000, which exceeds the calculated variable cost of $9,850 by $1,150. This excess amount of cost represents the fixed costs that will be incurred, irrespective of the level of activity. This information can be summarized into a formula that describes the line:

$$Y \text{ intercept} = \$1,150$$

$$\text{Slope of line} = \$9.85 \times \text{number of units produced}$$

or,

$$Y = \$1,150 + (\$9.85 \times \text{number of units produced})$$

The obvious problem with the high/low method is that it uses only two values out of the entire available set of data, which may result in a less accurate best-fit line than would be the case if all scattergram data were to be included in the calculation. The problem is particularly acute if one of the high or low values is a stray figure that is caused by incorrect data, and is therefore so far outside of the normal range of data that the resulting high/low calculation will be significantly skewed. This problem can be avoided to some extent if the high and low values are averaged over a cluster of values at the high and low ends of the data range, or if the data are visually examined prior to making the calculation, and clearly inaccurate data are either thrown out or corrected.

A formulation that avoids the high/low calculation's problem of using too few data items is called linear regression. It uses every data item in a data set to calculate the variable and fixed cost components of an activity within a specific activity range. This calculation is best derived on an electronic spreadsheet, which can quickly determine the best-fit line on the scattergram that comes the closest to all data points. It does so by calculating the line for which the sum of all squared deviations between the line and all data elements results in the

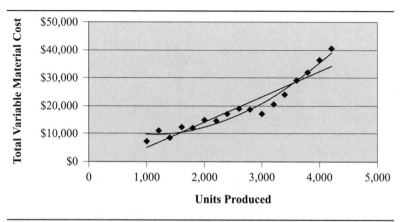

EXHIBIT 5.8 LINEAR AND CURVILINEAR REGRESSION ANALYSIS

smallest possible figure. The result is shown in Exhibit 5.8, where a line has been plotted through the scattergram by the computer. A variation on the process is shown in the same graph, which includes a curvilinear regression line that matches the data more closely. The curvilinear approach does not force the computer program to determine a straight line from the available data, thereby revealing trends in the data that may not otherwise be immediately apparent, such as higher or lower variable costs per unit at different volume levels.

The regression calculation method is the most accurate of all the cost prediction models, but suffers from several issues that one must be aware of when creating regression calculations. They are:

- *Verify a valid cause-and-effect relationship.* Even though the regression analysis may appear to have found a solid relationship between an activity and a cost, be sure to give the relationship a reality test to ensure that it is valid. For example, there is a long-running and completely irrelevant relationship between the length of women's skirts and variations in the stock market. Even though there may be a statistically valid relationship, there is no reason in fact for the relationship to exist, and so there is no reason for changes in the activity to accurately predict stock market volatility in the future. Similarly, make sure that the activity measure being included in a regression analysis bears some reasonable relationship to the cost being reviewed.

- *Pick a cost driver with a statistically strong relationship to the activity being measured.* No matter how obviously a cost driver appears to relate to an activity from the standpoint of common sense, it may not be suitable if the measured data do not support the relationship. Evidence of a tight relationship is one where the trend line in the regression analysis has a steep slope, and about which the data points are tightly clustered. If this is not the case, another cost driver should be found that results in a better statistical relationship.

- *Verify the accuracy of data collection methods.* A regression analysis may result in a weak correlation between a cost driver and an activity—not because there is in fact a weak correlation, but because the data collection system that compiles the activity data is not functioning properly. To correct this problem, one should examine the procedures, forms, training, and data entry methods used to accumulate all activity data, and have the system periodically audited to ensure that the correct information is being reported.

- *Include all relevant costs.* When comparing an activity to a cost, a common problem is to not include costs because they are recorded either in the wrong account or in the wrong time period. In the first case, this requires better attention to how costs are compiled and stored in the accounting system. In the latter case, the easiest way to ensure that costs are included in the correct time period is to lengthen the time period used for the study—for example, from a month to a quarter. By doing so, inter-period changes in costs are eliminated, and the sample size is so much larger that any remaining problems with the timing of costs are rendered statistically insignificant.

- *Ensure that the time required is worth the effort.* A regression analysis involves the determination of a cost driver, data collection, plotting on a scattergraph to find and correct outlying data items, and then (finally) the actual regression calculation. If the benefit of obtaining this information is less than the not-inconsiderable cost of the effort required to obtain it, then switch to a less accurate and less expensive prediction method that will yield a more favorable cost/benefit ratio.

No matter which of the preceding methods are used, there still will be the potential for errors in costing predictions, given the various problems inherent with each method. To counteract some of these problems, it is useful to combine methods. For example, the linear regression method can derive an accurate formulation of fixed costs and variable costs per unit, but only if the data being used are accurate; by preceding the regression analysis with a review of the data by an expert who can throw out or adjust inaccurate data, the resulting regression analysis will be significantly improved. This same principle can be applied to any of the quantitative measures noted here: Have the underlying data reviewed by experienced personnel prior to running the calculations, and the results will be improved.

NORMAL ACTIVITY

A significant consideration in the control of manufacturing overhead expense through the analysis of variances is the level of activity selected in setting the standard costs. While it has no direct bearing on the planning and control of the manufacturing expenses of each individual department, it does have an impact on the statement of income and expenses (both planned and actual) as well as on the statement of financial position. As to the income statement, it is desirable to identify the amount of manufacturing expense "absorbed" by or allocated to the manufactured product, with the excess expense identified as variance from the standard cost. This variance or excess cost ordinarily should be classified as to cause. As to the statement of financial position, the normal activity level has a direct impact on inventory valuation and, consequently, on the cost-of-goods-sold element of the income statement, in that it helps determine the standard product cost. It should be obvious that the fixed element of unit product costs is greatly influenced by the total quantity of production assumed. Of equal importance is the necessity of a clear understanding by management of the significance of the level selected, because in large part it determines the "volume" variance.

Generally speaking, there are three levels on which fixed standard manufacturing overhead may be set:

1. The expected sales volume for the year, or other period, when the standards are to be applied
2. Practical plant capacity, representing the volume at which a plant could produce if there were no lack of orders
3. The normal or average sales volume, here defined as normal capacity

Some general comments may be made about each of these three levels. If expected sales volume is used, all costs are adjusted from year to year. Consequently, certain cost comparisons are difficult to make. Furthermore, the resulting statements fail to give management what may be considered the most useful information about volume costs. Standard costs would be higher in low-volume years, when lower prices might be needed to get more business, and lower in high-volume years, when the increased demand presumably would tend toward higher prices. Another weakness is that the estimate of sales used as a basis would not be too accurate in many cases.

Practical plant capacity as a basis tends to give the lowest cost. This can be misleading because sales volume will not average this level. Generally, there will always be large unfavorable variances, the unabsorbed expense.

Normal sales volume or *activity* has been defined as the utilization of the plant that is necessary to meet the average sales demand over the period of a business cycle or at least long enough to level out cyclical and seasonal influences. This base permits a certain stabilization of costs and the recognition of long-term trends in sales. Each basis has its advantages and disadvantages, but normal capacity would seem to be the most desirable under ordinary circumstances.

Where one product is manufactured, normal capacity can be stated in the quantity of this unit. In those cases where many products are made, it is usually necessary to select a common unit for the denominator. Productive hours are a practical measure. If the normal productive hours for all departments or cost centers are known, the sum of these will represent the total for the plant. The total fixed costs divided by the productive hours at normal capacity results in the standard fixed cost per productive hour.

Volume variances can also cause costing problems in an ABC environment. Activity costs are derived by dividing estimated volumes of activity drivers into activity cost pools to derive costs for individual activities. If the estimated volume of an activity driver deviates excessively from the actual amount, then the activity cost applied to a product may significantly alter the product's ABC cost. For example, there are estimated to be 1,000 material moves associated with a product in a month, and the total cost of those moves in a month is $10,000, which is $10 per move. If the actual number of moves associated with the product is 2,000, then the cost per move that is applied to product costs is off by $5 per move. However, if the ABC system collects activity driver volume information for every accounting period, then the volume variance will not occur.

ALLOCATION OF INDIRECT PRODUCTION COSTS

This section discusses the methods for storing and allocating costs in a typical cost accounting system, as well as the types of costs that are typically found in an indirect production cost pool. The discussion is designed to leave the reader with a good understanding of how to organize costs into an adequate cost allocation system.

It is common for a company to have a large amount of overhead costs that are not readily identifiable to a specific product or service. These costs can include engineering, fixed asset charges, general supervision, and quality-related costs. Though it is possible to simply lump these costs into a massive overhead account," it is irresponsible to do so, because this means that there is minimal identification of or control over what may very well be the largest expense in the company. To attain greater control over these costs, it is best to first group costs into cost pools, from which they can be allocated to various activities.

Most companies still use just one cost pool to allocate costs to activities. This single overhead cost pool is frequently allocated to products based on the labor that goes into making them. For example, if all overhead costs during the period equal $1 million and the total direct labor incurred during that period equals $100,000, then a controller is theoretically justified in charging $10 to a product for every dollar of direct labor cost that it has absorbed. The problems with this allocation approach are that the costs contained in the single cost pool may not directly relate to the product, while the direct labor rate may not be the best way to allocate costs to the product. A better approach is to group costs into different cost pools related to specific activities, and then allocate those costs based better allocation measures. Examples of cost pools are:

- *Employee-related costs.* These costs can include benefits, the cost of payroll systems, and the entire cost of the human resources and payroll departments. This cost pool should be allocated out to activities based on their use of employees—for example, an activity like production, that normally uses a large proportion of a company's employees, should be charged with a large proportion of this cost pool.

- *Equipment-related costs.* Many costs directly relate to specific machines or groups of machines, such as depreciation, maintenance, and repairs. These costs can easily be charged back to the machines based on the amount of machine usage. It is common for each machine to have its own cost pool, which can then be charged out to production jobs based on the machine hours used by each job.

- *Materials-related costs.* There are significant costs associated with storing and moving materials, such as taxes insurance, a warehouse staff, and materials handling equipment. These costs can be charged to specific products based on the square footage occupied by finished goods, as well as by the space taken up by component parts.

- *Occupancy-related costs.* A building requires expenditures for utilities, repairs, insurance, and a maintenance staff, all of which can be stored in a cost pool and charged out to various activities based on the square footage they require.

- *Transaction-related costs.* Some activities require a considerable usage of transaction processing expenses, such as order entry time, the time to issue an invoice and collect on it, and procure materials for an order. There are significant staff expenses attached to these activities, which can be charged out based on order size or frequency, or even the number of invoices issued.

All of these cost pools have a different allocation method, because company activities use the costs in different ways. For example, a production job should be charged for the machine hours it uses on a specific machine, rather than direct labor hours, because the machine usage more correctly reflects the job's use of a company asset. Though this may seem like a relatively simple and accurate approach to allocating costs, there are a variety of problems to be aware of:

- *New cost-tracking systems needed.* A traditional cost allocation system uses only one cost pool, so this revised approach, with multiple pools, requires a different cost roll-up methodology in the general ledger, as well as the storage of information about the different allocation methods to be used. For example, the existing system may not track the usage of a specific machine by all production jobs, which is needed to properly allocate costs from the cost pool.

- *Multilevel allocations are probable.* Not all cost pools can be charged straight to an activity or customer, because there is no direct relationship. Instead, one cost pool may have to be charged to another cost pool, which in turn is charged to the final activity. For example, the cost pool for occupancy-related costs must first be charged (at least in part) to the machine cost pool, since each machine uses up some building space (which is the usual allocation method for occupancy costs); the enlarged machine cost pool is then charged to an activity.

• *Some costs do not fit into any cost pools.* There will always be some costs, such as the receptionist's salary or subscriptions, that do not easily fall into the usual cost pools, and which could not justifiably be charged to an activity in any event. These costs should be segregated and tracked; if the total of these costs becomes excessive, there should be a review to determine which costs actually can be shifted to a cost pool—an excessive amount of unallocatable costs leads one to conclude that there are too many costs that are probably not justified in order to run a company.

This section described the most common cost pools used to allocate indirect costs, as well as the allocation methods used to charge the pooled costs out to activities. Though presented in a simplified manner, this should be sufficient information for a controller to construct a simple indirect cost allocation system.

BUDGETARY PLANNING AND CONTROL OF MANUFACTURING EXPENSES

Having discussed those special factors that are important in the proper planning and control of manufacturing expense, we will now review some of the *budgetary* methods. It should be understood that manufacturing expenses can be controlled through the use of unit standards applied to the expense type or department under consideration. Probably budgetary control is the technique more useful in the overall planning of expense levels, as well as the control phase.

Three types of budgets might be applied in the manufacturing expense area:

1. A fixed- or administrative-type budget
2. A flexible budget, wherein certain expenses should vary with volume handled
3. A step-type budget

Fixed-Type Budget

The fixed-type budget is, as the name implies, more or less constant in the amount of budgeted or allowed expenses for each month. The permitted expense level does change somewhat to reflect a differing volume of manufacturing. Basically, the planning procedure is one wherein the department manager estimates the level of expenses, by account, for each month of the planning period, with some recognition given to expected differing amounts of production. These monthly estimates are subject to review by a superior (with the advice in some instances of the controller or budget director). The control phase consists in comparing actual expense incurred with the predetermined estimate.

An example of a summary planning budget of the fixed type for the manufacturing department is illustrated in Exhibit 5.9. While the budget estimate in this exhibit reflects only the annual and quarterly amounts, in practice the estimate is prepared on a monthly basis.

This fixed type of budget has the advantage of simplicity, and some recognition is given to the small changes in production level. Where production volume is nearly constant, perhaps the method is satisfactory. If the monthly budget in the example is predicated on a volume of 43,333 machine hours ($^1/_3$ of 130,000) and the actual level turns out to be 51,000, can the resulting budget comparison be deemed a good control tool? For expenses that are truly fixed, it would be satisfactory. For expenses that should vary by production volume, the "allowed" budget may be inadequate—if such a wide variance happens frequently.

THE JOHNSON CONTROLS CO.
MANUFACTURING DIVISION—ANNUAL BUDGET
MANUFACTURING EXPENSE

Item/Expense	Present Year Indicated Final	Plan Year Total	Quarter 1	2	3	4	Increase (Decrease) over Present Year
Planned production (machine hours)	412,000	440,000	110,000	130,000	100,000	100,000	28,000
Expenses							
Supervisory salaries	$ 170,000	$ 178,500	$ 44,625	$ 44,625	$ 44,625	$ 44,625	$ 8,500
Other salaries	66,000	70,000	17,500	17,500	17,500	17,500	4,000
Indirect wages	742,000	786,500	200,000	226,520	180,000	180,000	44,520
Subtotal	978,000	1,035,020	262,125	288,645	242,125	242,125	57,020
Fringe benefits (40%)	391,200	414,000	104,850	115,450	96,850	96,850	22,800
Repairs and maintenance	243,100	267,400	67,100	82,400	60,000	57,900	24,300
Power	191,300	200,860	50,600	59,800	46,000	44,460	9,560
Supplies	71,000	72,000	18,000	18,000	18,000	18,000	1,000
Depreciation	129,500	129,500	32,375	32,375	32,375	32,375	—
Communications	62,000	63,000	15,400	18,200	15,400	14,000	1,000
Occupancy	98,700	98,700	24,675	24,675	24,675	24,675	—
Other	10,200	9,000	2,000	3,000	2,000	2,000	(1,200)
Total	$2,175,000	$2,289,480	$577,125	$642,545	$537,425	$532,385	$114,480

EXHIBIT 5.9   MANUFACTURING EXPENSE—FIXED-TYPE BUDGET

Flexible Budget

The flexible or variable budget recognizes that some expense levels should change as the volume of production varies, and it is the type suggested for proper planning and control of manufacturing expenses in many instances. An illustrative annual planning budget is shown in Exhibit 5.10. An example of a related budgetary control report is presented in Exhibit 5.11.

Basically, the budgetary procedure is:

- By an examination and analysis of the expenses in each department, for each type of expense the budget structure of a fixed amount and a variable rate per factor of variability is determined. For an illustrative structure, see Exhibit 5.10.
- The department manager, when the planned production level is known, applies the budget structure to the planned volume level, probably by month, and arrives at the annual budget. (See Exhibit 5.10).
- The planned budget is reviewed by the manager's supervisors, etc.; after the iterative process is complete, the approved budget becomes part of the manufacturing division budget.
- This budget is incorporated in the company/division annual plan.
- Each month the actual expenses are compared to the flexible budget as applied to the actual volume level experienced. (See Exhibit 5.11).
- Corrective action, if necessary, is taken by the department manager.

For most applications this flexible-type budget probably is the more suitable.

Step-Type Budget

Some companies desire budgets that more or less reflect what expenses should be at particular levels, but wish to avoid a monthly calculation of the allowable budget based on the fixed amount and variable unit rate as in the flexible budget. Rather, the management prefers to establish a budget for each level of activity within a range of possible activity levels. Such a budget is illustrated in Exhibit 5.12.

Budgetary control consists of comparing actual expenses, by account, with the budget level closest to the activity level experienced. Some applications provide for interpolating between budget levels for the allowed budget.

Summarized Manufacturing Expense Planning Budget

In the context of planning, the annual planning budget should be prepared for each department in the manufacturing department, on a responsibility basis. Whatever type of budget is to be used—whether fixed or variable—the department budgets for the expected production level for the plan year should be summarized as part of the annual planning process. A summarized manufacturing expense budget, after completion of the iterative process and approval by the chief production executive, could be in the format reflected in Exhibit 5.13. This planning budget is then used in the process of determining the total cost of goods manufactured. While the illustrated budget is presented on an annual basis only, in fact the budget is prepared to show monthly data.

From a control viewpoint, each month the actual departmental expenses, by type of expense, under the control of the department manager, are compared with the monthly budget, reasons for variance are established, and corrective action taken. A representative departmental control report is shown in Exhibit 5.11, as already commented upon.

THE ADAMSON CONTROLS CO.
MANUFACTURING EXPENSE—ANNUAL BUDGET
FLEXIBLE TYPE
PLANNED ACTIVITY LEVEL

Department 62
Machine Hours 640,000

Item/Expense	Budget Structure (a)		Estimated Final–Current Year	Planning Year			
	Budget Fixed per Month	Variable Rate per Hour		Total	Fixed	Variable	Increase (Decrease) Annual
Machine hours			598,000	740,000			142,000
Expenses							
Supervisory salaries	$ 7,310	$ —	$ 82,000	$ 87,720	$ 87,720	$ —	$ 5,720
Other salaries	4,340	.10	112,000	116,080	52,080	64,000	4,000
Indirect wages	24,900	.50	493,400	618,800	298,800	320,000	125,400
Subtotal	36,550	.60	687,400	822,600	438,600	384,000	135,200
Fringe benefits (40%)	14,620	.24	274,960	329,040	175,440	153,600	54,080
Repairs and maintenance	6,000	.11	142,800	142,400	72,000	70,400	(400)
Power	10,000	.23	246,100	267,200	120,000	147,200	21,100
Communications	2,000	.10	81,100	88,000	24,000	64,000	6,900
Occupancy	30,000	—	334,800	360,000	360,000	—	35,200
Supplies	3,000	.05	61,400	68,000	36,000	32,000	6,600
Depreciation	40,000	—	420,000	480,000	480,000	—	60,000
Total	$142,170	$1.33	$2,248,560	$2,557,240	$1,706,040	$851,200	$308,680

Note: (a) Adjusted to reflect new expense levels (inflation, cost reduction, and restructuring).

EXHIBT 5.10 MANUFACTURING EXPENSE—FLEXIBLE BUDGET

THE ADAMSON CONTROLS CO.
BUDGET REPORT—DEPT. 62(B)
MONTH OF MARCH, 20XX

Activity Level ___52,100___ Machine Hours

Item/Expense	Month			Year to Date		
	Actual	Budget	(Over)/under Budget	Actual	Budget	(Over)/under Budget
Machine hours	52,100			162,000		
Expenses						
Supervisory salaries	$ 7,310	$ 7,310	$ —	$ 21,930	$ 21,930	$ —
Other salaries	9,220	9,550	330	29,000	29,220	222
Indirect wages	52,100	50,950	(1,150)	156,700	155,700	(1,000)
Subtotal	68,630	67,810	(820)	207,630	206,850	(780)
Fringe benefits (40%)	27,452	27,124	(328)	83,052	82,740	(312)
Repairs and maintenance	13,401	11,731	(1,670)	33,620	35,820	2,200
Power	20,012	21,983	1,971	63,260	67,260	4,000
Communications	6,910	7,210	300	22,000	22,200	200
Occupancy	30,000	30,000	—	90,000	90,000	—
Supplies	5,600	5,605	5	16,900	17,100	200
Depreciation	40,000	40,000	—	120,000	120,000	—
Total	$212,005	$211,463(a)	$(542)	$636,462	$641,970	$ 5,508

Notes: (Over)/under budget—not significant.

(a) Budget—Fixed	$142,170				$426,510	
—Variable	69,293				215,460	
Total	$211,463				$641,970	

(b) Despite the disruptions to his operations from ongoing construction, Foreman Johnson has done an excellent job controlling costs.

EXHIBIT 5.11 DEPARTMENTAL BUDGET REPORT

THE GENERAL CORPORATION
HEATER DIVISION
MONTHLY MANUFACTURING EXPENSE BUDGET

Department __Fabrication__
Department Head __Ship__

Year __20XX__
Normal Activity (month) __85,000__
Base __Standard Machine Hours__

	\$ 60%	70%	80%	90%	100% (N.A.)	110%	120%	130%
					Percent of Normal Activity (N.A.)			
Salaries and wages								
General foreperson	\$ 8,000	\$ 8,000	\$ 8,000	\$ 8,000	\$ 8,000	\$ 8,000	\$ 8,000	\$ 8,000
Foreperson	17,000	19,000	21,000	24,000	24,000	24,000	27,000	27,000
Clerical	1,500	1,500	2,000	2,000	2,000	2,000	2,500	2,500
Indirect labor	20,000	22,000	25,000	30,000	30,000	30,000	32,000	34,000
Subtotal	46,500	50,500	56,000	64,000	64,000	64,000	69,500	71,500
Fringe benefits (40%)	18,600	20,200	22,400	25,600	25,600	25,600	27,800	28,600
Maintenance and repairs	19,000	21,000	24,000	29,000	30,000	34,000	37,000	39,000
Power	38,000	39,000	41,000	43,000	45,000	47,000	50,000	52,000
Traveling	8,000	8,000	10,000	10,000	12,000	12,000	12,000	12,000
Communications	6,000	7,000	7,000	8,000	8,000	8,000	9,000	9,000
Supplies	8,000	8,000	9,000	9,000	10,000	11,000	12,000	12,000
All other controllable	1,600	1,700	1,800	2,000	2,000	2,000	2,500	3,000
Subtotal	145,700	155,400	171,200	190,600	196,600	203,600	219,800	227,100
Depreciation	40,000	40,000	40,000	40,000	40,000	40,000	40,000	40,000
Property taxes	5,000	5,000	5,000	5,000	5,000	5,000	5,000	5,000
Insurance	3,000	3,000	3,000	3,000	3,000	3,000	3,000	3,000
Total	\$193,700	\$203,400	\$219,200	\$238,600	\$244,600	\$251,600	\$267,800	\$275,100

EXHIBIT 5.12 MANUFACTURING EXPENSE BUDGET: STEP TYPE

THE ADAMSON CONTROLS CO.
SUMMARY MANUFACTURING EXPENSE BUDGET
FOR THE PLANNING YEAR 20XX
(DOLLARS IN THOUSANDS)

			Plan Year 20XX			
	Indicated Final	Annual		Quarter		
Department	Current Year	Plan	1	2	3	4
Standard machine hours (000)	11,780	12,500	3,125	3,500	2,700	3,175
Manufacturing administration	$ 212.1	$ 225.0	$ 56.25	$ 56.25	$ 56.25	$ 56.25
Fabrication	2,316.4	2,480.0	620.00	670.00	535.70	654.30
Subassembly	2,721.3	2,850.0	712.50	790.00	627.00	720.50
Final assembly	2,016.9	2,160.0	540.00	604.80	470.20	545.00
Production control	472.5	505.0	126.25	141.40	110.10	127.25
Industrial engineering	389.2	410.0	102.50	102.50	102.50	102.50
Quality control	140.0	150.0	37.50	42.50	32.50	37.50
Tooling	89.7	112.1	28.03	30.03	26.01	28.03
Purchasing	167.6	170.2	42.55	44.55	40.55	42.55
Shipping	212.4	225.3	56.00	60.10	52.50	56.70
Power	1,014.1	1,080.4	270.10	300.50	237.70	272.10
Maintenance	687.3	730.2	182.55	184.55	180.55	182.55
Less: Interdepartmental transfers(a)	(1,624.3)	(1,922.7)	(480.68)	(515.08)	(444.20)	(482.68)
Total	$ 8,815.2	$ 9,175.5	$2,293.55	$2,512.10	$2,027.30	$2,342.55

Note: (a) Represents allocation from tooling, power, and maintenance departments.

EXHIBIT 5.13 SUMMARIZED MANUFACTURING EXPENSE BUDGET, BY DEPARTMENT

REVISION OF MANUFACTURING EXPENSE BUDGETS

It is intended that any budget procedure be a useful function. Since the budget structure is founded on certain assumptions, standards, and criteria, these need to be periodically checked. Normally, the expense structure does not change very often, but there will be occasions when the data should be updated, such as when:

- There are major changes in the manufacturing process (e.g., introduction of JIT techniques) such as cellular manufacturing or departmental functions.
- Major changes take place in the salary, wage, or employee fringe benefits package.
- Major organizational changes take place (new departmental structure).
- Major inflationary or other external price changes occur in commodities or services purchased and so forth.

Many of these adjustments can be made in connection with the annual planning cycle. During the interim period, small cost level advances probably can be ignored, but major increases need to be instituted on a timely basis.

SECURING CONTROL OF OVERHEAD

As previously stated, the basic approach in controlling factory overhead is to set standards of performance and operate within the limits of these standards. Two avenues may be followed to accomplish this objective: one involves the preplanning or preventive approach; the other, the after-the-fact approach of reporting unfavorable trends and performance.

Preplanning can be accomplished on many items of manufacturing overhead expense in somewhat the same fashion as discussed in connection with direct labor. For example, the crews for indirect labor can be planned just as well as the crews for direct labor. The preplanning approach will be found useful where a substantial dollar cost is involved for purchase of supplies or repair materials. It may be found desirable to maintain a record of purchase commitments, by responsibility, for these accounts. Each purchase requisition, for example, might require the approval of the budget department. When the budget limit is reached, then no further purchases would be permitted except with the approval of much higher authority. Again, where stores or stock requisitions are the sources of charges, the department manager may be kept informed periodically of the cumulative monthly cost, and steps may be taken to stop further issues, except in emergencies, as the budget limit is approached. The controller will be able to find ways and means of assisting the department operating executives to keep within budget limits by providing this kind of information.

The other policing function of control is the reporting of unfavorable trends and performance. This involves an analysis of expense variances. Here the problem is somewhat different as compared with direct labor or material because of the factor of different levels of activity. Overhead variances may be grouped into the following classifications:

- Controllable by departmental supervision
  - Rate or spending variance
  - Efficiency variance
- Responsibility of top management
  - Volume variance

It is important to recognize the cause of variances if corrective action is to be taken. For this reason, the variance due to business volume must be isolated from that controllable by the departmental supervisors.

Activity-based costing is rarely used for budgeting, but if the controller wishes to use it, then bills of activity and bills of material should be used as the foundation data for standard costs. Multiplying the planned production quantities by the activity costs found in the bills of activity and direct costs found in the bills of lading will yield the bulk of all anticipated manufacturing costs for the budget period. The appropriate management use of budgeted activity costs is to target reductions in the use of activities by various products, as well as to reduce the cost of those activities. For example, the cost of paying a supplier invoice for a part used by the company's product can be reduced by either automating the activity to reduce its cost, or to reduce the product's use of the activity, such as by reducing the number of suppliers, reducing the number of parts used in the product, or grouping invoices and only paying the supplier on a monthly basis.

Analysis of Expense Variances

The exact method and degree of refinement in analyzing variances will depend on the desires of management and the opinion of the controller about requirements. However, the volume variance, regardless of cause, must be segregated from the controllable variances. *Volume variance* may be defined, simply, as the difference between budgeted expense for current activity and the standard cost for the same level. It arises because production is above or below normal activity and relates primarily to the fixed costs of the business. The variance can be analyzed in more detail about whether it is due to seasonal causes, the number of calendar days in the month, or other causes.

The controllable variances may be defined as the difference between the budget at the current activity level and actual expenses. They must be set out for each cost center and analyzed in such detail that the supervisor knows exactly what caused the condition. At least two general categories can be recognized. The first is the rate of spending variance. Simply stated, this variance arises because more or less than standard was spent for each machine hour, operating hour, or standard labor hour. This variance must be isolated for each cost element of production expense. An analysis of the variance on indirect labor, for example, may indicate what share of the excess cost is due to: (1) overtime, (2) an excess number of workers, or (3) use of higher-rated workers than standard. The analysis may be detailed to show the excess by craft and by shift. As another example, supplies may be analyzed to show the cause of variance as: (1) too large a quantity of certain items, (2) a different material or quality being used, or (3) higher prices than anticipated.

Another general type of controllable variance is the "production" or "efficiency" variance. This variance represents the difference between actual hours used in production and the standard hours allowed for the same volume. Such a loss involves all elements of overhead. Here, too, the controller should analyze the causes, usually with the assistance of production personnel. The lost production might be due to mechanical failure, poor material, inefficient labor, or lack of material. Such an analysis points out weaknesses and paves the way to corrective action by the line executives.

The accounting staff must be prepared to analyze overhead variances quickly and accurately to keep the manufacturing supervision and management informed. The variance analysis should relate to overhead losses or gains for which unit supervision is responsible and include such features as:

- The expenditure or rate variance for each cost element as an over or under the budget condition for the reporting period and year to date. The budgeted amount for controllable expenses may be calculated by multiplying the operating hours by the standard rate per cost element and compared to actual.

- The departmental variance related to the level of production.
- The amount of fixed costs, even though the particular supervisor may not be responsible for the incurrence.
- Interpretative comments as to areas for corrective action, trends, and reasons for any negative variances.

It is not sufficient just to render a budget report to the manufacturing supervision; this group must be informed about the reasons for variances. The information must be communicated and a continuous follow-up must be undertaken to see that any unfavorable conditions are corrected. This may take the form of reviewing and analyzing weekly or even daily reports. Abnormal conditions such as excess training, overtime, absenteeism, and excessive usage of supplies must be isolated and brought to the attention of the responsible individuals who can take remedial action. There also may be other data available such as repair records, material and supplies usage reports, personnel statistics—including turnover and attendance records that are useful.

Responsibility must be established for all significant variances in a timely manner so that appropriate corrective action is taken.

Incentives to Reduce Costs

It has been stated repeatedly that costs are controlled by individuals. In the control of manufacturing expenses, as in the case of direct labor and material, a most important factor is the first-line supervision. As representatives of management who are on the scene observing production the first-line supervisors can detect immediately deficient conditions and take action or influence the utilization of resources. Reports showing the performance of this group are of great assistance. However, the experience of many companies has shown that standard costs or budgets covering indirect costs are a more effective management tool when related to some type of incentive or financial reward. Usually, this incentive takes the form of a percentage of the savings or is based on achieving a performance realization above some predetermined norm. If a supervisor participates in the savings from being under the budget it is a powerful force in obtaining maximum efficiency. Since variances will fluctuate from month to month, it is advisable to consider an incentive plan for supervision on a cumulative performance basis—a quarter or a year.

INDIRECT LABOR: A MORE PRECISE TECHNIQUE

Indirect labor often is one of the largest controllable elements of manufacturing expense and therefore may warrant a special review. In the examples provided earlier in this chapter, an acceptable cost level for this type of expense was determined by measuring the historical cost against a factor of variability such as standard machine hours or direct labor hours. Sometimes the correlation may not be as close as desired and a more analytical technique may be necessary—which involves the aid of industrial or process engineers. The method, which closely resembles the calculation of the required direct labor for any given manufacturing operation, essentially is:

- The engineers study the specific function to be performed by the departmental indirect labor crew, including the exact labor hours required at differing activity levels.
- An activity base is selected, such as standard machine hours, that would be a fair and easily determinable measure of just what labor hours are needed for each function of the indirect labor crew.

- Estimates are made as to just what portion of the crew is fixed, and what portion can be treated as variable (perhaps by performing other functions), and the related labor hours are determined.

- The hours data are costed (by the cost accountants), the fixed budget allowance determined, and the variable rate calculated per unit of activity.

The process is summarized on the cost worksheet in Exhibit 5.14. First, the technical data are summarized, and then the cost bases are calculated.

Where deemed appropriate, this more exact method can be used in arriving at the flexible budget base.

OTHER ASPECTS OF APPLYING BUDGETARY CONTROL

In applying budgetary control to manufacturing expenses, an alert controller will generate ideas of how to make the budget report more usable to those managers who use it. There are many techniques that can be found; however, in any case it takes good communication. Normally, accountants will develop budgets in terms of dollars or value. Sometimes, production managers cannot relate their operations to monetary units. In most cases they think and manage in terms of labor hours. If this is more understandable, the budget can easily be stated in terms of labor hours per standard labor hours or some other factor. The budgeted allowances of other expenses may be expressed in units of consumption—kilowatt hours of power, gallons of fuel, tons of coal, pounds of grease, and so on.

One of the purposes of budgetary control is to maintain expenses within the limits of income. To this end, common factors of variability are *standard* labor hours or *standard* machine hours—bases affected by the quantity of approved production. If manufacturing difficulties are encountered, the budget allowance of all departments on such a base would be reduced. The controller might hear many vehement arguments by the maintenance foreperson, for example, that the budget should not be penalized because production was inefficient or that plans once set cannot be changed constantly because production does not come up to expectations. Such a situation may be resolved in one of at least two ways: (1) the forecast standard hours could be used as the basis for the variable allowance, or (2) the maintenance foreperson could be informed regularly if production, and therefore the standard budget allowance, will be under that anticipated. The first suggestion departs somewhat from the income-producing sources but does permit a budget allowance within the limits of income and does not require constant changes of labor force over a very short period. The second suggestion makes for more coordination between departments although it injects the element of instability to a slight degree.

Extraordinary or unanticipated expenditures of a manufacturing expense nature must frequently be made. These may fall well without the scope of the usual budget, even when the cumulative yearly condition is considered. In such instances, and if the expenditure is considered necessary and advisable, a special budget allowance will be made over and above the usual budget—something superimposed on the regular flexible budget structure.

Another point should not be overlooked by the accounting staff: The important consideration is not *how* flexibility is introduced into the standard or budget but rather that it *is* injected. Whether charts or tables are used to determine the allowable budget on a more or less automatic basis or whether the budget is adjusted monthly or quarterly on the basis of special review in relation to business volume is not too essential, because either method can be successfully employed. The major consideration is that of securing an adequate measuring stick that also keeps expenses at the proper level in relation to activity or income.

Account Name Indirect Labor
Account No. 6201
Length of Period Month

Normal Work Week: Shifts per day 1
Hours per shift 8
Days per week 5
Operating Range 70%–100%

Plant Sylvan
Dept. Machine Shop
Year 20XX
Activity base Standard Hours
Activity units at capacity 6,880

TECHNICAL DATA
(WORKERS PER SHIFT)

Job Code	Description	Requirement at Activity Level			Data at 100% Level	
		70%	80%	100%	Fixed	Variable
601	Janitorial	.5	.3	.5	.5	—
602	Moving	2.0	2.5	3.0	—	3.0
603	Testing	1.0	1.0	1.5	—	1.5
604	Preparation	.5	.7	1.0	.5	.5
605	Inspection	2.0	2.5	3.0	—	3.0
	Total	6.0	7.0	9.0	1.0	8.0

COST DATA

Job Code	Description	Requirement at Activity Level			Rate per Hour	100% Activity Level				Variable Rate per M Units	
						Fixed		Variable			
		70%	80%	100%		Man-hours	Amount	Man-hours	Amount	Man-hours	Amount
601	Janitorial	86	86	86	$15.00	86	$1,290	—	$ —	—	$ —
602	Moving	344	430	516	16.50	—	—	516	8,514	75.00	$1,237.50
603	Testing	172	172	258	18.50	—	—	258	4,773	37.50	693.75
604	Preparation	86	86	172	20.00	86	1,720	86	1,720	12.50	250.00
605	Inspection	344	430	516	22.50	—	—	516	11,610	16.15	1,687.50
485	All other	38	40	42	17.00	30	510	12	510	.38	74.12
	Total	1,070	1,244	1,590		202	$3,520	1,388	$27,127	141.53	$3,942.88

Supplementary Data and Comments:
1. Calculation of hours at capacity: a = 40 machines per shift, b = 8 hours per shift, c = 5 days per week, d = 4.3 weeks per month = a × b × c × d = 40 × 8 × 5 × 4.3 = 6,880 hours.
2. At a 100% operation, one tester will spend one-half of time on janitorial. At the 70% operation, preparation man will spend alternate days on janitorial.
3. Time for 80–90 codes will be offset by overtime if needed.
4. All other consists of union meetings, training, and physical inventory.

EXHIBIT 5.14 ENGINEERING-BASED INDIRECT LABOR BUDGET STRUCTURE

OTHER CONTROL PROCEDURES

The budgetary process has been emphasized for control of manufacturing overhead expenses in this chapter for these reasons:

- It more closely recognizes the cost behavior of the specific types of expense through its fixed and variable expense structure determination.
- It not only addresses the *control* process, but also is a *planning* device.
- It tends to promote coordination among functions.

There will be occasions when, for whatever reason, the top management and/or functional management does not wish to adopt budgetary procedures. Under these circumstances, in some departments other standards may be employed. In other instances, selected standards may supplement the budget standards. In fact, it is in the manufacturing function that standards were first employed in the control of not only direct labor and direct material, but also many of the indirect expenses.

Such a system involves the establishment of standards (see Chapter 2) and the comparison of actual expenses—either individual accounts, or departmental totals—against such standards, and the taking of corrective action where appropriate. Many manufacturing executives in particular industries know from observation that certain expense relationships are the key to a profitable operation. Their experience has led to the use of a number of standards or standard relationships for manufacturing expenses. These ratios are usually collected and distributed by industry trade associations or magazines devoted to the affairs of specific industries. Some comparisons often used, or trends followed, are shown in Exhibit 5.15.

For any *significant* expenses, trends can often be observed in the absolute and in relationship to selected or total manufacturing expenses.

ROLE OF THE CONTROLLER

Much has been said about the technique of setting manufacturing expense budgets or standards, but little mention has been made about *who* prepares the budgets and applies them.

Item	As Related to
Total manufacturing expenses	Total direct labor costs
(or selected departments)	Total direct costs
Indirect labor expense	Total standard direct labor
	Per direct labor hour
	Per actual direct labor hour
	Per machine hour
	Total manufacturing expense
Repair and maintenance expense	Per machine hour
Power	Per operating hour
Supplies	Per labor hour
Shipping and receiving	Per ton handled
Downtime expense	Per operating hour

EXHIBIT 5.15 SAMPLE EXPENSE COMPARISONS

This duty is usually delegated to the controller and staff and understandably so. Past experience is an important factor in setting expense budgets. An analysis of expenses and their behavior in relation to volume is required, and the principal source of information is the accounting records. The accountants are the best qualified to make these analyses of the historical information. Then, too, the accounting staff usually possesses the necessary technical qualifications for organizing the data into the desired shape. Furthermore, the approach must be objective, and the independent position of the accounting department makes it suitable for the setting of fair standards or budgets.

Although the controller "carries the ball" in preparing the budgets, he is only part of the team. Successful control of manufacturing expenses requires the cooperation of the operating departments' supervisors who are charged with the responsibility of meeting their budgets. For this reason, among others, each supervisor should agree to the budget before it is put into effect. Moreover, each supervisor's experience and knowledge of operating conditions must be utilized in the preparation of the budget. The controller and staff act as coordinators in seeing that the job gets done reasonably well and that it is accomplished on time.

The role of the controller and staff in the accounting for, and planning and control of, manufacturing expenses may be summarized in this fashion. The controller should:

- Provide that expenses are accumulated in such account categories that control is reasonably simple; that is, the natural expense groupings should originate from the same sources, or a comparable method of control or time or point of control should be employed. Thus, repairs done by outside sources and controlled on a purchase order basis, perhaps should be isolated from in-house repairs that are controlled by requisition.

- Arrange the departmental accounts on a responsibility basis, by natural expense classifications, so that costs are accumulated according to the authority delegated to plan and control the expenses. This categorization also should permit the accumulation of product costs in a suitable manner.

- Where a budgetary process is in effect, arrange that the *procedure* facilitates the preparation of the planning budget in an effective and timely manner (by provision of adequate instructions, forms, schedules, etc.); and that the control procedure provides a timely accumulation of actual expenses, compared with budget, together with reasons for any significant departure from plan, if known.

- Provide reasonable assistance to department managers in their preparation of the annual plan or budget (including requested analyses), and in searching out causes of standard deviation and perhaps methods of correction.

- Where flexible budgets are in use, either identify, or assist in the identification of, the fixed and variable portions.

- Where budget structures need revision by reason of changed expense levels (inflation, etc.) or new manufacturing processes, see that timely revisions are made to the end that the budgets are useful and not outdated.

- Evaluate the planned level of manufacturing expenses in the process of consolidating and testing the annual plan.

- If budgetary procedures, for whatever reason, are not used, see if some other sort of standard application may be of value in planning and controlling the manufacturing expenses.

- Determine that the costing methods provide reliable and acceptable accumulation and allocation by cost object—product, department (as to service operations), and so forth—and that variances are properly analyzed.

REPORTS FOR MANUFACTURING EXECUTIVES
Scope of Coverage

The supervisory staff of the production organization extends over several levels of authority and responsibility from the assistant foreperson, foreperson, general foreperson, division head, plant superintendent, and so on, up to the works manager. Likewise, the matters the supervisory staff controls relate to materials, labor, and overhead, and each of these subjects has special aspects to be reported on. Production reports must cover a wide field of both reader and subject matter. Effective production control is possible only when the production executives are aware of the necessary facts related to the plant operations, and the higher the executive the more reliance on reports instead of personal contacts and observations. As a result, a system of reports has been developed in most industrial organizations for presenting the pertinent facts on the production activities.

It will bear mentioning that the recent developments in computer hardware and software (programs) permit an improved monitoring of operations. Information on some activities must be, and is, available on a real-time basis. With the advent of personal computers, interesting combination reports consisting of commentary, tabulations, and graphs in an inviting appearance are now possible.

The number of variance reports that are used by manufacturing management will decline as cellular manufacturing becomes the standard form of production. Since cellular manufacturing uses minimal work-in-process (WIP), month-end variance reports from the accounting department will arrive far too late for the information to be useful. For example, if a machine produces a part out of specification, then a cellular layout will immediately detect the problem, because the part will not be hidden in a pile of WIP. Consequently, management can detect and correct the problem immediately without the need for a report.

Types of Reports on Actual Performance

The reports will differ from industry to industry from company to company so that no standardized reports can be set for business generally. However, they may be divided into two general categories according to their purpose. These may be classified as (1) control reports and (2) summary reports. As the name implies, control reports are issued primarily to highlight substandard performance so that corrective action may be taken promptly. These reports deal with performance at the occurrence level and are therefore usually detailed in nature and frequent in issuance. On the other hand, summary reports show the results of performance over a longer period of time, such as a month, and are an overall recapitulation of performance. They serve to keep the general executives aware of factory performance and are, in effect, a summary of the control reports.

Indicative of the subjects the reports to production executives may cover, including direct and indirect costs for which the executive may be responsible, are:

- *Material*
  - Inventories
  - Spoilage and waste
  - Unit standard costs
  - Material consumed
  - Actual versus standard usage
- *Labor*
  - Total payroll
  - Unit output per labor hour

    ○ Total production in units
    ○ Average hourly labor rates
    ○ Overtime hours and costs
    ○ Bonus costs
    ○ Turnover
    ○ Relationship of supervisory personnel to direct labor
    ○ Actual and standard unit and total labor costs

- *Overhead*
    ○ Actual versus budgeted costs
    ○ Idle facilities
    ○ Maintenance costs
    ○ Supplies used
    ○ Cost of union business
    ○ Subcontracted repairs
    ○ Ratio of indirect to direct labor

In a production environment that has adopted just-in-time (JIT) manufacturing systems, reports will no longer include standards, because JIT assumes that most cost improvements can be managed in the design phase, not in the production phase, and that collecting variance information costs more in effort than is gained in tangible results. A set of JIT reports would include:

- Inventory turnover
- Unit output per labor hour
- Total production in units
- Staff turnover
- Actual purchased costs versus planned costs
- Inventory accuracy
- Bill of material accuracy
- Bill of activities accuracy

Presentation of Data

Most production executives will make good use of data bearing on their operations provided three fundamental rules are followed:

1. The reports should be expressed in the language of the executive who is to use them and in the form preferred by him.
2. Reports should be submitted promptly enough to serve the purpose intended. Control reports are of little value if issued too late to take corrective action.
3. The form and content of the report should be in keeping with the responsibility of the executive receiving it. Minor executives are interested in details, whereas higher executives are interested in departmental summaries, trends, and relationships.

Some of the reports prepared by the accounting department will be on costs, and others will be expressed in nonfinancial terms. Some may be narrative; others will be in tabular or graphic form. But all should follow the principles just set forth.

OPERATIONS LABOR ANALYSIS
NDPIM-01

Report No. 97	Hours					Dollars				
	Weekly		Year to Date			Weekly		Year to Date		
	Plan	Actual	Plan	Actual	Var	Plan	Actual	Plan	Actual	Var
Operations Section										
Burden										
Supervisor	$574	$459	$7,860	$6,946	$914	$8,437	$6,822	$115,471	$103,099	$12,372
Clerical	341	418	4,517	6,096	1,579–	2,244	2,814	29,722	41,778	12,056–
V C Burden	32	19	445	238	207	227	157	3,125	2,026	1,099
Staff & Tech	463	504	6,339	6,291	48	5,651	6,017	77,352	75,040	2,312
Ops Lead	105	105	1,442	1,566	124–	1,061	1,002	14,869	16,090	1,221–
Key Lead	213	159	2,931	3,084	153–	1,776	1,348	249,413	25,676	1,265–
Comm Act										
Miscellaneous	69	22	920	445	475	493	157	6,578	2,987	3,591
Idle-Equip Fail				22	22–				153	153–
Conference				16	16–				244	244–
Training	131	510	1,698	4,675	2,977–	1,076	3,421	13,962	32,610	18,648–
Premium Pay				—		1,139	2,338	21,143	31,732	10,589–
Total Burden	1,928	2,196	26,152	29,379	3,227–	22,124	24,156	306,635	331,437	24,802–
Fringe										
Vacation Taken	248	409	3,423	3,152	271	2,128	3,574	29,547	26,203	3,344
Holiday			3,112	2,877	235			26,898	24,573	2,325
Paid Absence	263	280	3,488	3,445	43	2,262	2,026	30,096	27,812	2,286
Total Fringe	511	689	10,023	9,474	549	4,390	5,600	86,543	78,586	7,955
Sub Total	2,439	2,885	36,175	38,853	2,678–	26,514	29,756	393,178	410,025	16,847–
Adjustments										
Time Card Var										
Suspense/Correct		152		152	152–		1,079		1,079	1,079–
Vac Advances		40–		160–	160		402–		716–	716
Edit Rejects				40	40–		5		320	320–
Total Adjustments		112	—	32	32–	—	682	—	681	681–
Total Ops Payroll	$7,965	$7,958	$109,363	$106,055	$3,308	$69,671	$68,640	$964,202	$931,627	$32,575

EXHIBIT 5.16 LABOR ANALYSIS REPORT

165

Report No. ___C24.206___

SUMMARY OF ACCOUNTS

Account		Month			Year To Date		
		Budget	Actual	Variance	Budget	Actual	Variance
Other Expenses							
014-02 Training		16,642	4,130	12,512	30,421	14,420	16,000
014-03 Medical		333		333	999	603	396
014-07 Moving Exp		2,000	104–	2,104	6,000	13,879	7,879–
	Account Total	18,975	4,025	14,949	37,420	28,902	8,517
020-01 Adv Per Proc		8,333	9,695	1,362–	24,999	28,723	3,724–
020-02 Agency Fees		4,167	6,435	2,268–	12,501	15,435	2,934–
	Account Total	12,500	16,130	3,630–	37,500	44,158	6,658–
024-01 Mileage		417	750	333–	1,251	2,394	1,143–
024-02 Co. Vehicles		125		125	375	338	36
	Account Total	542	750	208–	1,626	2,732	1,106–
028-01 Bus. Conf.		25	128	128–	100	310	210–
028-02 O/T Meals		25		25	25		25
	Account Total	25	128	103–	125	310	185–
030-01 Telephone		15,834	13–	15,847	47,502	30,171	17,330
033-02 Depr Other		10,623	10,535	87	31,961	31,699	261
035-01 Due Non Memr		3,750		3,750	17,250	17,755	505–
035-02 Sci Tech		2,432	270	2,162	5,366	3,340	2,026
	Account Total	6,182	270	5,912	22,616	21,095	1,521
041-01 Emp Rel Misc							
015-01 Gen Ins		1,142		1,042	3,126	848	2,277
057-03 Consultants						1,569	1,569–
062-08 Rent-Off. Eq		1,225		1,225	3,675	2,212	1,462
065-07 Maint-Off Eq		4,708	4,636	71	17,624	23,533	5,909–
Purchased Services							
Offsite							
067-13 Pur Systems		162,416	211,637	49,221–	488,723	720,935	232,212–

EXHIBIT 5.17 FACTORY OVERHEAD BUDGET REPORT

Report No. ___C24.206___

SUMMARY OF ACCOUNTS

Account		Month			Year To Date		
		Budget	Actual	Variance	Budget	Actual	Variance
067-14	Pur Prg Labr	4,833	11,541	6,708–	31,499	17,241	14,257
067-19	Misc.						
	Account Total	342,404	358,783	16,379–	1,097,513	1,204,229	106,716–
	Sub Group Total	342,404	358,783	16,379–	1,097,513	1,204,229	106,116–
	Group Total	456,938	421,641	35,296	1,443,864	1,514,544	70,680–
Supplies							
DP Supplies							
071-20	Misc.	3,887	11,361	7,474–	9,795	39,188	29,393–
071-21	Mag. Tape	3,100	1,931	1,168	9,300	3,863	5,436
071-22	Paper Tape	2,583	2,560	22	6,749	5,507	1,241
071-23	Cards	3,975	2,954	1,020	11,925	11,963	38–
071-24	Paper	101,529	111,349	9,820–	316,544	321,759	5,215–
071-25	Ribbon	7,826	15,027	7,201–	24,322	29,039	4,717–
071-27	Form Paper	38,472	87,904–	126,376	95,380	11,507–	106,887
071-28	Microfilm Su	13,238	6,494	6,743	42,910	37,706	5,203
071-29	Fiche Supp.		236–	236		236–	236
	Account Total	174,610	63,539	111,070	516,925	437,284	79,640
	Sub Group Total	174,610	63,539	111,070	516,925	437,284	79,640
Other Supplies							
071-01	Office	3,175	3,087	87	9,525	8,375	1,149
071-03	M Eq Non Dp	12,500	622	11,877	37,500	13,237	24,262
	Account Total	15,675	3,709	11,965	47,025	21,613	25,411
	Sub Group Total	15,675	3,709	11,965	47,025	21,613	25,411
	Group Total	190,285	67,249	123,035	563,950	458,897	105,052

EXHIBIT 5.17 FACTORY OVERHEAD BUDGET REPORT *(CONTINUED)*

Illustrative Reports

As indicated previously, indirect manufacturing costs have increased significantly, resulting in the need for better visibility and control of these expenses. Exhibits 5.16 through 5.18 are examples of reports that may be adapted to a particular company or type of manufacturing operation.

Exhibit 5.19 provides an analysis of weekly and year-to-date hours and costs of the indirect labor and related fringe costs of a manufacturing department.

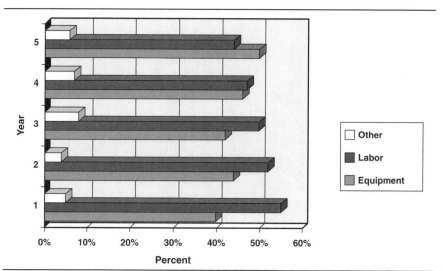

EXHIBIT 5.18   COMPARATIVE COST HISTORY CHART

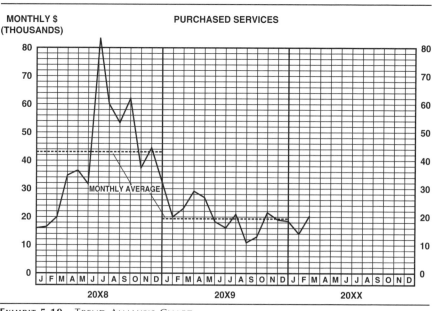

EXHIBIT 5.19   TREND ANALYSIS CHART

Exhibit 5.20 is a summary and analysis of the monthly and year-to-date expenses for the activity of three manufacturing expense accounts being monitored: supplies, purchased services, and "other" expenses.

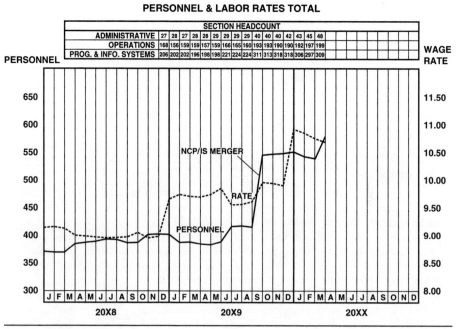

PERSONNEL & LABOR RATES TOTAL

SECTION HEADCOUNT														
ADMINISTRATIVE	27	28	27	28	28	29	29	29	29	40	40	40	42	43	45	48
OPERATIONS	168	156	159	159	157	159	166	165	160	193	193	190	190	192	197	199
PROG. & INFO. SYSTEMS	206	202	202	196	198	198	221	224	224	311	313	318	318	306	297	309

EXHIBIT 5.20   TREND ANALYSIS CHART

6

PLANNING AND CONTROL
OF RESEARCH AND
DEVELOPMENT EXPENSES

RESEARCH AND DEVELOPMENT ACTIVITIES

The terms *research* and *development* are often used imprecisely. Each may have a myriad of connotations, and even though these two words often are used together, each represents a different process with differing implications in terms of planning and control. Research as used herein relates to those activities in a business enterprise that are directed to a search for new facts, or new applications of accepted facts, or possibly new interpretations of available information, primarily as related to the physical sciences. It is the activities or functions undertaken, often in the laboratory, to discover new products or processes. Development, however, as discussed herein, denotes those activities that attempt to place on a commercial basis that knowledge gained from research. In another sense, the efforts discussed in this chapter are those that normally would be managed by the vice president or director of research and development (R&D).

Although R&D activities may be grouped in any number of ways—and proper classification is important in the planning and control function—this segregation is often used internally by those entities that do extensive work in these three areas:

1. *Basic or fundamental research.* This may be defined as investigation for the advancement of scientific knowledge that does not have any specific commercial objective. It may or may not be, in fields of present, or of possible, interest to a company or a customer.

2. *Applied research.* Activity in this area would relate to the practical application of new scientific knowledge to products or processes in which the company has an interest.

3. *Development.* Functions under this classification would include those efforts or studies to get the product or process into full-scale commercial production.

For those financial executives who deal with budgeting efforts in the R&D area, and who are desirous of having the activity defined, here are separate definitions for "research" and "development."

- *Research* is an organized search for new knowledge that may lead to the creation of an entirely new product, or that will lead to the development of a new process, or which will substantially improve an existing product or process.

- *Development* involves the systematic translation of new knowledge into the designs, tests, prototypes, and pilot production of new products or processes. It does not involve minor enhancements to existing products or processes.

IMPACT OF R&D ACTIVITIES ON CORPORATE EARNINGS

The most effective assistance of the financial discipline in respect to the planning and control of R&D expenses probably must recognize the role these expenditures can and should play in the economy as well as in a given business.

R&D in the United States is conducted by a diverse number of institutions: the federal government and other governments; industry; universities and colleges; nonprofit types of organizations; and professional firms that conduct research for others. Although the efforts of these groups have resulted in the technological superiority of the United States in the mid-twentieth century, now it has become evident that reduced expenditures at the federal level and a hostile climate for new ideas and products are threatening this position. Whether it be because of uncertain business conditions, shortsighted corporate management, lack of adequate incentive, unacceptable governmental regulation or procedures, the fact remains that such a trend may well have adverse implications for the U.S. economy.

There is evidence, in an aggregate sense, of the relationship between technical innovation and the stimulation of economic development. Within a given manufacturing company, in terms of a particular project or projects, perhaps no simple cause-and-effect relationship between R&D expenditures and net income can be found. However, statistical correlation suggests a tendency for earnings to increase, over a period of time, with an increase in research spending. Empirical data tend to show that under the private enterprise system, industrial firms grow and prosper by developing, or investing in new products or processes, or improving existing ones. It simply is not enough to do reasonably well that which is being done, for competitors will pass by such a business. Innovation or improvement and management of change are the intangible attributes that distinguish the progressive company from one on the road to decline. And the wise planning and control of research and development costs should recognize this relationship.

In a very real sense, the funds spent on R&D are quite different from many other expenses. They are an investment in the regeneration, growth, and continued existence of the business and should be evaluated, insofar as possible, as an investment.

R&D ACTIVITIES IN RELATION TO CORPORATE OBJECTIVES

From the strategic and long-range viewpoint, the important corporate activities should support the corporate goals and objectives. Certainly research and development efforts should fit this category. For example, if an entity is planning substantial growth in the compact disc field, then research and development in this area should be considered. Conversely, if strategic plans call for divestiture of a television operation, then it makes little sense to expend sizable sums on R&D in this field. Moreover, R&D input regarding acquisition targets, competitive R&D activity, or the state of the art should be helpful in strategic planning. Further, strategic planning should consider the alternative of performing research in-house or of purchasing an entity already active in the product line.

This preferred relationship between corporate objectives and the R&D plan is shown in Exhibit 6.1.

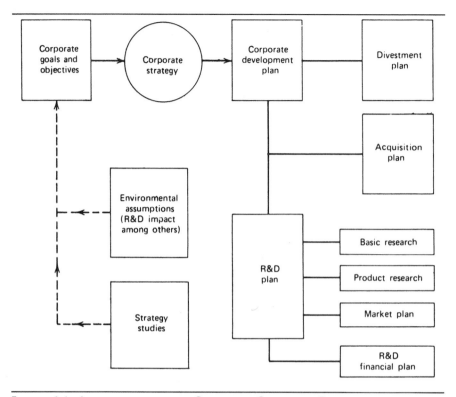

EXHIBIT 6.1   INTERRELATIONSHIP OF CORPORATE GOALS AND OBJECTIVES WITH THE R&D PLAN

INTEGRATION OF R&D WITH OTHER FUNCTIONS

Aside from understanding the proper relationship of R&D to corporate objectives, the increased competition, the often critical time factor in developing new products, and perhaps greater wisdom about the nature of R&D, is forcing a new approach in many complex R&D situations. This viewpoint has been denoted as *system focus* by one author.[1]

System focus is a philosophy which emphasizes the importance of technology integration *early* in the process: the mutual adaptation of new technology, product design, the manufacturing process, and user needs.

The traditional approach to R&D might be regarded as one group of executives after another adding its contribution to the developing product and then passing the task later to others down the line—in the engineering department and then in the manufacturing process and finally in marketing. This transfer of knowledge is mostly downstream. Often there is little incentive or no mechanism for sending knowledge back upstream so it can improve the technology in the next go-around. In the systems-focused organization, the goal of new product development shifts from a compartmentalized sequential approach to optimizing the whole system. Under such circumstances, the company early in the R&D process forms

---

1.   Marco Iansiti, "Real-World R&D: Jumping the Product Generation Gap," *Harvard Business Review*, May/June 1993, pp. 138–147.

an *integration team* composed of a core group of managers, scientists, and engineers. This team investigates the impact of various technical choices on the design of the product and the manufacturing system.

The purpose of this brief section is to alert the controller to the time and cost savings inherent in this systems integration. The controller should be aware of the potential in any relevant discussions with the R&D manager, and in the formulation of the planning and control system.

ORGANIZATION FOR THE R&D FINANCIAL FUNCTIONS

Another relevant background matter is organization. The importance of the R&D function in many companies has led to the establishment of separate organizational units, such as a division or subsidiary. Although the size of the company, scope of the research function, management philosophy, and type of research may influence the organization structure, a pattern is discernible in a review of different corporations. A self-contained unit is illustrated in Exhibit 6.2. The financial officer handling the financial aspects of R&D activity reports to the vice president of Research and Development, and provides the necessary financial analysis, accounting and reporting services, and coordination with the corporate finance group. In this instance, a "dotted line" relationship is maintained with the corporate vice president and controller.

The precise manner in which the R&D function is organized directly affects the accounting for the activity. The organization responsibilities, as defined by the functional outline or charter, provide the basis for budgeting and controlling the costs. The reporting and measurement of expenses must be guided by the organization plan; it must parallel the responsibilities of each organizational unit.

ACCOUNTING TREATMENT OF R&D IN FINANCIAL STATEMENTS

In public corporations, prior to the mid-1970s, there existed a wide difference in the balance sheet treatment of R&D costs. Given the tendency or desire in some quarters to report the highest possible earnings, as well as the high degree of uncertainty about the future economic benefits of *individual* R&D projects, such variations are understandable. Therefore, because of this reason, among others, and before deciding on the preferred accounting treatment of R&D costs, the Financial Accounting Standards Board (FASB) in 1973 considered four alternative methods of accounting for such costs as incurred:

1. Charge all costs to expense as incurred.
2. Capitalize all costs as incurred.
3. Capitalize costs when incurred, if specified conditions are fulfilled, and charge all other costs to expense.
4. Accumulate all costs in a special category until the existence of future benefits could be determined.

The FASB concluded that all R&D costs (except those covered by contract) should be charged to expense when incurred. This treatment was to be effective for fiscal years beginning on or after January 1, 1975.

The above comments relate to R&D costs exclusive of costs of developing of software. U.S. firms may account for the costs of development of similar software products in different ways. Some costs of development of software to be sold, leased, or otherwise marketed, may

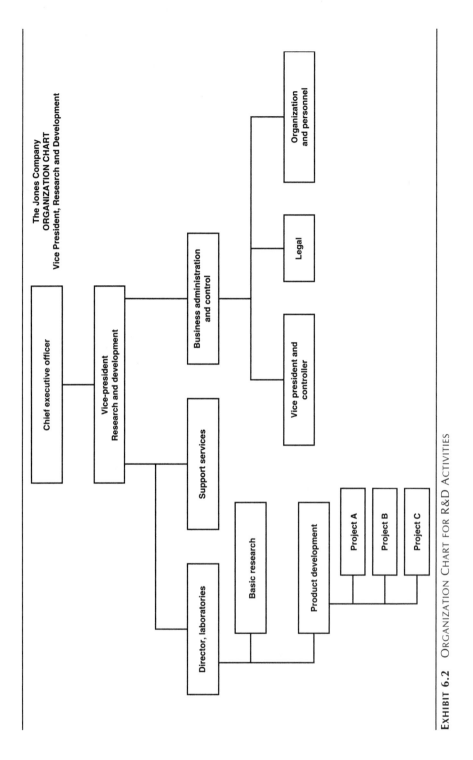

EXHIBIT 6.2 ORGANIZATION CHART FOR R&D ACTIVITIES

be capitalized. All the costs of development of similar software created for internal use may be expensed by some firms and capitalized by others.

There seem to be differences of opinion between the Institute of Management Accounting (IMA) and the FASB. The results of a survey by Kirsch and Sakthivel published in January 1993, covering 139 completed questionnaires mailed to 417 of the *Fortune 500* companies showed this treatment of software development costs:

Systems Software		Application Software
Expense	84%	78%
Capitalize	9	10
Expense and capitalize	7	12
	100%	100%

Readers, if interested, can keep updated on the directives concerning accounting for software development costs.

ELEMENTS OF R&D COSTS

The Statement of Financial Accounting Standards No. 2 does not apply to the costs of R&D conducted for others under a contractual arrangement; this is covered by statements relating to accounting for contracts in general. It does apply to the types of costs discussed in this chapter but not incurred under a contract to outside parties.

Elements of costs identified with R&D activities would include costs of (a) materials, equipment, and special facilities, (b) personnel, (c) intangibles purchased from others, (d) contract services, and (e) indirect costs. Illustrative activities, the costs of which typically would be included in R&D and would be expensed unless conducted for others under a contractual arrangement as outlined in the FASB's Statement No. 2, include:

- Basic research related to the discovery of entirely new uses or applications
- Applied research that attempts to adapt existing discoveries to specific applications
- Testing of new concepts or adaptations of new concepts to determine operating parameters
- Design, construction, and testing of prototypes
- Design, construction, and testing tools, molds, and dies involving new technological applications
- Design, construction, and testing of pilot production facilities that are strictly for the testing of new production concepts, and not for ongoing production for sale to customers

If an activity fits into one of the above categories, then a controller should categorize any related expenses into a format that clearly breaks down expenditures for each R&D activity. Before going into the details of this breakdown, however, it is reasonable for a controller to determine the size of expected R&D expenditures. If they are comparatively small, it may be easier to roll the R&D costs into overall engineering expenses and not go to the expense of creating a separate categorization. However, if the costs are significant, costs should be grouped into the following five categories for reporting purposes, or some similar format:

1. Cost of materials, equipment, and special facilities:
   - Building rental or lease fees
   - Building occupancy costs
   - Equipment capital costs

    ○ Equipment maintenance costs
    ○ Equipment operating costs
    ○ Equipment depreciation costs
    ○ Laboratory supplies

2. Personnel:
    ○ Department supervisory staff
    ○ Professional staff
    ○ Clerical and other personnel

3. Intangibles purchased from others:
    ○ Scholarly subscriptions
    ○ Outside services such as document reproduction
    ○ Legal fees for the filing and maintenance of patents

4. Contract services:
    ○ Any purchased service directly related to R&D, such as testing or analysis services

5. Indirect costs:
    ○ Allocated corporate or local overhead costs

Though it is important to group expenses into the proper R&D categories, it is equally important to exclude some expenses, primarily those that are no longer strictly concerned with R&D activities, but rather with commercial production. These excludable expenses are:

- Correction of production or engineering problems after a product has been released to the production department
- Ongoing efforts to improve existing product quality
- Slight product alterations
- Routine changes to molds, tools, or dies
- Any work related to full-scale commercial production facilities (as opposed to pilot plants)

ROLE OF THE FINANCIAL EXECUTIVE IN R&D

Now that much of the background information has been briefly reviewed, it might be useful to discuss some of the areas where the knowledge of the financial executive should be helpful to the research director before talking about the technical financial aspects relating to planning and control of R&D costs.

    Primary responsibility for the R&D activities rests with the officer in charge of the function. However, the corporate controller and the cognizant financial executive assigned to the R&D financial duties should be knowledgeable and exercise leadership in these areas (not necessarily in the order of importance):

- Provide the necessary *accounting* accumulation and reporting of the costs and expenses, and assets and liabilities, of the R&D activities in an economical way, and in a manner that provides useful financial data to the R&D executives. As to expenses, this will include accumulation by type of expense, by department, and, where appropriate, by project.
- Establish and maintain proper internal controls.

- In conjunction with the headquarters controller, if applicable, and the R&D executives and managers, establish and maintain an adequate budgetary planning and control system.
- Assist in developing guidelines for the *total amount* to be spent on R&D activities (for the annual plan and/or strategic planning).
- Where applicable, and where quantitative analysis may be helpful, and in those instances where an economic/business viewpoint is needed, provide data to guide in establishing budgets and cost/benefit and relative risk comparisons, for R&D projects. (See the discussion of "stage-gate systems" at the end of Section Section "Effectiveness of R&D Effort").
- Assist the R&D managers in developing the *planning budgets* for which each is responsible.
- Assist in preparing the annual capital budget (discussed in Chapter 11).
- Provide acceptable, practical expense control reports—either budgetary or otherwise (standards).

The remainder of this chapter relates to specific questions or tasks in the planning and control of R&D expenses.

GENERAL BUDGETARY PROCEDURE

By and large the planning and control of R&D expenses in the United States are handled through a budgetary process. The seven principal steps are:

1. Determine the *total* amount to be spent on R&D activities for the planning period.
2. Establish the individual project budgets and, where appropriate, provide related risks and costs/benefits information.
3. Where applicable, as in the overall administrative function, establish the individual departmental budgets.
4. After appraisal and consolidation, secure approval of the budget.
5. Provide the periodic comparisons of actual versus planned expenses and the cost to completion of project budgets.
6. Where needed, provide data on a standards basis—actual versus standard performance.
7. Where feasible, provide measures on the effectiveness of R&D activity.

DETERMINING THE TOTAL R&D BUDGET

"How much should the company spend on R&D this year?" A great many managers ask this question. And since expenditures should give weight to the long term, the query is really a multiyear one. There are innumerable projects which innovative R&D executives can conjure up; but there are limits on what a company should spend. Many constraints must be considered, including these, in determining the total R&D budget for any given time period:

- *Funds available.* Most entities have financial limitations; and the funds must be within reach, not merely in the one year, but perhaps extending over several years—depending on the projects.
- *Availability of manpower.* In the United States, companies often are unable to secure the needed professional or technical talent for a given project.

- *Competitive actions.* What the competitors are doing in R&D, or not doing, usually is a factor that management must weigh. The firm should be reasonably up to date on its R&D efforts.
- *Amount required to make the effort effective.* If the company embarks on some specific programs, sufficient amounts must be spent. It may be foolish to spend too little; better not to attempt the project.
- *The strategic plans.* Future needs over the longer term to meet the strategic plan may eliminate some proposed new projects.
- *General economic and company outlook.* Is the company about to enter a cyclical downturn? What is the expected trend in earnings? These factors may deter new projects if the outlook seems downbeat for a time.

So, if the constraints are known, there are several guidelines in current use for determining the limits of R&D spending. Some of these measures are useful guides in determining the overall budget:

- The amount spent in the past and/or current year, perhaps adjusted by a factor for inflation as well as growth
- A percentage of planned net sales, perhaps using past experience as a guide
- An amount per employee
- A percentage of planned operating profit
- A percentage of planned net income
- A fixed amount per unit of product sold (experience) or estimated to be sold
- A share of estimated cash flow from operations

INFORMATION SOURCES ON R&D SPENDING

Aside from internal experience data developed from company records by either the R&D director or the controller, some useful information may be obtained from several external sources. Thus, trade associations may have available data on a particular industry. The Industrial Research Institute, Inc., of Washington, DC, may be another source. If a company is required to file a Form 10-K with the Securities and Exchange Commission (SEC), this document may be available. Further, most of the national business publications such as *Business Week, Fortune,* or *Planning Review* and others periodically discuss the subject. One of the best sources is the annual "R&D Scoreboard" published in June or July of each year by *Business Week.* Typical material in each annual report is similar to this:

- The amount spent on company sponsored research and development as reported by each entity to the SEC on Form 10-K
- R&D expenditures for the year, by industry, as summarized in Exhibit 6.3
- Commentary on R&D's biggest U.S. spenders
- Comparison of R&D expenditures by U.S. companies versus those in other leading countries
- Significant recent developments in R&D activity

For example, in 2005 it was reported that R&D managers were learning to "make do" in a period of difficult economic times by such actions as:

1. Discontinuing marginal projects
2. Decentralizing R&D efforts

Industry	Total 2004 R&D Expenditures ($ Millions)	Per Employee R&D Expenditures	R&D as a % of Sales	R&D as a % of Profits
Aerospace & Defense	$ 4,210.4	$ 6,470.8	4.2%	77.7%
Automotive	13,441.4	8,975.9	4.0	115.0
Chemicals	4,993.0	6,987.4	4.1	66.3
Conglomerates	3,432.3	4,776.9	2.5	29.5
Consumer Products	2,322.9	2,294.7	1.5	16.6
Containers and Packaging	154.0	1,347.2	0.9	82.2
Electrical and Electronics	8,504.5	9,524.0	5.5	59.4
Food	640.8	1,390.8	0.8	10.7
Fuel	2,660.4	4,466.7	0.8	12.0
Health Care	13,886.9	18,247.8	10.6	72.7
Housing	494.7	2,743.6	1.8	22.3
Leisure Time Products	1,891.5	8,087.1	5.4	109.2
Manufacturing	3,931.1	4,314.7	3.0	49.8
Metals and Mining	360.6	1,541.5	0.9	neg
Office Equipment & Services	17,212.6	15,739.5	8.0	neg
Paper & Forest Products	440.6	2,051.7	1.1	27.8
Services Industries	205.8	1,141.1	1.0	31.1
Telecommunications	4,240.6	7,149.1	3.7	52.5
All Industry Composite	$83,023.8	$ 7,476.4	3.8%	64.1%

EXHIBIT 6.3 INDUSTRY SUMMARY—SELECTED R&D EXPENDITURE DATA FOR 2004

3. Collaborating with outside experts such as consortiums, universities, other companies, or government laboratories
4. Continuing internationalism in that
   (a) More research is now headquartered overseas.
   (b) Research efforts are more open to foreign participation.
   (c) New technology is being shared with developing countries.
   (d) Patent rights are being shared among certain participants.

Of course, any R&D statistical information must be carefully interpreted in that the start of major new projects or the cessation of completed ones can severely impact the quantified results of a company's effort.

ESTABLISHING THE R&D OPERATING BUDGETS

Determining the total amount to be spent on R&D for the planning year merely establishes a maximum limit on aggregate expenditures. In terms of effective planning and control, three related segments of the total operating expenses need to be determined:

1. The R&D specific "projects" and their related costs

2. The indirect expenses associated with the departmental R&D activities, but not part of the project direct expenses

3. The departmental expenses, developed following the organization structure and "responsibility" accounting and reporting—and consisting of the project expenses for which the department manager will be held responsible, and the related (or not related) indirect expenses

Because many departmental expenses depend on which projects will be undertaken and on the estimated cost of each, the project selection and cost estimating are discussed first.

Project Selection

The selection of the particular R&D projects is primarily the responsibility of the research director, giving weight to resources available, the amount of risk found acceptable by management, the strategic plan of the company, and a proper balance between the various types of projects.

In a practical way, a judgment will be made about the relative amount of effort to be spent on various categories of projects. A typical categorization might include these, perhaps in the order of ascending risk or cost, or reducing chance of economic return:

- Sales service (projects originated by the marketing department and involving field selling practices and delivery)
- Factory service (projects requested by the manufacturing arm and relating to manufacturing processes)
- Product improvement (includes efforts to improve appearance, or quality, or usefulness of the product)
- New product research (on products about which some facts are known, but which are not yet in the product line)
- Fundamental research (research of a fundamental or basic nature) where no foreseeable commercial application is yet envisioned, and which may or may not be in fields of interest to the company

Numerous influences will enter into the decision of project selection. The research director, for example, probably would consider these factors, among others:

- *Availability of qualified professional personnel.* In some time spans, the necessary professional skills simply might not be available.
- *Urgency of the project from a marketing or manufacturing viewpoint.* Some matters may be so important, that further manufacturing or marketing of the product is not feasible until the problem is solved.
- *Time required for the research.* It may be that some significant problem probably can be very quickly solved, and it is considered better to resolve the matter before proceeding to other projects with a longer time span.
- *Prior research already done by others.* Clues or significant beginnings, either within or without the organization (universities, joint ventures, etc.), may have been found or achieved. It might be the judgment of the head of research that this past effort should be capitalized upon in the present time span.
- *Prospect of economic gain as the predominant influence.* Perhaps the management may believe the possible economic returns from successful research or development are so high that a given project should be undertaken without delay.

The projects to be initiated will depend on the judgment of the research director and other members of top management. However, these general observations are made, including some comments as to how a controller or financial executive may be useful:

- Because the odds of economic benefit from an investment in pure or fundamental research is quite remote, some managements may wish to place modest limits on such expenditures.
- Development projects ordinarily should be given a high priority since successful applications would tend to be more likely.
- All development projects should be "ranked" or evaluated much as are capital budget projects (see Chapter 11). The financial discipline should be helpful, applying discounted cash flow techniques, or other quantitative methods, to information provided by the research and/or marketing staff in determining:
  - Total investment needed, anticipated revenue, operating expenses, and return on investment
  - The relative risk
  - Potential licensing income and the like

Some Quantitative Techniques in Evaluating R&D Expenditures

It is no easy task to decide on an economic basis whether R&D on a given project should be undertaken. However, there will be instances when it can be attempted.

Consider, first, return on assets (ROA), sometimes described as return on investment. The cost–volume–profit relationship may add a dimension to the R&D investment decision. Assume these five conditions:

1. Management has set a 10% return on gross assets, net after taxes, as the minimum acceptable rate.
2. In one or two years after development is complete, the estimated sales of the newly developed Product T ought to attain a stable level so that aggregate sales should total $100 million.
3. The typical gross margin in the business is 30%, and Product T should be no exception.
4. It is expected that, when research and development is complete, the required asset investment will be:

Working capital	$11,000,000
Plant and equipment	5,000,000
Total	$16,000,000

5. The expected income tax rate—federal, state, and local (netted) is 40%.

With this sales and gross margin expectation and a minimum 10% return on assets, how much can the company spend on research and development on Product T?

Some indication of the approximate expenditure level can be gained from this calculation:

$$\text{Return on assets} = \frac{\text{Net income}}{\text{Assets}}$$

$$\text{Net income} = \text{Gross margin} - \text{R\&D} - \text{Income taxes}$$

$$\text{Income tax} = (\text{Gross margin} - \text{R\&D}) \times 40\%$$

$$\text{Gross margin} = \text{Sales} \times 30\%$$

$$\text{ROA} = 10\%$$

By substitution:

$$\text{Net income} = \text{Gross margin} - \text{R\&D} - [(\text{Gross margin} - \text{R\&D} \times 40\%)]$$

$$\text{ROA} = \frac{\text{Gross margin} - \text{R\&D} - [(\text{Gross margin} - \text{R\&D} \times 40\%)]}{\text{Total assets}}$$

$$= \frac{(\$100,000,000 \times 30\%) - \text{R\&D} - [(\$100,000,000 \times 30\% - \text{R\&D}) \times 40\%]}{\$16,000,000}$$

Simplify:

$$\$1,600,000 = \$30,000,000 - \text{R\&D} - (\$30,000,000 - \text{R\&D})\,0.40$$
$$\$1,600,000 = \$30,000,000 - \text{R\&D} - \$12,000,000 - 0.40\,\text{R\&D}$$
$$1,600,000 = \$18,000,000 - \text{R\&D} - 0.40\,\text{R\&D}$$
$$-\$16,400,000 = -\text{R\&D} + 0.40\,\text{R\&D}$$
$$0.60\,\text{R\&D} = \$16,400,000$$
$$\text{R\&D} = \$27,333,333$$

Proof:

Sales	$100,000,000
Gross margin at 30%	$ 30,000,000
Less: R&D	27,333,333
Income before taxes	$ 2,666,667
Income tax at 40%	1,066,667
Net	$ 1,600,000
Assets	$ 16,000,000
ROA =	10%

The $27,333,333 permissible R&D can be converted to a budgeted amount per annum.

Another quantitative analysis related to percent return on net sales. Some managements judge the acceptability of a product by the adequacy of its percent return on sales.

Make these three assumptions and then decide how much can be spent on R&D for the product:

1. The minimum acceptable net return on product sales is 10%.
2. Sales of the new product are expected to aggregate $160 million.
3. The (net) income tax rate (federal and state) is 40%.

The calculation is:

$$\text{Return on sales} = \frac{\text{Net income}}{\text{Net sales}}$$

wherein again,

$$\text{Net income} = \text{Gross margin} - \text{R\&D} - \text{Income tax}$$
$$\text{Income taxes} = (\text{Gross margin} - \text{R\&D})\,40\%$$
$$\text{Gross margin} = \text{Sales} \times 20\%$$
$$\text{ROS} = 10\%$$

By substitution:

$$\text{Net income} = \text{Gross margin} - \text{R\&D} - (\text{Gross margin} - \text{R\&D}) \times 40\%$$

$$\text{ROS} = \frac{\text{Gross margin} - \text{R\&D} - (\text{Gross margin} - \text{R\&D}) \times 40\%}{\text{Sales}}$$

$$10\% = \frac{\$32,000,000 - \text{R\&D} - (32,000,000) - \text{R\&D}) 0.40}{\$160,000,000}$$

Simplify:

$$0.10 = \frac{\$32,000,000,000 - \text{R\&D} - \$12,800,000 + 0.40 \text{ R\&D}}{\$160,000,000}$$

$$\$16,000,000 = \$19,200,000 - 0.6 \text{ R\&D}$$
$$0.6 \text{ R\&D} = \$19,200,000 - \$16,000,000$$
$$0.6 \text{ R\&D} = \$3,200,000$$
$$\text{R\&D} = \$5,333,333$$

Proof:

Sales	$160,000,000
Gross margin 20%	$ 32,000,000
Less: R&D	5,333,333
Margin before income taxes	26,666,667
Income taxes 40%	10,666,667
Net income	$ 16,000,000
Sales =	$160,000,000
ROS =	10%

Project Risk

As previously mentioned, one factor in determining how much should be spent on a given project is the risk of that project. Although it may be difficult to calculate risk, analysis (by the controller) may provide management with some sense of the *relative* risk. One approach is based on the logical assumptions that (a) risk increases as a company ventures into new markets and new products, and (b) risks also increase with time from the completion of R&D until product sales commence. The concept is illustrated by the matrix in Exhibit 6.4 wherein the market objective and the time span are the factors of risk. The objective of a completed matrix is to graphically illustrate how relative risk for the planning year compares with the prior year, or how risks on R&D in one division compare with another or how one project may relate to another.

The four steps in identifying the *relative* risk are:

1. The various proposed R&D projects for each division or marketing group or the entity as a whole are grouped by market objective (new product in new market or new product in existing market, etc.) in order of risk
2. The year when the product will be initially sold is estimated

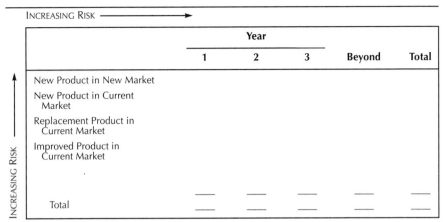

EXHIBIT 6.4 Market Objective and Relative R&D Risk

3. The proposed spending for each product having the same market objective is tabulated, as in Exhibit 6.5

4. The results are summarized by market objective, translated to percent as in Exhibit 6.6

As illustrated in Exhibit 6.6, 30% of the expenditures in planning year 1 (20XX) are contemplated in the area of most risk—new products in new markets, as compared with only 5% in the market area deemed least risky.

The research director must judge how prudent such risk is, together with the return on assets for completing products, the total potential return, and so on.

DETAILED BUDGETING PROCEDURE

Having reviewed how the overall expenditures for R&D for a given year might be determined, some of the influences in determining what projects might be considered, and a couple of illustrations of a possible quantitative approach to judging the desirability of a given project, it might help to summarize a typical budgeting procedure and provide budgetary examples.

HEALTH CARE DIVISION
PLANNED 20XX R&D EXPENDITURES
MARKET OBJECTIVE: NEW PRODUCT IN CURRENT MARKET
(DOLLAR AMOUNTS IN THOUSANDS)

Project	Year of Initial Impact				
	20X1	20X2	20X3	Beyond	Total
1	$140				$140
2	90				90
3		$ 80	$ 50	$30	160
4		60	40	10	110
5			30	10	40
Total	$230	$140	$120	$50	$540

EXHIBIT 6.5   ILLUSTRATIVE R&D EXPENDITURES FOR A MARKET
OBJECTIVE—NEW PRODUCT, CURRENT MARKET

JOHNSON COMPANY
DISTRIBUTION OF 20XX R&D EXPENDITURES
BY MARKET OBJECTIVE AND YEAR OF INITIAL COMMERCIAL IMPACT

Market Objective	Effective Year (%)				
	20X1	20X2	20X3	Beyond	Total
New products in new market	30	20	10		60
New product in current market	15	10		5	30
Replacement product in current market	5				5
Improved product in current market	5	—	—	–	5
Total	55	30	10	5	100

EXHIBIT 6.6 DISTRIBUTION OF 20XX PLANNED R&D BY MARKET OBJECTIVE AND YEAR OF INITIAL IMPACT

These are the eight steps that the research director might take, with the assistance of the controller or financial executive, in some phases:

1. Determine the total budget for the planning period. This may include the comparisons with some of the measures discussed earlier.

2. Review the individual projects. Select those deemed the more suitable and determine the total cost in some reasonable degree of detail, as in Exhibit 6.7. Some managements may want the "other expenses" broken down into more detail.

3. Determine each departmental budget, based on the project costs determined in step 2, and the necessary indirect expenses, as in Exhibit 6.8. This well may involve an iterative procedure as between project costs and total departmental budgets.

4. Summarize the project and departmental budgets to arrive at the proposed total R&D planning budget, as in Exhibit 6.9. Supporting this summary would be the project and departmental budgets.

5. Secure necessary approval of the R&D budget (board of directors, etc.). This should be regarded as approval in principle.

6. As specific projects are to begin, prepare a project budget request, with adjusted or updated data, if applicable, and secure *specific* budget approval.

7. Provide periodic control reports, comparing, as in Exhibit 6.10, actual project costs to date and cost to complete, with the budget, and comparing department actual costs with budget, as in Exhibit 6.11. In this latter case, costs are controlled by department, but not by project.

8. Take any necessary corrective action.

OTHER CONTROL METHODS

As previously explained, the *control* phase of the budgeting process consists of comparing actual expenses and budgeted expenses for the indirect or administrative type expenses of the R&D function. Project direct expenses also could be judged in the same fashion. But it makes more sense, in this latter case, to compare estimated total expenses to complete the project—a continuous or monthly updating process—with the project budget. In this manner, if it appears that expenses are going over budget, perhaps steps can be taken to reduce some of the anticipated costs. Budgetary control probably is the most widely used method of monitoring expense trends, and correcting over-budget conditions.

THE PLASTICS COMPANY
PROJECT BUDGETS
FOR PLANNING YEAR 20XX
(DOLLARS IN THOUSANDS)

Dept.	Project	Project No.	Prior Year(s) Professional Labor Hours (100s)	Prior Year(s) Total Costs	Planning Year Professional Labor Hours (100s)	Professional Salaries	All Other Wages	Total Salaries and Wages	All Other Expenses	Total Costs	Future Years Costs	Estimated Total Cost
New Product Research												
102	Alkyd resin "Q"	1026	—	$ —	100	$ 300	$ 76	$ 376	$ 526	$ 902	$ 90	$ 992
102	Paint thinner "S"	1029	—	—	60	150	38	188	264	452	90	542
105	Melamine "P"	1057	—	—	100	250	65	315	457	772	—	772
105	Urea surface "L"	1059	65.6	2,624	80	120	30	150	215	365	—	2,989
107	Urea mold "N"	1073	—	—	140	350	90	440	618	1,058	180	1,238
109	Urea filler "R"	1095	91.0	546	460	960	240	1,200	1,740	2,940	—	3,486
	Subtotal		156.6	3,170	940	2,130	539	2,669	3,820	6,489	360	10,019
Product Improvement												
102	Alkyd dryer "K"	1028	—	—	60	138	55	193	267	460	—	460
102	Wet agent "T"	1022	—	—	40	52	13	65	90	155	—	155
107	Urea composite "U"	1072	—	—	20	37	15	52	75	127	—	127
107	Urea fast mold "Y"	1079	—	—	480	840	294	1,134	1,587	2,721	—	2,721
109	Phenolic resin "Z"	1091	—	—	180	365	106	471	660	1,131	450	1,581
214	Adhesive "D"	2143	—	—	80	320	104	424	590	1,016	110	1,126
	Subtotal		—	—	860	1,750	587	2,339	3,271	5,610	560	6,170

EXHIBIT 6.7 SUMMARY PROJECT BUDGET

THE PLASTICS COMPANY
PROJECT BUDGETS
FOR PLANNING YEAR 20XX
(DOLLARS IN THOUSANDS)

Dept.	Project	Project No.	Prior Year(s) Professional Labor Hours (100s)	Prior Year(s) Total Costs	Planning Year Professional Labor Hours (100s)	Professional Salaries	All Other Wages	Total Salaries and Wages	All Other Expenses	Total Costs	Future Years Costs	Estimated Total Cost
Manufacturing Service												
102	Anti-caker	102M	—	—	40	60	30	90	128	218	—	218
105	Solvent remover	105M	—	—	20	35	12	47	69	116	—	116
112	Antipollutant "K"	112M	—	—	60	120	45	165	247	412	—	412
	Subtotal		—	—	120	215	87	302	444	746	—	746
Sales Service												
216	Product storage	216S	—	—	20	30	12	42	59	101	—	101
219	Curing rate—#7	219S	—	—	60	110	40	150	221	371	—	472
	Subtotal		—	—	80	140	52	192	280	472	—	472
Fundamental Research												
301	Reflective surfaces	3012	—	—	100	200	70	270	380	650	—	650
303	Hardening compounds	3033	—	—	160	240	80	320	460	780	—	780
	Subtotal		—	—	260	440	150	590	840	1,930	—	1,430
Grand total R&D project budget			156.6	$3,170	2,260	$4,677	$1,415	$6,092	$8,655	$14,747	$920	$18,837

EXHIBIT 6.7 SUMMARY PROJECT BUDGET *(CONTINUED)*

THE PLASTICS COMPANY
DEPARTMENT 102—TOLEDO—R&D BUDGET
PLANNING YEAR 20XX

Item	Total Professional Labor Hours (100s)	Professional Salaries	All Other (2) Costs	Budget Total
Projects				
New Project Research				
Alkyd resin "Q"	100	$300,000	$ 602,000	$ 902,000
Paint thinner "S"	60	150,000	302,000	452,000
Subtotal	160	450,000	904,000	1,354,000
Product Improvement				
Alkyd dryer "K"	60	138,000	322,000	460,000
Wet agent "T"	40	52,000	103,000	155,000
Subtotal	100	190,000	425,000	615,000
Manufacturing Service				
Anti-caker	40	60,000	158,000	218,000
Total projects	300	$700,000	$1,487,000	$2,187,000
Administrative Expenses				
General				290,000
Library				46,000
Research associates				12,000
Total administrative (1)				348,000
Grand total budget				$2,535,000

Notes:
(1) Ratio of indirect to project costs	16%	
(2) Other Costs: Salaries and wages	$ 212,000	
Fringe benefit costs	84,800	
Supplies	210,000	
All others	980,200	
	$1,487,000	

EXHIBIT 6.8   DEPARTMENT PLANNING BUDGET (DEPT. 102)

In some instances, performance standards also may be used to control costs—or to supplement budgetary control. While many phases of the R&D effort are varied and not easily subject to measurement, there are circumstances where performance standards may be useful in evaluating some of the quantitative phases of the work. Some suggested performance standards for those functions that are repetitive and perhaps voluminous include:

- Number of tests per employee, per month
- Number of formulas developed per labor week
- Cost per patent application
- Cost per operating hour (pilot plant or lab)
- Number of requisitions filled per worker, per month (lab supply room)
- Number of pages of patent applications created per man-day
- Cost per professional man-hour of total research or departmental expense

THE PLASTICS COMPANY
SUMMARY BUDGET FOR R&D
PLANNING YEAR 20XX
(DOLLARS IN THOUSANDS)

Item	Year 20XX			Estimated Current Year Costs
	Professional Labor Hours (100s)	Professional Salaries	Total Expense	
Project Costs by Category				
Fundamental research	260	$ 440	$ 1,430	$ 1,220
New-product research	940	2,130	6,489	5,200
Product improvement development	860	1,752	5,610	5,080
Manufacturing services	120	215	746	750
Sales service	80	140	472	460
Total direct project costs/hrs.	2,260	$4,677	$14,747	$12,710
Administrative				
General administration			580	520
Department administration			1,160	1,040
Libraries			120	110
Patent activity			240	170
Other			110	90
Total administrative			2,210	1,930
Grand total			$16,957	$14,640
Ratio indirect to project costs			15%	15%

EXHIBIT 6.9 SUMMARY R&D BUDGET

EFFECTIVENESS OF R&D EFFORT

Management has often asked, and still asks, "Are the R&D expenditures worthwhile?" or "Is the company research effective?" Questions such as these do not relate to budgetary performance or performance standard results. Rather, they go to the heart of the contribution that the R&D activity, or segments of it, makes to the economic well being of the company.

Some research efforts, such as basic research, are difficult to measure because no specific or direct objective is discernible. But the reason for some projects is clearly economic, such as the discovery of a cheaper manufacturing process or a new product. For these, a kind of measurement is possible.

Some economic measures or indices that the accountant might suggest, or perhaps assist in developing, include:

- *For a lower-cost manufacturing process.* The savings over 1 to 5 years versus the development expense

- *For a new product*

  ○ The operating profit of the product over X years as compared to the cost of development

  ○ Rate of return on new products (DCF)

THE PLASTICS COMPANY
PROJECT BUDGET STATUS REPORT
FOR THE PERIOD ENDED MARCH 31, 20XX
(DOLLARS IN THOUSANDS)

Project	Project No.	Current Month Labor Hours (100's)	Current Month Total Costs	Cumulative Year to Date Labor Hours (100's)	Cumulative Year to Date Costs	Purchase Order Commitments	Estimated Cost to Complete Labor Hours (100's)	Estimated Cost to Complete Costs	Prior Year Labor Hours (100's)	Prior Year Costs	Indicated Project Total Costs	Indicated Project Budget	Indicated (Over) Under Budget
New Product Research													
Alkyd resin "Q"	1026	8.33	$ 72	25	$ 220	$ 4	75	$ 693	—	—	$ 917	$ 992	$ 75
Paint thinner "S"	1029	5.00	4	15	112	—	45	433	—	—	545	542	(3)
Melamine "P"	1057	8.50	66	25	197	8	75	565	—	—	770	772	2
Urea surface "L"	1059	6.67	31	20	89	7	55	2,880	65.6	$2,624	5,600	5,613	13
Urea mold "N"	1073	11.67	93	35	271	12	105	932	—	—	1,215	1,238	23
Urea filler "R"	1095	38.33	245	115	742	83	350	2,808	91.0	546	4,179	4,032	(147)
Subtotal		78.50	511	235	1,631	114	705	8,311	156.6	3,170	13,226	13,189	(37)
Product Improvement													
Alkyd dryer "K"	1028	5.00	38	15	117	12	45	320	—	—	449	460	11
Wet agent "T"	1022	3.33	12	10	36	7	30	110	—	—	153	155	2
Urea composite "Z"	1072	1.67	10	5	30	2	15	98	—	—	130	127	(3)
Urea fast mold "Y"	1079	40.00	229	120	697	47	360	2,066	—	—	2,810	2,721	(89)
Phenolic resin "Z"	1091	15.00	90	45	280	31	135	1,259	—	—	1,570	1,581	—
Adhesive "O"	2143	6.67	81	20	250	14	60	962	—	—	1,126	1,126	—
Subtotal		71.67	460	215	1,410	113	645	4,715	—	—	6,238	6,170	(68)

EXHIBIT 6.10 PROJECT BUDGET STATUS REPORT

THE PLASTICS COMPANY
PROJECT BUDGET STATUS REPORT
FOR THE PERIOD ENDED MARCH 31, 20XX
(DOLLARS IN THOUSANDS)

Project	Project No.	Current Month		Cumulative Year to Date		Purchase Order Commitments	Estimated Cost to Complete		Prior Year		Indicated Project		Indicated (Over) Under Budget
		Labor Hours (100's)	Total Costs	Labor Hours (100's)	Costs		Labor Hours (100's)	Costs	Labor Hours (100's)	Costs	Total Costs	Budget	
Manufacturing Service													
Anti-caker	102M	3.33	18	10	54	2	30	154	—	—	210	218	8
Solvent remover	105M	1.67	9	5	30	1	15	85	—	—	116	116	—
Antipollutant "K"	112M	5.00	35	15	101	12	45	300	—	—	415	412	(3)
Subtotal		10.00	62	30	185	15	90	541	—	—	741	746	5
Sales Service													
Product storage	216S	1.67	6	5	27	2	15	71	—	—	100	101	1
Curing rate #7	219S	5.00	31	15	90	6	45	284	—	—	380	371	(9)
Subtotal		6.67	37	20	117	8	60	355	—	—	480	472	(8)
Fundamental Research													
Reflective surfaces	3012	8.33	57	25	155	7	75	491	—	—	653	650	(3)
Hardening compounds	3033	13.33	64	40	192	6	120	579	—	—	777	780	3
Subtotal		21.66	121	65	347	13	195	1,070	—	—	1,430	1,430	—
Grand total—project budgets		188.50	$1,221	565	$3,690	$263	1,695	$14,992	156.6	$3,170	$22,115	$22,007	$(108)

EXHIBIT 6.10 PROJECT BUDGET STATUS REPORT *(CONTINUED)*

○ An index of market share:

$$\frac{\text{Sales}}{\text{Market potential}}$$

○ An index of share of sales from new products:

$$\frac{\text{Sales of new products}}{\text{Total sales}}$$

ACE MANUFACTURING COMPANY

BUDGET REPORT

MONTH __October__

DEPT. HEAD __R.R. Jones__
DEPARTMENT __TECHNICAL DIVISION__   NO. ____

DESCRIPTION	CURRENT MONTH			YEAR TO DATE		
	BUDGET	ACTUAL	(OVER)/UNDER	BUDGET	ACTUAL	(OVER)/UNDER
SUMMARY OF TECHNICAL DIVISION EXPENSE BY DEPARTMENTS						
RESEARCH & DEVELOPMENT						
901 Aluminum	$ 5,327	$ 5,195	$ 132	$ 29,129	$ 28,073	$1,056
902 Plastic	1,959	1,752	207	11,165	10,583	583
903 Rubber	3,074	3,246	(172)	16,454	16,333	121
904 Other Metals	3,169	2,815	354	16,941	16,090	851
TECHNICAL SERVICE						
911 Automotive	870	757	113	4,800	4,510	290
913 Aircraft	1,285	1,162	123	7,196	6,718	478
914 Boats	1,120	1,257	(137)	6,870	6,675	195
917 Military	1,573	1,444	129	8,293	8,075	218
918 Appliances - Small	1,194	1,162	32	6,996	6,823	173
OTHER						
920 General	129	129	-	1,527	1,527	-
930 Pilot Plant	9,587	9,587	-	55,455	54,369	1,086
945 Patents	6,355	6,941	(586)	38,130	38,557	(427)
949 Chicago Project	21,424	20,716	708	72,198	69,621	2,577
950 Library	752	752	-	752	752	-
TOTAL DEPARTMENT PERFORMANCE	$ 57,818	$ 56,915	$ 903	$ 275,906	$ 268,706	$7,200
PER CENT (OVER)/UNDER BUDGET			1.6%			2.7%

ISSUED BY THE ACCOUNTING DEPT. __November 14__

EXHIBIT 6.11 PROJECT BUDGET REPORT

- *For improved products*

  o The operating profit from the estimated additional sales over X years versus the development cost

  o Some of the ratios or measures suggested above for new products can be adapted for improved products

The effectiveness of R&D effort is principally the responsibility of the executive in charge of such activity. With the high level of foreign competition, in those instances where research and development is a critical success factor for the business, the process of benchmarking may be a means of increasing R&D productivity. Although this method has been used extensively with regard to manufacturing and marketing functions, it can be applied also to R&D activity. As discussed in Chapter 1, benchmarking is the measuring of a company's functions against those of companies considered to be the best in their class, and the initiation of actions to improve the activity under review.

In the event the controller is asked for advice regarding the application of benchmarking in R&D activities, the controller should be aware that the process has been a factor in creating (for the R&D function) the following benefits in some companies:

- Significant acceleration of the time-to-market for new products and new processes
- Assistance in transferring technology from the R&D organization to the business unit involved (an operating division or subsidiary)
- Identification and definition of the core R&D technologies needed to support the companies' planned long-term growth
- Help with the companies' efforts to tap global technical resources
- Assistance in evaluating research project selection
- Improvement in cross-functional participation in many R&D projects

Finally, in judging the effectiveness of product development, a broad business viewpoint must be considered—not merely the R&D project and/or revenue calculated for budget purposes. Management must allow for the right combination or trade-offs between cost, time, and performance requirements. This is where the financial executive, and especially the controller, can be of assistance to other management in the periodic evaluation of product development projects. Increasingly, the controller is a member of the "stage gate" group that monitors the progress of the project.

The "stage-gate" system segregates a company's new-product process into a series of development stages. These stages are partitioned by a series of "gates" which are periodic check points for such matters as cost escalation, market changes, quality control, and other risks. Each project must meet certain criteria before it can pass through the gate and down the development path. The senior managers involved, as well as the financial executive, review progress as the product approaches its market launch. Typically, in the early development phase, accurate information is lacking and financial risk is low. As the project reaches a critical point, a detailed financial analysis is desirable. The controller's department, or chief financial officer (CFO) integrates financial analysis, technical analysis, and manufacturing and marketing plans. Revealed are sales forecasts, prices, profit margins, and possibly impact of a discontinued project. The end result is said to be more efficient development operation, more new product successes, and a more flexible cost latitude (e.g., recognizing the time factor in the product success).

The stage-gate system offers a strong role for finance, but also provides sometimes beneficial cost-time trade-offs and plan changes for the product developers.

7

PLANNING AND CONTROL
OF GENERAL AND
ADMINISTRATIVE EXPENSES

INTRODUCTION

In this chapter, the planning for and control over the area of general and administrative (G&A) expenses are discussed. Typically an amorphous and poorly controlled area, the G&A expense area hides a significant number of expenses that a careful company can take many steps to avoid, or to at least keep from becoming larger. This chapter describes the most common elements of G&A expenses and how to control them, offers a number of pointers on how to reduce them, and finishes with a discussion of the best budgeting methods a controller can use to plan for as well as mitigate the impact of G&A expenses.

By reviewing this chapter, a controller will reach a better understanding of the components of G&A, as well as how to manage them.

COMPONENTS OF G&A EXPENSE

The G&A expense includes costs for a specific set of departments and expenses, which are both described in this section. These departments and expenses are ones that cannot be directly related to production or sales activities and so are segregated in the chart of accounts under a separate account category. This section not only describes the G&A departments, but also the accounts that are most commonly used within those departments.

For a typical company, there are a set of departments that do not relate in any way to production or sales activities, and so by default must be included in the G&A category. These departments address the overall management of the corporation, as well as its financial, computer systems, and legal activities. The departments are:

- The office of the chairman of the board
- The office of the president
- The accounting department
- The management information systems department
- The treasurer's department
- The internal audit department
- The legal department

For each of these departments, there is a common set of expenses, irrespective of the function of each department. These expenses relate to the ongoing salary, operating, and occupancy costs that any functional area must incur in order to do business. The expenses are:

- Salaries and wages
- Fringe benefits
- Travel and entertainment
- Telephones
- Repairs and maintenance
- Rent
- Dues and subscriptions
- Utilities
- Depreciation
- Insurance
- Allocated expenses
- Other expenses

A controller can use the above expenses when setting up any department that falls within the G&A category. However, in addition to these common expenses, there are a large number of additional expenses that do *not* fall into any clear-cut category, nor can they be listed as being production or sales specific. These expenses, as shown below, cannot be allocated to other departments (or at least not without the use of a very vague basis of allocation), and so must be grouped into the G&A heading:

- Director fees and expenses
- Outside legal fees
- Audit fees
- Corporate expenses (such as registration fees)
- Charitable contributions
- Consultant fees
- Gains or losses on the sale of assets
- Cash discounts
- Provision for doubtful accounts
- Interest expense
- Amortization of bond discount

A controller can use this information to set up a chart of accounts for the G&A expense area.

CONTROL OVER G&A EXPENSES

Some companies get into trouble with investors and lenders, because they have inadequate controls over their G&A costs, which leads to lower profits. It is possible to eliminate these issues by implementing a variety of controls that are useful for keeping G&A costs within an expected range. This section describes a number of controls that serve this purpose.

The potential savings that can be realized through tight control over G&A expenses are usually not as great as those in the manufacturing or sales areas. This is to be expected, because the volume of expenses is far smaller in the G&A area. However, depending on the size of the gross margin, tight control over G&A costs can still lead to a significant change in profits, because it is easier to increase profits by reducing costs than it is to increase profits by increasing sales. In the following example, we show the revenues required to cover the cost of a person with a $50,000 salary:

Salary Level	Gross Margin	Revenue Required
$50,000	90%	$55,556
$50,000	80%	$62,500
$50,000	70%	$71,429
$50,000	60%	$83,333
$50,000	50%	$100,000
$50,000	40%	$125,000
$50,000	30%	$166,666
$50,000	20%	$250,000
$50,000	10%	$500,000

The table makes it clear that for a low-margin company in particular, it is necessary to increase sales by an enormous amount in order to cover a small additional expense. Thus, it is much easier to increase profits by cutting costs for most companies than it is to increase revenues. Accordingly, the controls noted in this section and the expense reduction ideas listed in the next section are well worth the effort of implementing, even in the G&A area, which does not normally comprise a large percentage of a company's costs.

One of the easier controls to implement is to assign a number of control points to a company's internal audit group for periodic reviews. The internal audit team can observe operations, procedures, and process flows, and compare expenditures to activity levels, thereby acquiring enough information to determine where control points are at their weakest, and require strengthening. Examples of good internal audit targets in the G&A area include:

- Compare process efficiencies to those of best-practice companies and recommend changes based on this review.
- Confirm the results of consulting engagements, and construct cost-benefit analyses for them to determine which consultants are creating the largest payoff.
- Review the bad debt expense to see if there is an unusual number of write-offs, and recommend changes to the credit granting policy based on this review.
- Verify that all dues and subscriptions have been properly approved.
- Verify that all paychecks cut are meant for current employees.
- Verify that assets are categorized in the correct depreciation pools.
- Verify that cellular phone usage is for strictly company business.
- Verify that charitable contributions are approved in advance.
- Verify that insurance expenses are competitive with market rates.
- Verify that legal expenses are at market rates.
- Verify that office equipment is not incurring excessive repair costs.
- Verify that phone expenses are in line with market rates.
- Verify that scheduled rent changes have been paid.
- Verify that there are proper deductions from paychecks for benefits.
- Verify that there is approved backup for current employee pay rates.

- Verify that travel and entertainment expenses are approved.
- Verify that travel and entertainment expenses are in accordance with company policy.

Besides the internal audit team, another good control point is the budget. A controller should always hand out a comparison of actual expenses to the budget after each month has been closed, so that all managers in the G&A area can gauge their performance against expectations. In addition, there should be a report that lists the amount of money left in each manager's budget, so that there is no reason for anyone to demand extra funds towards the end of the fiscal year. The strongest control in this area is to have the purchasing system automatically check on remaining budgeted funds, so that a purchase order will be rejected if there are not sufficient funds on hand through the accounting period. Thus, a budget can be used in several ways to create tight control over G&A costs.

Another control method is to divide up all G&A costs by responsibility area and tie employee bonuses and pay rate changes to those costs. For example, the building manager can be made directly responsible for all occupancy costs, and will only receive a pay raise by reducing the overall occupancy costs by a preset percentage. When using this method, it is best to set up a range of compensation goals, so that an employee can still go after a lesser target, even when it becomes apparent that the main cost goal is not reachable. To expand on the previous example, there can be a large pay raise if occupancy costs are reduced by 5 percent, a modest pay raise if the reduction is only 2 percent, and a very minor pay raise if the person can do nothing but maintain occupancy costs at their current level. By using this multitiered compensation system that is tied to direct responsibility for G&A costs, there is a much greater chance that managers will pay close attention to those G&A costs that are assigned to them.

One problem with dividing up G&A costs by responsibility area is to find a reasonable method for doing so, since it is quite possible to erroneously charge G&A costs to the wrong person, which may lead to behavior that does not match company objectives. Fortunately, there are several allocation methods available that allow one to assign costs to facilitate planning and control, by responsibility center, and to cost pools, in case a company is using activity-based costing. The preferred method of allocating G&A costs is based on a hierarchy of alternatives, which are listed in descending order of usability:

1. *Allocated based on the amount of resources consumed by the cost center that is receiving the service.* For example, if a division is using the central accounting staff to create invoices for it, costs should be allocated to that division based on the cost of creating an invoice, multiplied by the total number created for that division.

2. *Allocated based on the relative amount caused by the various cost centers.* This method is less precise, because there is not a direct relationship between the activity and the cost, only a presumed one. For example, medical costs can be allocated to a department based on the number of people in a department; we assume that the people in that department take up a proportionate share of medical costs, even though this may not be the case. Other examples are allocating costs based on the material cost of an item (such as material handling costs), based on square footage (such as physical facility costs), or based on energy consumption (such as the rated horsepower of a machine). Though not as accurate as the first method, this approach allows one to allocate most costs on a fairly rational basis.

3. *Allocated based on the overall activity of a cost center.* This method is the least precise, because it is only based on a general level of activity, which may have no bearing on a cost center's actual expense consumption. An example of an overall activity measure is the three-factor Massachusetts Formula, which is a simple average of a

cost center's payroll, revenue, and assets as a proportion of the same amounts for all cost centers. This approach essentially charges costs to those areas that have the greatest ability to pay for services, irrespective of whether or not they are using them.

Exhibit 7.1 shows a number of ways to allocate costs. The exhibit covers activities in a variety of areas, and notes allocation methods that are based on one or more of the preceding allocation methods. The exact allocation method chosen will depend on an individual company's circumstances.

No matter which of these allocation methods is used, one should keep in mind the end result—attaining a greater degree of control over costs. If the allocation method is excessively time consuming or expensive to implement, one must factor this issue into the assumed savings from having a greater degree of control over G&A costs and make a determination regarding the cost effectiveness of the allocation method.

When allocating costs, one should also consider the impact on the recipient of the allocation. It is best to allocate only those costs over which a recipient has direct control, since the recipient can take direct action to control the cost. If a cost is allocated that the recipient can do nothing about, there is much less reason to make the allocation. For example, computer programming costs can be charged to a cost center for the exact amount of the time

General and Administrative Costs	Possible Allocation Bases
Research and development	Estimated time or usage Sales Assets employed New products developed
Personnel department functions	Number of employees Payroll Number of new hires
Accounting functions	Estimated time or usage Sales Assets employed Employment data
Public relations and corporate promotion	Sales
Purchasing function	Dollar value of purchase orders Number of purchase orders Estimated time or usage Percentage of material cost of purchases
Corporate executives' salaries	Sales Assets employed Pretax operating income
Treasurer's functions	Sales Estimated time or usage Assets or liabilities employed
Legal and governmental affairs	Estimated time or usage Sales Assets employed
Tax department	Estimated time or usage Sales Assets employed
Income taxes	Net income
Property taxes	Square feet Real estate valuation

EXHIBIT 7.1   ALLOCATION BASES FOR G&A COSTS

needed to develop a requested report—if the manager of that cost center does not want to incur the cost, then he or she should not request that any reports be developed. Alternatively, if senior management wants to encourage the use of certain internal resources, such as legal, accounting, or computer services, it can reduce the activity costs of these functions to below-market rates, which will encourage managers to use them. Either approach involves cost allocations that managers can directly impact by choosing to consume or not consume G&A services.

Another way to control G&A costs is to create standards for each activity performed, which can then be used to compare against actual performance, in the same way that labor standards have been used in the manufacturing arena for decades. By tracking performance based on these standards and modifying systems to match or beat the standards, a controller can achieve a high performance G&A function. To create standards for this purpose, use the following steps:

- *Observe work tasks.* Carefully note the steps and duration of a task. This step is fundamental in securing the necessary overall understanding of the problem and in picking those areas of activity that lend themselves to standardization. For example, it will not be possible to create a standard if there are an excessive number of variations that are commonly part of a work routine. In addition, the preliminary review will spot any obviously major weaknesses in a routine.

- *Select tasks to be standardized.* The preliminary review will reveal those routines that are the best candidates for standard creation. The two main criteria for this will be that a routine has enough volume to justify the work of setting a standard, and that a routine does not include so much variation that it is impossible to create a reliable standard. These two criteria will quickly reduce the number of standards to a modest percentage of the total number of routines used in the G&A area.

- *Determine the unit of work.* There must be a measurement base upon which to set a work standard. Examples of units of work follow:

Function	Unit of Standard Measurement
Billing	Number of invoice lines
Check writing	Number of checks written
Customer statements	Number of statements
Filing	Number of pieces filed
Mail handling	Number of pieces handled
Order handling	Number of orders handled
Order writing	Number of order lines
Posting	Number of postings
Typing	Number of lines typed

- *Determine the best way to set each standard.* Various kinds of time and motion studies can be applied to each work routine, depending on the nature of the work.

- *Test each standard.* After a standard has been set, it should be tested with varying workloads to determine whether it is a reasonable standard. Keep in mind that a standard is much less effective if an employee has many tasks to perform, since it is often necessary to jump repeatedly between tasks. In these cases, it may not even be practical to install standards for any but the most high-volume routines.

- *Apply the standard.* This step involves explaining the standard to each employee on whom it will be used, as well as to supervisors. In addition, one should set up a reporting system for tracking this information, and a feedback loop that tells employees how they are doing against the standard.

- *Audit the standard.* There should be a regular schedule of reviews for each standard, so that there is not a problem with a standard becoming so out of date that it no longer reflects the current level of efficiency of each routine. In addition to the scheduled reviews, there should also be a review every time there are major changes to a routine, possibly due to the implementation of a best practice, which would invalidate a standard.

In addition to performance standards, unit cost standards can be applied to measure an individual function or overall activity. Thus, applying cost standards to credit and collection functions may involve these functions and units of measurement, depending on the extent of mechanization. (See Exhibit 7.2.)

By applying the standard creation methods noted in this section to G&A activities, it is possible to exercise additional control over the more repetitive tasks within the G&A area.

There are a number of controls that a controller can implement to ensure that G&A expenses stay within an expected range. These controls include periodic reviews by the internal audit department, both manual and automated comparisons of budgeted to actual costs, and the development of unit cost standards. By using a selection of these controls, there is much less chance that there will be any significant variations from expected G&A costs.

Functional Activity	Unit Cost standard
Credit investigation and approval	Cost per sales order Cost per account sold Cost per credit sales transaction
Credit correspondence records and files	Cost per sales order Cost per letter Cost per account sold
Preparing invoices	Cost per invoice line Cost per item Cost per invoice Cost per order line Cost per order
Entire accounts receivable records, including posting of charges and credits and preparation of customer statements	Cost per account Cost per sales order Cost per sales transaction
Posting charges	Cost per invoice Cost per shipment
Preparing customers' statements	Cost per statement Cost per account sold
Posting credits	Cost per remittance Cost per account sold
Calculating commissions on cash collected	Cost per remittance

EXHIBIT 7.2 APPLYING COST STANDARDS TO CREDIT
AND COLLECTION FUNCTIONS

REDUCING G&A EXPENSES

Unfortunately, many controllers feel that the G&A expense is a fixed one, and consequently make little effort to reduce it. Although it is true that there are better methodologies for cost reduction in other functional areas of a company, there are still a considerable number of cost reduction techniques that a controller can implement to reduce G&A costs.

The principle issue to remember when trying to cut costs is that one must attack the underlying assumptions that are protecting G&A expenses, rather than trying to make incremental adjustments to those expenses by using greater efficiencies. In many cases, the only way to bring about massive reductions in G&A costs is to completely eliminate some categories of costs. Why go to this extreme? Because G&A costs do not directly contribute to revenue gains or production efficiencies—they are dead weight—and must be constantly reviewed to ensure that they are kept at an absolute minimum, even if the company as a whole is growing at a great rate.

If a company consists of a central headquarters that oversees the functions of a large number of facilities or subsidiaries, there may be a chance to reduce a very large proportion of the existing G&A expense. This reduction can be achieved by altering the management concept of the headquarters group. By altering this key underlying assumption of how to manage a company, it becomes possible to decentralize and push management functions down into the various facilities or subsidiaries, thereby vastly reducing the need for most of the staff in the headquarters facility. This approach is the single most effective way to reduce G&A costs.

Another general cost reduction concept that applies to nearly all parts of the G&A area is the use of outsourcing. This approach questions the underlying assumption that there is a need for an in-house staff to handle every G&A function. For example, a legal staff can be eliminated in favor of using an outside law firm that handles company legal issues. Though the hourly cost of using this approach may be quite high, it can be cheaper over time, for several reasons. First, the in-house staff tends to find work for itself to do, even though that work may not be entirely necessary. Second, there tends to be a greater emphasis on cost reduction when an expensive outside service is used that charges by the hour (or minute), especially when that cost can be traced back and charged to a specific department. Finally, the cost becomes a variable one when the fixed cost of the in-house staff is eliminated in favor of one that is incurred only when needed. Thus, outsourcing is a valid approach for reducing G&A costs.

Besides the general cost reduction methods just noted, there are a variety of specific cost areas that deserve the attention of the controller. The following list notes a variety of techniques that can be used to reduce costs in specific G&A areas:

- *Audit expense.* Most companies hire a group of outside auditors to review the year-end financial statements. The cost of this audit can be substantial, especially if company operations are widely separated or if the accounting records are not well organized. A controller can succeed in reducing the audit expense by changing to a different type of review. Instead of a full audit, it may be possible to have the auditors conduct a compilation or review, both of which are less expensive. However, these alternatives do not provide for as complete a review of the accounting records, so the switch may meet with resistance from lenders, who rely on the results of the audit to determine the risk of continued lending to a company. Another way to reduce expenses in this area is to volunteer the services of the accounting staff in assisting the external auditors. Though these services will be limited to a supporting role, it will reduce the hours charged to the company by the auditors, which will reduce the overall cost of the audit.

- *Bad debt expense.* A controller can have some of the accounting or internal auditing employees assist the external auditors during the annual audit of a company's financial records. This can reduce the size of the audit fee, since the hourly rate charged by an external auditor is typically several times the hourly rate paid to employees. This approach has its limitations, since there are only so many tasks that an audit team will allow the in-house staff to take over.

- *Charitable contributions.* This is a rare area for a company to exercise much cost control over, perhaps because there are so many worthy nonprofit organizations that are in need of a company's cash. However, it is reasonable to target a company's charitable giving to specific organizations that best meet its charitable giving goals. By creating an approved giving list at the beginning of each year, a company can avoid giving to organizations that are not on the approved list, thereby bringing about a reduction in the cost of contributions while still achieving the company's overall charitable giving goal.

- *Equipment lease expense.* Many companies purchase all of their office equipment at wide intervals, and obtain leases to pay for them without much thought for the terms of those leases, which tend to be high. A better approach is to consolidate all of the leases into a single master lease, which a controller can then shop to a variety of lenders to obtain the best possible lease rate.

- *Forms expense.* Some companies have such a large expense for the printing of a multitude of forms that they even have a separate line item in the budget to track it. This is a particular problem for paper-intensive companies such as those in the insurance industry. A controller can reduce this expense by conducting a complete review of all forms to see which ones are no longer necessary. Another option is to combine forms, so that the functions performed by many forms can now be completed with just a few. It may also be possible to convert paper-based forms to on-line ones, so that there is no printing expense at all. Another possibility is to reduce the number of copies of each form, so that they are routed to fewer people within a company. This has the double benefit of reducing the paper cost while also reducing the volume of paper working its way through a company. All of these steps can significantly reduce a company's forms expense.

- *Interest expense.* Interest expense is generally classified with G&A expenses; however, the underlying reason for the expense lies elsewhere. Interest expense is caused by debt, and debt is needed, to a large extent, to fund working capital requirements, such as accounts receivable and inventory. By paying close attention to accounts receivable collections and inventory usage, a controller can have a major impact on the amount of cash being funded through debt, which will shrink the amount of interest expense.

- *Officer salaries.* An exceedingly large part of the G&A expense is officer salaries. It is quite unlikely that a controller can persuade more senior executives to cut their pay, but it may be possible to influence the decision to alter the components of officer salaries, so that a larger proportion of it is tied to profitability or other similar performance-related targets. By inserting a large variable component into the officer salary expense, it is possible to reduce the expense substantially during periods when performance goals are not reached.

- *Reproduction expense.* The cost of copying documents is astronomical at many companies. There are several ways to reduce it. One way is to focus on the expense of the copiers used. For most employees, a very simple copier model that replicates and sorts is all that is needed, with only a small minority of the staff needing a copier with more advanced functions. Accordingly, a controller can replace expensive copiers with simpler ones, while still retaining a few complicated machines for the most complex printing jobs. Another option is to standardize on a single type of copier, which allows a company to stock a limited number of service and replacement parts for all of them, rather than a wide range of parts for a wide range of copiers. In addition, it may be possible to outsource the larger print jobs to a supplier, allowing a controller to specifically trace the billings for these jobs to the person requesting the work, which brings home to management the exact cost of reproduction, which would otherwise be buried in the overall cost of G&A expenses.

- *Storage space.* A great deal of the office space allocated to the G&A function is filled with documents. A controller can reduce the amount of prime office space devoted to record storage by reviewing the documents and consigning all but the most current ones to cheaper off-site storage facilities. Also, a good archiving policy will allow a company to throw away records that have reached the limit of their usefulness, both from a legal and operational perspective, which also reduces the amount of storage space. Finally, some or all documents can be scanned into a database for retrieval through the computer system, which not only eliminates storage space, but also reduces the time that would otherwise be spent finding records and returning them to storage.

- *Telephone expense.* There are a plethora of options that allow a controller to drop telephone expenses down to just a few pennies a minute, even for long-distance calls. To achieve such a large cost reduction, a controller should first review all existing phone invoices to determine the number and cost of extra phone services, and then determine the need for those services. Next, one must determine the number of phone lines used, as well as the need for special phone lines that carry extra charges (usually because they offer extra bandwidth), such as ISDN or T1 lines. Finally, after adjusting the types of services and number of lines, a controller can review the prices offered by different carriers to determine the lowest possible per-minute charges. With Internet phone service now becoming available, the possibility of acquiring phone service for under five cents a minute is in sight. Since some companies have extremely complex phone systems, it may be best to hire a company that specializes in reviewing phone systems, since they can provide a more knowledgeable view of phone options.

Besides the general and specific cost reduction options that have already been noted in this section, there is also the cost contained in the efficiencies of the tasks performed under the umbrella of G&A expenses. By paying close attention to the efficiency of these processes, a controller can wring out additional cost savings. The methodology to use when improving G&A efficiencies is a simple one. Essentially, one must clear out any unnecessary tasks or paperwork that are cluttering the work area, thereby allowing a clearer view of the underlying processes that require fine tuning. One can then review and eliminate a number of types of duplication, and then focus on automation, reduced cycle times, training, and benchmarking to achieve extremely high levels of efficiency. The specific efficiency improvement steps are:

- *Clean up the area.* Though a seemingly simple task, this is one that many people never get past. By reviewing all documents in an area and archiving anything more than a few months old, one can quickly reduce the volume of work that appeared to be part of the backlog of a job. If possible, as much of this old material as possible should be thrown out, in order to save on archiving costs, but just getting it out of the primary work area is the main target, not shifting it into a dumpster.

- *Eliminate duplicate documents.* Once the old paperwork has been eliminated or moved, it is time to compare the remaining documents to determine whether there are any duplicates. If so, it is only necessary to keep one copy. The remainder can be thrown out or archived.

- *Eliminate duplicate tasks.* It is entirely possible that some information is being prepared by more than one person in the same organization. The best way to spot this problem is to bring people together into teams, and review each other's work. It can be very helpful to include people from widely separated parts of a company, since they will have a better knowledge of any data being prepared in their areas that is already being prepared elsewhere (as they will find out by interacting with the review teams).

- *Eliminate reports.* Now it is time to shrink the work being performed. A classic case of work reduction is to make a list of all the reports generated, and then walk them through the organization to see if they are really needed anymore. In addition, one can review the elements of a report to see if some items can be eliminated that require large amounts of data collection or analysis. Thus, either a report can be eliminated, or some of the information in it.

- *Eliminate multiple approvals.* A review team can plot out the flow of documents through an organization, which frequently reveals a large number of unnecessary and redundant approvals that are lengthening the time required to complete processes. By identifying only the most crucial approvals and eliminating all others, the time wasted while waiting for all the other approvals can be removed from processes, dramatically shrinking cycle times.

- *Use automation.* There are many types of automation that can be used to reduce the workload of people in the G&A area. Some are common, such as the automated voice response system that replaces the receptionist, while others, such as document imaging systems, are less well known but also offer significant monetary savings. When using automation, it is important to first review the capital and ongoing costs of the new systems in comparison to the existing costs, to ensure that there is a sufficient pay back to make the projects worth the time and effort of installation and maintenance.

- *Provide training.* Too many companies make the mistake of assuming that their staffs need no extra training, and then even if they do, the company that foots the bill will not see an adequate return on its training dollars. To avoid these problems, a company should carefully compile a set of training classes for each job title, so that each person receives extremely job-specific information, rather than generic information that does not give a recipient much practical knowledge. By focusing on targeted training, it is much easier to improve the quality of employees, who return the favor by applying their new knowledge to improve the efficiency of their jobs.

- *Rearrange the workspace.* Most employees do not work in areas that allow them to complete the majority of their work while sitting in one place. Instead, they must walk to distant filing cabinets, copiers, or fax machines. By altering the office layout to reduce the amount of movement, a controller can achieve a significant productivity improvement. Sometimes, the best approach is to multiply the amount of inexpensive office equipment. For example, if someone is a heavy user of a copier, typewriter, or fax machine, then procure an inexpensive variety of each one of these office tools and set it up right next to that employee; some very low-end copiers are now so cheap that a controller can give one to every employee, if necessary.

- *Staff for low volume.* Some G&A functions have large swings in the volume of transactions they process, especially if the business is a seasonal one. If so, it may be possible to maintain a small core staff that handles a modest volume of work and then bring in temporary workers to cover the workload when the volume of work rises. This approach reduces the overall labor cost, although the temporary staff will be less efficient than the permanent employees, who are more experienced.

- *Benchmark G&A.* Once all of the preceding tasks have been completed, management should not become complacent and think that it has a world-class G&A function. Instead, this is an ideal time to benchmark a company's operations against those of companies who have become acknowledged masters in certain functional areas. Another way to collect benchmarking information is to use recommendations by the company's auditors, who see the operations of many companies, and can recommend practices used by other organizations. By seeing how much better these companies handle their G&A areas, management is spurred on to loop back through the preceding tasks and find better and better ways to improve the efficiency and effectiveness of the function.

- *Cross-train the staff.* Once a company has gone through several of the steps in this process, it will find that there are fewer people in the G&A area—so few in some areas that there may be only one person left with a knowledge of how a process works. To avoid the danger of losing this information with a departing employee, it now becomes important to cross-train employees in multiple functional areas. Also, this allows for further reductions, so that one employee can handle multiple functions.

There are a multitude of possibilities for reducing G&A costs. These options fall into three main categories. One is to question the underlying assumptions for incurring broad categories of costs. For example, there may be no need for any headquarters staff if the management philosophy is changed to emphasize control at a local level, rather than from headquarters. The next category is changes that target specific expenses, of which numerous examples were cited. Finally, one can focus on the overall efficiency of transactions, for which a variety of steps were noted; by following these steps, a controller can reduce the cycle time and cost of many G&A operations. Taken together, the steps noted in this section can have a dramatic impact on G&A expenses.

BUDGETING G&A EXPENSES

In most companies, G&A expense is not budgeted as a percentage of sales, since it is relatively fixed and does not vary with sales. However, many G&A functions can be viewed as step costs. For example, accounts receivable volume will decline as sales drop; if there is a signified reduction in sales volume, then the budget for a receivables position would be eliminated. On the other hand, there are many fixed costs. For example, director expenses are fixed, since the same number of board meetings will occur, no matter how much sales volume may vary.

However, there are many discretionary costs. Withholding expenditures on discretionary items can have a marked impact on profits, so a separate analysis of discretionary G&A costs should be made available to management, especially if profitability is expected to be a problem.

Areas where costs may verge on variable costs instead of step costs are the salaries of the payroll, cost accounting, cashier's, and internal audit departments.

The budget preparation procedure for G&A varies somewhat from the procedure used for production, since there is no budget for purchased materials, inventory, cost of goods sold, or direct labor. A typical G&A budget preparation procedure includes:

1. The controller or budget director makes available to each functional executive and/or department head, in either worksheet form or computer accessible data:

   (a) Actual year-to-date expenses and head count

   (b) Assumptions to be used for budgetary purposes: percent of pay raise, fringe benefit cost percent, inflation rate, generally acceptable rate of expense increase, etc.

   (c) Any relevant information on the business level, economic conditions, etc.

   (d) Instructions on preparing the planning budget

2. The department head completes the budget proposal and sends it to his supervisor for approval, who then forwards it to the budget director.

3. The individual department budget requests are reviewed by the budget director, checked for reasonableness and completeness, and, when acceptable, summarized for the central office by responsibility.

   When the aggregate G&A budget is accepted, it becomes part of the annual business plan.

4. Monthly, the department expenses—actual and budget—are compared by the department head, who takes corrective action where appropriate. This report shows any significant over- or underrun. Budget performance could also be reported on a graphic basis. This report also explains significant overruns. The monthly trend of performance, by group and in total, could be displayed in vertical bar chart or line graph. The entire group performance could be summarized as to budget and actual expense by natural expense category (salaries and wages, travel and entertainment, etc.).

8

PLANNING AND CONTROL OF CASH AND SHORT-TERM INVESTMENTS

INTRODUCTION

Most business executives have long been aware of the need for cash. Supplier bills must be paid by cash. Payrolls must be met with cash. The ability of an entity to generate adequate cash has assumed more importance. Witness the attention given cash flow in leveraged buy-outs (LBOs) or other proposed mergers or acquisitions. Or consider the standard issued by the Financial Accounting Standards Board (FASB) for cash flow reporting—FAS No. 95, Statement of Cash Flows.

In any event, sound cash management is a basic financial function. While it is usually the responsibility of the senior financial officer, the controller has an important role to play. This chapter reviews the phases that the controller either handles or has a direct interest in:

- Cash planning, with emphasis on the annual plan
- Some aspects of cash control, including internal control
- Limited comments on temporary investments, given their close relationship to cash

OBJECTIVES OF CASH PLANNING AND CONTROL

Cash is a particularly vulnerable asset because, without proper controls, it is easily con-cealed and readily negotiable. But it is something every business needs. From an overall viewpoint, cash management would have these six objectives:

1. Provision of adequate cash for operations—both short and long term
2. Effective utilization of company funds at all times
3. Establishment of accountability for cash receipts and provision of adequate safe-guards until the funds are placed in the company depository
4. Establishment of controls to ensure that disbursements are made only for approved and legitimate purposes
5. Maintenance of adequate bank balances, where appropriate, to support proper com-mercial bank relations
6. Maintenance of adequate cash records

DUTIES OF THE CONTROLLER VERSUS THE TREASURER

With respect to cash management, a cooperative relationship should exist between the controller and treasurer. Duties and responsibilities will vary, depending on the type and size of the business firm. Under ordinary circumstances, the treasury staff has custody of cash funds and administers the bank accounts. Usually, it is the treasurer who is responsible for maintaining good relations with banks and other investors, providing the timely interest and principal payments on borrowed debt, and investing the excess cash. The treasurer usually would have primary responsibility for cash receipts and disbursement procedures.

The controller may have these responsibilities in companies large enough for separate treasury and controllership functions:

- Development of some, or all, of the cash forecasts
- Review of the internal control system with respect to both receipts and disbursements to assure its adequacy and effectiveness
- Reconciliation of bank accounts—as part of a sound internal control system (and not to be done by members of the treasurer's department who have access to funds or by accounting personnel who record the transactions)
- As may be deemed appropriate, preparation of selected cash reports

THE CASH FORECAST

Purposes of Cash Forecasting

A *cash forecast,* or cash plan, or cash budget, is a projection of the anticipated cash receipts and disbursements and the resulting cash balance within a specified period. This is a necessary function in any well-managed plan of cash administration.

The operation of any business must be planned within the limits of available funds, and, conversely, the necessary funds must be provided to carry out the planned business operations.

In these days of increasing sales and earnings, and taxes, business management is rediscovering that profits are not the same as cash in the bank. The company may show a small profit, or even a loss, and have a very sizable cash balance. Particularly in those industries requiring heavy capital investment, the cash generation by the operations, the "cash flow," may be very heavy and yet result in mediocre profits. For reasons such as these, cash forecasting is being recognized as a vital management function.

The basic purpose behind the preparation of the cash budget is to plan so that the business will have the necessary cash—whether from the short-term or long-term viewpoint. Further, when excess cash is to be available, budget preparation offers a means of anticipating an opportunity for effective utilization. Aside from these general purposes, some specific uses to which a cash budget may be put are:

- To point out peaks or seasonal fluctuations in business activity that necessitate larger investments in inventories and receivables
- To indicate the time and extent of funds needed to meet maturing obligations, tax payments, and dividend or interest payments
- To assist in planning for growth, including the required funds for plant expansion and working capital
- To indicate well in advance of needs the extent and duration of funds required from outside sources and thus permit the securing of more advantageous loans

- To assist in securing credit from banks and improve the general credit position of the business
- To determine the extent and probable duration of funds available for investment
- To plan the reduction of bonded indebtedness or other loans
- To coordinate the financial needs of the subsidiaries and divisions of the company
- To permit the company to take advantage of cash discounts and forward purchasing, thereby increasing its earnings

Cash Forecasting Methods

At least two methods are in widespread use for developing a cash forecast. Although the end product is the estimated cash balance, the methods differ chiefly in terms of the starting point of the forecast and the detail made available. These two techniques are described as:

1. *Direct estimate of cash receipts and disbursements.* This is a detailed forecast of each cost element or function involving cash. It is essentially a projection of the cash records. Such a method is the one most commonly used in business and is quite essential to giving a complete picture of the swings or gyrations in both receipts and disbursements. It is particularly applicable to those concerns subject to wide variations in activity. Moreover, it is very useful for controlling cash flow by comparing actual and forecasted performance. A cash forecast prepared on this basis is shown in Exhibit 8.1. The individual line items will depend on what items are significant, and/or on those in which the management is especially interested— presuming the actual data are also readily available from the cash records for comparing budget with actual results. The cash inflows and outflows from operations are shown; thus, management can easily see the cash flow generated by operations, and the cash flows from investing activities and financing activities are readily determinable.If changes in the annual plan (e.g., sales) cause adjustments in cash flow, the use of the computer for this detailed cash planning makes such modifications rather easy.

2. *Adjusted net income (or indirect or reconciliation) method.* As the name implies, the starting point for this procedure is the estimated income and expense statement. This projected net income is adjusted for all noncash transactions to arrive at the cash income or loss and is further adjusted for cash transactions that arise because of non-operating balance sheet changes. A worksheet showing the general method is illustrated in Exhibit 8.2.

    Because net income is used, the true extent of the gross cash receipts or disbursements is not known. Where a company must work on rather close cash margins, this method probably will not meet the needs. It is applicable chiefly where sales volume is relatively stable and the out-of-pocket costs are fairly constant in relation to sales.

    This format identifies the cash flows according to source—from operating activities, from investing activities, or from financing activities. This segregation is that suggested by the FASB for inclusion in published financial statements. It may or may not be used for internal planning purposes. If this style is utilized, it permits management to readily see the relative size of each estimated cash flow source approximately as it will appear in the annual report to shareholders.

THE MANUFACTURING COMPANY
STATEMENT OF ESTIMATED CASH RECEIPTS AND DISBURSEMENTS
FOR PLAN YEAR 20XX
(DOLLARS IN THOUSANDS)

Item	January	February	March	First Quarter Total	December	Fourth Quarter Total	Year Total
Cash and cash equivalents at beginning of period	$1,330	$756	$842	$1,330	$2,339	$7,245	$1,330
Cash receipts							
From operations:							
Collections on account	2,985	3,255	3,975	10,215	4,087	12,413	47,946
Cash sales	70	40	110	220	200	710	1,730
Interest receivable	20	20	15	55	20	50	205
Insurance proceeds	—	—	360	360	—	—	360
Miscellaneous	20	20	20	60	20	20	240
Total from operations	3,095	3,335	4,480	10,910	4,327	13,233	50,481
From other activities:							
Common stock issue	—	2,000	2,000	—	—	2,000	
Short-term borrowings	—	—	500	500	3,725	3,725	7,725
Long-term debt issue	—	—	1,000	1,000	—	—	1,000
Total from other activities	—	—	3,500	3,500	3,725	3,725	7,725
Total cash receipts	3,095	3,335	7,980	14,410	8,052	16,958	58,206
Total cash available	4,425	4,091	8,822	15,740	10,391	24,203	59,536

EXHIBIT 8.1 STATEMENT OF ESTIMATED CASH RECEIPTS AND DISBURSEMENT

THE MANUFACTURING COMPANY
STATEMENT OF ESTIMATED CASH RECEIPTS AND DISBURSEMENTS
FOR PLAN YEAR 20XX
(DOLLARS IN THOUSANDS)

Item	January	February	March	First Quarter Total	December	Fourth Quarter Total	Year Total
Cash disbursements							
For operations							
Accounts payable and accrued items	1,972	2,117	2,300	6,389	1,865	5,806	24,089
Payrolls	1,096	1,067	1,240	3,403	1,380	4,610	13,700
Interest	—	—	150	150	600	710	2,170
Federal and state income taxes	185	—	—	185	3,100	3,100	7,185
Total from operations	3,253	3,184	3,690	10,127	6,945	14,226	47,144
For other activities							
Repayment on long-term debt	416	65	500	981	—	1,081	3,496
Dividends	—	—	650	650	650	2,600	2,600
Capital expenditures	—	—	2,000	2,000	—	3,500	3,500
Total for other activities	416	65	3,150	3,631	650	7,181	9,596
Total cash disbursements	$3,669	3,249	6,840	13,758	7,595	21,407	56,740
Cash and cash equivalents at end of period	756	$ 842	1,982	1,982	$ 2,796	$ 2,796	$ 2,796

EXHIBIT 8.1 STATEMENT OF ESTIMATED CASH RECEIPTS AND DISBURSEMENT *(CONTINUED)*

THE RANDOM COMPANY
STATEMENT OF ESTIMATED CASH FLOWS
FOR PLAN YEAR 20XX
(DOLLARS IN THOUSANDS)

Item	January	February	March	First Quarter Total	December	Fourth Quarter Total	Year Total
Cash Flows from Operating Activities							
Net income	$ 500	$ 450	$ 600	$ 1,500	$ 800	$ 2,100	$ 7,000
Adjustments (all related to operations)							
Depreciation and amortization	20	20	20	60	25	75	265
Provision for losses on accounts receivable	10	8	12	30	15	40	125
Increase in receivables	(12)	(14)	(14)	(40)	(5)	(10)	(90)
Decrease in inventories	20	10	30	60	10	20	110
Decrease in accounts payable and accrued items	(70)	(10)	(20)	(100)	(20)	(40)	(220)
Increase in income taxes payable	10	10	10	30	10	30	120
Increase in other liabilities	5	5	5	15	—	5	30
Total adjustments	(17)	29	43	55	35	120	340
Net cash provided by operating activities	483	479	643	1,605	835	2,220	7,340

EXHIBIT 8.2 STATEMENT OF ESTIMATED CASH FLOWS (INDIRECT METHOD)

THE RANDOM COMPANY
STATEMENT OF ESTIMATED CASH FLOWS
FOR PLAN YEAR 20XX
(DOLLARS IN THOUSANDS)

Item	January	February	March	First Quarter Total	December	Fourth Quarter Total	Year Total
Cash flows from investing activities							
Purchases of companies M and P, net of Cash acquired	—	—	(700)	(700)	—	—	(2,575)
Capital expenditures	(100)	(300)	(2,100)	(2,500)	(200)	(400)	(3,300)
Proceeds-sale of facility	70	—	—	70	—	—	70
Net cash used in investing activities	(30)	(300)	(2,800)	(3,130)	(200)	(400)	(5,805)
Cash Flows from Financing Activities							
Proceeds for long-term debt	—	—	1,000	1,000	—	—	1,000
Proceeds from stock issue	—	—	2,000	2,000	—	—	1,000
Dividends paid	—	—	(600)	(600)	(650)	(650)	(2,550)
Net cash flows provided by financing activities	—	—	2,400	2,400	(650)	(650)	(550)
Net change in cash and equivalents	453	179	243	875	(15)	1,170	(550)
Cash and cash equivalents at beginning of period	1,400	1,853	2,032	1,400	2,400	1,215	1,400
Estimated cash and cash equivalents at end of period	$ 1,853	$ 2,032	$ 2,275	$ 2,275	$ 2,385	$ 2,385	$ 2,385

EXHIBIT 8.2 STATEMENT OF ESTIMATED CASH FLOWS (INDIRECT METHOD) *(CONTINUED)*

Estimating Cash Receipts

The sources of cash receipts for the typical industrial or commercial firm are well known: collections on account, cash sales, royalties, rent, dividends, sale of capital items, sale of investments, and new financing. These items can be predicted with reasonable accuracy. Usually, the most important recurring sources are collections on account and cash sales. Experience and a knowledge of trends will indicate what share of total sales probably will be for cash. From the sales forecast, then, the total cash sales value can be determined. In a somewhat similar fashion, information can be gleaned from the records to enable the controller to make a careful estimate of collections.

Once the experience has been analyzed, the results can be adjusted for trends and applied to the credit sales portrayed in the sales forecast.

An example illustrates the technique. Assume that an analysis of collection experience for June sales revealed the following collection data:

Description	% of Total Credit Sales
Collected in June	2.1
July	85.3
August	8.9
September	2.8
October	.3
Cash discounts	.5
Bad debt losses	.1
Total	$ 100.0

If next year's sales in June could be expected to fall into the same pattern, then application of the percentages to estimated June credit sales would determine the probable monthly distribution of collections. The same analysis applied to each month of the year would result in a reasonably reliable basis for collection forecasting. The worksheet (June column) for cash collections might look somewhat as:

	Description		
Month of Sale	% Total	Net Sales	June Collections
February	.4	$149,500	$ 598
March	1.9	160,300	3,045
April	7.7	290,100	22,338
May	88.3	305,400	269,668
June	2.1	320,000	6,720
Total collections			302,369
Cash discounts (May)	.5	305,400	(1,527)
Losses	.1		(320)
Total			$ 300,522

Anticipated discounts must be calculated, since they enter into the profit forecast.

These experience factors must be modified, not only by trends developed over a period of time but also by the estimate of general business conditions as reflected in collections, as well as contemplated changes in terms of sale or other credit policies. Refinements in the approach can be made if experience varies widely between geographical territories, types of customers, or channels of distribution. The analysis of collections need not be made every month; it is sufficient if the distribution is checked occasionally.

Exhibit 8.3 is an example of a typical statement of estimated cash receipts by customer type. In this instance receipts from particular contracts are set out in addition to the usual collections from customer sales.

Estimating Cash Disbursements

If a complete operating budget is available, the controller should have little difficulty assembling the data into an estimate of cash disbursements. The usual cash disbursements in the typical industrial or commercial firm consist of salaried and hourly payrolls, materials, taxes, dividends, traveling expense, other operating expenses, interest, purchase of equipment, and retirement of stock.

From the labor budget, the manufacturing expense budget, and the commercial expense budget, the total anticipated expense for salaries and wages can be secured. Once this figure is available, the period of cash disbursement can be determined easily, for payrolls must be met on certain dates, closely following the time when earned. Reference to a calendar will establish the pay dates. Separate consideration should be given to the tax deductions from the gross pay, since these are not payable at the same time the net payroll is disbursed—unless special bank accounts are established for the tax deductions.

The material budget will set out the material requirements each month. The more important elements probably should be treated individually (e.g., power units or engines). Other items will be grouped together. Only in a few instances is material purchased for cash. However, reference to required inventories and to delivery dates as well as assistance from the purchasing department will establish the time allowed for payments. If 30 days are required, then usage of one month can be moved forward for the purpose of estimating cash payments. The effect of cash discounts should be considered in arriving at the estimated disbursements.

The various manufacturing and operating expenses should be considered individually because they are by no means all the same. Some are prepayments or accruals, paid annually, such as property taxes and insurance. Some are noncash items, such as depreciation expense or bad debts. For a large number of individually small items, such as supplies, telephone and telegraph, and traveling expense, an average time lag may be used.

Cash requirements for capital additions should be determined from the plant budget or other known plans. No particular difficulty presents itself because the needs are relatively fixed and are established by the board of directors or other authority.

Usual practice requires the determination of cash receipts and disbursements exclusive of transactions involving voluntary debt retirements, purchase of treasury stock, or funds from bank loans. Decisions relative to these means of securing or disbursing cash are reached when the cash position is known and policy formulated accordingly. When branch plants are involved, all such outlying activities must be consolidated to get the overall picture.

A typical cash disbursements budget is illustrated in Exhibit 8.4, with a format found practical for estimating purposes. The treatment of payments on other than a monthly basis is shown.

CONSOLIDATED ELECTRONICS CORPORATION
STATEMENT OF ESTIMATED CASH RECEIPTS
FOR THE PERIOD JANUARY 1, 20XX THROUGH MARCH 31, 20XX

Description	January	February	March	Total
Electronics				
Fixed Price Contracts				
U.S. Government				
Progress Payments	$625,000	$820,000	$1,150,000	$2,595,000
Collections on delivery	333,500	470,200	695,000	1,498,700
Total	958,500	1,290,200	1,845,000	4,093,700
Foreign governments				
Advances	21,500	—	10,000	31,500
Collections on delivery	32,500	21,000	8,500	62,000
Miscellaneous	8,000	6,000	5,200	19,200
Total	62,000	27,000	23,700	112,700
Total receipts—FP contracts	1,020,500	1,317,200	1,868,700	4,206,400
Incentive—Commercial				
Refinery				
Advances from customers	20,000	—	—	20,000
Collections on account	35,900	39,500	28,000	103,400 ·
Cash sales	4,300	4,000	4,500	12,800
Total	60,200	43,500	32,500	136,200
Automotive				
Advances from customers	890,000	410,000	300,000	1,600,000
Collections on delivery	245,000	390,000	250,000	885,000
Total	1,135,000	800,000	550,000	2,485,000
Total collections—electronics	2,215,700	2,160,700	2,451,200	6,827,600
Heavy Machine Tools				
Petroleum				
Deposits	5,500	—	2,000	7,500
Collections on account	8,300	9,200	6,400	23,900
Cash sales	2,000	2,000	2,000	6,000
Total	15,800	11,200	10,400	37,400
Chemical				
Collections on account	12,500	11,300	8,100	31,900
Deposits	500	200	300	1,000
Cash sales	1,000	750	500	2,250
Total	14,000	12,250	8,900	35,150
Total machine tools collections	29,800	23,450	19,300	72,550
Miscellaneous	1,000	1,000	1,000	3,000
Total cash receipts	$ 2,246,500	$ 2,185,150	$ 2,471,500	$ 6,903,150

EXHIBIT 8.3   STATEMENT OF ESTIMATED CASH RECEIPTS BY SOURCE

CONSOLIDATED SPACECRAFT CORPORATION
STATEMENT OF ESTIMATED CASH DISBURSEMENTS
FOR THE PERIOD JANUARY 1 THROUGH DECEMBER 31, 20XX

Description	January	February	March	November	December	Total
Inventory Items						
Raw Material and Purchased Parts						
Project 615						
Power units	$1,350,000	$1,325,000	$1,375,000	$1,300,000	$1,300,000	$15,840,000
Landing gears	325,000	325,000	320,000	325,000	415,000	3,900,000
Radios	115,000	117,500	117,500	115,000	115,000	1,380,000
Tires and tubes	120,000	110,000	110,000	110,000	122,500	1,320,000
Other	35,000	30,000	35,000	30,000	25,000	360,000
Total	1,945,000	1,907,500	1,957,500	1,880,000	1,997,500	22,800,000
Project 616						
Power units	80,000	76,000	84,000	160,000	168,000	1,200,000
Radios	10,000	10,000	12,000	24,000	30,000	132,000
Other	4,000	3,500	5,000	10,000	12,000	72,000
Total	94,000	89,500	101,000	194,000	210,000	1,404,000
Total Raw Materials and Purchased Parts	2,039,000	1,997,000	2,058,500	2,074,000	2,187,500	24,204,000
Subcontracted Production						
Project 615	420,000	510,000	480,000	105,000	120,000	3,600,000
Project 616	20,000	10,000	10,000	—	23,000	150,000
Total Subcontracted Production	440,000	520,000	490,000	105,000	143,000	3,750,000

EXHIBIT 8.4 STATEMENT OF ESTIMATED CASH DISBURSEMENTS

CONSOLIDATED SPACECRAFT CORPORATION
STATEMENT OF ESTIMATED CASH DISBURSEMENTS
FOR THE PERIOD JANUARY 1 THROUGH DECEMBER 31, 20XX

Description	January	February	March	November	December	Total
Expenses						
Salaries and wages—direct	560,000	458,000	562,000	657,000	665,000	7,380,000
Salaries and wages—indirect	36,500	36,000	36,500	36,000	37,000	432,000
Total salaries and wages	596,500	494,000	598,500	693,000	702,000	7,812,000
Payroll taxes, etc.	35,900	31,300	37,800	24,900	18,400	373,000
Property taxes	—	—	122,000	—	—	122,000
Property insurance	—	72,500	—	—	—	72,500
Supplies	2,000	1,800	2,100	2,000	2,000	22,800
Other	11,000	11,000	11,000	11,000	11,000	132,000
Total Expenses	645,400	610,600	771,400	730,900	733,400	8,534,300
Total Inventory Items	3,124,400	3,127,600	3,319,900	2,909,900	3,063,900	36,488,300
Other Cash Disbursements						
Administrative expense	12,000	12,000	17,000	15,500	12,000	168,000
Selling and advertising	17,000	12,000	45,000	11,500	22,500	310,000
Advances to vendors	20,500	—	—	—	—	20,500
Additions to fixed assets	101,000	51,000	19,500	—	17,000	397,500
Other	2,000	2,000	3,000	3,000	2,000	30,000
Total	152,500	77,000	84,500	30,000	53,500	926,000
Total Cash Disbursements	$ 3,276,900	$ 3,204,600	$ 3,404,400	$ 2,939,900	$ 3,117,400	$ 37,414,300

EXHIBIT 8.4 STATEMENT OF ESTIMATED CASH DISBURSEMENTS *(CONTINUED)*

FASB Statement of Financial Accounting Standards No. 95: Statement of Cash Flows

Having discussed the two methods in general use for estimating cash flows, it may be appropriate to review the standard issued by the FASB relating to statements of cash flow. It could be relevant to the cash forecasting process if management desires that the internal estimating procedure closely parallel the format to be used in reporting cash flow to the investor or security analysts and others.

The cash reporting procedure prior to this standard in many instances suffered from these weaknesses:

- *No common definition of cash.* Should it include cash equivalents, compensating balances, postdated checks, and so forth?
- *No common format.* The format for the issuance of a cash flow statement was not distinguished from the statement of changes in financial condition.
- In many instances, it was difficult to identify the cash flows from normal operating activity. (They were combined with other cash producing/generating activities.) Thus, the potential investor was at a disadvantage in gauging the cash generating potential of the normal everyday activities.

The complete FASB Statement of Financial Accounting Standards No. 95, Statement of Cash Flows should be reviewed in its entirety by the controller. Though lengthy, the standard should be useful for many reasons, including:

- It provides examples of the cash flow formats that meet the standard for general purpose external financial accounting and reporting.
- It includes the many helpful definitions regarding cash flows from the three basic sources: operating, investing, and financing activities.
- It contains useful background data on cash flow statements and the basis of the FASB for reaching the conclusions it did.
- In addition to examples of statements of cash flow for a domestic manufacturing company, it provides an example of a statement of cash flows under the direct method for a domestic manufacturing company with foreign operations.

Some examples of current reporting practices are provided later in this chapter.

Relation of Cash Budget to Other Budgets

From the preceding discussion, it is readily apparent that preparation of the cash budget is generally dependent on other budgets—the sales forecast, the statement of estimated income and expense, the various operating budgets, the capital budget, and the long-range strategic plan. It is in reality part of a coordinated program of sales and costs correlated with business sheet changes and expected revenues and expenditures.

It can be appreciated, also, that the cash budget is a check on the entire budgetary program. If the operating budget goals are achieved, the results will be reflected in the cash position. Failure to achieve budgeted performance may result in the treasurer seeking additional sources of cash.

Depending on the financial position of the company, the cash forecast may have a high priority. Many executives prefer to review the cash forecast ahead of other projected statements, and it may, therefore, take the number one spot in the complete report on expected operations.

Length of Cash Budget Period

The length of the budget period depends on several factors, including the purpose the budget is to serve, the financial condition of the company, and the opinion of the executives about the practicality and accuracy of estimating. For illustration, a short-term forecast would be used in determining cash requirements, perhaps for one to three months in advance. But if the cash margin is low, an estimate of cash receipts and disbursements may be necessary on a weekly basis or even daily. On the other hand, a firm with ample cash may develop a cash forecast, by months, for six months, or a year in advance. For the determination of general financial policy a longer-term budget is necessary. Some companies feel that estimating beyond three months is inaccurate and restrict the cash budget to this period. Other companies maintain a running budget for three or more months in advance, always adding one month and dropping off the present month. A controller will have to adapt forecasting to the existing conditions. It may be necessary to prepare a short-term cash budget for cash requirements purposes and also a long-term forecast for use in financial policy decisions.

Putting the Cash Budget to Work

The controller can prepare the cash budget in the usual manner, indicating the extent of additional cash funds needed, if any, and the probable duration of such need. However, the responsibility for securing these funds on the most advantageous basis rests with the treasurer or chief financial officer. The treasurer, and not the chief accounting officer, would usually negotiate with banks for loans, or would invest surplus funds. Yet the part played by the controller is not always as routine as might appear. In times of adversity, the controller must be prepared to furnish extra information. Thus the treasurer may need to know the exact cash needs of the following week. This can be furnished by manually adding the bills payable at that time, as well as the payrolls. If the accounts payable are in the computer file, the requirements can be readily determined by tabulating the applicable due date file. The same procedure can be used in determining the funds, if any, to be transferred to each branch for the weekly period.

Cash requirements must be planned just as other operations are planned. It simply is not satisfactory to assume that a high volume of sales will automatically result in a sound financial position or that with a satisfactory budgeted profit and loss statement finances will take care of themselves. The controller can be an effective voice in establishing the necessity for a well-developed financial program.

CASH COLLECTIONS

Administration of Cash Receipts

One of the primary objectives of financial management is the conservation and effective utilization of cash. From the cash collection viewpoint, there are two phases of control: (1) the acceleration of collections, and (2) proper internal control of collections.

Acceleration of Cash Receipts

Two methods are commonly used to speed up the collection of receivables: the lockbox system and area concentration banking. The lockbox system involves the establishment of depository accounts in the various geographical areas of significant cash collections so that remittances from customers will take less time in transit, preferably not more than one day.

Customers mail remittances to the company at a locked post office box in the region served by the bank. The bank collects the remittances and deposits the proceeds to the account of the company. Funds in excess of those required to cover costs are periodically transferred to company headquarters. Supporting documents accompanying remittances are mailed by the bank to the company. Collections are thus accelerated through reduction in transit time with resultant lower credit exposure. Arrangements must be made, however, for proper control of credit information.

Under the system of area concentration banking, local company units collect remittances and deposit them in the local bank. From the local bank, usually by wire transfers, expeditious movement of funds is made to a few area or regional concentration banks. Funds in excess of compensating balances are automatically transferred by wire to the company's banking headquarters. By this technique in-transit time is reduced.

The controller is expected to be aware of these and other devices for accelerating collections, and to assist the treasurer, should that be necessary.

While checks are the predominant means of collecting accounts receivable, an increasing amount of business is handled through electronic fund transfer (EFT). Moreover, there are various combinations of methods and instruments that speed collections:

- Lockbox
- Depository transfer check (DTC)
- Preauthorized draft (PAD)
- Automated clearinghouse (ACH) transfer (from one bank to another through the ACH system)
- Wire transfer

"Reports on Cash" on page 229 includes limited comments on the employment of the new technology in use and services that might be expected from the company's banking institutions.

Internal Control of Cash Receipts

In most business organizations, the usual routine cash transactions are numerous. The following sources are typical: mail receipts, over-the-counter cash sales, sales or collections made by salesmen, solicitors, and so on, and over-the-counter collections on account. Naturally, all businesses have other cash transactions of a less routine nature, such as receipts from the sale of fixed assets, that may be handled by the officers or require special procedures. Most of the cash problems will be found to center on the transactions just listed, because the more unusual or less voluminous cash receipts are readily susceptible to a simple check.

Regardless of the source of cash, the very basis for the prevention of errors or fraud is the principle of internal check. Such a system involves the separation of the actual handling of cash from the records relating to cash. It requires that the work of one employee be supplemented by the work of another. Certain results must always agree. For example, the daily cash deposit must be the same as the charge to the cash control account. This automatic checking of the work of one employee by another clearly discourages fraud and locates errors. Under such conditions, any peculations are generally restricted to cases of carelessness or collusion.

The system of internal control must be designed on the groundwork of the individual organization. However, there are some general suggestions that will be helpful to the controller in reviewing the situation:

- All receipts of cash through the mail should be recorded in advance of transfer to the cashier. Periodically, these records should be traced to the deposit slip.

- All receipts should be deposited intact daily. This procedure might also require a duplicate deposit slip to be sent by the bank or person making the deposit (other than the cashier) to an independent department—for use in subsequent check or audit.

- Responsibility for handling of cash should be clearly defined and definitely fixed.

- Usually, the functions of receiving cash and disbursing cash should be kept entirely separate (except in financial institutions).

- The actual handling of cash should be entirely separate from the maintenance of records, and the cashiers should not have access to these records.

- Tellers, agents, and field representatives should be required to give receipts, retaining a duplicate, of course.

- Bank reconciliations should be made by those not handling cash or keeping the records. Similarly, the mailing of statements to customers, including the check-off against the ledger accounts, should be done by a third party. The summarizing of cash records also may be handled by a third party.

- All employees handling cash or cash records should be required to take a periodic vacation, and someone else should handle the job during such absence. Also, at unannounced times, employees should be shifted in jobs to detect or prevent collusion.

- All employees handling cash or cash records should be adequately bonded.

- Mechanical and other protective devices should be used where applicable to give added means of check—cash registers, the tape being read by a third party; duplicate sales slips; daily cash blotters.

- Where practical, cash sales should be verified by means of inventory records and periodic physical inventories.

Illustrative Cash Receipts Procedure

A simple and effective cash receipts procedure can be executed that embodies some of the controls mentioned in the preceding section and that is adaptable by most industrial firms receiving cash by mail. All incoming mail not addressed to a specific individual is opened in the mailroom. Any mail containing remittances is listed on a daily remittance sheet prepared in triplicate. The name, check number, date, and amount are detailed on the record (Exhibit 8.5). One copy is forwarded, with the envelopes and remittance slips, to the cashier; a second goes to the auditor, treasurer, or controller; and the third copy is retained by the mailroom. The cashier records the cash received via the mailroom on a daily cash sheet or computer recording (Exhibit 8.6), indicating the nature of the receipt, along with any other receipts from other sources. This cash record is subsequently sent to the accounting department for posting, details as well as summary, after the cashier has made a summary entry. The deposit slip is prepared in quadruplicate. The cashier retains one copy. Three copies go to the bank for receipting, one of which is retained by the bank; another is returned to the cashier as evidence the bank received the funds; and a third is sent to the auditing department or controller's office. This is then compared in total, and occasionally in detail, with the daily cash register. The remittance sheet is also test-checked against the deposit slip. The cashier, of course, does not have access to the accounts receivable records, general ledger, or disbursements.

These basic methods may be adapted, in large degree, to personal computer systems.

The Blank Company
MAILROOM REMITTANCE SHEET
Receipts of   July 19, 20XX

Check No., etc.	Source if Not Check	Sender	City and State	Amount
1602		The Rush Airplane Company	Scranton, Pa.	$ 126.12
195692	P.M.O.	Rentaul Air Service	Stamford, Conn.	19.50
2402		Automatic Service Company	Los Angeles, Calif.	316.00
1613		Voe Parts Dealer	Toledo, Ohio	2.90
9865		Brush Electric Company	Chicago, Ill.	25.50
2915		Ajax Manufacturing Company	Cleveland, Ohio	1,002.60
8512		Apex Machine Tool Co.	New York City	18.60

Total.. $1,511.22

Prepared by __J. J. B.__
Date __7/19/XX__

Original: Cashier

EXHIBIT 8.5   MAILROOM REMITTANCE SHEET

Common Methods of Misappropriating Cash

An enumeration of some of the more common methods of misappropriating company funds may be a guide to the controller in recognizing points to guard against:

1. Mail receipts
   (a) Lapping—diverting cash and reporting it some time after it has been collected; usually, funds received from one account are credited against another account from which cash has been diverted earlier
   (b) Borrowing funds temporarily, without falsifying any records, or simply not recording all cash received
   (c) Falsifying totals in the cashbook
   (d) Overstating discounts and allowances
   (e) Charging off a customer's account as a bad debt and pocketing the cash
   (f) Withholding of miscellaneous income, such as insurance refunds

DAILY CASH SHEET

Date April 20, 20xx

Check No.	Description	Debit Cash (101)	Trade Accounts Receivable (108)	Deposits (104)	Cash Sales (501)	Employees Accounts Receivable (106)	Credit Other — Account	Description	Amount
1242	Jones Chemical Co.	$ 622.50	$ —	$ —	$ 622.50	$ —			$ —
846	Witmer Candy Co.	9,875.00	9,875.00						
101	Prescott Molding Co.	4,322.50	4,322.50						
10	Rush Mfg. Co.	12,500.00		12,500.00					
322	Monsanto Cyanamid Co.	16,321.50	16,321.50						
464	Laughlin Stamping Co.	421.12			421.12				
422	Aero Company	3,820.00	3,820.00						
	Marjorie Jones	16.00				16.00			
	Adela Castle	1.20				1.20			
	Pierre's Restaurant	19.70					662	Vending Machine Income	19.70
	Total	$47,919.52	$34,339.00	$12,500.00	$1,043.6	$17.20			$19.70

EXHIBIT 8.6 DAILY CASH SHEET

2. Over-the-counter sales

   (a) Failing to report all sales and pocketing the cash

   (b) Underadding the sales slip and pocketing the difference

   (c) Falsely representing refunds or expenditures

   (d) Registering a smaller amount than the true amount of sale

   (e) Pocketing cash overages

3. Collections by salespeople

   (a) Conversion of checks made payable to "cash"

   (b) Failure to report sales

   (c) Overstating amount of trade-ins

Where adequate internal control is used, most of these practices cannot be carried on without collusion.

Other Means of Detecting Fraud

In addition to the segregation of duties that has been described, certain other practices may be adopted to further deter any would-be peculator or embezzler. One of these tools is surprise audits by the internal auditor as well as by the public accountants. Another is the prompt follow-up of past-due accounts. Proper instructions to customers about where checks should be mailed, and a specific request that they be made payable to the company, and not to any individual, also will help. Bonding of all employees, with a detailed check of references, is a measure of protection. Special checking of unusual receipts of a miscellaneous nature will tend to discourage irregularities.

For additional comments on internal control and fraud prevention, see Chapter 7.

CASH DISBURSEMENTS

Control of Cash Disbursements

In this area of cash administration, also, there are two aspects of control: (1) the timing of payments, and (2) the system of internal control.

Experience indicates the value of maintaining careful controls over the timing of disbursements to ensure that bills are paid only as they are due and not before. In such a manner, cash can be conserved for temporary investment.

Another consideration in payment scheduling is the conscious use of cash "float." By recognizing in-transit items and the fact that ordinarily bank balances are greater than book balances because of checks not cleared, book balances of cash may be planned at lower levels. The incoming float may be balanced against the outgoing payments.

The relationship between the time a check is released to the payee and the time it clears the bank, the disbursement float, is made up of three elements:

1. The time needed for the check to travel by mail or other delivery from the issuer to the payee

2. The time required by the payee to process the check

3. The period required by the banking system to clear the check, that is, the time from deposit by the payee to the time the item is charged to the issuer's account

In controlling this "float," it often is helpful to trace the time interval of large checks to estimate the proper allowance for the period required for checks to clear. The controller should take measures to assure there is no abuse of float (e.g., writing of checks on banks in some remote location far from the recipient's address, so as to secure an additional three or four days of float).

Administrative Bank Accounts

In the control of disbursements, particularly where subsidiary or field office divisional transactions are involved, several special purpose bank accounts may be used (e.g., imprest accounts, zero balance accounts, and automatic balance accounts).

Under an imprest system, the unit operates with a fixed maximum balance. Periodically, such as weekly, or when the fund is below a minimum level, receipted bills are submitted for reimbursement.

With a zero balance account system, the clearing account for the organizational segment is kept at a zero balance. When checks are presented for payment, arrangements are such that the bank is authorized to transfer funds from the corporate general account to cover the items. Payment may be made by draft. Comparable arrangements can be made for the treasurer to make wire transfers to the zero bank account on notification of the items being presented for payment. Zero bank balance arrangements can facilitate control of payments through one or a limited number of accounts. The system may facilitate a quick check of the corporate cash position.

Automatic balance accounts use the same account for receipts and disbursements. When the account is above a specified maximum level, the excess funds are transferred to the central bank account; conversely, when the balance drops below a minimum level, the bank may call for replenishment.

INTERNAL CONTROL

Importance of Internal Control

Once the cash has been deposited in the bank, it would seem that the major problem of safeguarding the cash has been solved. Control of cash disbursements is a relatively simple matter—if a few rules are followed. After the vendor's invoice has been approved for payment, the next step usually is the preparation of the check for executive signature. If all disbursements are subject to this top review, how can any problem exist? Yet it is at precisely this point that the greatest danger is met. Any controller who has had to sign numerous checks knows that it is indeed an irksome task—the review to ascertain that receiving reports are attached, the checking of payee against the invoice, and the comparison of amounts. Because it is such a monotonous chore, it is often done in a most perfunctory manner. Yet this operation, carefully done, is essential to the control of disbursements. Where two signatures are required, both signatures need not make the detailed review, but certainly one should. The other can review on a spot-check basis only. There are too many instances where false documents and vouchers used a second time have been the means of securing executive signatures. Prevention of this practice demands careful review before signing checks, as well as other safeguards. It cannot be taken for granted that everything is all right. Those who sign the checks must adopt a questioning attitude on every transaction that appears doubtful or is not fully understood. Indeed, the review of documents attached to checks will often bring to light foolish expenditures and weaknesses in other procedures.

Some Principles of Internal Control

The opportunities for improper or incorrect use of funds are so great that a controller cannot unduly emphasize the need for proper safeguards in the cash disbursement function. Vigilance and sound audit procedures are necessary. Although the system of internal control must be tailored to fit the needs of the organization, some general suggestions may be helpful:

- Except for petty cash transactions, all disbursements should be made by check.
- All checks should be prenumbered, and all numbers accounted for as either used or voided.
- All general disbursement checks for amounts in excess of $x (e.g., $5000) should require two signatures.
- Responsibility for cash receipts should be divorced from responsibility for cash disbursements.
- All persons signing checks or approving disbursements should be adequately bonded.
- Bank reconciliations should be made by those who do not sign checks or approve payments.
- The keeping of cash records should be entirely separate from the handling of cash disbursements.
- Properly approved invoices and other required supporting documents should be a prerequisite to making every disbursement.
- Checks for reimbursement of imprest funds and payrolls should be made payable to the individual and not to the company or bearer.
- After payment has been made, all supporting documents should be perforated or otherwise mutilated or marked "paid" to prevent reuse.
- Mechanical devices should be used to the extent practical (check writers, safety paper, etc.)
- Annual vacations or shifts in jobs should be enforced for those handling disbursements.
- Approval of vouchers for payment usually should be done by those not responsible for disbursing.
- Special authorizations for interbank transfers should be required, and a clearing account, perhaps called Bank Transfers, should be maintained.
- All petty cash vouchers should be written in ink or typewritten.
- It may be desirable to periodically and independently verify the bona fide existence of the regularly used suppliers of recurring services (e.g., consultants, lawyers).

Methods of Misappropriating Funds

The safeguards just listed are some of those developed on the basis of experience by many firms. Some common means of perpetrating fraud are:

- Preparing false vouchers or presenting vouchers twice for payment
- "Kiting," or unauthorized borrowing by not recording the disbursement, but recording the deposit, in the case of bank transfers
- Falsifying footing in cash records
- Raising the amount on checks after they have been signed

- Understating cash discounts
- Cashing unclaimed payroll or divided checks
- Altering petty cash vouchers
- Forging checks and destroying them when received from the bank, substituting other canceled checks or charge slips

Bank Reconciliations

An important phase of internal control is the reconciling of the balance per bank statement with the balance per books. This is particularly true with respect to general bank accounts as distinguished from accounts solely for disbursing paychecks. If properly done, the task is much more than a listing of outstanding checks, deposits in transit, and unrecorded bank charges. For example, the deposits and disbursements as shown on the bank statement should be reconciled with those on the books. A convenient form to handle this is illustrated in Exhibit 8.7. Then, too, it is desirable to compare endorsements with the payee and to check the payee against the record.

It has been mentioned previously that bank reconciliations should be handled by someone independent of any cash receipts or disbursements activities. The job can be handled by the controller or may be performed by the bank itself. Particular attention should be paid to outstanding checks of the preceding period and to deposits at the end of the month to detect kiting.

Petty Cash Funds

Most businesses must make some small disbursements. To meet these needs, petty cash funds are established that operate on an imprest fund basis, that is, the balances are fixed. At any time the cash, plus the unreimbursed vouchers, should equal the amount of the fund. Numerous funds of this type may be necessary in the branch offices or at each plant. A uniform receipt and uniform procedure should be provided, including limits on individual disbursements through this channel, proper approvals, and so forth. If it is practicable, the person handling cash receipts or disbursements should not handle petty cash. Other safeguards would include surprise cash counts, immediate cancellation of all petty cash slips after payment, and careful scrutiny of reimbursements. Although the fund may be small, very considerable sums can be expended. The controller should not neglect checking this activity.

Payrolls

In most concerns, payroll disbursements represent a very sizable proportion of all cash payments. Proper safeguards for this disbursement are particularly desirable. The use of a special payroll account is a very common procedure. A check in the exact amount of the total net payroll is deposited in the payroll account against which the individual checks are drawn. This has advantages from an internal control standpoint, and it may facilitate the reconciling of bank accounts.

The preparation of the payroll, of course, should be separate from the actual handling of cash. Special payroll audits are advisable—by the internal audit staff—to review procedures, verify rates, check clerical accuracy, and witness the payoff.

The Jones Company
BANK RECONCILIATION

Bank   <u>National Trust Co.</u>

Account   <u>General</u>

As of   <u>December 31, 20XX</u>

	Balance 11/30/XX	Receipts	Disburse-ments	Balance 12/31/XX
Per Bank...............	$126,312.50	$92,420.00	$85,119.00	$133,613.50
Add:				
Deposits in Transit				
Date per Bank *Per Book*				
12/1 11/30	5,600.00	(5,600.00)		
1/2 12/31		12,500.00		12,500.00
Deduct:				
Outstanding Checks				
Nov................	4,320.00		(4,115.00)	205.00
(Per List Attached)				
Dec................			6,110.00	6,110.00
Other Items:				
Bank Charges Not Re-corded.............			(5.01)	5.01
Per Books..............	$127,592.50	$99,320.00	$87,108.99	$139,803.51

Prepared by   <u>R. S.</u>

Date   <u>1/12/XX</u>

EXHIBIT 8.7   BANK RECONCILIATION

REPORTS ON CASH
Cash Reports for Internal Use

The cash reports used in most businesses are rather simple in nature but still provide important information. Reports on estimated cash requirements and balances or receipts or disbursements are illustrated in Exhibits 8.1 through 8.4.

For information purposes, a simple daily cash report is prepared in some companies for the chief executive and treasurer. It merely summarizes the cash receipts and cash disbursements, as well as balances of major banks. An example is shown in Exhibit 8.8. Such a report may be issued daily, weekly, or monthly, depending on needs. A detailed statement of cash receipts is illustrated in Exhibit 8.9.

THE DAY COMPANY
DAILY CASH REPORT
AS OF THE CLOSE OF BUSINESS, JUNE 16, 20xx

Balance, June 15, 19xx	$ 135,300
Receipts	10,200
Total	$ 145,500
Disbursements	15,300
Balance, June 16, 19xx	130,200
Bank Balances, etc.	
National City Bank—General	65,900
Commerce National Bank—General	22,100
Ohio Trust Company—General	30,500
Total	$ 118,500
Petty Cash and Payroll Funds	11,700
Total	$ 130,200

EXHIBIT 8.8 DAILY CASH REPORT

THE XYZ COMPANY
STATEMENT OF DAILY CASH RECEIPTS
DATE

Account No.	Name	Amount
201-1	Accounts Receivable—Aircraft	$
201-2	Accounts Receivable—Parts	
201-3	Accounts Receivable—Employees	
201-5	Accounts Receivable—Intercompany	
201-6	Accounts Receivable—Miscellaneous	
303	Claims Receivable	
801	Deposits on Account	
1001-1	Cash Sales—Aircraft	
1001-2	Cash Sales—Parts	
1001-3	Cash Sales—Scrap	
1001-4	Cash Sales—Miscellaneous	
6001	Revenue—Vending Machines	
6005	Royalty Income	
6010	Miscellaneous Income and Expense	
Total		$

EXHIBIT 8.9 STATEMENT OF DAILY CASH RECEIPTS

From the control viewpoint, it is desirable to know how collections and disbursements compare with estimates. Such information is shown in Exhibit 8.10, as well as the expected cash balance at month end.

THE ROTH COMPANY
WEEKLY CASH REPORT
FOR THE WEEK ENDED NOVEMBER 16, 20XX
(THOUSANDS OF DOLLARS)

| Description | Actual Week Ended 11/16/xx | Month to Date | |
		Actual	Estimated
Beginning Cash Balance	$ 17,890	$32,511	$32,510
Cash Receipts			
Government	10,810	18,310	18,000
Wholesale	19,620	67,730	65,500
Retail	8,330	21,100	23,400
Total	38,760	107,140	106,900
Cash Disbursements			
Accounts Payable-Expenses	12,330	12,860	12,300
Payrolls	12,660	37,010	36,900
Material Purchases	1,890	19,340	14,300
Federal Taxes	2,790	8,640	8,920
Capital Expenditures	13,370	39,990	40,190
Other	1,060	2,030	2,000
Total	44,100	119,870	114,610
Ending Cash Balance	$ 12,550	$ 19,781	$ 24,800
Estimated Month-End Balance			$ 30,000

EXHIBIT 8.10 COMPARISON OF ACTUAL AND ESTIMATED CASH ACTIVITY

In addition to comparing actual and forecasted cash activity, it is also useful to periodically compare book balances with those required to meet service charges of the banks and compensating balances. Such a report compares the "objective" balance with actual book and actual bank balances. This type of report provides a periodic check on effective cash utilization by recording the absence of excessive balances and the progress in keeping bank balances adequate to fairly compensate the financial institution. A cash management report is shown in Exhibit 8.11.

There are any number of variations in cash reports, including some that are greatly detailed about daily cash receipts and the like. The suggested reports are merely examples; many may be adapted to computer applications.

Cash Flow Analysis for Investment Purposes

Cash flow is a broad measure of company performance. "Free cash flow," a further refinement of cash flow in that from "cash flow" is subtracted a provision for required capital expenditures and, in some calculations, the dividend payments. In this latter case, the subtrahend is the equivalent of "discretionary funds," and it represents sums that can be spent on acquisitions, stock buybacks, inventory, and many other items.

Where reported earnings are heavily reduced by depreciation, cash flow in some industries is an analytical yardstick of choice. It is useful to investors in spotting companies with ample resources to make them rewarding acquisitions. Additionally, corporate raiders are

THE STEVEN COMPANY
QUARTERLY REPORT ON BANK BALANCES
AS AT JUNE 30, 20XX
(THOUSANDS OF DOLLARS)

Bank	Actual per Books	Objective	(Over) Under Objective	Balance per Bank Statement
First National City	$ 19,870	$ 20,200	$ 330	$ 23,070
Chase Manhattan	17,440	17,800	360	19,120
Morgan Guaranty	16,850	16,500	(350)	17,180
Bank of America	14,310	15,700	1,390	15,810
Chemical Bank	10,870	10,250	(620)	12,300
First Interstate	6,430	5,900	(530)	7,110
American Trust	5,510	5,800	290	5,840
Anglo-American	4,380	4,500	120	4,760
National Bank of Commerce	2,890	3,000	110	3,020
Other Local	490	—	(490)	520
Total Cash in Banks-U.S.	99,040	99,650	610	108,730
Subsidiaries-Foreign	8,190	7,000	(1,190)	8,600
Cash Funds	760	750	(10)	—
Total Cash	$ 107,990	$ 107,400	$ (590)	$ 117,330

EXHIBIT 8.11 ACTUAL AND OBJECTIVE BANK BALANCES

attracted to high cash flow situations because the cash stream may be used to pay down heavy debt incurred in a takeover. Periodically, listings appear comparing stock prices in terms of cash flow.

The controller should be aware that cash flow may rank high in judging the investment worth of a company. It is a feature that usually deserves comment in any analytical effort.

CASH FLOW RATIO ANALYSIS

The requirement by the FASB for companies to provide shareholders (with access to the public and to potential investors) with a statement of cash flows, which identifies cash flows from operating activities, as well as that from investing activities and financing activities, has facilitated and encouraged the use of certain cash flow ratios. These ratios are useful in the planning and control of cash in that they may provide benchmarks or standards to measure the cash performance of a given company against other entities. Such comparisons may be helpful in evaluating financial performance of an acquisition target or other investments. Equally valuable, the ratios may be used to judge trends in the controller's own company and as compared with competitors or other selected best-in-their class entities.

The cash flow ratios are of two types. The *sufficiency* ratios directly measure the ability of a company to generate enough cash flow to meet the needs of the entity, such as the ability to pay long-term debt, provide for needed plant and equipment, and pay dividends to the owners. The *efficiency* ratios indicate how well a company generates cash from selected measures, such as sales, income from continuing operations, and from total assets (or total assets employed).

Some *sufficiency* ratios and their derivatives are:

Ratio	Derivation
Cash flow adequacy	$= \dfrac{\text{Cash from operations}}{\text{Long-term debt paid 1 Funds for assets purchased 1 Dividends paid}}$
Long-term debt repayment	$= \dfrac{\text{Long-term debt payments}}{\text{Cash from operations}}$
Dividend payout	$= \dfrac{\text{Dividends}}{\text{Cash from operations}}$
Reinvestment	$= \dfrac{\text{Purchase of assets}}{\text{Cash from operations}}$
Debt coverage	$= \dfrac{\text{Total debt}}{\text{Cash from operations}}$
Depreciation-amortization relationship	$= \dfrac{\text{Depreciation 1 Amortization}}{\text{Cash from operations}}$

Some *efficiency* cash flow ratios are:

Ratio	Derivation
Cash flow to sales	$\dfrac{\text{Cash flow from operations}}{\text{Sales}}$
Cash flow return on assets	$\dfrac{\text{Cash flow from operations}}{\text{Total assets (or total assets employed)}}$

The cash efficiency ratios reflect the effectiveness or efficiency by which cash is generated from either operations or assets. Specifically:

- The cash flow-to-sales ratio reflects the percentage of each sales dollar realized as cash.
- The operations index reflects the ratio of cash generated to the income from continuing operations.
- The cash flow from assets reflects the relative amount of cash which the assets (or assets employed) are able to generate.

These ratios will assist in the analysis of financial statements. However, there is still a need for a consensus as to what are useful cash flow ratios, and the development of norms or standards for companies and industries.

IMPACT OF NEW INFORMATION TECHNOLOGY AND ORGANIZATIONAL STRUCTURES

The vast majority of the basic cash management functions described earlier in this chapter have been performed for years and will continue to be accomplished. But *how* they will be done, and what organization structure will do them (*who*) is subject to change. The pressures or influences that are causing or accelerating adjustments are many and include:

- The substantial improvements in information technology, or computer technology
- Growth in the global nature of business
- Economic pressures that are causing entities to integrate horizontally, to reduce staff size (such as treasury or controllership functions), to focus on the principal business, and to do more subcontracting or outsourcing
- Closer electronic integration with supplier, customer, or other third parties (such as banks)

The personal computer and the related software greatly aid in the analysis of data required for a cash forecast, as well as the actual preparation of the cash plan. As corporations and banks electronically integrate, there are many possibilities that should be of interest to the controller (for internal control and other purposes) including:

- Using an electronic data interchange (EDI) file, a customer can supply selling company's bank directly with invoice data and arrange payment. The bank will then update the payee's account.
- Where banks handle the lockbox operations, they can book images of remittance documents in a computer file and avoid enormous sorting and reassociation of check copies and the like. Less paperwork means less cost.
- Arrangements can be made with a company's bank for automatic payment of taxes and/or other designated items. This reduces float and provides greater control over the payment.
- Companies can arrange a system for electronic payment of selected supplier invoices thus reducing paperwork.
- For faster information, arrangements can be made for electronic account analysis.
- Banks can provide an automated check reconcilement through data transmission.
- Other systems have been developed by banks, using modern technology at the time of check presentments to reduce fraud.

Aside from the technology involved, companies can select banks to perform duties regularly handled by their own internal departments, such as portfolio management; cash collections, cash disbursements; payroll check preparation, retirement funds custody, accounting, and disbursements. Outsourcing of some financial activities is no longer a dirty word. Hopefully, the treasurer will have close contact with the company's banks in order to keep abreast of what services can be proved (more cheaply) on an outsourcing basis.

INVESTMENT OF SHORT-TERM FUNDS

In many companies, surplus or excess funds not needed for either operating purposes or compensating bank balances are available for investment, even over weekends. Prudent use of otherwise idle funds can add to income. Although the financial officer ordinarily will direct the investment of these funds, the controller may be concerned with adequate reporting and control and generally should be somewhat knowledgeable about the subject.

Criteria for Selecting Investments

Given the opportunity for earning additional income from temporary excess funds, what are some of the criteria to be considered in selecting the investment vehicle? There probably are five, and all somewhat related:

1. *Safety of principal.* A primary objective should be to avoid instruments that might risk loss of the investment.

2. *Price stability.* If the company is suddenly called on to liquidate the security to acquire funds, price stability would be important in avoiding a significant loss.

3. *Marketability.* The money manager must consider whether the security can be sold, if required, rather easily and quite quickly.

4. *Maturity.* Funds may be invested until the demand for cash arises, perhaps as reflected in the cash forecast. Hence maturities should relate to prospective cash needs. Temporary investments usually involve maturities of a day or two to as much as a year.

5. *Yield.* The financial officer of course is interested in optimizing the earnings or securing at least a competitive return on the investment and is thus interested in the yield. This is not necessarily the most important criterion, because low-risk, high-liquidity investments will not provide the highest yield.

The importance attached to each of these factors will depend on the management philosophy, condition of the market, and inclinations of the investing person. Restrictions placed on the operation will influence the weighting of each.

Investment Restrictions

Sometimes the board of directors will place restrictions on just how short-term funds may be invested. In other instances, the senior financial officer will provide such guidelines. Subjects covered would include:

- Maximum maturity
- Credit rating of issuer
- Maximum investment in selected types of securities
    - By user
    - By type of instrument
    - By country
    - By currency

Instruments for investment vary widely, and market conditions may dictate the most desirable at any particular time. Typical money market instruments include:

- U.S. Treasury bills
- U.S. Treasury notes and bonds
- Negotiable certificates of deposit
- Banker's acceptances
- Selected foreign government issues
- Federal agency issues
- Repurchase agreements
- Prime commercial paper
- Finance company paper
- Short-term tax exempts

An illustration of the guidelines of an aerospace company for use in making temporary investments is shown in Exhibit 8.12.

THE AEROSPACE SERVICE CORPORATION
INTERNAL GUIDELINES FOR TOTAL SHORT-TERM INVESTMENTS
EFFECTIVE NOVEMBER 1, 20XX

Objective

To invest excess cash in only top-quality-short-term investments, for optimum total return, commensurate with corporate liquidity requirements.

Liquidity

Liquidity shall be provided by minimum and maximum limits as follows:

1. At least $80 million shall be invested in overnight investments and in negotiable marketable obligations of major U.S. issuers.

2. No more than 50% of the total portfolio shall be invested in time deposits or other investments with a lack of liquidity such as commercial paper for which only the dealer and issuer make a market.

Diversification

Diversification shall be provided through a limit on each nongovernment issuer as listed next. These are general limits, and in each case quality review may result in elimination or a lower limit for an issuer. Overnight or repurchase investments must meet quality criteria but are not subject to limits on the amount invested.

1. U.S. Government and agencies—no limit.

2. Domestic bank certificates of deposit, time deposits and banker's acceptances—$30—million limit for banks with capital accounts in excess of $800 million (top 10 banks); $20 million for banks with capital accounts of $350 to $800 million (second 11 banks); $5 million for all other banks with capital accounts in excess of $250 million (11 banks).

3. U.S. dollar (or fully hedged foreign currency) obligations of foreign banks, each with capital accounts exceeding $500 million—limited to $15 million each for Canadian banks and $10 million each for other foreign banks, subject to an aggregate limit of $75 million for non-Canadian foreign banks.

4. Domestic commercial paper with P-1/A-1 rating only—$20—million limit for issuers with long-term senior debt rating of Aa or better; $10 million for issuers with debt rating of A; and $10 million for commercial bank-holding companies with capital accounts in excess of $500 million, within the overall limit of the flagship bank described in 2 above.

5. Foreign commercial paper unconditionally guaranteed by a prime U.S. issuer and fully hedged, subject to the guarantor's issuer limit described in 4 above.

6. Obligations of savings and loan associations, each with capital accounts exceeding $250 million—limited to $10 million each.

Operating Procedure

Payment shall be made only against delivery of a security to a custodian bank. Securities shall be delivered from custody only against payment.

Due bills issued by a bank will be accepted for delivery only under exceptional conditions. No due bills issued by a dealer will be accepted.

Maturity Limits

The average maturity of the entire fund shall be limited to an average of two years. The maximum maturity for each category is as follows:

U.S. government	5 years
Municipal obligations	2 years
Banks CDs and BAs	1 year
Bank TDs	90 days
Commercial paper	270 days

EXHIBIT 8.12   GUIDELINES FOR SHORT-TERM INVESTMENTS

Investment Controls

Many securities that companies purchase as short-term investments are negotiable. Additionally, these investments often are paid for through bank wire transfers. Given the nature and frequency of transactions, the control system should be adequate.

Many corporations contract with a major commercial bank to serve as custodian of the securities, to make payment on incoming delivery, and to receive funds on outgoing delivery. The form of contract should provide maximum safeguards to the company.

Because opportunities for fraud exist, given telephonic transactions and wire transfer of funds, care must be exercised in the form and nature of confirmation secured and the internal controls used in authorizing payment.

Reports to Management

Periodic reports to top management, including the board of directors, will depend in part on this group's interest and the size of the investment portfolio. However, it is suggested, as a minimum, that where investments are significant, information should be conveyed regarding the type of investment and yield. Suggested report content would include:

- Detail of individual securities, grouped by type and/or maturity
- Summary by type
- Summary by maturity
- Summary by yield
- Overall portfolio yield, by maturity
- Comparison of yield with selected index or by money manager, if appropriate

An illustrative report comparing in-house performance with an outside money manager is shown in Exhibits 8.13 through 8.14.

THE CORPORATION SHORT TERM FUNDS
DISTRIBUTION BY ISSUER (CONTINUED)
AUGUST 31, 20XX
(DOLLARS IN MILLIONS)

	INTERNAL	MANAGER	TOTAL
U.S. GOVERNMENT			
COLLATERAL FOR RESALES	—	4	4
U.S. BANK OBLIGATIONS			
BANK OF AMERICA			
BANK OF NEW YORK			
BANKERS TRUST			
CHASE			
CHEMICAL			
CITIBANK			
CONTINENTAL ILLINOIS			
FIRST INTERSTATE			
FIRST NATIONAL CHICAGO			
HOME SAVINGS & LOAN			
MANUFACTURERS HANOVER			
MARINE MIDLAND			
MORGAN GUARANTY			
REPUBLIC NATIONAL NEW YORK			
SECURITY PACIFIC			
WELLS FARGO			

THE CORPORATION SHORT TERM FUNDS
DISTRIBUTION BY ISSUER (CONTINUED)
AUGUST 31, 20XX
(DOLLARS IN MILLIONS)

	INTERNAL	MANAGER	TOTAL
FOREIGN BANK OBLIGATIONS			
ALGEMENE	10	—	10
BANK OF MONTREAL	—	5	5
BNP	11	—	11
BANK OF NOVA SCOTIA	—	5	5
BARCLAYS	5	—	5
CREDIT LYONNAIS	—	5	5
DAI-ICHI KANGYO	5	—	5
NATIONAL WESTMINSTER	5	—	5
SWISS BANK CORP	—	5	5
TORONTO DOMINION	3	5	8
INDUSTRIAL			
SPERRY RAND	5	—	5
TAX EXEMPTS			
NEW YORK STATE	5	—	5
GRAND TOTAL	216	104	320

EXHIBIT 8.13   REPORT TO MANAGEMENT, BY ISSUER, ON SHORT-TERM INVESTMENTS

THE CORPORATION SHORT TERM FUNDS
DISTRIBUTION BY MATURITY-AVERAGE YIELDS
AUGUST 31, 20XX

	INTERNAL		MANAGER		TOTAL	
	$ MILL	%	$ MILL	%	$ MILL	%
UNDER 1 MONTH	47	22	94	90	141	44
1 – 3 MONTHS	71	33	10	10	81	25
3 – 6 MONTHS	98	45	—	—	98	31
	$216	100%	$104	100%	$320	100%

AVERAGE MATURITY, MONTHS	3.2
AVERAGE YIELD, 4 MONTHS MAY – AUGUST	
MARK TO MARKET	8.19%
BOOK ACCOUNTING	8.28%
MARKET PRICES, SEPTEMBER 1 FOR PRIME CO'S:	
1 MONTH	8.15%
3 MONTHS	8.38%
6 MONTHS	8.80%

THE CORPORATION SHORT TERM FUNDS
DISTRIBUTION BY TYPE OF OBLIGATION
AUGUST 31, 20XX

	INTERNAL		MANAGER		TOTAL	
	$ MILL	%	$ MILL	%	$ MILL	%
RESALES AND OVERNIGHT TIME DEPOSITS	8.0	3.7	7.7	7.4	15.7	4.9
U.S. BANKS – U.S. DOLLAR CD'S AND BA'S	128.5	59.4	18.0	17.4	146.5	45.8
CANADIAN BANKS – U.S. DOLLAR TIME DEPOSITS	—	—	15.0	14.5	15.0	4.7
FOREIGN BANKS – U.S. DOLLAR CD'S AND BA'S	30.9	14.3	10.0	9.7	40.9	12.8
U.S. BANKS – EURODOLLAR TIME DEPOSITS	35.0	16.2	25.0	24.1	60.0	18.7
COMMERCIAL PAPER	9.0	4.1	27.9	26.9	36.9	11.5
TAX EXEMPTS	5.0	2.3	—	—	5.0	1.6
TOTALS	$216.4	100.0%	$103.6	100.0%	$320.0	100.0%

EXHIBIT 8.14   REPORT TO MANAGEMENT ON SHORT-TERM INVESTMENTS BY MATURITY AND TYPE OF OBLIGATION

9

PLANNING AND CONTROL
OF RECEIVABLES

INTRODUCTION

The typical goals of the accounts receivable area are to keep the receivable amount as low as possible, in order to reduce working capital needs, while reducing bad debts to a very low level. Unfortunately, a controller may also be subjected to the opposing pressure of granting very high credit levels to customers in order to spur revenue growth, which inevitably leads to high levels of accounts receivable and larger amounts of bad debt. Although it is not possible to fully reconcile these conflicting goals and instructions, this chapter describes a number of methods for setting up rational systems for granting credit, analyzing customers, and collecting funds from them. In addition, a number of control methods for ensuring that established credit levels are strictly followed are discussed, as well as how to predict the investment in accounts receivable for budgeting purposes. In short, this chapter describes how to control accounts receivable and predict receivable levels.

GRANTING CREDIT TO CUSTOMERS

When reducing the amount of accounts receivable outstanding, it is best to view the collections process as a funnel. The collections person is dealing with a continuous stream of poor credit risks that are emerging from a funnel full of accounts receivable. Going into the other end of the funnel are sales to customers; unless those sales are filtered somehow, there will be an unending stream of potential bad debt problems. Clearly, then, the best way to avoid collection problems is to pay strict attention to the process of granting credit to customers before the company ever sells them anything. This section discusses the issues related to the important process of granting credit to customers.

First of all, why grant credit to a customer? Some companies insist on cash payments, but they find that this limits the number of customers who are willing to deal with them. Thus, granting credit widens the range of potential customers. Another reason is that many customers view credit terms as part of the price of the product, and may pay more for a product if a company is willing to grant generous credit terms. Yet another reason is that some industries have a customary number of payment days, and a company will be viewed as "playing hardball" if it demands cash payments at the time of delivery. Consequently, there are a variety of good reasons to grant credit to customers.

However, there are a number of pitfalls that a company must be mindful of when granting credit. Some are so important that a company can be dragged into bankruptcy if it does not closely monitor the process. One danger is of granting too much credit to customers, because this may seriously reduce the amount of available working capital that a company has available for other purposes. Another danger is that improper review of customer financial statements or payment history may result in the extension of credit that results in large bad debts. Either problem can reduce a company's available credit to the point where it cannot issue credit to good customers who deserve to have the credit, resulting in a loss of business. Consequently, a company must maintain tight control over the credit granting process, so that just enough credit is issued to encourage business with a company's best customers, without going so far as to enhance sales by issuing excessive amounts of credit to customers with poor credit histories.

It is difficult to balance the pros and cons of granting credit, since granting an excessive amount of credit will tie up valuable working capital, while a restriction on credit will turn away potential sales. The balance between these two offsetting factors is usually influenced by the overall corporate strategy. For example, if there is a strong drive in the direction of increasing company profits, it is likely that management will clamp down on the amount of credit granted, since management does not want to incur any extra expense for bad debts. Alternatively, an aggressive management team that wants to increase revenues and market share will probably loosen the credit granting policy to bring in more sales, even though there is a greater risk of increasing the level of bad debt. In either case, the controller or treasurer will be on the receiving end of an order from top management regarding the level of credit to be granted. This is not an area in which middle management is given much say in the type of credit policy that a company will follow.

Within the strictures of a company's established credit policy, there are many steps that a controller can take to ensure that credit is granted in a reliable and consistent manner, and that the policy is strictly followed. The focus of a company's credit granting policy is in the areas of customer investigation, credit granting, and subsequent control:

- *Investigate the customer.* The easiest and most thorough source of information about a customer is the credit report. The premier issuer of this information is Dun & Bradstreet, which provides phone or computer access to credit report information, so that a credit report can be in the requester's hands a minute after making the request. Other sources of information are trade references, though these tend to be biased in favor of the customer, since most customers will always be sure to make timely payments to their trade references. A limited amount of information can also be gleaned from a customer's bank, but this is rarely sufficient information on which to make a credit decision. There may also be detailed financial reports available from the Securities and Exchange Commission (SEC) if a company is publicly held, but even this excellent source can be rendered invalid if a company is only dealing with a subsidiary of a publicly held company, since the financial results of the subsidiary will not be broken out in the financial reports.

- *Grant credit.* Once there is a sufficient amount of financial information about a customer, one must determine the amount of credit to give to the customer. This should be a consistent methodology; otherwise, there will be great variations in the amounts of credit granted to customers. Also, a wide range of credit amounts will make salespeople think that credit levels are highly negotiable, so they will attempt to sway the person granting credit to increase the amounts of credit given to their customers. The best approach is to come up with a formula that can be applied consistently to all customers. Though the exact method devised will vary by industry, a simple method is to use the median credit level granted by a customer's other suppliers, as noted in the credit report, and then reduce this amount by a standard percentage for every day that the customer is late in making payments to its other suppliers. For example, a customer who receives a median amount of $100,000 in credit from its suppliers, and who pays them ten days late, will receive a total credit amount of $50,000 if the controller decides to apply a 5 percent penalty to each day that a customer is late in making payments; this approach assumes that there is a direct correlation between a customer's ability to pay on time and the risk that the customer will default on its payments.

- *Control subsequent credit transactions.* The amount of credit granted will not matter if a company makes a habit of ignoring the established credit limit. This matter is discussed more fully in the Control over Accounts Receivable section later in this chapter; the key point is that there should be an automated check in the order entry system that automatically halts any new customer order that results in a level of credit that exceeds the preestablished limit that is already recorded in the system. If the level of automation is not sufficient to allow this method, a controller can authorize a continuing internal audit of credit levels to ensure that they are not being deliberately or inadvertently avoided by the order entry staff. Either approach ensures that credit levels, once established, will be maintained.

A key issue in the credit granting process is when the credit investigation is performed. If a company finds customers first and then asks the controller or treasurer to grant credit, it is common for the salespeople who worked hard to bring in the new customers to lobby equally hard on the customers' behalf to give them the largest possible amount of credit. This gives the salesperson the best chance of earning a large commission, which can come only from a large amount of sales volume. Granting credit after a sale is made makes the credit granting job an intense one, because there is great pressure from the sales staff to grant credit, which is especially difficult if the credit investigation reveals that a customer is a poor risk. A better approach is to implement some sales planning with the sales staff in advance, so that there is a target list of customers that the sales staff is asked to contact for orders. Using this approach, the controller can investigate potential customers in advance and advise the sales staff to avoid certain ones if their credit histories are poor. By using advance credit checks, a controller can avoid requests for excessive levels of credit by the sales staff.

While there is a need to grant credit to customers, one should note the pitfalls of extending too much credit. A methodical company will position credit investigations before new customer contacts, in order to avoid wasted efforts by the sales staff in contacting poor credit risks.

CUSTOMER MARGIN ANALYSIS

Although a formula can be used to grant credit to customers, there will be times when a customer or a salesperson calls to ask for more credit. If an excessive amount of credit is granted and then the customer defaults, the controller may have some explaining to do to a company officer or owner. However, there are some cases where a customer is so important to a company's survival that it is nearly mandatory to give the customer an inordinate amount of credit. How is a controller to make a judgment call regarding when to grant additional credit and when to turn it down?

The answer is to use a customer margin analysis. As shown in Exhibit 9.1, a margin analysis is really a matrix that divides up customers into various categories based on the margins and volume that a company experiences with each one. Using the example, if a customer with both low margins *and* sales volume calls to demand an increase in credit, the controller's best response may be to chuckle warmly and hang up the phone—adding credit to a customer who yields minimal profits is simply making a bad situation worse. Alternatively, a request to increase credit for any customer with high margins should be looked at very seriously, since there will be a major increase in company profits if sales to this customer increase. Finally, credit to customers with low margins and high revenue volume may require scaling back to a lower level, since there is no reason to support sales volume on which there is no return. Thus, the credit granting decision should be strongly driven by the margins and sales volumes of each customer.

It is important to factor customer margins and sales volumes into the decision to grant credit; however, a controller should always keep in mind a customer's ability to pay down the credit—after all, making lots of money on a customer will not last if the high margins are offset by bad debts.

COLLECTIONS TASK

This section discusses a variety of ways to bring in accounts receivable as soon as possible, resulting in reduced working capital requirements and less risk of accounts becoming

	Low Sales Volume	High Sales Volume
High Margin	7 customers 17% of sales Acme Distribution Barton Warehousing Chemical Distributor Francis Distribution General Warehouses International Storage	4 customers 55% of sales Serious Storage Terrific Moving and Storage Unitary Storage Vehicular Movers
Low Margin	6 customers 3% of sales Mexican Storage Nascent Movers Omnipresent Storage Publican Moving Quarterly Long-haul Roadway Moving	8 customers 25% of sales Women Only Movers Yearly Storage Facilities Zorro Motor Vehicles Kustomary Storage Long-Term Storage Short-Haul Movers Alfred's Moving Fine Auto Storage Facility

EXHIBIT 9.1 CUSTOMER MARGIN MATRIX

significantly overdue. The methods for enhancing collections fall into several categories. The first is collection techniques, which describes ways to bring in payments on existing debts. The second is altered payment methods, which looks at accelerating the speed with which payments travel from a customer to the accounting department. The final method is shrinking the entire billing and collection cycle, which focuses on ways to reduce the time needed to process orders, issue credit, generate invoices, and other matters. The methods are outlined in greater detail as:

1. *Collection techniques.* This section covers several ways to enhance the efficiency and effectiveness of the collections staff in bringing in accounts receivable payments on time. The methods are:

   (a) *Involve the sales staff.* The people with the best customer contacts are the sales staff. They can frequently collect on accounts receivable that the collections staff cannot, because the salesperson can contact a different person within the customer's organization who can order an immediate payment that is otherwise frozen in the accounts payable area. This method is especially effective when the sales staff's commissions are tied to cash received, rather than sales, so that the sales personnel have a major interest in resolving any collection problems.

   (b) *Create a relationship.* It is much easier to collect money from someone you know. The best way to build up this kind of relationship is to take a few extra moments on the phone to chat with the customer's accounts payable person; by creating even such a minor relationship as this, the collections person has a much greater chance of obtaining money from the customer. The relationship can be enhanced by carefully avoiding any confrontations or heated discussions, actions which are common for an inexperienced collections person to make.

   (c) *Follow overdue accounts closely.* A customer who is deliberately delaying payments will be much more inclined to make payments to a company that is consistently persistent in calling about overdue accounts, since it is easier to pay these companies at the expense of other companies that are conveniently *not* calling to inquire about their accounts. It is especially effective to tell a customer when to expect a follow-up call, and then make that call on the predicted day, which reinforces in the customer's mind the perception that the collections person is not going away, and will continue to make inquiries until the debt is paid.

   (d) *Use leverage.* When there is no response from making a multitude of calls and other forms of contact with a customer regarding a payment, it is time to kick the issue upstairs to the controller, or even higher in the organization. When a customer's accounts payable person is not responding, it is quite possible that a different response can be obtained when the controller contacts his or her counterpart, since there may be a better relationship at that level. In some cases, though usually only for the largest debts, the two presidents may need to correspond. If none of these approaches work, a different kind of leverage may be necessary—cutting off service or shipments until payment is made.

However, this approach must be used with care, since such a cutoff may have a drastic effect on customer relations.

(e) *Create a contact log.* All of the previously cited collection methods can be made more effective by using a contact log. This is a simple device that lists the last date on which contact was made, and the next date on which action is required. A collections person can then flip through the log each day to see what actions are needed. It is helpful to include the most recent accounts receivable aging in the log, for easy reference when talking to customers.

2. *Altered payment methods.* Besides jawboning customers to pay on time, it may be possible to alter the underlying method used to make payments, which can greatly reduce the time required to make collections. Any of the following approaches should be considered to alter the payment method.

(a) *Lockbox.* This is a post office box that is opened in a company's name, but accessed and serviced by a remittance processor, which is normally a bank. By having a bank open mail containing checks and deposit these funds directly into a company's account, it is possible to reduce the time interval before the money would have been deposited by other means. In addition, lockboxes can be set up close to customers, so that there is a minimal mail float time. This also reduces the time before a company must wait to receive payment.

(b) *Wire transfer.* This is a set of telegraphic messages between banks, usually through a Federal Reserve bank, whereby the sending bank instructs the Federal Reserve bank to charge the account of the sending bank and credit the account of the receiving bank.

(c) *Automated clearinghouse (ACH) transfer.* This method allows banks to exchange electronic payments. Usually, the customer initiates a payment directly to the company's bank account.

(d) *Depository transfer check (DTC).* Under this approach, a bank prepares a DTC on behalf of its customer against the customer's deposit account at another bank. It is a means for rapidly shifting funds from deposit accounts into concentration accounts from which investments can be made.

(e) *Preauthorized draft (PAD).* This is a draft drawn by the company against the bank account of the customer. The method is most commonly used by insurance companies or other lenders where the payment is fixed and repetitive.

3. *Shrink the cycle.* Besides altering collection methods and changing the type of customer payment, there are many other ways to shrink the cycle that begins with issuing an invoice to a customer and ends with the collection of cash. This last category is a catchall of ways to reduce the time required to complete the entire process. The shrinking methods are:

(a) *Accelerate billing frequency.* If a company only issues invoices once a week, some billings will sit in a pile until the end of the week, when they could have been on their way to a customer much sooner. Daily invoicing should be the rule.

(b) *Alter payment terms.* Sometimes a customer will radically alter its payment timing if there is a large enough early payment discount placed in front of them. Usually, a 2 percent discount for early payment is a sufficient enticement to bring in cash much earlier than was previously the case. However, such a large discount may have a major impact on profits if margins are already low, or if customers were already paying relatively quickly, so it should only be offered to those customers who are extremely late in paying. Although this approach may seem like a reward to those customers who are late in paying, it only reflects the realities of the collection situation.

(c) *Reduce billing errors.* One of the most important reasons why customers do not pay is that they disagree with the information on a company invoice. Accordingly, it is imperative that a controller systematically track down errors (which are most easily revealed through the collections process, when customers tell the collections staff about invoicing errors) and fix them as soon as possible. A common mistake is sending an invoice to the wrong address or contact person, while others are to incorrectly price a product or to bill for the wrong product or service, either in type or quantity. There are usually a number of problems to be fixed before all errors are corrected. Even then, careful watch must be maintained over the invoicing process to ensure that errors are kept out.

(d) *Use electronic billings.* Rather than sending a paper invoice, it is possible to use an electronic one, which has the advantage of avoiding the time required to move through the postal system. In addition, such a transmission can be automatically processed by a customer's computer system without ever being punched in again by a data entry clerk, so there are fewer chances of an error occurring on the customer's side when paying the invoice. An electronic billing is usually sent by electronic data interchange (EDI), which requires a considerable amount of advance preparation by a company and its customers to set up; because of the advance work required, it is generally best to only use this method with long-term customers with whom a company has a significant volume of business.

Although a major portion of collecting accounts receivable is contacting customers to request payment, a variety of other techniques have a major impact on the speed with which payments are collected. These techniques include using early payment discounts, electronic invoice delivery, and lockboxes. It takes a complete implementation of all these methods before a company will experience a significant decline in the amount of its outstanding accounts receivable.

MEASUREMENT OF ACCOUNTS RECEIVABLE

A controller may feel that, by making many collection improvements, the investment in accounts receivable is being reduced; however, it is impossible to be sure without using several performance measurements. Not all of the measures described in this section need to be implemented, but a controller should use a selection of them to gain a clear picture of the state of a company's accounts receivable. The measurements are:

- *Accounts receivable turnover ratio.* The simplest and one of the most effective ways to see if there are problems with accounts receivable is the turnover ratio. This measure illustrates how rapidly accounts receivable are being converted into cash. To calculate the measure, divide net sales by accounts receivable. For example, if the turnover ratio is 12, then accounts receivable are being collected after precisely one month. If turns are only six, then accounts receivable are going uncollected for two months, and so on. To gain a better idea of ongoing performance, it is best to track the turnover measure with a trend line.

- *Days old when discount taken.* When a customer takes a discount for early payment, it is understood that the payment will be made within the previously agreed-upon guidelines, such as taking a discount *only* if payment is made within a certain number of days. This measure is designed to spot those customers who take the discount, but who stretch the payment out beyond the standard number of terms. To calculate the measure, one must write a program for the accounting software that lists the date of each invoice paid and the date when cash was applied against the invoice. The difference between these two dates, especially when grouped by customer, will be a good indicator of any ongoing problems with late payments on discount deals.

- *Days' sales outstanding.* A common measure that may be swapped with the accounts receivable turnover measure is days' sales outstanding (DSO). This measure converts the amount of open accounts receivable to a figure that shows the average number of days that accounts are going unpaid. The measure is used somewhat more frequently than turnover, since the number of days outstanding is considered to be somewhat more understandable. To measure it, divide the average accounts receivable by annual credit sales, and multiply by 365. To determine if DSO is reasonable, compare it to the standard payment terms. For example, a DSO of 40 is good if standard terms are 30 days to pay, whereas it is poor if standard terms are only 10 days. If collections are well managed, the DSO should be no more than one third beyond the terms of sale. For a more precise view of the collection operations, the DSO can be calculated for each customer.

- *Percent of bad debt losses.* It is necessary to track the proportion of sales that are written off as bad debts, because a high percentage is a strong indicator of either lax collection practices or an excessively lenient credit granting policy. To calculate the measure, divide the bad debt amount for the month by credit sales. An alternative measure may be to divide the bad debt by sales from several months ago, on the theory that the bad debts were more specifically related to sales in a previous time period.

- *Percent of unexplained credits taken.* Some customers take credits on a whim, resulting in considerable write-offs for which there is no explanation. If this comes to a reasonable percentage of sales to a customer, that customer should be terminated, since it is cutting into company margins. Researching the credits also requires a large proportion of accounting staff time. To calculate the measure, track all invoices that are not completely paid and divide by sales to customers; this measure should be completed on a customer-by-customer basis to gain a better understanding of which customers are causing the problem.

- *Reasons for bad debt write-offs.* A less common measure is to manually accumulate the reasons why sales are written off as bad debts, and to summarize total bad debts by these explanations. One can then sort the reasons by declining dollar volume to see what problems are arising most frequently, which can lead to steps to fix various credit granting or collection problems. It is also worthwhile to accumulate bad debt information by customer, to see which ones are responsible for the largest number of write-offs.

The measurements discussed in this section are useful for determining how rapidly accounts receivable are collected, as well as the size of and reasons for bad debts. Properly tracking these measures results in a fine management tool for altering the methods used to collect accounts receivable, as well as the credit granting policy, resulting in faster receivable turnover and fewer bad debt losses.

CONTROL OVER ACCOUNTS RECEIVABLE

This chapter is primarily concerned with the processes needed to grant credit and then collect it. However, an astute controller must be sure that these processes are operational, or else incorrect credit levels will be granted, and collections will not occur as expected. Proper controls are required to ensure that processes function as planned. This section discusses the key controls that one should install to make sure that the accounts receivable function produces results that are within expectations.

This section is divided into two parts: controls over the credit granting process, and controls over collections. The first part, credit granting, involves controls over the timing of credit processing, ongoing customer monitoring, excess credit, and process reviews:

- *Control the timing of granting credit.* One of the largest problems with granting credit is that it is always a rush—a salesperson runs in with a new customer order and demands an immediate credit check, so that the order can be accepted and the salesperson can earn a commission. Unfortunately, the compressed time period forces a controller to dispense with an appropriate number of credit checks, and may even result in granting credit with no review work at all. A good control over this process is to enforce the early identification of sales prospects and the communication of this information to the accounting or treasury departments, so that a thorough credit review can be completed prior to the conclusion of a sale.

- *Monitor the financial condition of customers.* A customer may suffer financial reverses and suddenly be unable to pay its bills. To avoid being caught with a large amount of outstanding credit in such situations, there should be a control that requires the credit granting staff to annually review the financial condition of all customers with significant credit lines; this information can come from either the customers or a credit reporting agency. Unfortunately, some companies suffer financial reverses that are so sudden that an annual financial review will not catch the decline; for these situations, there should be an additional control requiring financial reviews for any customer who suddenly begins to stretch out payment dates on open invoices. This control results in rapid action to shrink credit balances where customers are clearly unable to pay.

- *Review excess credit taken.* Some accounting systems allow customers to exceed the credit limits programmed into the accounting database. In such situations, the official credit level is essentially meaningless, since it is not observed. To avoid this problem, the controller should create and review a report that lists all customers who have exceeded their preset credit limits. A controller can then use this report to follow up with the order entry department to ensure that, in the future, credit limits are examined prior to accepting additional orders from customers.

- *Review the process.* Many credit granting processes are excessively cumbersome, for a variety of reasons: They involve too many people, require input from too many sources, and need multiple approvals. The result is a long time period before credit levels are set, as well as too much cost invested in the process. To avoid this problem, there should be a periodic review, preferably by the internal auditing staff, that flowcharts the entire credit granting process, makes recommendations to reduce its cost and cycle time, and which follows up to verify that recommendations have been implemented. An annual review of this type will ensure that the process is lean, as well as responsive to the needs of customers and other departments.

Once there are a sufficient number of controls over the credit granting process, one must still be concerned with a company's ability to collect on credit that has been issued to customers. The controls that assist in this task include using the services of other departments, reviewing cycle time, and watching over bad debt approvals. The controls are:

- *Enroll other departments in the effort.* The accounting staff cannot be completely successful in collecting money from customers unless it uses the efforts of other departments. A good control over this issue is to have the internal audit staff check on the collection team's efforts to use other departments prior to writing off accounts receivable. For example, there should be an effort to capitalize on the services of the sales staff to collect from their customers (which can be made easier if the sales staff's commissions are only paid when payment is received from customers), or to use other personal relationships, such as between the presidents of the company and the customer, to pay off a debt.

- *Look for special payment deals.* Sometimes, it is difficult to collect payment on an invoice, not because the collections staff is doing a poor job, but because the sales staff agreed to a special payment deal with the customer. Though it is occasionally necessary to agree to special deals, sometimes they happen without proper approvals from management. To detect such deals, there should be an occasional confirmation process with customers, whereby the customers are asked to confirm the payment terms of their invoices. Any disparity between the company's payment terms and those recorded by the customer should be investigated.

- *Match invoices to the shipping log.* Collection problems can arise when there are incorrect billings, such as when an invoice lists the wrong quantity of a shipped product. To maintain control over this issue, one can conduct a periodic comparison of the quantities noted on invoices to the quantities actually shipped, as noted in the shipping log. Since the amount billed is usually taken from a copy of the bill of lading (BOL), the BOL can also be compared to the bill and the shipping log to see where record inaccuracies are occurring.

- *Remove other accounts receivable for the receivable account.* It is difficult to gain a true understanding of the amount of overdue accounts receivable if the accounts receivable balance is skewed by the presence of miscellaneous items, such as amounts owed from company officers or taxing authorities. It is best to strip these accounts out of any receivable turnover calculation, thereby arriving at a "pure" turnover figure that will reveal the need for additional collection activities.

- *Report on collection actions taken.* It is difficult to collect an account receivable unless there is a history of the efforts previously taken to bring in a payment. Such a record should include the name of the person contacted, the date when this happened, and the nature of the discussion. A good control here is to conduct a periodic review of the contact data for all overdue accounts receivable, and to require better recordkeeping where appropriate.

- *Report on receivable items by customer.* The accounts receivable aging report is the single best control over the collections process, because it clearly shows any invoices that are overdue for payment. The report is sorted by invoice for each customer, and lists invoice amounts by category—current, 30 to 60 days old, 61 to 90 days old, and over 90 days old. By reviewing the totals for each customer, it is an easy matter to determine where the problem accounts and invoices are located, and where additional collection actions are needed.

- *Review billing frequency.* One problem with collections is the time needed to issue an invoice to the customer. A lazy billing person may wait several days or even a week between issuing invoices, which can seriously delay the time before customers will return payments for them. To detect this problem, there should be a continuing audit of the billing process that compares the date on which invoices were created to the date when products actually shipped. Any large disparity between these two dates should be investigated.

- *Review credits taken.* A common problem is that someone in the accounting department "cleans up" the accounts receivable aging by processing a number of credits that write off old accounts. This practice is fine if there is a proper approval process for the credits, but is otherwise only a lazy way to get rid of old accounts without any real effort to collect them. The best way to control this practice is to conduct a periodic review of all credits taken, and to verify that each one was approved by an authorized manager. To save time, it may make sense to allow credits on small balances without any associated approval.

- *Segregate the accounts receivable and cash receipts functions.* When the person who collects cash and applies it to accounts receivable records is the same one who creates invoices, there may be a temptation to keep some of the cash and alter the receivable records with false credits to hide the missing money. The best way to control this potential problem is to split the two functions among different people, so that the problem can only arise if there is collusion between multiple personnel, which is a much less likely occurrence.

- *Verify pricing.* Customers may not want to pay for invoices if the per-unit prices charged to them are incorrect. To control this problem, it is useful to occasionally compare the prices listed on invoices to the official company price list. Any pricing problems require immediate follow-up, as well as rebilling customers if the prices charged to them were incorrect.

There were many controls that can be installed to ensure that the credit granting and collection tasks operate as planned. This is an area in which the best intentions for setting up a quality system are not good enough. There must also be a set of firmly enforced controls that are regularly reviewed and enforced, so that credit is granted only after a reasonable amount of review and collection efforts are made in a timely manner, resulting in the minimal amount of bad debt.

BUDGETING FOR ACCOUNTS RECEIVABLE BALANCES

The *planning* function of the controller as related to accounts receivable largely has to do with the preparation of the annual business plan, and perhaps plans for a shorter time span. Working closely with the treasurer and/or credit manager, the controller's responsibilities include:

- Determining, within suitable interim time periods, the amount to be invested in accounts receivable for the planning horizon—the accounts receivable budget. Typically this is the month-end balance for each month of annual plan.

- Testing the receivable balances to determine that the planned turnover rate or daily investment is acceptable or within the standard.

- Based on past experience, or other criteria, estimating the amount required for a reasonable reserve for doubtful accounts.

- Consolidating the accounts receivable budget with other related budgets to determine that the entity has adequate funds to meet the needed receivables investment.

The determination of the monthly investment in accounts receivable would produce a plan for the next business year substantially similar to that shown in Exhibit 9.2.

Additions to the monthly customer accounts receivable balance would be based on the sales plan. Collections would be determined as described in the preceding chapter on cash planning. Essentially the same "entries" would be made using the estimated data as are made for the actual monthly activity. The same process used in calculating the receivables balance for the annual plan may be used for the long-range plan, although only annual (not monthly) estimates need be used. Computer software programs are available to determine the receivable balance and to age the accounts.

While the illustration reflects the customer accounts receivable activity, a comparable procedure would be used to estimate the "other miscellaneous receivable" balances for such typically small transactions as:

- Amounts due from officers and employees
- Claims receivable
- Accounts receivable—special transactions
- Notes receivable—miscellaneous

THE JOHNSTON COMPANY
CUSTOMER ACCOUNTS RECEIVABLE BUDGET
FOR THE YEAR ENDING DECEMBER 31, 20XX
(DOLLARS IN THOUSANDS)

Month	Beginning Balance	Sales	Cash Collections	Adjustments Dr. (Cr.)	Ending Balance
January	$ 15,620	$ 10,340	$ 9,760	$ —	$ 16,200
February	16,200	11,110	9,890	—	17,420
March	17,420	12,370	10,100	(80)	19,610
April	19,610	11,480	11,200	—	19,890
May	19,890	10,270	12,430	—	17,730
June	17,730	9,420	10,300	(60)	16,790
July	16,790	9,240	9,850	—	16,180
August	16,180	9,450	9,610	—	16,020
September	16,020	9,140	9,330	—	15,830
October	15,830	9,090	9,180	—	15,740
November	15,740	9,860	9,010	(110)	16,480
December	16,480	10,430	9,720	(120)	17,070
Total or balance	$ 15,620	$ 122,200	$ 120,380	$ (370)*	$ 17,070

* Represents accounts written off.

EXHIBIT 9.2   PLANNED INVESTMENT IN ACCOUNTS RECEIVABLES

10

PLANNING AND CONTROL
OF INVENTORIES

INTRODUCTION

A controller who is not familiar with the intricacies of inventory management may have a difficult time determining whether a company has an inventory problem at all, the nature of the problem, and how to fix it. This chapter solves these problems by describing all key aspects of inventory that a controller should be concerned with, including the costs and benefits of having inventory on hand; the various materials management systems and how they impact inventory; types of reordering methodologies; the impact of obsolete inventory on overall valuations, accuracy, and turnover; and how to budget for projected inventories in future periods. Only a thorough grounding in all of these areas will allow a controller to master the art of keeping inventory levels to a minimum without upsetting a company's customer service levels or its ability to produce to a predetermined production schedule.

COSTS AND BENEFITS OF CARRYING INVENTORY

This chapter deals with a wide range of issues dealing with inventory, to an extent that is greater than in other chapters dealing with other parts of the balance sheet. Why the hoopla? This section notes the many critical factors surrounding inventory, all of which a controller should keep in mind before making a decision that will change the mix or amount of inventory kept on hand.

First, what are the benefits of keeping inventory on hand? One is that it covers up mistakes in the production area. For example, if the production process is damaging parts that are being assembled, it makes sense to keep a supply of extra parts on hand to fill in for any shortfalls caused by damage to parts. Similarly, it is useful to keep inventory on hand if the supply of parts from suppliers is questionable, which is a common occurrence if a supplier has a track record of not delivering on time or in the expected quantities. Of course, it is also possible to solve the root problem in both cases and fix the reason for damage to parts or replace a supplier. However, these options may require a considerable amount of time; in the meantime, it is useful to keep inventory on hand to cover any problems that may arise.

Another reason for keeping a healthy level of inventory on hand is to meet the demands of customers. In particular, if there is a seasonal demand for a company's products, it makes sense to keep a considerable quantity on hand for those periods when regular production capacity cannot keep up with surging demand. It may also be necessary to keep extra quantities available if demand is not predictable and fluctuates broadly. In these cases, it is difficult to shave inventory levels to reduce working capital requirements, because there is a risk of losing sales.

These are good reasons for keeping inventory in stock; however, there are powerful reasons for keeping inventory levels down as much as possible. Even though it is not always mandatory to adhere to the following reasons for reducing inventory, a controller should at least pay close attention to them before approving of a change in inventory strategy that will lead to *more* on-hand quantities. The following reasons for *not* keeping inventory on hand are all related to cost:

- *Building cost.* Most forms of inventory must be stored indoors, so one must factor in the cost of either owning or leasing building space, which includes building maintenance, utilities, and taxes.

- *Carrying cost.* When inventory is purchased, a company must expend working capital, which is not free. The best way to determine the cost of working capital is to assume that the money could otherwise have been invested or used to pay off debt, so the interest cost of doing so is the cost of carrying inventory.

- *Change control cost.* Of particular concern to a company that undergoes frequent product redesigns is the cost of moving from old to new component parts. When this happens, there must be a clearly defined breaking point when the new part is used, resulting in the immediate obsolescence of the old part. If a company wants to avoid this type of obsolescence, it must carefully track inventory levels and switch to new parts only when inventory levels of old parts are at a low point. However, this type of close management requires additional staff time. No matter how the issue is handled, change control when inventory is present is expensive.

- *Counting cost.* Most companies still conduct a year-end inventory count, while others prefer ongoing cycle counts to ensure record accuracy. In either case, there is a cost associated with paying employees to count the inventory, which can be exacerbated by sometimes having to shut down the production facility in order to ensure an accurate count.

- *Damage cost.* The problem with having piles of inventory is that one must move it around a lot in order to get at the inventory that is currently needed; when doing so, it is easy to damage inventory. In addition, every time something is moved in or out of the inventory, there is a risk that it will be damaged. The greater the number of moves, the greater the risk of damage.

- *Handling cost.* Moving inventory requires a staff to do the moving. If there is a large amount of inventory, there must be a large staff to do the moving, frequently armed with forklifts or similar equipment to assist the moves. A large warehouse staff adds no value to the product, and consequently is nothing more than a wasteful addition to overhead costs.

- *Insurance cost.* There is a risk that inventory can be destroyed, so there should be an insurance policy that covers damage to it. Though the cost of this policy can be reduced by increasing the deductible, the deductible becomes a cost in the event of an insurance claim.

- *Obsolescence cost.* Inventory may become unusable over time, which is a considerable risk when there is a large amount of inventory on hand, and especially if a company is in an industry with high product change rates, such as the personal computer industry. In these cases, a large proportion of inventory may have to be thrown away or disposed of at a substantial discount.

- *Pilferage cost.* If there is inventory, someone may want to steal it, especially if it is a consumer article that is readily used by employees, or an extremely valuable item that can be easily converted into cash, such as consumer electronics or computer parts. By reducing the amount of inventory, there is less need to incur expenses to guard it, while there is also proportionally less inventory available to be stolen.

- *Racking cost.* Most forms of inventory do not just sit in piles on the warehouse floor. Instead, they are stored in an orderly manner in storage racks, which can be exceedingly expensive, especially if they must be strong enough to support a large amount of storage weight.

The above list shows that the costs associated with inventory add up to a substantial amount, so much that a controller must hesitate to support any kind of increase in the amount of inventory kept on hand. Yet, there are good reasons for keeping inventory in specific situations. How does one reconcile these issues? The best solution is to keep inventory only until systems can be fixed that allow a company to reduce the need for the inventory. System changes that will allow this include switching to a just-in-time (JIT) manufacturing system, using express delivery to avoid storage fees, and using drop shipping straight from suppliers to customers to avoid any in-transit storage by the company. In short, inventory is needed by most companies in the short term, but there may be options over the long term that will allow the amount of inventory to be reduced or even eliminated.

ROLE OF THE CONTROLLER

One of the underlying functions of a controller is to report on the operations of other departments. Due to this staff function, a controller usually does not take direct responsibility for the operations of the materials management function, but rather reports on its operation by a line manager. This section notes the variety of tasks in which a controller can be involved that relate directly to inventory. The tasks are outlined as:

1. *Create overall inventory policy.* Though the controller must create policy in concert with other members of the management team, he or she has an opportunity to forcefully state the advantages of keeping inventory levels as low as possible, thereby reducing the risk of inventory obsolescence, scrap costs, warehousing costs, and the size of a company's investment in working capital.

2. *Verify that inventory records are accurate.* A large part of the typical company's assets reside in the warehouse. A controller must verify that the inventory listed in a company's general ledger is actually stored in the warehouse. All of the following inventory information is subject to audit:

   (a) *Overall accuracy.* To audit overall inventory accuracy, one must print an inventory report that sorts inventory by location, and compare a sample of items from the report to the actual inventory. However, there may be inventory that does not show up on the report at all, and will therefore never be counted, so one must also pick a number of items at random from the inventory and trace them back to the database. The total number of errors resulting from this audit can then be divided by the total number of items inspected to determine the percentage of inaccuracy for the inventory.

   (b) *High-dollar accuracy.* A small inaccuracy in the amount of the most expensive inventory can have a major impact of profits, so a separate audit can review the accuracy of a large proportion of the high-dollar items in stock. This can even be an audit of virtually *all* high-dollar items.

(c) *No locations.* Despite the most extensive searches, it is probable that there will be inventory that cannot be located. If so, the controller should regularly review a report that lists all inventory in the database for which a location code has not been assigned and determine the company's monetary exposure if that inventory does not exist.

(d) *Low usage.* Low usage parts take up valuable warehouse space, and should probably be disposed of rather than kept on hand. A controller can easily determine the amount of low usage items simply by printing a list of inventory for which there has been no or low activity for a prespecified number of months.

(e) *Unusual costs.* Most controllers tend to focus an excessive amount of energy on achieving perfect quantity accuracy, to the detriment of achieving equal levels of cost accuracy. One can avoid this difficulty by reviewing inventory reports that list the lowest and highest dollar unit costs in the inventory. Such reviews can spot items that have incorrect costs, resulting in massively high or low inventory values. This is a common problem when a part is assigned a cost based on a specific unit of measure, but someone changes the unit of measure, resulting in a vastly different cost. For example, a roll of tape may have a cost in the database that is based on the number of *rolls* of tape, but the engineering department then changes the unit of measure to inches, so that it can more easily enter tape amounts into bills of material. The result is an inventory value that is several thousand times higher than it really should be.

3. *Audit inventory controls.* A controller must ensure that all current inventory controls operate in their intended manner, which helps to keep inventory quantities from diverging from their intended levels. This function can also be performed by a company's internal audit department, assuming that it is large enough to have one.

4. *Install control points.* A controller has a considerable amount of knowledge regarding how to create controls for a variety of systems and situations; this knowledge should be turned toward creating controls that will ensure that inventory is only used for its intended purpose, and not scrapped or diverted for other purposes. These controls should also make it extremely difficult for anyone to illicitly remove inventory from the company.

5. *Supervise the annual physical inventory count.* If the perpetual inventory system is not accurate, the controller must conduct a physical inventory count, which involves setting up counting procedures and supervising the counting teams that check all inventory quantities.

6. *Report on inventory costs.* A controller's prime responsibility is to ensure that the reported cost of inventory is accurate. If it is not, the amount of the cost of goods sold will be inaccurate, which can lead to major inaccuracies in a company's reported levels of profit.

7. *Know how inventory management systems work.* A controller must know how a company's inventory management systems operate, because the type of system used has a direct impact on the control systems needed, as well as the inventory levels needed to feed a company's production systems.

8. *Measure warehouse functions.* The results of any audits of the inventory should be posted in a place where the warehouse staff can see them. The measurements should include the overall accuracy of the inventory, the accuracy of high-dollar items, the total number of items in stock and their total cost (in case there is a push to reduce the overall amount of inventory), and also the percentage of jobs that were fully kitted on time (which is used only if the warehouse is supplying a job shop production operation). These measures give the warehouse staff a complete knowledge of the most important operating results of the warehouse.

9. *Create inventory management policies and procedures.*

(a) *Low-cost, high-usage items policy.* All high-usage, low-cost items shall be removed from the inventory database and maintained in bulk on the production floor, using visual reorder systems. Exceptions must be approved by management.

(b) *Inventory accuracy policy.* Whatever actions necessary shall be taken to ensure that inventory accuracy is maintained at a level of at least 95%, with a level of 98% for high-dollar items.

(c) *Measurement policy.* The controller shall provide warehouse performance and status measurements to the warehouse staff on a weekly basis.

(d) *Purchase quantity policy.* Items shall be purchased only for immediate production needs. Blanket purchase orders shall be used whenever possible to assist in reducing the paperwork requirements of this policy.

(e) *Obsolescence review policy.* The materials review board shall review the inventory database for obsolete items no less than once a week. All items that have not been used within the last 12 months shall be disposed of, unless approved by management.

(f) *Inventory disposition procedure.* All items that have not been used in the last 12 months shall be considered obsolete. Of this group, all items with an extended cost of $50 or less shall be thrown out or donated, with no approval required. If the extended cost is between $50 and $500, the purchasing department shall first attempt to return it to a supplier, after which it may be thrown out or donated with no additional approval. Items with an extended cost exceeding $500 shall be disposed of only with the prior approval of the vice president of materials management.

Given the length and breadth of the discussion in this section, it is obvious that a controller can take a very large role in the management control and review of inventory. This sort of activity is normally welcomed by personnel in the materials management function, because the upshot of these activities is better control over inventory, which leads to reduced time by the materials management staff in looking for missing parts, making rush orders, and other unnecessary activities.

MATERIAL REQUIREMENTS PLANNING SYSTEMS

As noted in the "Role of the Controller" Section, a controller should be well grounded in materials management techniques, in order to know how to make recommendations to improve inventory tracking systems, as well as how to reduce inventory levels to save working capital and other costs. This section provides a brief overview of the most common materials management system, which is material requirements planning, or MRP.

There are two types of MRP. One is material requirements planning, and the other is manufacturing resource planning (MRP II). The first variety is concerned solely with inventory management, whereas MRP II is a more sophisticated version that also controls direct labor and machine usage. We will confine this discussion to MRP, since it is concerned only with the primary focus of this chapter—inventory. Material requirements planning uses several key databases in the manufacturing system to predict when inventory is needed for the production process. Its purpose is to form an orderly flow of parts to the production department, thereby ensuring that there will be no production stoppages due to parts shortages. When properly used, it can also keep inventory levels down, so that the working capital investment in inventory is minimized.

An MRP system works with three databases. The first is the production schedule. It takes the quantities and due dates on the production schedule for each product and multiplies it by the second database, which is the bill of materials for each product. The result is a list showing the quantities of parts needed for production, as well as their due dates. The system then compares the parts list to the on-hand inventory, to determine which parts are already in stock. Any parts that are not currently in stock or on order are then ordered, which can be done either manually or automatically by the MRP system, with the option of a manual review by the purchasing department. A final feature is that the purchase dates are based on the purchasing lead times required by each supplier, so that amounts ordered will arrive just when needed. In short, an MRP system combines the most common production databases to achieve timely delivery of a sufficient number of parts to complete the production schedule.

A controller should be aware of the various advantages and disadvantages of using an MRP system. One problem is that it is highly dependent on a large amount of computing power; the system must recalculate the purchasing schedule at least once a week, which can take many hours of processing time, even with today's super-fast computers. Another issue is that the system's results will be incorrect if the underlying databases contain incorrect data. For example, incorrect information in the bill of materials will result in parts overages or shortages on the production floor. Also, an MRP system allows for purchasing parts in economic order quantities, which means that not all parts ordered will be used at once. This opens the door to the possibility of having unused and obsolete inventory. However, MRP is an excellent way to gain control of a materials management process, ensuring reasonable inventory levels and the efficient marshaling of resources to ensure that products are produced on time.

By being aware of the inner workings of an MRP system, a controller can make recommendations to senior management regarding the need to have such a system, or to make modifications that will result in reduced inventory levels.

JIT MANUFACTURING SYSTEMS

Though JIT manufacturing is widely praised in the press for its ability to streamline entire organizations, improve delivery times, and shrink inventory levels, surprisingly few companies use any of its elements, let alone the entire range of JIT applications. Perhaps a greater understanding of JIT is needed to spur its deployment. Accordingly, this section gives a brief overview of the components of JIT and the impact it can have on inventory levels.

Many of the basic factors involved in good inventory management have been briefly reviewed, but a key one yet to be discussed is the inventory and production system the management has chosen to use. None has drawn more attention recently than the just-in-time inventory system. The controllers may have little voice in which system is selected by the manufacturing executives. But they should be generally aware of the central philosophy—which basically is that all inventories are undesirable and should be eliminated or minimized—and the impact on purchasing and delivery systems, as well as the manufacturing system itself.

Adopting the just-in-time system requires major changes in purchasing and manufacturing strategies. In purchasing, the JIT system requires the manufacturers to select a few reliable suppliers who deliver, when needed, dependable materials and component parts with zero defects. The JIT manufacturing function is characterized by smaller lot sizes than traditional manufacturing, fixed production schedules for shorter periods, possible machine and process reconfiguration, as well as automation and a more flexible or multifunction workforce.

The objective of a JIT system is to produce and deliver:

- Finished goods just in time to be sold
- Subassemblies just in time to be assembled into finished goods
- Fabricated parts just in time to be made into subassemblies
- Raw materials and purchased parts just in time to be converted to fabricated parts

JIT has been described as a "pull" system of production control wherein the final assembly line production schedule triggers the withdrawal of materials or required parts at the needed time from the work centers that precede them in the manufacturing process. Workers secure the right quantity of parts to complete an order. Sequentially, each work center supplies parts to the next manufacturing operation and then manufactures parts to replace them. Thus, there is no stockpiling of work-in-process to offset lead times or to meet safety stock levels or the economic order quantities of subsequent production functions. (See the later discussion.) The results of this system are:

- Lower inventories and lower carrying costs
- Reduced rework and scrap
- Improved quality control
- Shorter production time and lead time, which assists the next result
- Increased productivity

JIT Purchasing

A successful JIT system depends, in the first instance, on a few reliable and dependable suppliers who maintain a very close buyer-vendor relationship. JIT manufacturers enter into long-term contracts with fewer suppliers. Moreover, the suppliers handle smaller lot sizes, and use statistical quality control techniques to improve the quality of their products (rather than after-the-fact inspection). The suppliers essentially become specialized makers to the manufacturers, with facilities close to the JIT manufacturer's plant, so as to make easier delivery of their products; and they are involved with the manufacturer in the product design and manufacturing process from the very outset.

The controller should be involved in the following special issues regarding JIT purchasing:

1. *Target Costing.* The controller must include projected product costs in the budgeting process. Under the JIT concept, there is more opportunity to influence product costs

during the design process than later, in the manufacturing process. Thus, the controller should be involved in setting a target product cost and assigning targeted subsidiary part costs to suppliers. Based on this targeted cost information, the controller can prepare the material cost budget.

2. *Collusion with Suppliers.* Another accounting issue involving JIT purchasing is the possibility of collusion between buyers and suppliers. Since JIT precludes competitive bidding, it may be possible for buyers to select suppliers who will kickback profits to the buyers in exchange for the business. This problem is real, but is mitigated somewhat by the amount of interaction between company employees and the supplier. The product design function under JIT purchasing requires that the company's design engineers work closely with suppliers, so these people should recognize a sham supplier. A control that the controller can use is to compare supplier prices against those of the market on a spot basis. If prices seem excessive, then the controller should investigate further. Also, the controller can investigate whether or not previously agreed part price changes (usually downwards, for JIT suppliers) have taken place.

3. *Purchasing Paperwork.* JIT purchases tend to occur frequently and involve small part quantities. Under a traditional accounting system, this would present an increased paperwork problem, for there would be more receiving documentation to match to more invoices, and more checks to cut. Consequently, the controller should consider recording receipts based on the number of parts used in production (based on bills of material), plus parts that were damaged at the fault of the buyer. This system would require very accurate bills of material.

4. *Supplier Rating Systems.* Before JIT, suppliers ratings were based on the average unit price of parts sold to the company. Under the JIT philosophy, suppliers ratings should include ability to attain part cost targets, percentage of parts arriving on time ("on time" also means "not arriving too early," for such materials must be moved and stored, creating problems for the buying company), part defect rates, and the percentage of shipments containing the exact amounts ordered. The controller should be involved not only in the design of these information gathering systems, but also in the auditing of them for accuracy.

5. *Buyer Measurement Systems.* Before JIT, buyer ratings were based on the cost savings achieved from a standard cost for a part. JIT purchasing requires buyers to be facilitators rather than clerks, so that their new jobs require coordinating design teams from the two companies, assisting in qualifying suppliers, and shrinking the supplier base. Under JIT, continuing to judge a buyer based on the purchase price variance would be dysfunctional, since the buyer would be forced to put parts out to bid for the lowest price instead of working with one supplier to achieve a targeted cost. The controller should point out such dysfunctional performance measures to management, and recommend that they be eliminated. New performance measures for buyers are difficult to derive for individual buyers. Instead, the controller should consider formulating performance measures for groups, such as new product design teams that include buyers. A typical performance measure under this scenario would be achieving a product's cost that was originally targeted by management.

JIT Delivery

JIT manufacturers closely link their production schedules to the suppliers' delivery schedules. Hence, suppliers and manufacturers are not only relocating, they are also eliminating storage areas and loading docks where delivered material can accumulate. Suppliers may feed materials and parts directly to the assembly lines.

JIT Manufacturing

As would be expected, with the emphasis on small rather than large lot sizes, changes in manufacturing processes and machine arrangements usually are necessary. Under the typical U.S. production line, similar machines performing similar tasks are grouped together. This supposedly increases labor efficiency as well as the economy of large lot size production. Under the JIT system, "group technology" is used so that the small lot work moves rapidly through a common routing over several different types of machines. Hence there is little need for work-in-process inventory.

Moreover, rather than performing the task on only one machine, the worker is trained to operate all the machines of the work center. This leads to less boredom and assists in reducing defects, which, in the process, can be identified rather quickly.

For group technology to work, employees must be heavily cross-trained in the use of several pieces of equipment, since one employee will typically operate several machines. Also, since the company must invest in employee training, the cost of losing an employee is higher than would be the case in an assembly line environment, where less training is required. Finally, the employees must be willing to take responsibility for the quality of products produced; since an entire product can be produced by one employee or work group using group technology, part defects can be directly traced to individuals.

It is beyond the scope of this volume to discuss in detail the many operational aspects of just-in-time inventory planning and control. However, a review of one company's experience relative to purchased assemblies will give a good example of the pervasive impact that a JIT system can have on traditional financial controls. In this illustration, a high-cost subassembly is purchased from a single supplier with a long time association and under a long-term contract. There is one such assembly in each finished product. Each day all assemblies needed for that day's production are delivered at 8:00 A.M. A routine was established between the supplier and the manufacturer whereby the supplier was paid weekly based on the number of finished products shipped by the *manufacturer* that week.

This procedure eliminated the preparation and handling of purchase orders, receiving reports, inventory details (receipts and disbursements), and invoices—the new control being that if a product were manufactured, tested, and shipped, then the subassembly must have been delivered. This is a very different process from the usual matching of purchase orders, receiving report, and invoice in order to effect payment.

Just-in-time concepts strongly impact several accounting processes, reports, and performance measures. The controller should be aware of the following items:

1. *Product cost tracking.* Under traditional assembly line production techniques, there were many opportunities to reduce product costs by closely examining the production process. However, with JIT, the glaring cost issues (e.g., excessive scrap and inventory levels) are eliminated from the production process. The controller may find that cost tracking systems on the production floor are not revealing cost savings. In fact, the tracking systems may cost more than the savings they generate. Consequently, the controller should consider cutting back on cost tracking systems on the shop floor and turn more attention to how well in-house and supplier design teams are achieving targeted cost goals when creating new products.

2. *Direct labor cost tracking.* Traditionally, accountants have closely tracked all direct labor variances with the help of extensive shop floor labor reporting. However, in many companies, direct labor now accounts for less than 20 percent of a product's cost, so the cost expended to track direct labor may not be worth the benefit gained by reviewing labor variance reports. Therefore, the controller should consider eliminating direct labor reporting.

3. *Accounting reports.* Most accounting reports are issued after the end of the month. Line managers review them and take action sometime well into the following month. With JIT operations, there is no work-in-process buffer to hide manufacturing problems, so line managers can spot most problems within minutes or hours of their occurrence. In short, JIT manufacturing personnel do not need monthly accounting reports as much as they used to. As JIT is implemented, the controller should periodically meet with line manager to ascertain their need for the information. The likely result will be fewer reports.

4. *Operational auditing.* Under assembly line systems, operational audits focused on sources of waste from the system, such as pilferage, obsolete inventory, and scrap. With the greatly reduced inventory levels used by a JIT system, auditors must now shift their focus to issues that will slow down JIT, such as problems with setup time reductions, process flow and workstation designs, and product designs.

5. *JIT performance measures.* Under assembly line systems, performance measures related to variances for direct labor and materials. With the assumptions under a JIT system that direct labor and materials costs are fixed and will have few variances, performance measures should shift to attaining targeted output and quality goals, the number of employee suggestions received, and the percentage implemented.

6. *Cost generators.* Under assembly line systems, cost generators were viewed as direct labor and materials. With the assumptions under a JIT system that direct labor and materials costs are fixed, the controller should target other items. For example, close attention should be paid to:

   o *Engineering change orders,* which can slow the product release process

   o *Space utilization,* since excess space should be sublet for additional revenues

   o *Inventory levels,* since less inventory leads to less space requirements, fewer obsolete items, less inventory tracking time, and reduced insurance costs

   o *Equipment downtime,* since product ship dates cannot be achieved if production facilities are not functioning

Though this description of a JIT system may lead one to believe that it is entirely different from the previously described MRP system, it is possible to transition from MRP to JIT in an orderly manner. Because a JIT system requires a minuscule amount of inventory, the underlying management principle needed to bring about this transition is an alteration in purchasing policy. A traditional policy under the MRP system is for a company to purchase inventory in those quantities that minimize inventory carrying and ordering costs, which usually results in excess quantities of inventory on hand. The controller must convince management that the more appropriate technique is to purchase only the exact amounts required, which leaves no excess to be stored in inventory. By choking off the flow of incoming inventory, the warehouse and purchasing staffs can then concentrate on gradually reducing the remaining inventory stocks by a variety of means, such as donations, throwaways, and returns to suppliers. Over time, this approach will drastically reduce the inventory to the point where this aspect of a JIT system has been achieved.

Result of System	JIT	MRP
Reduces setup time	Yes	No
Reduces scrap	Yes	No
Reduces raw material inventory	Yes	Yes
Reduces work-in-process inventory	Yes	No
Emphasizes zero-defect production	Yes	No

Exhibit 10.1 Comparison between JIT and MRP Systems

If management does not feel that there is any reason to transition from an MRP system to a JIT system, a controller can present them with the information in Exhibit 10.1.

Exhibit 10.1 shows that MRP is deficient in a number of areas, which may spur management into making a change away from MRP. However, if there is still some hesitation in moving away from an existing MRP system, it may be possible to effect a partial transition by slowly adding JIT features, such as cellular manufacturing groups and reduced setup times, which work well in either operating environment.

In short, JIT principles can effect a drastic reduction in the amount of inventory a controller must contend with, while also improving product quality and the reliability of delivery times to customers. It is a system well worth implementing, either totally or in part.

INVENTORY REORDERING SYSTEMS

The type of inventory reorder system should be of great concern to a controller, because the wrong method can greatly increase the amount of inventory on hand. This section presents a list of reordering methods, shown in declining order of desirability, with the first one resulting in the smallest amount of inventory on hand, and the last one the largest. The first method, JIT, requires the greatest attention to management systems, while the last is a simple approach that can be easily installed with minimal continuing supervision, which is perhaps why the last approach is the one most commonly used in practice. The reordering systems are:

- *JIT.* This method requires a company to issue a request for the immediate delivery of parts to a supplier as soon as it needs the parts in the production process, with the supplier immediately delivering the exact amount required to the production line. Although this appears to be an elegantly simple approach, it actually requires great attention to the accuracy of bills of material, as well as the selection of suppliers and the quality of incoming goods. It results in almost no on-hand inventory (with the exception of work-in-process), and is therefore the best reordering system from the perspective of reducing a company's investment in inventory.

- *MRP.* This method calculates the exact amount of inventory needed for scheduled production, based on bills of material, the production schedule, and existing inventory levels. The computer system then generates a recommended ordering level, which is executed by a purchasing person. This is an excellent ordering method, but can result in too much inventory if the ordering levels are supplemented by an economic order quantity, which may result in too much inventory being purchased.

- *Visual check system.* This method is a simple check of stocking levels, with reordering taking place based on the knowledge of the checker of the movement of each inventory item. A more modern variation is to mark lines on storage bins; reordering takes place as soon as inventory falls below the lines. Another variation is to have two storage bins for each item; reordering takes place when the larger, main storage bin is empty, while the smaller emergency bin is used until the reordered amount arrives. This is a good approach for the reordering of large-volume, low-cost items that are otherwise difficult to track, such as fittings and fasteners.

- *Reservation method.* This method recognizes the available stock as well as the physical stock. Available stock is defined as stock on order, plus physical stock, less the unfilled requirement. The reorder point is based on the available stock rather than the physical stock.

- *Minimum–maximum.* A very common means for reordering inventory is to use the "minimum–maximum" system, or "MinMax." The minimum is the lowest acceptable amount of inventory that should be kept on hand, while the maximum is the highest acceptable amount. The minimum represents a margin of safety, while the maximum is usually the minimum level plus the standard ordering quantity. As a general rule, the use of a MinMax system is practical where the rate of sale or use of products is fairly stable and not subject to wide fluctuations or sporadic movements and where the order time is fairly short. However, it is based on a historical view of inventory data and can become inaccurate over time as usage rates vary. For this reason, it is generally inferior to a forward-looking system, such as material requirements planning.

The best way to still have an operational MinMax system while keeping the inventory investment low is to modify the "min/max" report so that it also shows the time period since a part was used, and its usage volume during the past 12-month period. If the computer system contains information from previous years, this can also be included, so that the report notes any trends in item usage. This additional information can be used by the purchasing staff to modify the minimum and maximum levels "on the fly," so that the figures are constantly trimmed to match actual usage. Without this additional information, the minimum and maximum levels for each part will probably be adjusted only once every few years, which may lead to significant shortages or surpluses of parts. Thus, modifying the "min/max" report to include usage information allows buyers to change the preset ordering levels to match actual usage.

As companies place more and more emphasis on reducing their working capital investments in inventory, the reorder point system will come under more attack. This is because it is based on prior usage, not expected usage. Any reorder system based on what has happened in the past may very well result in orders for inventory items that have declining usage, resulting in excess inventory. The controller should regularly review the usage trends for those parts that are reordered with reorder points, and also correspond with the engineering department to see what parts are to be discontinued. Any part that is to be excluded from future products should immediately have its reorder point removed from the computer system, which will keep a company from ordering more of it when it is no longer needed.

In this section, the pros and cons of various inventory reordering systems, with a particular emphasis on their impact on inventory levels, were discussed. A controller who cares about a company's overall inventory investment would be wise to pay close attention to the types of reordering systems currently in use.

OBSOLETE INVENTORY

A controller should be deeply concerned with the extent and cost of obsolete inventory, because it can have a dramatic effect on a company's profits. Accounting rules state that the value of all obsolete inventory shall be written off as soon as it is identified, so a controller should always have current information on the state of this portion of the inventory. This section describes how to obtain information about obsolete inventory, as well as how to track down the causes of obsolescence and eliminate or at least reduce them.

The easiest way to determine whether a part is already obsolete or heading in that direction is to create a report that extracts the last usage date for a part from the production or inventory databases. This extracted information can then be sorted by date, with the oldest parts appearing at the top of the report. It is then a simple matter to review this list with the engineering staff to see which of the old parts are not going to be used again. These old parts can also be sorted by extended dollar value and totaled, providing an easy calculation of the total amount of obsolete inventory that a controller must write off on the financial statements.

An additional approach for determining whether a part is obsolete is reviewing engineering change orders. These documents note those parts being replaced by different ones, as well as when the changeover is scheduled to take place. One can then search the inventory database to see how many of the parts that are being replaced are still in stock, which can then be totaled, yielding another variation on the amount of obsolete inventory on hand.

A final method for determining the amount of obsolescence is to run a "where used" report, which is a common one when a computer system contains a bill of materials for each product a company produces. The report lists all of the products for which a part is used. If the report lists parts for which there are no product uses, then those parts can be considered obsolete (unless they are new parts being purchased for a new product that does not yet have a bill of materials in the system). To be absolutely certain of a part's status as being obsolete, it may be possible to use all three methods to derive three lists of obsolete parts, which can then be reviewed with the engineering staff periodically to determine which parts are truly obsolete. In truth, because of the overwhelming workload of the accounting and engineering departments, it is most common to simply run the first report, showing those parts with the longest period since use, and record those items as obsolete. The preferred approach, however, is to use all the methods, thereby avoiding the disposal of some inventory for which there may still be a use.

No matter what approach is used to identify obsolete inventory, it is uncommon to rely only on reports to verify that something is obsolete. Instead, the reports should be examined by a group of people who represent several departments and are authorized to throw out inventory. This group represents the engineering, accounting, production, and materials management departments, and is commonly known as the Materials Review Board (MRB). The group is tasked with not only throwing out obsolete inventory, but also examining parts that are suspected to be defective, and authorizing either rework, scrapping, or the delivery of parts back to suppliers for replacement or credit. The MRB must decide, based on visual inspection, if something is truly obsolete.

Although a controller may believe that it is only his or her responsibility to *identify* obsolete inventory, it is better to provide some value to the company by going a step further and tracking down the causes of obsolescence, so that they can be reduced or even eliminated. This extra step can eliminate a great deal of expense. The primary issues causing obsolescence are:

- *Excessive purchasing volumes.* The purchasing department may be purchasing in very large quantities, in order to save itself the trouble of issuing a multitude of purchase orders for smaller quantities, or because it can obtain lower prices by purchasing in large quantities. This problem can be avoided by attaching purchasing performance goals to minimal on-hand inventory, and can be verified by continuing reviews by the internal audit staff.

- *Inadequate bills of material.* A well-run purchasing department will use bills of material to determine the parts needed to build a product, and then order them in the correct quantities. If the bill of material is incorrect, then the items purchased will either be the wrong ones, or the correct ones but in the wrong quantities. To avoid this problem, the bills of material must be audited regularly for accuracy.

- *Low inventory turnover.* If there is too much inventory sitting in the warehouse, it will take so long to work through it that some of the inventory is bound to become obsolete before being used. This is partly the fault of the purchasing staff (see previous point), but may also be caused by a conservative production manager who wants to have enormous volumes of all parts kept on hand, so that there is no chance of a stock-out occurring that can interfere with the smooth completion of production goals. Attaching a high inventory turnover target to the goals of the production manager can reduce this problem.

- *Poor engineering change control.* If the engineering department does not verify that old parts are completely used up before installing a new part in a product, the remaining quantities of the old part will be rendered obsolete. This can be a major source of obsolescence. To avoid it, there should be tight control over using up old parts first, which can be verified by the internal audit staff and enforced by top management.

- *Poor inventory tracking systems.* It is easy for a part to become obsolete if no one knows where it is. If it is buried in an odd corner of the warehouse, there is not much chance that it will be used up. To avoid this problem, there should be location codes in the inventory database for every part, along with continual cycle counting to ensure that locations are correct. A periodic audit of location codes will give management a clear view of the accuracy of this information.

If a controller can identify any of the above problems as being the cause of obsolescence, quantify the cost of the problem, and aggressively push for changes, there can be a very significant cost savings.

Many companies that have not reviewed their inventories for a long time will find that obsolescence is a much larger problem than they would care to believe. It is not impossible for an older company to find that 80 percent of its inventory is obsolete. One can look upon such a problem as a major opportunity, because a company can write off a very large amount and reduce profits, thereby avoiding paying taxes. However, highly leveraged companies are probably using their inventories as collateral for loans and will face a reduction in the amount of debt that creditors are willing to lend if the amount of inventory is reduced; in these cases, it is best for a company to embark on an intensive campaign of inventory returns to suppliers, so that it can realize as much cash as possible from the disposition of inventory. Thus, obsolescence can have a major impact on a company's tax and debt situation.

REDUCING INVENTORY

A controller may be faced with suspected inaccuracies of unknown size in a company's inventories. If the number of items in stock is minor, then this problem is an easy one to correct—enroll a group of counters and descend on the warehouse for a few hours of counting. However, there are usually many parts, frequently scattered throughout the facility, which are improperly identified (if at all). In these cases, a controller is faced with a serious problem, since any significant inaccuracy has a direct impact on the cost of goods sold and profits. This section briefly describes the tasks a controller can complete in order to reduce the chore of counting inventory, which essentially means reducing the amount of inventory to count.

The best way to reduce the work associated with reviewing the accuracy of a perpetual inventory's cost is to reduce the size of the perpetual inventory. This can be done by using JIT manufacturing techniques. This involves moving goods straight from the supplier to the shop floor, thereby avoiding the warehouse entirely. To bypass the warehouse, these shipments must be in small enough quantities to avoid the storage of excess amounts in the warehouse, and they must arrive precisely on time to avoid storage until they are needed in the production process. If these two criteria can be met, the quantity of goods stored in the warehouse can be limited to those items that must be ordered in bulk and those items that are delivered too early to be immediately used by the production department. The result for the controller is a minimal inventory quantity to audit, cost, and report on.

Another important consideration in establishing sound inventory management is the standardization of materials and products and the simplification of the line. Simplification is merely the elimination of excess types and sizes. The elimination of those items that do not sell readily can contribute greatly to reducing the inventory which must be carried. Simplification is labor-intensive once inventory has been received, for considerable effort is needed to sell off excess inventory and ship it out of the warehouse. Less work is required if simplification is treated as a key step in designing new products, so that existing parts are used, rather than stocking new parts that may become obsolete.

Standardization is a more general term having to do with the establishment of standards. In the application to inventories, it has reference to the reduction of a line to fixed types, sizes, and characteristics that are considered to be standard. The object is to reduce the number of items, to establish interchangeability of manufactured parts and products, and to establish standards of quality in materials. With a reduction in the possible number of inventory items to be carried, the control problem is facilitated. Standardization extends even to such insignificant items as fasteners. If similar products can be designed to be assembled with a single bolt instead of ten slight variations on the same bolt size and material, then nine items can be eliminated, and no longer have to be tracked. Every time an item is removed from inventory, cost is reduced in the areas of cycle counting, obsolescence reserves, insurance, material moves, kitting, and receiving.

A more efficient inventory tracking system can be achieved if all obsolete inventory is removed from stock. The reason for improved efficiency when this happens is that a considerable amount of cycle counting is required to maintain a perpetual inventory. If some of the inventory is deleted, there is less inventory left to cycle count, resulting in a more accurate inventory with less counting effort by the staff. The controller should be aware, however, that overall inventory accuracy may initially decline if obsolete inventory is removed from stock; the reason for this decline is that obsolete inventory represents the most stable part of the inventory (since it is never used). By removing it, the usage level (and therefore the volatility) of the remaining inventory will *increase,* resulting in reduced initial levels of accuracy.

One of the major inventory-related problems for a controller is subtracting the value of consignment stock from inventory. This is inventory that is owned by another entity (e.g., a supplier or customer) and therefore cannot be included in the company's inventory valuation. Because this inventory may have the same appearance as inventory that is owned by the company, the best solution is to immediately store the consignment stock in a segregated area as soon as it is received. The other problem with consignment inventory is identifying it when it first arrives on the receiving dock. If the controller enforces the use of purchase orders for all receipts, then either the lack of a purchase order or its identification on a special purchase order should be sufficient to identify the consignment stock. If this separate storage requirement is enforced, the accuracy of the physical inventory's extended cost will be greatly improved.

A final method for reducing the amount of inventory to count is to shift as much inventory as possible to the shop floor and expense it as shop supplies. This approach works very well for fittings and fasteners, which are typically of low cost as well as being difficult to count. The approach has an added benefit of making it much easier for production personnel to access the parts, which not only improves employee morale, but also reduces the amount of materials handling, because there are fewer materials to move to the production facility.

There are a number of approaches for reducing the amount of inventory that must be counted. By segregating consignment stock, eliminating obsolete inventory, moving small parts to the shop floor, and using JIT systems, a controller can drastically reduce the inventory counting chore.

INVENTORY CUTOFF

One of the most common problems for a controller is not obtaining a proper period-end cutoff of inventory. The problem stems from receiving inventory while not recording a corresponding account payable. Without the payable amount being listed in the accounting records, inventory will be overstated, resulting in an understated cost-of-goods-sold figure, which yields an inordinately large profit number. The reverse problem of recording a payable before inventory is recorded is also possible but uncommon, because suppliers tend to send invoices *after* the shipment of goods, resulting in the inventory arriving first and being recorded first. If this cutoff problem is not properly dealt with at the end of each reporting period, a controller may end up reporting incorrect profit figures, which can lead to the hiring of a new controller.

How can a controller avoid the cutoff problem? The answer is a simple one, but the execution of the solution is not that simple, because it requires absolutely rigid adherence to an established receiving procedure, as well as the construction and implementation of a computerized matching system. If the procedure and computer system are not adhered to, there will continue to be cutoff problems, no matter what other solutions a controller may attempt to implement.

The solution to the cutoff problem is the proper maintenance and use of a receiving log. If the receiving staff religiously and accurately logs all incoming materials into the receiving log, the controller has an excellent tool for comparing accounts payable to receipts, which effectively solves the cutoff problem. For example, a controller can take all incoming invoices that have arrived near the end of the month and manually compare them to the receiving log, to see when items were actually received. If an item was not received until the beginning of the next reporting period, then the corresponding supplier invoice should also not be recorded until the following reporting period. The log can also be used to determine whether any supplier invoices have not been received at all, simply by matching every receipt in the log to an invoice. If there is no invoice, the controller can accrue for the expected amount of the supplier billing. One problem with using a receiving log is that it must be totally accurate—it must include the exact amount received, identify from whom it was sent, and note the correct date of the receipt. It is also important that the items noted as being received in the log are also recorded in the inventory database on the same date and in the correct quantities; otherwise, all of the work performed to match invoices to the receiving log will be in vain, because an inaccurate inventory database will still result in incorrect period-end inventory numbers. Given these problems, an accurate receiving log is still the best way to attain an accurate period-end inventory cutoff.

The trouble with manually matching supplier invoices to the receiving log is that it is *manual*—the controller must expend a respectable amount of accounting staff time on the matching process, which can interfere with the timely completion of financial statements (which are dependent on the completion of the cutoff analysis). However, it is possible to use automation to avoid nearly all of the matching work. To achieve this, the receiving log must be on-line, not a written document, so that the receiving staff enters information into a database that can then be compared to supplier invoices, which must also be entered into the database in a timely manner. If the receiving log includes a company purchase order number that was used to purchase materials, this number can be used as an index to compare receipts to invoices (which should also note the purchase order number). This automated cross-reference can be performed automatically by the computer, which can then print out a list of receipts for which there are no invoices, as well as a list of invoices for which there are no receipts. The only manual labor is to then review this list and determine whether the information is accurate. If it is, the accounting staff can make accruals that will result in a perfect match of receipts to invoices. Thus, the use of automation and the receiving log will give a controller excellent control over the period-end cutoff problem.

The solution to the cutoff problem seems simple; it is easy for it to fail, however, because there are always situations that will result in the incorrect recording of information, usually in the receiving log, that will alter the period-end inventory results. For example, a new receiving person who has not been properly trained may not enter information into the receiving log properly. Also, an overwhelmed receiving department may not enter receipts into the receiving log for several days, which may result in incorrect inventory balances. Also, there may be special situations, such as the receipt of consignment inventory that the company does not own, that are recorded improperly. For all of these situations, the best method of detection is to employ a company's internal audit staff to conduct an ongoing review of receiving procedures, to determine where problems are arising. Other types of fixes are to periodically retrain the receiving staff, provide extra receiving staffing during periods of high transaction volume, and produce clear procedures for the receipt of all possible items. Only by implementing all of these error checking and error prevention methods will a controller avoid period-end cutoff problems.

BUDGETING FOR RAW MATERIALS

There are basically two methods of developing the inventory budget of raw materials, purchased parts, and supplies:

1. Budget each important item separately based on the production program.
2. Budget materials as a whole or classes of materials, based on selected production factors.

Practically all concerns must employ both methods to some extent, although one or the other predominates. The former method is always preferable to the extent that it is practicable, since it allows quantities to be budgeted more precisely.

Budgeting Individual Items of Material

The following steps should be taken in budgeting the major individual items of materials and supplies:

1. Determine the physical units of material required for each item of goods to be produced during the budget period.

2. Accumulate these into total physical units of each material item required for the entire production program.

3. Determine for each item of material the quantity that should be on hand periodically to provide for the production program with a reasonable margin of safety.

4. Deduct material inventories that are expected will be on hand at the beginning of the budget period to ascertain the total quantities to be purchased.

5. Develop a purchasing program which will ensure that the quantities will be on hand at the time they are needed. The purchase program must give effect to such factors as economically sized orders, economy of transportation, and margin of safety against delays.

6. Test the resulting budgeted inventories by standard turnover rates.

7. Translate the inventory and purchase requirements into dollars by applying the expected prices of materials to budgeted quantities.

In many instances, it is the controller's staff that translates the *unit* requirements and balances into values, based on the data received from production control or purchasing, and so on. In some cooperative efforts, the accounting staff may undertake the entire task of determining quantities and values, based on computer programs agreed to by the manufacturing arm (the explosion of finished goods requirements into the raw material components, etc.).

In practice, many difficulties arise in executing the foregoing plan. In fact, it is practicable to apply the plan only to important items of material that are used regularly and in relatively large quantities. Most manufacturing concerns find that they must carry hundreds or even thousands of different items of materials and supplies to which this plan cannot be practically applied. Moreover, some concerns cannot express their production programs in units of specific products. This is true, for example, where goods are partially or entirely made to customers' specifications. In such cases, it is necessary to look to past experience to ascertain the rate and the regularity of movement of individual material items and to determine maximum and minimum quantities between which the quantities must be held. This necessitates a program of continuous review of material records as a basis for purchasing and frequent revision of maximum and minimum limits to keep the quantities adjusted to current needs.

Budget Based on Production Factors

For those items of materials and supplies that cannot be budgeted individually, the budget must be based on general factors of expected production activity, such as total budgeted labor hours, productive hours, standard allowed hours, cost of materials consumed, or cost of goods manufactured. To illustrate, assume that the cost of materials consumed (other than basic materials which are budgeted individually) is budgeted at $1,000,000 and that past experience demonstrates that these materials and supplies should be held to a rate of turnover of five times per year; then an average inventory of $200,000 should be budgeted. This would mean that individual items of material could be held in stock approximately 73 days (one fifth of 365 days). This could probably be accomplished by instructing the executives in charge to keep on hand an average of 60 days' supply. Although such a plan cannot be applied rigidly to each item, it serves as a useful guide in the control of individual items and prevents the accumulation of excessive inventories.

In the application of this plan, other factors must also be considered. The relationship between the inventory and the selected factor of production activity will vary with the degree of production activity. Thus a turnover of five times may be satisfactory when materials consumed are at the $1,000,000 level, but it may be necessary to reduce this to four times when the level goes to $750,000. Conversely, it may be desirable to hold it to six times when the level rises to $1,250,000. Moreover, some latitude may be necessitated by the seasonal factor, since it may be necessary to increase the quantities of materials and supplies in certain months in anticipation of seasonal demands. The ratio of inventory to selected production factors at various levels of production activity and in different seasons should be plotted and studied until standard relationships can be established. The entire process can be refined somewhat by establishing different standards for different sections of the materials and supplies inventory.

The plan, once in operation, must be closely checked by monthly comparisons of actual and standard ratios. When the rate of inventory movement falls below the standard, the records of individual items must be studied to detect the slow moving items.

Materials Purchasing Budget Illustrated

Some of the problems and methods of determining the total amount of expected purchases may be better understood by illustration. Assume, for example, that this information is made available regarding production requirements after a review of the production budget:

| | | Class | | | |
| | | Units | | | Amount |
Period		W	X	Y	Z
January		400	500		
February		300	600		
March		500	400		
Subtotal		1,200	1,500		
2nd quarter		1,500	1,200		
3rd quarter		1,200	1,500		
4th quarter		1,000	1,700		
Total		4,900	5,900	10,000	$ 20,000

Solely for illustrative purposes, the following four groups of products have been assumed:

Class W	Material of high unit value, for which a definite quantity and time program is established in advance-such as for stock items. Also, the material is controlled on a MinMax inventory basis for budget purposes.
Class X	Similar to item W, except that, for budget purposes, MinMax limits are not used.
Class Y	Material items for which definite quantities are established for the budget period but for which no definite time program is established, such as special orders on hand.
Class Z	Miscellaneous material items grouped together and budgeted only in terms of total dollar purchases for the budget period.

In actual practice, of course, decisions about production time must be made regarding items using Y and Z classifications. However, the bases described later in this chapter are applicable in planning the production level.

Class W. Where the items are budgeted on a MinMax basis, it usually is necessary to determine the range within which purchases must fall to meet production needs and stay within inventory limits. A method of making such a calculation is shown next:

	Units	
	For Minimum Inventory	For Maximum Inventory
January production requirements	400	400
Inventory limit	50	400
Total	450	800
Beginning inventory	200	200
Limit of receipts (purchases)	$ 250	$ 600

Within these limits, the quantity to be purchased will be influenced by such factors as unit transportation and handling costs, price considerations, storage space, availability of material, capital requirements, and so forth.

A similar determination would be made for each month for each such raw material, and a schedule of receipts and inventory might then be prepared, somewhat in this fashion:

	Units					
Period	Beginning Inventory	Receipts	Usage	Ending Inventory	Unit Value	Purchases Budget
January	200	400	400	200	$200	$ 80,000
February	200	400	300	300		80,000
March	300	400	500	200		80,000
Subtotal		1,200	1,200			240,000
2nd quarter	200	1,350	1,500	50		270,000
3rd quarter	50	1,200	1,200	50		240,000
4th quarter	50	1,200	1,000	250		240,000
Total		$ 4,950	$ 4,900			$ 990,000

Class X. It is assumed that the class X materials can be purchased as needed. Since other controls are practical on this type of item and since other procurement problems exist, purchases are determined by the production requirements. A simple extension is all that is required to determine the dollar value of expected purchases:

Period	Quantity	Unit Price	Total
January	500	$10	$ 5,000
February	600		6,000
March	400		4,000
Subtotal	1,500		15,000
2nd quarter	1,200		12,000
3rd quarter	1,500		15,000
4th quarter	1,700		17,000
Total	$ 5,900		$ 59,000

Class Y. The breakdown of the class Y items may be assumed to be:

Item	Quantity	Unit Price	Cost
Y-1	1,000	$1.00	$ 1,000
Y-2	2,000	1.10	2,200
Y-3	3,000	1.20	3,600
Y-4	4,000	1.30	5,200
Total	$ 10,000		$ 12,000

A determination about the time of purchase must be made, even though no definite delivery schedules and the like have been set by the customer. In this instance, the distribution of the cost and units might be made on the basis of past experience or budgeted production factors, such as budgeted machine hours. The allocation to periods could be made on past experience, as:

Period	Past Experience Regarding Similar Units Manufactured	Units					Values (Purchases Budget)
		Y-1	Y-2	Y-3	Y-4	Total	
January	10%	100	200	300	400	1,000	$ 1,200
February	15	150	300	450	600	1,500	1,800
March	10	100	200	300	400	1,000	1,200
Subtotal	35	350	700	1,050	1,400	3,500	4,200
2nd quarter	30	300	600	900	1,200	3,000	3,600
3rd quarter	20	200	400	600	800	2,000	2,400
4th quarter	15	150	300	450	600	1,500	1,800
Total	100%	1,000	2,000	3,000	4,000	10,000	$ 12,000

The breakdown of units is for the benefit of the purchasing department only, inasmuch as the percentages can be applied against the total cost and need not apply to individual units. In practice, if the units are numerous regarding types and are of small value, the quantities of each might not be determined in connection with the forecast.

Class Z. Where the materials are grouped, past experience again may be the means of determining estimated expenditures by the period of time. Based on production hours, the distribution of class Z items may be assumed to be (cost of such materials assumed to be $2 per production hour):

Period	Productive Hours	Amount
January	870	$ 1,740
February	830	1,660
March	870	1,740
Subtotal	2,570	5,140
2nd quarter	2,600	5,200
3rd quarter	2,230	4,460
4th quarter	2,600	5,200
Total	10,000	$ 20,000

THE BLANK COMPANY
PURCHASES BUDGET
FOR THE YEAR 20XX

Period	Class W	X	Y	Z	Total
January	$ 80,000	$ 5,000	$ 1,200	$ 1,740	$ 87,940
February	80,000	6,000	1,800	1,660	899,460
March	80,000	4,000	1,200	1,740	86,940
Subtotal	240,000	15,000	4,200	5,140	264,340
2nd quarter	270,000	12,000	3,600	5,200	290,800
3rd quarter	240,000	15,000	2,400	4,460	261,860
4th quarter	240,000	17,000	1,800	5,200	264,000
Total	$ 990,000	$ 59,000	$ 12,000	$ 20,000	$ 1,081,000

EXHIBIT 10.2   SAMPLE PURCHASES BUDGET

When all materials have been grouped and the requirements have been determined and translated to cost, the materials budget may be summarized as in Exhibit 10.2.

Exhibit 10.2 relates to raw materials. A similar approach would be taken with respect to manufacturing supplies. A few major items might be budgeted as the class W or X items just cited, but the bulk probably would be handled as Z items.

Once the requirements as measured by delivery dates have been made firm, it is necessary for the financial department to translate such data into cash disbursement needs through average lag time and so forth.

BUDGETING FOR WORK-IN-PROCESS

The inventory of goods actually in process of production between stocking points can be best estimated by applying standard turnover rates to budgeted production. This may be expressed either in units of production or dollars and may be calculated for individual processes and departments or for the factory as a whole. The former is more accurate. To illustrate this procedure, assume the following inventory and production data for a particular process or department:

Process inventory estimated for January 1	500 units	(a)
Production budgeted for month of January	1,200 units	(b)
Standard rate of turnover (per month)	4 times	(c)
Average value per unit of goods in this process	$10	

With a standard turnover rate of four times per month, the average inventory should be 300 units (1,200 + 4). To produce an average inventory of 300 units, the ending inventory should be 100 units:

$$\frac{500 + 100}{2} = 300$$

Using the symbol X to denote the quantity to be budgeted as ending inventory, the following formula can be applied:

$$X = \frac{2b}{c} - a = \frac{2(1200)}{4} - 500 = 100 \text{ units}$$

Value of ending inventory is $1,000 (100 \times $10)$.

Where the formula produces a minus quantity (as it will if beginning inventory is excessive), the case should be studied as an individual problem and a specific estimate made for the process or department in question.

Control over the work-in-process inventories can be exercised by a continuous check of turnover rates. Where the individual processes, departments, or plants are revealed to be excessive they should then be subjected to individual investigation.

The control of work-in-process inventories has been sorely neglected in many concerns. The time between which material enters the factory and emerges as the finished product is frequently much longer than necessary for efficient production. An extensive study of the automobile tire industry revealed an amazing spread of time between five leading manufacturers, one company having an inventory float six times that of another. This study indicated also, by an analysis of the causes of the float time, that substantial reductions could be made in all five of the companies without interference with production efficiency.

Although it is desirable to reduce the investment in goods actually being processed to a minimum consistent with efficient production, it is frequently desirable to maintain substantial inventories of parts and partially finished goods as a means of reducing finished inventories.

Parts, partial assemblies, processed stock, or any type of work-in-process that is stocked at certain points should be budgeted and controlled in the same manner as materials. That is, inventory quantities should be set for each individual item, based on the production program; or inventory limits should be set that will conform to standard rates of turnover. In the former case, control must be exercised through the enforcement of the production program; in the latter case, maximum and minimum quantities must be established and enforced for each individual item.

With the planned cost input to work-in-process known from the materials usage budget, the direct labor budget, and the manufacturing expense budget (see Chapters 4 and 5), and the quantities of planned completed goods furnished by manufacturing, the controller may develop the planned work-in-process, time-phased (condensed), as shown in Exhibit 10.3. The reasonableness of the budgeted inventory level should be tested by one of the several methods suggested in this chapter (turnover, etc.).

BUDGETING FOR FINISHED GOODS

The budget of finished goods inventory (or merchandise in the case of trading concerns) must be based on the sales budget. If, for example, it is expected that 500 units of item A will be sold during the budget period, it must be ascertained what number of units must be kept in stock to support such a sales program. It is seldom possible to predetermine the exact quantity that will be demanded by customers day by day. Some margin of safety must be maintained by means of the finished goods inventory so that satisfactory deliveries can be made. With this margin established, it is possible to develop a program of production or purchases whereby the stock will be replenished as needed.

THE ILLUSTRATIVE COMPANY
BUDGET FOR WORK-IN-PROCESS
FOR THE PLAN YEAR 20XX
(DOLLARS IN HUNDREDS)

Month/Quarter	Beginning Inventory	Charges to Work-in-Process				Transfers to Finished Goods	Ending Inventory
		Direct Material	Direct Labor	Manufacturing Expense	Total		
January	$ 264,800	$ 110,000	$ 84,700	$ 105,900	$ 300,600	$ 307,100	$ 258,300
February	258,300	120,000	92,400	115,500	327,900	314,400	271,800
March	271,800	145,000	110,200	137,750	392,950	402,800	261,950
Total-Quarter 1	264,800	375,000	287,300	359,150	1,021,450	1,024,300	261,950
Quarter 2	261,950	432,000	332,640	415,800	1,180,440	1,186,210	256,180
Quarter 3	256,180	353,000	271,800	338,700	963,500	969,100	250,580
Quarter 4	250,580	327,000	250,800	314,600	892,400	880,300	262,680
Grand Total	$ 264,800	$ 1,487,000	$ 1,142,540	$ 1,428,250	$ 4,057,790	$ 4,059,910	$ 262,680

EXHIBIT 10.3 BUDGET FOR WORK-IN-PROCESS

Budgeting Finished Goods by Individual Items

Two general methods may be employed in budgeting the finished goods inventory. Under the first method, a budget is established for each item separately. This is done by studying the past sales record and the sales program of each item and determining the quantity that should be on hand at various dates (usually, the close of each month) throughout the budget period. The detailed production or purchase program can then be developed to provide such quantities over and above current sales requirements. The total budget is merely the sum of the budgets of individual items. This total budget can then be tested by the rate of turnover desired as proof that a satisfactory relationship will be maintained between inventory and sales and that it harmonizes with the general financial program. If it fails in either respect, revision must be made in the program of sales, production, or finance until a proper coordination is effected.

Under this plan, control over the inventory is effected by means of enforcement of the sales and production programs. If either varies to any important degree from the budget, the other must be revised to a compensating degree and the inventory budget revised accordingly.

Where the sales and production programs can be enforced with reasonable certainty, this is the preferable method. It is particularly suitable for those concerns that manufacture a comparatively small number of items in large quantities. The application is similar in principle to that illustrated in connection with raw materials controlled budget-wise by minimums and maximums.

Budgeting Total Finished Quantities and Values

Where the sales of individual items fluctuate considerably and where such fluctuations must be watched for hundreds or even thousands of items, a second plan is preferable. Here basic policies are adopted relative to the relationship that must be maintained between finished inventory and sales. This may be done by establishing standard rates of turnover for the inventory as a whole or for different sections of the inventory. For example, it may be decided that a unit turnover rate of three times per year should be maintained for a certain class of goods or that the dollar inventory or another class must not average more than one fourth of the annual dollar cost of sales. The budget is then based on such relationships, and the proper executives are charged with the responsibility of controlling the quantities of individual items in such a manner that the resulting total inventories will conform to the basic standards of turnover.

With such standard turnover rates as basic guides, those in charge of inventory control must then examine each item in the inventory; collect information about its past rate of movement, irregularity of demand, expected future demand, and economical production quantity; and establish maximum and minimum quantities, and quantities to order. Once the governing quantities are established, they must be closely watched and frequently revised if the inventory is to be properly controlled.

The establishment and use of maximum, minimum, and order quantities can never be resolved into a purely clerical routine if it is to be effective as an inventory control device. A certain element of executive judgment is necessary in the application of the plan. If, for example, the quantities are based on past sales, they must be revised as the current sales trend indicates a change in sales demand. Moreover, allowance must be made for seasonal demands. This is sometimes accomplished by setting different limits for different seasons.

The most frequent cause of the failure of such inventory control plans is the assignment of unqualified personnel to the task of operating the plan and the failure to maintain a continuous review of sales experience relative to individual items. The tendency in far too many cases is to resolve the matter into a purely clerical routine and assign to it clerks capable only of routine execution. The danger is particularly great in concerns carrying thousands of items in finished stock, with the result that many quantities are excessive and many obsolete and slow-moving items accumulate in stock. The successful execution of an inventory control plan requires continuous study and research, meticulous records of individual items and their movement, and a considerable amount of individual judgment.

The plan, once in operation, should be continually tested by comparing the actual rates of turnover with those prescribed by the general budget program. If this test is applied to individual sections of the finished inventory, it will reveal the particular divisions that fail to meet the prescribed rates of movement. The work of correction can then be localized to these divisions.

Whenever possible, the plan of finished inventory control should be exercised in terms of units. When this is not practicable, it must be based on dollar amounts.

In the context of preparing the annual business plan in monetary terms, and based on the quantities of finished goods (furnished by the cognizant executive) deemed necessary for an adequate inventory, the controller can develop the budget for the finished goods inventory, much as is shown in condensed form in Exhibit 10.4. When the total of the inventory segments is known, the total inventory budget for the company can be summarized as in Exhibit 10.5. Such a summary can be useful in discussing inventory levels with management. Any pertinent ratios can be included. Again, in testing the reasonableness of the annual business plan, the inventory—by segments, or perhaps in total—should be tested by turnover rate or another device suggested for control (or planning) purposes.

THE ILLUSTRATIVE COMPANY
FINISHED GOODS INVENTORY BUDGET
FOR THE PLAN YEAR 20XX
(DOLLARS IN HUNDREDS)

Month/Quarter	Beginning Inventory	Transfers from Work-in-Process	Purchased Parts (a)	Cost of Goods Sold	Ending Inventory
January	$ 329,600	$ 307,100	$ 71,000	$ 365,400	$ 342,300
February	342,300	314,400	72,000	419,100	309,600
March	309,600	402,800	80,000	472,500	319,900
Total-Quarter 1	329,600	1,024,300	223,000	1,257,000	319,900
Quarter 2	319,900	1,186,210	64,500	1,243,700	326,910
Quarter 3	326,910	969,100	41,400	1,017,500	319,910
Quarter 4	319,910	880,300	49,600	932,900	316,910
Grand total	$ 329,600	$ 4,059,910	$ 378,500	$ 4,451,100	$ 316,910

EXHIBIT 10.4   BUDGET FOR FINISHED GOODS INVENTORY

Note: (a) Certain purchased parts are acquired for sale to customers, and do not enter work-in-process

THE ILLUSTRATIVE COMPANY
SUMMARY OF BUDGETED INVENTORIES
FOR THE PLAN YEAR 20XX
(DOLLARS IN THOUSANDS)

Item	Raw Materials and Purchased Parts	Work-in-Process	Finished Goods	Total
Beginning inventory	$ 186,400	$ 264,800	$ 329,600	$ 780,800
Quarter ending inventory				
March	183,400	261,950	319,900	765,250
June	176,400	256,180	326,910	759,490
September	169,400	250,580	319,910	739,890
Year ending inventory	$ 200,400	$ 262,680	$ 316,910	$ 779,990
Total annual usage—estimated	$ 1,487,000	$ 4,059,910	$ 4,451,100	
Daily average (255 days)	$ 5,831	$ 15,921	$ 17,455	
Number of days usage on hand—year end	34.4	16.5	18.2	

EXHIBIT 10.5 SUMMARY OF BUDGETED INVENTORIES

11

PLANNING AND CONTROL OF PLANT AND EQUIPMENT OR CAPITAL ASSETS

IMPACT OF CAPITAL EXPENDITURES

Capital expenditure planning and control are critical to the long-term financial health of any company operating in the private enterprise system. Generally, expenditures for fixed assets require significant financial resources, decisions are difficult to reverse, and the investment affects financial performance over a long period of time. The statement "Today's decisions determine tomorrow's profits" is pertinent to the planning and control of fixed assets.

Investment in capital assets has other ramifications or possible consequences not found in the typical day-to-day expenditures of a business. First, once funds have been used for the purchase of plant and equipment, it may be a long time before they are recovered. Unwise expenditures of this nature are difficult to retrieve without serious loss to the investor. Needless to say, imprudent long-term commitments can result in bankruptcy or other financial embarrassment.

Second, a substantial increase in capital investment is likely to cause a much higher break-even point for the business. Large outlays for plant, machinery, and equipment carry with them higher depreciation charges, heavier insurance costs, greater property taxes, and possibly an expanded maintenance expense. All these tend to raise the sales volume at which the business will begin to earn a profit.

In today's highly competitive environment, it is mandatory that companies make significant investments in fixed assets to improve productivity and take advantage of the technological gains being experienced in manufacturing equipment. The sophisticated manufacturing and processing techniques available make investment decisions more important; however, the sizable amounts invested allow for greater rewards in increased productivity and higher return on investment. This opportunity carries with it additional risks relative to the increasing costs of a plant and equipment.

These conditions make it imperative that wisdom and prudent judgment be exercised in making investments in capital assets. Management decisions must be made utilizing analytical approaches. There are numerous mathematical techniques to assist in eliminating uneconomic investments and systematically establish priorities. Since these investment decisions have a long-term impact on the business, it requires an intelligent approach to the problem.

CONTROLLER'S RESPONSIBILITY

What part should the controller play in the planning and control of capital commitments and expenditures? The board of directors and the chief executive officer (CEO) usually rely on first-level management to analyze the capital asset requirements and determine, on a priority basis, which investments are in the best long-term interests of the company. The controller has a key role to play in making the determinations. All the functional departments, like sales or manufacturing, will have valid reasons for expansion or cost savings through the purchase of new plant and equipment. In addition, each operating unit will have a real need to increase the capital asset expenditures to meet its goals and objectives. The controller, with the financial knowledge of all company operations, should be able to apply objectivity by making a thorough analysis of the proposed expenditures. In many cases, heavy losses have been incurred because the decision was made with an optimistic outlook but without adequate financial analysis. The responsibility is placed on the controller's staff to make an objective appraisal of the potential savings and return on investment. The board of directors and the CEO must have a proper evaluation of proposed expenditures if they are to carry out their responsibilities effectively.

After the decisions have been made to make the investments, the controller must establish proper accountability, measure performance, and institute recording and reporting procedures for control.

The following is a list of thirteen functions that relate in some way to the planning and control of fixed assets and that typically come within the purview of the controller:

1. Establish a practical and satisfactory procedure for the planning and control of fixed assets.

2. Establish suitable standards or guides, also called hurdle rates, as to what constitutes an acceptable minimum rate of return on the types of fixed assets under consideration.

3. Review all requests for capital expenditures, which are based on economic justification, to verify the probable rate of return.

4. In the context of the business plans—whether short term or long range—ascertain that the plant and equipment expenditures required to meet the manufacturing and sales plans (or plans for research and development [R&D] or any other function) are included in such plan, and that the funds are available.

5. As required, establish controls to assure that capital expenditures are kept within authorized limits.

6. As requested, or through initiative, review and consider suitable economic alternatives to asset purchases, such as leasing or renting, or buying the manufactured item from others—a part of the "make-or-buy" decision.

7. Establish an adequate reporting system that advises the proper segment of management on matters related to fixed assets, including:

   ○ Maintenance costs by classes of equipment

   ○ Idle time of equipment

   ○ Relative productivity by types or age of equipment and so forth

   ○ Actual costs versus budgeted or estimated costs (as in the construction or purchase of plant and machinery, etc.)

8. Design and maintain property records, and related physical requirements (numbering, etc.) to accomplish:

   ○ Identifying the asset

   ○ Describing its location, age, and the like

   ○ Tracking transfers

   ○ Properly accounting for depreciation, retirement, and sale

9. Develop and maintain an appropriate depreciation policy for each type of equipment—for book and tax purposes, each separate, if advisable.

10. Develop and maintain the appropriate accounting basis for the assets, including proper reserves.

11. Ascertain that proper insurance coverage is maintained.

12. See that asset acquisition and disposition is handled in the most appropriate fashion taxwise.

13. Ascertain that proper internal control procedures apply to the machinery and equipment or any other fixed asset.

While the controller and staff have certain accounting, evaluation, auditing, and reporting requirements to meet, it should be understood that the line executives have the major responsibility for the acquisition, maintenance, and protection of the fixed assets.

CAPITAL BUDGETING PROCESS

Having mentioned the responsibilities related to fixed assets that are typically assigned to the controller, we devote the principal part of this chapter to the capital budgeting process. Most of the accounting and reporting duties are known to the average controller, but more involvement in the budget procedure needs to be encouraged. Given the relative inflexibility that exists once capital commitments are made, it is desirable that the CEO and other high functional executives be provided a suitable framework and basis for selecting the essential or economically justified projects from among the many proposals—even though their intuitive judgment may be a key factor. And when the undertaking begins, the expenditures must be held within the authorized limits. Moreover, for the larger projects at least, management is entitled, once the asset begins to operate, to be periodically informed how the actual economics compare with the anticipated earnings or savings.

The sequential steps in a well-conceived capital budgeting process are outlined below. It should be understood that these steps are not all performed by the controller, but rather by the appropriate line executive. (In separate sections, some of the more analytical facets are explored.)

1. For the planning period of the short-term budget, which may be a year or two, *determine* the outer *limit* or a permissible range for capital commitments or expenditures for the company as a whole, and for each major division or function. This is desirable so that the cognizant executive has some guidance as to how much he can spend in the planning period. (There must be a starting point, and this is as good a one as any.) Depending on the circumstances, this may be an iterative procedure.

2. Through the appropriate organizational channels, *encourage* the presentation of worthy capital investment projects. For major projects, the target rate of return should be provided, and any other useful guidelines should be furnished (corporate objectives, plans for expansion, etc.).

3. When the proposals are received (and presumably there are many) make a preliminary screening to eliminate those that do not support the strategic plan, or that are obviously not economically or politically supportable.

4. After this preliminary screening:

    (a) Classify all projects as to urgency of need.

    (b) Also, calculate the supposed economic benefits. Those performing this task must be given guidance as to (1) the method of determining the rate of return and (2) the underlying data required to support the proposal.

5. When the data on proposed projects are submitted for top management approval, the financial staff should review and check the material as to:

   (a) Adequacy and validity of nontechnical data

   (b) Rate of return and the related calculations

   (c) Compatibility with

      (i) Other capital budget criteria

      (ii) Financial resources available

      (iii) Financial constraints of the total or divisional budget and so forth

6. When the proposals have been reviewed and analyzed, and approved by top management, the data must be presented to the board of directors and approval secured *in principle.*

7. When the time approaches for starting a major project, the *specific* authorization should be reviewed and approved by the appropriate members of management. This process may require a recheck of underlying data to be sure no fundamentals have changed.

8. As a control device, when a project has started, periodic reports should be prepared to indicate costs incurred to date, and estimated cost to complete—among other information deemed critical.

9. At stipulated times, and for a stated period, after a major project has been completed, a post-audit should be made comparing actual and estimated cash flow.

As can be deduced, the role of the controller and staff as to capital budgeting relates to the financial planning, the establishment and monitoring of the capital budgeting procedure, the economic analyses, and the control reports during and after completion.

ESTABLISHING THE LIMIT OF THE CAPITAL BUDGET

A common beginning point in the annual planning process is to set a maximum amount that may be spent on capital expenditures. There will be occasions when the "normal" limit is set aside because of an unusual investment opportunity or other extraordinary circumstances. Normally, however, top management will set a capital budget amount, based on its judgment and considering such factors as:

- Estimated internal cash generation (net income plus depreciation and changes in receivables and inventory investment, etc.)
- Availability and cost of external funds
- Present capital structure of the company (too much debt, etc.)
- Strategic plans and corporate goals and objectives
- Stage of the business cycle
- Near- and medium-term growth prospects of the company and the industry
- Present and anticipated inflation rates
- Expected rate of return on capital projects as compared with cost of capital or other hurdle rates
- Age and condition of present plant and equipment
- New technological developments and need to remain competitive
- Anticipated competitor actions
- Relative investment in plant and equipment as compared to industry or selected competitors

At different times, each of these factors will seem more compelling than others. As an additional rule of thumb for "normal" capital expenditures, some managements determine the limit based on the (a) amount of depreciation, plus (b) one third of the net income. The remaining two thirds of net income are used equally: one half for dividend payout to shareholders, and the other half for working capital.

In considering the company investment in plant and equipment versus the industry, these two ratios may provide some guidance:

1. *Ratio of fixed assets to net worth.* This ratio, when compared with those of competitors, indicates how much of the net worth is used to finance plant and equipment vs. working capital.

2. *Turnover of plant and equipment.* The ratio of net sales to plant and equipment, when compared to industry data, to specific companies, or to published ratios such as those issued by Dun & Bradstreet, shows whether too much is invested in fixed assets for the sales volume being achieved.

INFORMATION SUPPORTING CAPITAL EXPENDITURE PROPOSALS

An important element in a sound capital budgeting procedure is securing adequate and accurate information about the proposal. In this connection, the reason for the expenditure is a relevant factor in just what data are needed.

In a sense, a capital expenditure may call for a *replacement* decision, that is, an existing piece of equipment is to be replaced. For such a decision the information necessary would include:

- The investment and installation cost of the new piece of equipment
- The salvage value of the old machinery
- The economic life of the new equipment
- The operating cost of the new item over its life

Presumably, the economic decision would relate directly to the lower cost of production with the new piece of equipment, and possibly the opportunity to produce a greater quantity of output.

In contrast, consider an *expansion* type of decision. Assume a company wants to produce a new product to be sold in a new market. Then, not only must the economic data on the acquisition and operation of the new equipment be available, but also marketing information is required, such as estimates of:

- The market potential for the new product
- The probable sales quantity and value of the output for X years
- The marketing or distribution cost

Such a capital investment obviously will involve more risk than a replacement decision.

One other comment may be germane to securing good ideas and adequate information about new capital items. First, those who would use the equipment and are knowledgeable should be consulted. Too often management does not listen to this valuable source of information. Secondly, management should encourage the flow of ideas about capital expenditures, especially new processes and perhaps new products. It is far better to have too many good ideas than not enough. Ideas should be sought from many elements of the organization and compared. What is most desirable is a balanced agenda, rather than a limiting of ideas to any one department or single source.

As is discussed later, economic data on proposals normally should include all relevant cash flow information—cash outgo—the complete installation costs and operating expense, and cash inflow—the expected net sales revenues less related marketing expense, and so on. Any relevant economic data should be made available, such as tax data, inflation outlook, economic life of the project, other equipment needed, capacity data, cost information, and salvage value.

Here is an expanded list of the reasons that capital expenditures are made, all of which have a bearing on input data:

- To enable continued operation of the business
- To meet pollution control requirements
- To meet safety needs
- To reduce manufacturing or marketing (distribution) costs through more efficient use of labor, material, or overhead
- To improve the quality of the product
- To meet product delivery requirements
- To increase sales volume of existing or new products
- To diversify operations
- To expand overseas and so forth

METHODS OF EVALUATING PROJECTS

In an effort to invest funds wisely in capital projects, companies have developed several evaluation techniques. It is these expenditures that provide the foundation for the firm's growth, efficiency, and competitive strength. Because most companies do not have sufficient funds to undertake all projects, some means must be found to evaluate the alternate courses of action. Such decisions are not merely the application of a formula. The evaluation of quantitative information must be blended with good judgment, and perhaps good fortune, to produce that aggregate wisdom in capital expenditures that will largely determine the company's future earning power.

As will be seen, some entities have rather simple procedures while some of the more capital intensive managements feel a need for more sophisticated methods. Those companies using the more analytical tools find these three elements essential:

1. An estimate of the expected capital outlay, as well as the amount and timing of the estimated future benefits—the cash flow
2. A technique for relating the expected future benefits to a measure of cost—perhaps the cost of capital, or other "hurdle rates"
3. A means of evaluating the risk—which relates to (a) the probability of attaining the estimated rate of return, and (b) a sense of how changes in the assumptions can affect the calculated return

The two more important valuation methods in use, which are quantitative in nature, consist of the following or some variation thereof:

1. *Payback method.* This is the simple calculation of the number of years required for the proceeds of the project to recoup the original investment.
2. *Rate of return methods.* Among them are:
   (a) The *operators' method,* so called because it is often used to measure operating efficiency in a plant or division. It may be defined as the relationship of annual cash return, plus depreciation, to the original investment.

(b) The *accountants' method,* perhaps so named because the accounting concept of average book value and earnings (or book profit) is employed. This method is merely the relationship of profit after depreciation to average annual outstanding investment.

(c) The *investors' method* or discounted cash flow method. This rate of return concept recognizes the time value of money. It involves a calculation of the present worth of a flow of funds.

PAYBACK METHOD

Assume that project A calls for an investment of $1,000,000 and that the average annual income before depreciation is expected to be $300,000. Then the payback in years would be 3.3 years, calculated thus:

$$\text{Payback time in years } = \frac{\text{Investment}}{\text{Yearly net income} + \text{Depreciation}}$$

$$= \frac{\$1,000,000}{\$200,000 + \$100,000}$$

$$= 3.3 \text{ years}$$

In circumstances where the net income and depreciation are not approximately level each year, then the method may be refined to reflect cash flow each year to arrive at the payback time—instead of the *average* earnings. For example, assume an increasing stream of cash inflow followed by a decrease, then a matrix as in Exhibit 11.1, can be completed. In this illustration, the payback is completed in 5 1/2 years (5 years plus a $900,000/$1,800,000 fractional year).

Briefly stated, the payback method offers these four advantages:

1. It may be useful in those instances where a business firm is on rather lean rations cashwise and must accept proposals that appear to promise a payback, for example, in two years or less.

2. Payback can be helpful in appraising very risky investments where the threat of expropriation or capital wastage is high and difficult to predict. It weighs near-year earnings heavily.

3. It is a simple manner of computation and easily understood.

4. It may serve as a rough indicator of profitability to reject obviously undesirable proposals.

Year	Cash Outflow	Cash Inflow	Net Investment (Recovery)
0	$10,000,000	—	$10,000,000
1	—	$1,200,000	8,800,000
2	—	$1,500,000	7,300,000
3	—	$1,800,000	5,600,000
4	—	$2,500,000	3,100,000
5	—	$2,200,000	900,000
6	—	$1,800,000	(900,000)

EXHIBIT 11.1 PAYBACK PERIOD—UNEVEN CASH FLOW

There are, however, three very basic disadvantages to the payback method:

1. *Failure to consider the earnings after the initial outlay has been recouped.* Yet the cash flow *after payback* is the real factor in determining profitability. In effect, the method confuses recovery of capital with profitability. In the foregoing example, if the economic life of the project is only 3.3 years, there is zero profit. If on the other hand, the capital life is 10 years, the rate of return will differ significantly from that produced by a 4-year life.

2. *Undue emphasis on liquidity.* Restriction of fund investment to short payback may cause rejection of a highly profitable source of earnings. Liquidity assumes importance only under conditions of tight money.

3. *Capital obsolescence or wastage is not recognized.* The gradual loss of economic value is ignored—the economic life is not considered. This deficiency is closely related to item 1. Similarly, the usual (average) method of computation does not reflect irregularity in the earning pattern.

OPERATORS' METHOD

A manner of figuring return on investment, using the figures of the payback method, is:

$$\text{Return on investment} = \frac{\text{Annual earnings} + \text{Depreciation}}{\text{Original investment}}$$

$$= \frac{\$200,000 + \$100,000}{\$1,000,000}$$

$$= 30\%$$

The technique may be varied to include total required investment, including working capital.

The operators' method has these three advantages:

1. It is simple to understand and calculate.
2. In contrast with the payout method, it gives some weight to length of life and overall profitability.
3. It facilitates comparison with other companies or divisions or projects, especially where the life spans are roughly comparable.

The basic disadvantage is that it does not recognize the time value of cash flow. Competing projects may have equal returns, but the distribution of earnings, plus depreciation, may vary significantly between them year by year and/or the total period over which equal annual returns are received may vary between projects.

ACCOUNTANTS' METHOD

This technique relates earnings to the average outstanding investment rather than the initial investment or assets employed. It is based on the underlying premise that capital recovered as depreciation is therefore available for use in other projects and should not be considered a charge against the original project.

There are variations in this method, also, in that the return may be figured before or after income tax, and differing depreciation bases may be employed.

The rate of return using the accountants' method and assuming a 10-year life and straight-line depreciation on project A is shown in Exhibit 11.2.

RETURN ON INVESTMENT—THE ACCOUNTANTS METHOD AVERAGE BOOK
INVESTMENT AND AVERAGE PROFIT PROJECT A

Year	Net Earnings Before Depreciation	Depreciation	Net Profit	Average Instrument Outstanding
1	$300,000	$100,000	$200,000	$950,000
2	$300,000	$100,000	$200,000	$950,000
3	$300,000	$100,000	$200,000	$950,000
4	$300,000	$100,000	$200,000	$950,000
—	—	—	—	—
—	—	—	—	—
—	—	—	—	—
—	—	—	—	—
9	$300,000	$100,000	$200,000	$950,000
10	$300,000	$100,000	$200,000	$950,000
Total	$ 3,000,000	$ 1,000,000	$ 2,000,000	$ 5,000,000

$$\text{Rate of return} = \frac{\text{Profit after depreciation}}{\text{Average outstanding investment}}$$

$$= \frac{\$2,000,000}{\$5,000,000}$$

$$= 40\%$$

EXHIBIT 11.2   RETURN ON INVESTMENT-THE ACCOUNTANTS METHOD

This basic procedure has two chief shortcomings. First, it is heavily influenced by the depreciation basis used. Double-declining balance depreciation will, of course, reduce the average investment outstanding and increase the rate of return. Second, it fails to reflect the time value of funds. In the example, if the average investment was the same but income was accelerated in the early years and decelerated in later years (with no change in total amount) the rate of return would be identical. Such conditions are reflected in Exhibit 11.3. By many measures, the cash flow shown in this illustration is more desirable than that reflected in Exhibit 11.2, because a greater share of the profit is secured earlier in the project life, and is thus available for other investment.

Most projects do vary in income pattern, and the evaluation procedure probably should reflect this difference.

The accountants' method offers the advantage of simplicity over the discounted cash flow approach.

DISCOUNTED CASH FLOW METHODS

Given the importance of capital expenditures to business, especially the capital intensive enterprises such as steel or chemicals, much thought has been directed to ways and means of comparing investment opportunities. It becomes very difficult to compare one project with another, particularly when the cash flow patterns vary or are quite different. *When* cash is received becomes very important in that cash receipts may be invested and earn something. The sooner the funds are in hand, the more quickly they can be put to work.

RETURN ON INVESTMENT—THE ACCOUNTANT METHOD DECREASING PROFIT PROJECT A

Year	Net Earnings Before Depreciation	Depreciation	Net Profit	Average Instrument Outstanding
1	$400,000	$100,000	$300,000	$950,000
2	400,000	$100,000	$300,000	850,000
3	400,000	$100,000	$300,000	750,000
4	400,000	$100,000	$300,000	650,000
5	400,000	$100,000	$300,000	550,000
6	200,000	$100,000	$100,000	450,000
7	200,000	$100,000	$100,000	350,000
8	200,000	$100,000	$100,000	250,000
9	200,000	$100,000	$100,000	150,000
10	200,000	$100,000	$100,000	50,000
Total	$ 3,000,000	$ 1,000,000	$ 2,000,000	$ 5,000,000

$$\text{Rate of return} = \frac{\text{Profit after depreciation}}{\text{Average outstanding investment}}$$

$$= \frac{\$2,000,000}{\$5,000,000}$$

$$= 40\%$$

EXHIBIT 11.3 TRIAL AND ERROR—COMPUTATION OF INTERNAL RATE OF RETURN

Accordingly, the discounted cash flow principle has been adopted as a far superior tool in ranking and judging the profitability of the investments. The principle may be applied in two forms:

1. The investors' method, also known as the internal rate of return (IRR)
2. The net present value (NPV)

The first one actually involves the determination of what rate of return is estimated. The second method applies a predetermined rate, or hurdle, to the estimated stream of cash to ascertain the present value of the proposed investment.

Investors' Method: Internal Rate of Return

Technically, the rate of return on any project is that rate at which the sum of the stream of after-tax (cash) earnings, discounted yearly according to present worth, equals the cost of the project. Stating it another way, the rate of return is the maximum constant rate of return that a project could earn throughout the life of the outstanding investment and just break even.

The method may be simply described by an example. Assume that an investment of $1,000 may be made and, over a five-year period, cash flow of $250 may be secured. What is the rate of return? By a cut-and-try method, and the use of present value tables, we arrive at

8%. The application of the 8% factor to the cash flow results in a present value of approximately $1,000 is:

Year	8% Annual Cash Flow (a)	Discount Factor (b)	Present Value (a) × (b)
1	$ 250	.926	$ 232
2	250	.857	214
3	250	.794	198
4	250	.735	184
5	250	.681	170
	Total present value		$ 998

The proof of the computation is the determination of an 8% annual charge with the balance applicable to principal, just as bankers calculate rates of return.

Year	Cash Flow (a)	Return at 8% of Investment Outstanding at Beginning of Year (b)	Balance Applicable to Investment (c) = (a − b)	Outstanding Investment at Year-End (d)
0	$—	$—	$—	$1,000
1	250	80	170	830
2	250	66	184	646
3	250	52	198	448
4	250	36	214	234
5	250	19	231	3*

* Due to rounding.

By trial and error, application of the proper discount factor can be explored until the proper one is found. Using a 10% discount factor and a 40% discount factor, the $1,000,000 assumed investment, discussed in connection with other evaluation methods, to be recouped over 10 years, results in a 36% rate of return, as shown in Exhibit 11.4.

The steps in application of the method may be described as:

• Determine the amount and year of the investment.
• Determine, by years, the cash flow after income taxes by reason of the investment.
• Extend such cash flow by two discount factors to arrive at present worth.
• Apply various discount factors until the calculation of one comes close to the original investment and interpolate, if necessary, to arrive at a more accurate figure.

The disadvantages of the discounted cash flow method are:

• It is somewhat more complex than other methods; this apparent handicap is minor in that those who must apply the technique grasp it rather readily after a couple of trials.
• It requires more time for calculation. However, the availability of handheld computers, or desktop computers, with a software package or built-in programs, makes the calculations rather painless.
• An implicit or inherent assumption is that reinvestment will be at the same rate as the calculated rate of return.

		INTERNAL RATE OF RETURN			
		PRESENT VALUE OF STREAM CASH			
		10% Discount Rate		40% Discount Rate	
Years from Start of Operation	(Expenditure) or Income	Discount Factor	Amount—M	Discount Factor	Amount—M
0	$ (1,000,000)		$ (1000.0)		$ (1,000,000)
0 to 1	300,000	.953	285.9	.844	253.2
2	300,000	.866	259.8	.603	180.9
3	300,000	.788	236.4	.431	129.3
4	300,000	.716	214.8	.308	92.4
5	300,000	.651	195.3	.220	66.0
6	300,000	.592	177.6	.157	47.1
7	300,000	.538	161.4	.112	33.6
8	300,000	.489	146.7	.080	24.0
9	300,000	.444	133.2	.060	18.0
10	300,000	.404	121.2	.041	12.3
Total Cash Flow	$ 3,000,000				
Discounted cash flow			$ 1,932.3		$ 856.8

Discounted rate of return:

$$10\% \ 1 \ 30\% \left[\frac{1,932 - 1,000}{1,932 - 857} \right] = 36\%$$

EXHIBIT 11.4   TRIAL AND ERROR—COMPUTATION OF INTERNAL RATE OF RETURN

These disadvantages are more than offset by the benefits. Among them are:

- Proper weighting is given to the time value of investments and cash flow.
- The use of cash flow minimizes the effect of arbitrary decisions about capital versus expenses, depreciation, and so on.
- Is comparable with the cost-of-capital concept.
- Is a valuable tool for the financial analyst in evaluating alternatives.
- Brings out explicit reasoning for selecting one project over another.

Net Present Value

The typical capital investment is composed of a string of cash flows, both in and out, that will continue until the investment is eventually liquidated at some point in the future. These cash flows are comprised of many things: the initial payment for equipment, continuing maintenance costs, salvage value of the equipment when it is eventually sold, tax payments, receipts from product sold, and so on. The trouble is, since the cash flows are coming in and going out over a period of many years, how do we make them comparable for an analysis that is done in the present? By applying the discount rate to each anticipated cash flow, we can reduce and then add them together, which yields a single combined figure that represents the current value of the entire capital investment. This is known as its net present value.

For an example of how net present value works, we have listed in Exhibit 11.5 the cash flows, both in and out, for a capital investment that is expected to last for five years. The year is listed in the first column, the amount of the cash flow in the second column, and the discount rate in the third column. The final column multiplies the cash flow from the second column by the discount rate in the third column to yield the present value of each cash flow. The grand-total cash flow is listed in the lower right corner of the exhibit.

Notice that the discount factor in Exhibit 11.5 becomes progressively smaller in later years, since cash flows further in the future are worth less than those that will be received sooner. The discount factor is published in present value tables, which are listed in many accounting and finance textbooks. They are also a standard feature in midrange handheld calculators. Another variation is to use the following formula to manually compute a present value:

$$\text{Present value of a future cash flow} = \frac{(\text{Future cash flow})}{(1 + \text{Discount rate})^{(\text{squared by the number of periods of discounting})}}$$

Using the above formula, if we expect to receive $75,000 in one year, and the discount rate is 15%, then the calculation is:

$$\text{Present value} = \frac{\$75,000}{(1 + .15)^{1}}$$

$$\text{Present value} = \$65,217.39$$

The example shown in Exhibit 11.5 was of the simplest possible kind. In reality, there are several additional factors to take into consideration. First, there may be multiple cash inflows and outflows in each period, rather than the single lump sum that was shown in the example. If a CFO wants to know precisely what is the cause of each cash flow, then it is best to add a line to the net present value calculation that clearly identifies the nature of each item, and discounts it separately from the other line items. An alternative way is to create a net present value table that leaves room for multiple cash flow line items while keeping the format down to a minimum size. Another issue is which items to include in the analysis and which to exclude. The basic rule of thumb is that it must be included if it impacts cash flow, and stays out if it does not. The most common cash flow line items to include in a net present value analysis are:

- *Cash inflows from sales.* If a capital investment results in added sales, then all gross margins attributable to that investment must be included in the analysis.
- *Cash inflows and outflows for equipment purchases and sales.* There should be a cash outflow when a product is purchased, as well as a cash inflow when the equipment is no longer needed and is sold off.

Year	Cash Flow	Discount Factor*	Present Value
0	-$100,000	1.000	-$100,000
1	+$25,000	.9259	+$23,148
2	+$25,000	.8573	+$21,433
3	+$25,000	.7938	+$19,845
4	+$30,000	.7350	+$22,050
5	+$30,000	.6806	+$20,418
		Net Present Value	+$6,894

* *Note:* Discount factor is 8%.

EXHIBIT 11.5 SIMPLIFIED NET PRESENT VALUE EXAMPLE

- *Cash inflows and outflows for working capital.* When a capital investment occurs, it normally involves the use of some additional inventory. If there are added sales, then there will probably be additional accounts receivable. In either case, these are additional investments that must be included in the analysis as cash outflows. Also, if the investment is ever terminated, then the inventory presumably will be sold off and the accounts receivable collected, so there should be line items in the analysis, located at the end of the project time line, showing the cash inflows from the liquidation of working capital.

- *Cash outflows for maintenance.* If there is production equipment involved, then there will be periodic maintenance needed to ensure that it runs properly. If there is a maintenance contract with a supplier that provides the servicing, then this too should be included in the analysis.

- *Cash outflows for taxes.* If there is a profit from new sales that are attributable to the capital investment, then the incremental income tax that can be traced to those incremental sales must be included in the analysis. Also, if there is a significant quantity of production equipment involved, the annual personal property taxes that can be traced to that equipment should also be included.

- *Cash inflows for the tax effect of depreciation.* Depreciation is an allowable tax deduction. Accordingly, the depreciation created by the purchase of capital equipment should be offset against the cash outflow caused by income taxes. Though depreciation is really just an accrual, it does have a net cash flow impact caused by a reduction in taxes, and so should be included in the net present value calculation.

The net present value approach is the best way to see if a proposed capital investment has a sufficient rate of return to justify the use of any required funds. Also, because it reveals the amount of cash created in excess of the corporate hurdle rate, it allows management to rank projects by the amount of cash they can potentially spin off, which is a good way to determine which projects to fund if there is not enough cash available to pay for an entire set of proposed investments.

HURDLE RATES

A hurdle rate is the minimum rate of return that a capital project should earn if it is to be judged acceptable. In reviewing this subject, on which there are a variety of opinions, perhaps these aspects are the more important ones:

- Value of using any hurdle rate
- Value of using a single hurdle rate
- Value of using multiple hurdle rates

Value of Hurdle Rates

Many companies do not establish hurdle rates, for a variety of alleged reasons, including:

- There is a large element of subjectivity in capital investments, and management wishes to review all proposals. It does not want to eliminate any from consideration simply because of the rate of return.

- When new business areas are to be considered, it is difficult to set a suitable hurdle rate.

- Many projects must be undertaken regardless of economic reasons: pollution abatement, safety equipment, and the like.
- If hurdle rates are used, then data will be manipulated so that the minimum profit rate will seem attainable.

If management wishes to maintain flexibility in its capital budgeting process, it seems this can still be done with proper instructions or guidelines, despite the existence of hurdle rates. Thus, provision can be made for some expenditures that do not relate directly to a given profit rate. Moreover, sound analytical procedures, including dismissal, can minimize any efforts to fabricate justification data. Additionally, if a for-profit business is an economic institution, and the authors think it is, and if the management task is to enhance shareholder value, then it seems guidelines must include profit rates which by and large do not dilute the shareholder's equity.

A Single Hurdle Rate?

A great many companies that employ the hurdle rate concept use a single rate, as distinguished from different rates for various kinds of expenditures. The reasoning in the application of one hurdle rate is basically this:

- The cost of capital, a good point of departure, is about the same for all segments of the company (divisions, subsidiaries, product lines, etc.).
- The additional risk in attempting to earn an acceptable return on equity is essentially the same for all parts of the company.
- Given the elements of error in estimating the rate of return on the capital project, the future cost of capital, and the subjective nature of the decision, it isn't worth the effort to establish several hurdle rates.

One of the common single hurdle rates employed is closely associated with the cost of capital, discussed in the next section. Some projects do not earn the cost of capital, so a factor must be added as the goal of other projects so that, on average, the proper earnings level is maintained.

A single hurdle rate might be established thus:

Cost of capital	17%
Allowance to offset sublevel projects	5
Profit goal for capital projects	22%

COST OF CAPITAL—A HURDLE RATE

Technically, the cost of capital is the rate of return the long-term debt holders and shareholders require to persuade them to furnish the required capital. Thus, assume that:

- A company capital structure target objective is $500,000,000 composed of 25% debt and 75% equity.
- In the current market environment long-term bondholders require a 10% return (6% cost to the company after income taxes); a 17% return on equity is the going earnings rate.

Then the cost of capital would be calculated as:

Structure	Capitalization	Required Rate of Return (After Income Taxes)	Required Amount of Return
Senior debt	$ 125,000,000	6.0%	$ 7,500,000
Common stock	375,000,000	17.0%	63,750,000
Total	$ 500,000,000		$ 71,250,000

$$\text{Cost of capital} = \frac{\$71,250,000}{500,000,000}$$

$$= 14\%$$

It could be argued that if the company is to attract the capital required to stay in business, then, on average, all its capital investments should earn at least 14% after taxes. If this does not occur, then the shareholder return would be diluted. Of course, it would be well to consult with the investment bankers as to the bondholder and shareholder expectations on earnings of the company and industry for the next several years. Depending on their views, a cost of future capital might be determined based on the relation of expected earnings to expected market value of the stock, plus the yield the bondholders might require. In this manner, the minimum return for capital projects could be estimated.

This calculation represents the average cost of capital and seems a fair basis for capital investment decisions viewed on the thesis that the true cost of capital is calculated on a pool basis. However, there might be some circumstances where the marginal or incremental cost of capital basis may be calculated for informational use. This is the cost of capital for the most recent capital transaction considered, such as the opportunity cost of not repurchasing common stock, or of not repaying debt. However, this application would be viewed as the cost of a specific source of capital. It seems to the authors that the pool concept of capital is the more appropriate basis for evaluating capital expenditures.

In any event, cost of capital, or cost of capital adjusted for some subnormal rates of return on some projects, might be a suitable hurdle rate.

Multiple Hurdle Rates

In these days of multinational companies, and conglomerates operating in many business sectors, a case could be made for using multiple hurdle rates. The use of multiple hurdle rates could be justified for different segments of a business where:

- Different business risk exists (threat of expropriation, adverse business environment, etc.).
- Rates of return expectations are markedly different (as in some non-U.S. geographical areas).
- Experienced earnings rates are much different.
- Differing business strategies may apply and require different hurdle rates for a time.

However, whether different hurdle rates should be determined, or whether management should make mental adjustments to a single hurdle rate, depends on management inclinations. Intuitive judgment still plays an important role in capital expenditure decisions.

INFLATION

Those involved in analyzing capital investments may ponder how inflation should be handled. Even so-called "modest" inflation rates of 5% or 6% can significantly influence results. In the budgetary process, these questions should be considered:

- Should adjustments be made for inflation in the cash flows?
- Should one inflation rate be applied to the entire period, or should year-to-date adjustments be made?
- If available, should specific estimated inflation rates be used on each factor (i.e., wages, material costs, product prices)?
- Should the hurdle rate be adjusted to provide for inflation?

Four comments on these questions are:

1. Many companies do not adjust for inflation. The reasons for not recognizing inflation range from the pragmatic—that product prices and revenues changes probably will at least match cost movements—to the recognition of the difficulty in getting a reliable rate estimate.

    However, those more analytical souls, and those using DCF techniques and the computer, are more likely to adjust for inflation.

2. Many analysts engaged in long-range planning use an average inflation rate because of the difficulty of getting more realistic data. However, if estimates of inflation by near-term years are available, perhaps these should be used, with an average "guess" for the later years.

3. Specific price indices exist for some materials, or groups of materials, and for wages in particular industries.

    With the availability of computers, if the company believes there will be wide variations of inflation in segments of the business, it might be well to test the results of applying specific inflation indexes.

4. If cash flows are adjusted for inflation, then the hurdle rate also probably should be adjusted for estimated inflation. However, if constant dollars are used in projections, then obviously the hurdle rate should not be adjusted for estimated inflation.

In reaching conclusions on any of these points the analysts probably should secure estimates of inflation, and experiment on the computer with the impact on the answer.

FOREIGN INVESTMENTS

Investments by the multinationals in countries with hyperinflation rates must separately consider the effect of these conditions on the real rate of return—and the desirability of making any capital investments at all.

When a discounted cash flow method (or, indeed, any method) is used to evaluate investments in another country, it is to be emphasized that the significant test is the cash flow to the *parent*—not to the foreign subsidiary or entity. Among the impediments to cash flow to the parent, which must be considered (for each year) and factored into the decision, are such items as:

- Currency restrictions
- Fluctuations in the foreign exchange rate

- Political risk
- Withholding taxes
- Inflation (as mentioned)

Limited discussion of these topics is contained in Chapter 10.

IMPACT OF THE NEW MANUFACTURING ENVIRONMENT

Investments are made in capital assets with the expectation that the return will be sufficiently high not only to recoup the cost but also to pass the hurdle rate for such an expenditure. But the nature of the investment is changing, as are the attendant risks, in the new manufacturing environment.

The nature of this net setting is reflected in these characteristics:

- While automation is viewed as a primary source of additional income, this often is preceded by redesigning and simplifying the manufacturing process, before automation is considered. Many companies have achieved significant savings simply by rearranging the plant floor, establishing more streamlined procedures, and eliminating the non-value-adding functions such as material storage and handling. After this rearrangement is accomplished, then automation might be considered.

- Investments are becoming more significant in themselves. While a stand-alone grinder may cost $1 million, an automated factory can cost $50 million or $100 million. Moreover, much of the cost may be in engineering, software development, and implementation.

- The equipment involved often is more complex than formerly, and the benefits can be more indirect and perhaps more intangible. If there are basic improvements in quality, in delivery schedules, and in customer satisfaction (which seems to be the emphasis today), then methods can be found to measure these benefits. (These gains may lie in improvements or lower costs in the support functions—such as purchasing, inventory control, and greater sales volume.)

- Because of the high investment cost, the period required to earn the desired return on investment is longer. This longer-term horizon, together with the intangibles to be considered and the greater uncertainty, require the controller, budget officer, or management accountant to be more discerning in his evaluation. Usually the indirect savings and intangible benefits need to be recognized and included in the investment analysis. (The direct benefits may be insufficient to justify the investment.)

IMPACT OF ACTIVITY-BASED COSTING

One output of the cost system may be used to determine the real net cash flow from the capital investment—and that is the sales revenues less the variable costs or direct cash costs of the specific products to be manufactured. Often, the allocation methods and the depreciation system do not reflect the realities of the manufacturing process. Hence, the relevant cost of sales may be substantially incorrect, leading to an improper cash flow calculation. Alternatively, the technology costs related to the product may be in error and, the larger the technology costs, the greater the impact of misallocation of product costs. Accordingly, the controller as well as the financial analyst developing, or reviewing, the capital investment justification should ascertain that the costing system accurately mirrors the resources needed in the relevant decision.

CLASSIFYING AND RANKING PROPOSED CAPITAL PROJECTS

When the reviews and analyses have been completed, it is necessary to bring order out of chaos, and to classify and rank the projects in some order of priority for discussion purposes. This is a necessary procedure because usually there are many more proposed capital expenditures than would normally be undertaken within the bounds of financial capability. Projects are ranked for discussion with top management (and the board of directors) on the basis of perceived need. While *profitability* may be a ranking factor for some categories, it does not follow that it is the only basis.

A practical grouping that would be understood by management and operation executives alike might be in some such order as:

1. Absolutely essential:
    (a) Installation of equipment required by government agencies, such as:
        (i) Safety devices
        (ii) Pollution abatement vehicles without which the business would be shut down
    (b) Replacement of inoperable facilities without which the company could not remain in business

2. Highly necessary:
    (a) State-of-the-art quality control devices
    (b) New flame-retardant painting facilities
    (c) High-intensity laser drills

3. Economically justified projects:
    (a) New facilities in Vancouver, British Columbia
    (b) Robot assembly line for casings
    (c) Warehouse in Denver, Colorado

4. All other:
    (a) Community center in Delaware, Maryland (public relations)
    (b) New lighting facilities in parking area (two shifts will be starting)
    (c) Outdoor cafeteria facilities for employees

For projects based on the economic return, usually these projects may be ranked by rate of return. An example is shown in Exhibit 11.6. It will be noted that a profitability index also is provided. As explained under the "mutually exclusive projects" section, on some occasions the proposal with the highest rate of return may not be the one with the highest profitability index.

While a ranked list of economically desirable projects may be provided, which keeps the total capital budget request within the guideline amount, sometimes a "contingent capital budget project" listing also is prepared in the event management or the board of directors decides to appropriate more funds than originally contemplated. These projects would rank just below the formal proposals as to rates of return.

THE MONEY COMPANY
PROPOSED CAPITAL PROJECTS
RANKED BY INTERNAL RATE OF RETURN
FOR THE 20XX CAPITAL BUDGET

Priority Ranking	Description and Location	Internal Rate of Return	Profitability Index	Cost
1	Electronics Assembly Plant—Wayne, Michigan	37.90%	1.62	$ 7,980,000
2	Robot Assembly Line—Hawthorne, Calif.	29.75	1.40	6,300,000
3	Computer Assisted Design Facility— Hawthorne, Calif.	28.00	1.25	4,500,000
4	Spray Equipment—Boston, Mass.	25.00	1.20	2,500,000
5	Material Handling System—San Francisco, Calif.	25.00	1.24	4,610,000
6	Composite Materials Equipment— Pomona, Calif.	22.00	1.10	5,100,000
	Total			$ 30,990,000

EXHIBIT 11.6 PROPOSED CAPITAL PROJECTS BY ECONOMIC RANKING

BOARD OF DIRECTORS' APPROVAL

Under normal circumstances, when management has decided what capital budget projects should be undertaken and be included in the annual business plan, approval of the board of directors is sought. Usually either the chief operating officer of the vice president in charge of facilities makes the presentation, perhaps with a visual aid much like that shown in Exhibit 11.7. The data are presented in some logical form and display the significant facts. The objective is to make the board aware of the reason for, benefits of, and risks attached to, each project. The information included in the proposal as reflected in Exhibit 11.7 contains:

- An identification of each project
- The priority and category of each project
- The reason for the proposed item
- The total anticipated cost
- The rate of return (where this is the basis of selection)
- The timing of the expenditures
- A contingency fund in the event of cost overruns

Any cost estimates, the rate of return, and availability of funds, and so forth should be checked, or calculated, by the controller's office before submission to the board (or management).

In securing the approval of the board of directors, there is one other aspect that often should be brought to the attention of the board and that has to do with GAAP.

THE CALIFORNIA COMPANY
ANNUAL CAPITAL BUDGET REQUEST—20X4
(DOLLARS IN THOUSANDS)

Project Description	Appropriation — New						Return on Investments (DCF)	Expenditures				
	Prior Years	1st Quarter	2nd Quarter	Last Half	Total 20X4	Total Commitments		Prior Years	20X4	20X5	Later Years	Total
Replacements and Substitutions												
Absolutely essential												
Safety equipment—Plant 5	$ —	$ 512	$ 460	$ 128	$ 1,100	$ 1,100		$ —	$ 1,100	$ —	$ —	$ 1,100
Solvent disposal—Chicago	—	—	—	500	500	500		—	250	250	—	500
Cadmium grinders—Toronto	—	—	400	350	750	750		—	750	—	—	750
Total	$ —	$ 512	$ 860	$ 978	$ 2,350	$ 2,350		$ —	$ 2,100	$ 250	$ —	$ 2,350
Competitive necessity												
Quality control upgrading—all plants	200	50	100	300	450	650		100	510	40	—	650
Delivery equipment—Denver	—	—	375	—	375	375		—	375	—	—	375
Total	$ 200	$ 50	$ 475	$ 300	$ 825	$ 1,025		$ 100	$ 885	$ 40	$ —	$ 1,025
Total replacements, etc.	$ 200	$ 562	$ 1,335	$ 1,278	$ 3,175	$ 3,375		$ 100	$ 2,985	$ 290	$ —	$ 3,375

EXHIBIT 11.7 ANNUAL CAPITAL BUDGET REQUEST

THE CALIFORNIA COMPANY
ANNUAL CAPITAL BUDGET REQUEST—20X4
(DOLLARS IN THOUSANDS)

Project Description	Appropriation New					Total Commitments	Return on Investments (DCF)	Expenditures				
	Prior Years	1st Quarter	2nd Quarter	Last Half	Total 20X4 Commitments			Prior Years	20X4	20X5	Later Years	Total
Expansion												
Manufacturing facility, Cleveland	850	1,800	2,300	700	4,800	5,650	26.50%	750	4,900	—	—	5,650
Warehouse, Toronto	—	400	600	2,000	3,000	3,000	17.50	—	2,400	600	—	3,00
Pneumatic loading system, Chicago	—	—	—	1,400	1,400	1,400	14.00	—	1,000	400	—	1,400
Total expansion	850	$2,200	$2,900	$4,100	$9,200	$10,050		$750	$8,300	$1,000	—	$10,050
Other												
Community facilities, Cleveland	—	—	140	—	140	140		—	140	—	—	140
Landscaping, Plant 5	—	—	—	75	75	75		—	75	—	—	75
Total	$ —	$ —	$ 140	$ 75	$ 215	$ 215		$ —	$ 215	$ —	$ —	$ 215
Contingency	—				630	630			630			630
Grand total	$1,050	$2,762	$4,375	$5,453	$13,220	$14,270		$ 850	$12,130	$1,290	$ —	$14,270

EXHIBIT 11.7 ANNUAL CAPITAL BUDGET REQUEST (CONTINUED)

Impact of Generally Accepted Accounting Principles

Just as the discussion of activity-based costing (ABC) has stimulated management accountants to recheck the cost drivers and allocation methods of the cost systems used in their companies, so also recent articles about the tendency of GAAP applications to discourage needed investment in new equipment such as computer integrated technology, is causing some thought about the accounting methodology in use in certain circumstances. Some of the alleged difficulty arises because of the practice of expensing, and not capitalizing, the startup costs of the new project, or perhaps the tendency to focus on short-term earnings, or the failure to recognize life-cycle accounting. The impact of a capital expenditure on earnings may cause the small company to reflect a loss in the initial years after the investment, even though the ultimate rate of return is excellent. Allegedly, a prospective loss might deter some banks from making a loan. (A diligent bank will carefully examine the cause of any expected loss.) This brings us to a consideration of what information should be provided to the board of directors and top management about the impact of new product development or major capital expenditures on the *earnings* of the company. It has nothing to do directly with the rate of return or project justification; these are separate considerations. It does relate to making the decision makers aware of the profit impact of capital investments and the related costs.

Perhaps these three supplemental forecast earnings statements may be useful to an informed management when considering any *major* expenditure (as well as for the purpose of obtaining necessary financing):

1. A statement of estimated income and expense without the new investment—for a number of years in the future

2. A statement of estimated income and expense, with the new investment, using GAAP (with emphasis on startup expenses and depreciation)—if that is a point to emphasize

3. A statement of estimated income and expense, with the new investment, with a modified or alternative capitalization and depreciation practice.

These are illustrated in Exhibits 11.8 through 11.10.

Exhibit 11.8 shows the anticipated decline in the operating profit of the Electronics Division without the investment under consideration (new manufacturing equipment also having additional capacity).

THE JOHNSON COMPANY
ELECTRONICS DIVISION
STATEMENT OF ESTIMATED INCOME AND EXPENSES
WITHOUT PROJECT X INVESTMENT
20XX THROUGH 20X6
(DOLLARS IN THOUSANDS)

	Year						
Item	20XX	20X1	20X2	20X3	20X4	20X5	20X6
Net sales	$2,500	$2,400	$2,100	$1,900	$1,700	$1,500	$1,200
Cost of sales	1,500	1,440	1,300	1,200	1,100	1,050	1,000
Gross profit	1,000	960	800	700	600	450	200
Selling expense	200	200	200	200	200	200	200
General and administrative expense	100	100	90	90	90	90	80
Operating profit or (loss)	$ 700	$ 660	$ 510	$ 410	$ 310	$ 160	$ (80)

EXHIBIT 11.8 STATEMENT OF ESTIMATED INCOME AND EXPENSE WITHOUT PROJECT X INVESTMENT

THE JOHNSON COMPANY
ELECTRONICS DIVISION
STATEMENT OF ESTIMATED INCOME AND EXPENSES
WITH PROJECT X INVESTMENT USING CURRENT ACCOUNTING PRACTICES
(GAAP) 20XX THROUGH 20X6
(DOLLARS IN THOUSANDS)

	Year						
Item	20XX	20X1	20X2	20X3	20X4	20X5	20X6
Net sales	$2,500	$2,700	$3,200	$4,000	$5,000	$6,000	$7,000
Cost of sales	1,500	1,620	1,920	2,400	2,500	3,000	3,500
Gross profit	1,000	1,080	1,280	1,600	2,500	3,000	3,500
Selling expense	200	200	200	200	200	200	250
General and administrative expense	100	100	100	100	100	100	100
Operating profit before start-up expenses and additional depreciation	700	780	980	1,300	2,200	2,700	3,150
Start-up expenses	500	100	—	—	—	—	—
Additional depreciation	150	300	300	300	300	150	—
Operating profit	$ (50)	$ 380	$ 680	$1,000	$1,900	$2,550	$3,150

EXHIBIT 11.9 STATEMENT OF ESTIMATED INCOME AND EXPENSE WITH PROJECT X INVESTMENT USING CURRENT ACCOUNTING PRACTICES (GAAP)

THE JOHNSON COMPANY
ELECTRONICS DIVISION
STATEMENT OF INCOME AND EXPENSES
WITH PROJECT X INVESTMENT AND WITH
MODIFIED CAPITALIZATION AND DEPRECIATION PRACTICE
20XX THROUGH 20X6
(DOLLARS IN THOUSANDS)

	Year						
Item	20XX	20X1	20X2	20X3	20X4	20X5	20X6
Net sales	$2,500	$2,700	$3,200	$4,000	$5,000	$6,000	$7,000
Cost of sales	1,500	1,620	1,920	2,400	2,500	3,000	3,500
Gross profit	1,000	1,080	1,280	1,600	2,500	3,000	3,500
Selling expense	200	200	200	200	200	200	250
General and administrative expense	100	100	100	100	100	100	100
Operating profit before start-up expenses and additional depreciation	700	780	980	1,300	2,200	2,700	3,150
Start-up cost capitalized	500*	100*					
Additional depreciation capitalized	150*	300*					
Amortization of start-up costs (1)			300	300			
Amortization of capitalized depreciation (2)			225	225			
Additional depreciation	—	—	300	300	300	150	—
Operating profit	$ 700	$ 780	$ 155	$ 475	$ 1,900	$ 2,550	$ 3,150

* See related write-offs (1) and (2).

EXHIBIT 11.10 STATEMENT OF ESTIMATED INCOME AND EXPENSE WITH PROJECT X INVESTMENT AND WITH MODIFIED ACCOUNTING PRACTICES

Exhibit 11.9 reflects the tremendous increase in operating profit, after the first two years, by making the investment in Project X. It also shows the effect of the write-off, in the years of incurrence of the startup costs, and the depreciation of the capital asset cost of $1,500,000 over a five-year life (straight line depreciation, with a one-half year of depreciation in 20XX). The use of a generally accepted accounting practice involving immediate write-off of startup costs in the years of occurrence, and commencement as early as possible of depreciation charges on a straight line five-year basis (not on a per unit of output), causes an operating loss in 20XX and a severe reduction in operating profit in 20X1.

Exhibit 11.10 shows the impact of a less conservative accounting practice—the immediate capitalization of the startup costs, with the subsequent amortization of the charge over a two-year period of operation, and the deferment of immediate depreciation of the capital assets, also for a two-year period, and a subsequent write-off over a five-year period. Such a practice avoids an operating loss in the first year of operations and avoids a large reduction in the operating profit of the second year of operation—with the heavier additional costs being deferred until there is a significant pickup in sales and operating profit (before such additional charges).

Providing such data to the board of directors advises them of the impact on expected operating profit of the proposed investment on two different accounting bases. This information would be in addition to that listed earlier. It rounds out the financial picture and perhaps avoids later questions. The annual plan and strategic plan should incorporate the effect of the expenditures on the statement of income and expense, the statement of financial position, and the statement of cash flows. This same data should be made available to the commercial banks, or other financial sources, who are asked to provide the financing. The authors suggest full disclosure of the financial statements of the annual plan and long-range plan to the financing institution, including the schedule for complete payment of the obligation.

When and if the board approves the project, the cognizant officer is notified. This constitutes an approval *in principle*. Specific project approval, as discussed in the next section, is required before the project may proceed.

PROJECT AUTHORIZATION

Under most circumstances, the analysis and review done in connection with securing project approval by the board of directors should be sufficient to complete a detailed authorization request. However, circumstances do change, and a period of six months might pass between the gathering and analysis of data for the board review. So sometimes this re-review is worthwhile. Also, it causes the project sponsors to commit in writing to the project. An illustrative form is shown in Exhibit 11.11.

It should be mentioned that authority required to commence a project depends on the amount of the request. While approval of the president for all projects might be needed in a small firm, in larger ones there might be an ascending scale of required approvals, perhaps as:

Amount	Required Approval
Less than $10,000	Plant Manager
$10,000–99,999	General Manager
$100,000–499,999	Chief Operating Officer
Over $500,000	Chief Executive Officer

The sample form provides for comments and recommendations by the controller as well as the line approval (depending on the amount).

REQUEST FOR EQUIPMENT AND FACILITY AUTHORIZATION

A.F.E. No. _____

Date: _____

Division	Plant

This request for authorization of a capital commitment and expenditure is made necessary by:

☐ Normal replacement   ☐ New product

☐ Change in manufacturing process   ☐ Increased volume

☐ Cost reduction   ☐ Styling changes

☐ Environmental regulations

Title: Pneumatic bagging equipment

Description and Justification: The present conveyor and manual handling system is too slow. It is anticipated that the state-of-the-art equipment will permit a volume of 1,500,000 2-lb. bags per year, with a reduction of 5 operators.

Use added pages if necessary.

Estimated Cost:

		Return on Investment	
Machinery and equipment . .	$105,700	(DCF method)	43%
Installation	25,000		
Total.	130,700	Payback period	2.1 yrs.
Contingency 5%	6,535	Estimated useful life	8 yrs.
Total	$ 137,235	Salvage value	$ 2,000

Controller Comments and Recommendations:

Cash flow appears conservative

Return is above hurdle rate of 20% for this type of investment

Approval recommended

Accounting Dept.		
Acct. No.		Amount
Capital M&E 21–310		$131,235
Expense—sales tax 21-407		6,000
Total		$137,235

_____
Controller

Approval and Authorization: Date

Requested by _____

	Approved	Rejected
Approved by _____		
Department head _____		
Plant manager _____		
Division manager _____		
Executive Committee _____		

Reason for Rejection:

EXHIBIT 11.11   REQUEST FOR EQUIPMENT AND FACILITY AUTHORIZATION

ACCOUNTING CONTROL OF THE PROJECT

When the work authorization has been properly approved, then the task of the controller is to keep tabs on both commitments and expenditures as well as expected costs to complete the project, and periodically report the data to the cognizant executive. Typically these figures are reported by project or work order:

- Amount authorized
- Actual commitments to date
- Actual costs incurred to date
- Estimated cost to complete
- Indicated total cost
- Indicated overrun or underrun compared to the project budget

An illustrated report, prepared monthly and in which control is by appropriation number, is shown in Exhibit 11.12.

For large and complicated projects a computer application may be appropriate.

POSTPROJECT APPRAISALS OR AUDITS

In many companies adequate analyses are made as to the apparent economic desirability of a project, and acquisition costs are held within estimate. Yet the project may not achieve the estimated rate of return. A sad truth is that some managements are unaware of such a condition because there is no follow-up on performance.

For large projects, especially, after a limited or reasonable period beyond completion— perhaps two years on a very large capital investment—when all the "bugs" are worked out, it is suggested that a postaudit be made. The review might be undertaken by the internal audit group, or perhaps a management team consisting of line managers involved with the project (but not among the original justification group) and some members of the controller's staff. The objective, of course, is to compare actual earnings or savings with the plan, ascertain why the deviation occurred, and what steps should be taken to improve capital investment planning and control. The scope might range from the strategic planning aspects (should the company be in the business?) through to the detailed control procedures.

The following advantages may accrue from an intelligently planned postaudit:

- It may detect weaknesses in strategic planning that lead to poor decisions, which in turn impact the capital budget procedures.
- Environmental factors that influence the business but were not recognized might be detected.
- Experience can focus attention on basic weaknesses in overall plans, policies, or procedures as related to capital expenditures.
- Strengths or weaknesses in individual performance can be detected and corrected— such as a tendency to have overly optimistic estimates.
- It may enable corrections in other current projects prior to completion of commitments or expenditures.
- It affords a training opportunity for the operating and planning staff through the review of the entire capital budgeting procedure.
- Prior knowledge of the follow-up encourages reasonable caution in making projections or preparing the justification.
- It may detect evidence of manufactured input data.

MAGRAUDY MANUFACTURING CO.
CAPITAL APPROPRIATION AND EXPENDITURE STATUS REPORT
FOR THE PERIOD ENDED APRIL 30, 20XX
(DOLLARS IN THOUSANDS)

Appropriation No.	Description	Work Order No.	Amount Appropriated	Actual Completion Date	Original Estimate	Outstanding Commitments	Actual Expenditures to Date	Estimated Cost to Complete	Indicated Total Cost	Amount (Over)/Under Appropriation	Amount (Over)/Under Original Estimate
42	Northridge Plant		$2,500								
	Site clearance	460		2/20/20XX	$ 125	$ —	$ 107	$ —	$ 107		$ 18
	Buildings	461		9/01/20XX	1,475	740	394	316	1,450		25
	Machinery and equipment	462		10/31/20XX	850	500	—	360	860		(10)
	Total appropriation 42				2,450	1,240	501	676	2,417	$ 83	33
46	Delivery Fleet		950								
	4 ton	495		6/30/20XX	360	300	40	10	350		10
	1 ton	496		6/30/20XX	180	75	30	60	165		15
	1/2 ton pick-up	497		6/30/20XX	400	140	260	—	400		—
	Total appropriation 46				940	515	330	70	915	35	25

EXHIBIT 11.12 CAPITAL APPROPRIATIONS AND EXPENDITURES

MAGRAUDY MANUFACTURING CO.
Capital Appropriation and Expenditure Status Report
For the Period Ended April 30, 20XX
(DOLLARS IN THOUSANDS)

Appropriation No.	Description	Work Order No.	Amount Appropriated	Actual Completion Date	Original Estimate	Outstanding Commitments	Actual Expenditures to Date	Estimated Cost to Complete	Indicated Total Cost	Amount (Over)/Under Appropriation	Amount (Over)/Under Original Estimate
50	Miscellaneous		1,750								
	Robot assemblers	525		5/19/20XX	350	100	214	20	334		16
	Security system—plant 5	529		3/31/20XX	100	—	97	—	97		3
	Profiler—plant 6	533		6/30/20XX	90	10	80	10	100		(10)
	Fleet communications	534		7/01/20XX	75	30	50	5	85		(10)
	Lab pilot plant	542		11/30/20XX	290	40	160	55	255		35
	Pallets	549		4/30/20XX	50	—	52	—	52		(2)
	Forklift trucks	550		9/30/20XX	150	75	70	5	150		—
	New gates—employee parking	562		8/31/20XX	75	—	5	67	72		3
	All others—complete				500	—	515	—	515		(15)
	Total appropriation 50				1,680	255	1,243	162	1,660	90	20
	Grand total		$ 5,200		$ 5,070	$ 2,010	$ 2,074	$ 908	$ 4,992	$ 208	$ 78

* Estimated

EXHIBIT 11.12 Capital Appropriations and Expenditures *(CONTINUED)*

CHART OF CUMULATIVE NET CASH POSITION – ACTUAL VS JUSTIFICATION

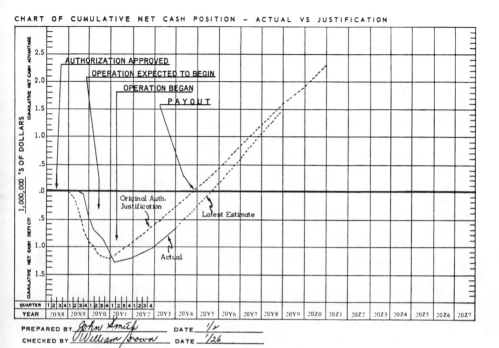

EXHIBIT 11.13 CAPITAL EXPENDITURE PERFORMANCE REPORT

The scope and postcompletion period of the review will depend on circumstances. Some companies limit the audit only to major projects over $1 million and only until the payback period is completed.

A simple form of graphic report quickly summarizing actual and expected performance is illustrated in Exhibit 11.13. The postaudit report commentary, of course, can touch on estimated cash flow to date of the audit as compared with actual cash flow, old versus new break-even points, and operating expenses, planned versus actual, as well as other pertinent observations.

OTHER ASPECTS OF CAPITAL EXPENDITURES

Working Capital

This chapter, up to this point, has dealt with capital expenditures in the strictest sense. In many cases this is proper in that, when a capital expenditure other than cash outflow is made, there is no impact on working capital. Yet, many instances, such as growth or expansion in the business, will require additional investment in inventory and receivables as well as the plant and equipment needs. Suffice it to say that if additional working capital is necessary, then it should be reflected in the investment requirement and in the rate of return calculation. It is partially offset by the salvage value recovery when the business ceases.

Lease versus Buy Decisions

Technically speaking, the acquisition of a long-term asset, whether purchased or leased, should be included in the capital budget. However, the rental of the asset or leasing it on a short-term basis would not warrant this treatment.

The discounted cash flow technique may be useful in reaching a decision whether to lease or buy, and several good reference sources are available on the subject. The best method to be used is either IRR or NPV, and treatment of some of the variables is controversial. The authors suggest the NPV method is perhaps easy to apply. If the marginal financing (net of taxes) cost of funds to purchase the asset is known, the same discount rate can be applied to the stream of lease payments to arrive at the net present value. Usually the alternative with the lower NPV, and the higher savings, should be the one selected. The comparative net present values of lease vs. purchase (with no investment tax credit) are shown in Exhibit 11.14. This application assumes a 15% interest borrowing rate, less a 40% tax rate, or a net cost of 9%. The net savings through purchase may be calculated as:

Present value of purchase	$ 1,000,000
Less: Present value of related tax savings	311,120
Net purchase cost	$ 688,880
Savings (NPV) by purchase over lease	
Present value of lease cost	$ 733,632
Net purchase cost (above)	688,880
Net savings	$ 44,752

Mutually Exclusive Capital Proposals

In the capital budgeting process there may be instances when the estimated rate of return on any two projects is the same, but funds are available for only one. The two projects, by definition, are mutually exclusive. How should a decision be made as to which proposal to accept? One complicating factor is that the IRR method may rank projects somewhat differently than the NPV approach. Such a condition can arise because the IRR method assumes that funds generated are reinvested at the discounted rate calculated for the initial investment. The NPV method assumes funds are reinvested at the rate used for discounting, which is often the cost of capital. Other reasons for differing evaluations relate to different project lines and different initial investments. When the projects are mutually exclusive, one way of making a decision is to (1) calculate the differences in cash flow, and (2) apply the opportunity cost rate, or cost of capital rate, to these cash flow differences.

Assuming the incremental or opportunity cost rate is higher than the capital budget cut-off rate, then the proposal with the higher value should be selected. As reflected in Exhibit 11.15, Project B should be accepted.

Plant and Equipment Records

Adequate plant and equipment records are a necessary adjunct to effective control. They provide a convenient source of information for planning and control purposes as well as for insurance and tax purposes. Some of the advantages may be enumerated as:

1. Provide necessary detailed information about the original cost (and depreciation reserves) of fixed assets by type of equipment or location.

NPV CALCULATION
LEASE VS. BUY
A. PURCHASE BASIS

Year	Accelerated Cost Recovery	Income Tax Savings (40% Rate)	Discount Factor (9%)	Present Value
1	$ 200,000	$ 80,000	.917	$ 73,360
2	200,000	80,000	.842	67,360
3	200,000	80,000	.772	61,760
4	200,000	80,000	.708	56,640
5	200,000	80,000	.650	52,000
6	—	—		—
7	—	—		—
8	—	—		—
9	—	—		—
Total	$ 1,000,000	$ 400,000		$ 311,120

NPV CALCULATION
LEASE VS. BUY
B. LONG-TERM LEASE BASIS

Year	Pretax Lease Rental	Tax Savings at 40% Rate	After-Tax Lease Cost	Discount Factor (9%)	Net Present Value
1	$ 280,000	$112,000	$ 168,000	.917	$154,056
2	280,000	112,000	168,000	.842	141,456
3	270,000	108,000	162,000	.772	125,064
4	270,000	108,000	162,000	.708	114,696
5	120,000	48,000	72,000	.650	46,800
6	120,000	48,000	72,000	.596	42,912
7	120,000	48,000	72,000	.547	39,384
8	120,000	48,000	72,000	.502	36,144
9	120,000	48,000	72,000	.460	33,120
Total	$ 1,700,000	$ 680,000	$ 1,020,000		$ 733,632

EXHIBIT 11.14   NPV CALCULATION—LEASE VERSUS BUY

2. Make available comparative data for purchase of new equipment or replacements.

3. Provide basic information to determine proper depreciation charges by department or cost center and serve as a basis for the distribution of other fixed charges such as property taxes and insurance.

4. Establish the basis for property accountability.

5. Provide detailed information on assets and depreciation for income tax purposes.

6. Are a source of basic information in checking claims and supporting the company position relative to personal and real property tax returns?

MUTUALLY EXCLUSIVE PROJECTS
COMPARATIVE CASH FLOWS
(DOLLARS IN THOUSANDS)

| Year | Cash Flows | | | Present Value at 20%* | |
	A	B	B–A Difference	Factor	Amount
0	$(50,000)	$(90,000)	$(40,000)	1.00	$(40,000)
1	12,000	30,000	18,000	.833	14,994
2	14,000	35,000	21,000	.694	14,574
3	15,000	35,000	20,000	.579	11,580
4	15,000	35,000	20,000	.482	9,640
5	15,000	34,000	19,000	.402	7,638
6	15,000	30,000	15,000	.335	5,025
7	10,000	21,000	11,000	.279	3,069
Total	$ 46,000	$ 130,000	$ 84,000		$ 26,520

* Incremental rate of 20% exceeds cut-off rate of 17%

EXHIBIT 11.15   INCREMENTAL INVESTMENT—MUTUALLY EXCLUSIVE PROJECTS

7. Serve as evidence and a source of information for insurance coverage and claims.
8. Provide the basis for determining gain or loss on the disposition of fixed assets.
9. Provide basic data for control reports by individual units of equipment.

Property records include the plant ledgers and detailed equipment cards. The ledgers will follow the basic property classifications of the company. Detailed records must be designed to suit the individual needs of the company. Information in a data bank, preferably stored in a computer, should include:

- Name of asset
- Type of equipment
- Control number
- Description
- Size
- Model
- Style
- Serial number
- Motor number
- Purchased new or used
- Date purchased
- Vendor
- Invoice number
- Purchase order number
- Location
  - Plant
  - Building
  - Floor
  - Department

- Account number
- Transfer information
- Original cost information
  - Purchase cost
  - Freight
  - Tax
  - Installation cost
  - Material
  - Labor
  - Overhead

- Additions to
- Date retired
- Sold to
- Scrapped
- Cost recovered
- Depreciation data
  - Estimated life
  - Annual depreciation
  - Basis

Additional information may be required in particular companies. However, a database should be complete so that appropriate reports can be prepared.

There are numerous software packages available that permit the generation of most conceivable needs as regards reports or fixed assets.

Internal Control and Accounting Requirements

Once the property has been acquired, the matter of proper accounting and control arises. Usually, such duties become the responsibility of the controller. The problem is essentially very simple, but a few suggestions may prove helpful:

- All fixed assets should be identified, preferably at the time of receipt; a serial number may be assigned and should be affixed to the item. Use of metal tags or electrical engraving is a common method of marking the equipment.
- Machinery and equipment assigned to a particular department should not be transferred without the written approval of the department head responsible for the physical control of the property. This procedure is essential to know the location for insurance purposes and to correctly charge depreciation, etc.
- No item of equipment should be permitted to leave the plant without a property pass signed by the proper authority.
- Periodically, a physical inventory should be taken of all fixed assets.
- Detailed records should be maintained on each piece of equipment or similar groups.
- Purchase requisitions and requests for appropriations should be reviewed to assure that piecemeal acquisitions are not made to avoid the approval of higher authority. Thus if all expenditures over $100 require the signature of the general manager, individual

requisitions may be submitted for each table or each chair to avoid securing such approval.

- Retirement of fixed assets by sale or scrapping should require certain approvals to guard against the disposal of equipment that could be used in other departments.
- If possible, bids should be secured on any sizable acquisitions.
- Provision should be made for proper insurance coverage during construction as well as on completion.
- Expenses should be carefully checked to decrease the possibility that portions of capital expenditures are treated as expenses to avoid budget overruns.

Idle Equipment

Another phase of control over fixed assets relates to unused facilities, whether only of short duration or for more extended periods. In every business, it can reasonably be expected that some loss will be sustained because of idle facilities and/or idle workers. The objective is to inform management of these losses and place responsibility in an attempt to eliminate the avoidable and unnecessary costs. But aside from stimulating action to eliminate the causes of short-term idleness, such information may be a guide in determining whether additional facilities are necessary. Also, such knowledge may encourage disposal of any permanently excess equipment, giving consideration to the medium-term plans.

Losses resulting from unused plant facilities are not limited to the fixed charges of depreciation, property taxes, and insurance. Very often idle equipment also results in lost labor, power, and light, as well as other continuing overhead expenses, to say nothing of startup time and lost income from lost sales.

Causes of idle time may be threefold:

1. *Those controllable by the production staff.* These may result from:
   (a) Poor planning by the foreperson or other production department staff member
   (b) Lack of material
   (c) Lack of tools or other equipment
   (d) Lack of power
   (e) Machine breakdown
   (f) Improper supervision or instructions, etc.

2. *Those resulting from administrative decisions.* For example, a decision to build an addition may force the temporary shutdown of other facilities. Again, management may decide to add equipment for later use. Here certain idle plant costs may be incurred until the expected demand develops.

3. *Those arising from economic causes.* Included are the causes beyond the control of management, such as cyclical or seasonal demand. In somewhat the same class is idle time resulting from excess capacity in the industry. The effect of such conditions may be partially offset by efficient sales planning and aggressive sales effort.

The cause of idle time is important in determining the proper accounting treatment. Where idle facilities result from economic causes or are otherwise highly abnormal—such as a prolonged strike—it may be desirable for the controller to have such costs segregated and handled as a separate charge in the statement of income and expense. Such expenses should not be included in inventory or cost of sales.

Some companies isolate in the manufacturing expenses the cost of idle time that is controllable by the production staff. In other cases, a simple reporting of the hours is all that is necessary. Where it is desirable to charge the costs of idle time to a separate account the segregation is simple through a comparison of normal and actual hours and the use of standard rates.

Depreciation Accounting

Depreciation has been defined in many ways, such as a dictionary definition, "decline in value of an asset due to such causes as wear and tear, action of the elements, obsolescence and inadequacy." The accounting profession has considered several definition, and after long consideration the American Institute of Certified Public Accountants (AICPA) Committee on Terminology formulated the following definition:

> Depreciation accounting *is a system of accounting which aims to distribute the cost or other basic value of tangible capital assets, less salvage (if any), over the estimated useful life of the unit (which may be a group of assets) in a systematic and rational manner. It is a process of allocation, not of valuation.* Depreciation for the year *is the portion of the total charge under such a system that is allocated to the year. Although the allocation may properly take into account occurrences during the year, it is not intended to be a measurement of the effect of all such occurrences.*[1]

In arriving at the applicable charges for depreciation, there are at least three related objectives of proper accounting: (1) to state earnings correctly; (2) to protect the investment of owners and creditors by maintaining the integrity of the fixed capital accounts (a write-off of plant and equipment over the useful life, by charges against income, tends to avoid the payment of dividends out of capital); and (3) to secure useful costs through proper depreciation allocations to cost centers. Another objective might be to maximize tax deductions (depreciation) under the applicable IRS code.

The accomplishment of these objectives must lie largely in the controller's hands. The determination of the useful life of the plant and equipment is largely an engineering problem. However, the ramifications and implications of depreciation policy—such matters as treatment of obsolescence, accounting for retirements, determination of allocation methods, and selection of individual or group rates—are best understood by the accountant. For these reasons, the controller should be the primary force in recommending to management, as may be necessary, the policies to be followed.

Obsolescence

Obsolescence, sometimes called *functional depreciation* as distinguished from physical depreciation, can be a highly significant factor in determining useful economic life. More often than not, the usefulness of facilities is likely to be limited by obsolescence, so that it may outweigh the depreciation factor. Such a condition can occur as a result of two causes. The product manufactured may be replaced by another, so that the need no longer exists for the facility. Or a new type of asset—one that produces at a much lower cost—may be developed to supersede present manufacturing equipment. Sometimes the need for expanded capacity has the effect of rendering obsolete or inadequate the existing asset.

Obsolescence may be of two kinds—normal or special. The former is the normal loss in value and can be anticipated in the same degree as other depreciation factors. It should be included in the estimate of useful life. Extraordinary or special obsolescence, on the other hand, can rarely be foreseen. The controller's responsibility generally should extend to a

---

1. Paul Grady, Inventory of Generally Accepted Accounting Principles of Business Enterprises.

review of past experience and trends to determine whether obsolescence is an important consideration in his industry. If so, then it should be duly recognized in the useful life estimates.

In accounting for obsolescence, the question must be settled about whether a distinction should be made in the accounts between charges for obsolescence and depreciation. In practice, the normal obsolescence will be combined with depreciation in both the provision and the reserve. A highly abnormal and significant obsolescence loss probably should be segregated in the income and expense statement. Aside from this, circumstances may indicate the desirability of segregating a reserve for obsolescence. It may not be possible to identify obsolescence with a particular asset, although experience will indicate the approximate amount. This can be handled as a general provision without regard to the individual piece of equipment.

Fully Depreciated Assets

In properly stating on the balance sheet the value of fixed assets and in making the proper charge to manufacturing costs for the use of the plant and equipment, the question is raised about the correct accounting treatment of fully depreciated assets. If the facilities are no longer of use, they should be retired and the amount removed from both the asset and the reserve. If the item is fully depreciated but still in use, then the depreciation charge to the earnings statement must be discontinued—unless a composite useful life estimate or a composite depreciation rate is being used. The controller should consider these conditions, as well as increased maintenance costs, in evaluating operating performance and in preparing useful reports for management.

Appraisals and Appraisal Records

Management may request appraisals of property for any one of several reasons: for the purchase or sale of property, for reorganization or liquidations, for financing when the property is collateral, for insurance purposes, for taxation purposes, and for control purposes when the records do not indicate investment by process or cost center.

The basis of valuing fixed assets has already been reviewed, and the desirability of stating such property at original cost has been emphasized. However, occasions arise when management directs the valuation of property on another basis, perhaps to remove extremely high depreciation charges. When appraisals are recorded, the original cost and depreciation on original cost should continue to be reflected in the detail records, along with the appraised value and depreciation thereon.

Loss or Gain on the Sale of Fixed Assets

The matter of accounting for the loss or gain on the sale or other disposition of fixed assets is primarily one of accounting theory. Some have supported the proposition that losses resulting from premature retirement or technological advances are properly capitalized and charged against future operations. Most authorities do not concur in this view. The sound value—or asset value, less accumulated depreciation—for all assets retired is a loss that should be charged off as incurred. It is in the nature of a correction of prior profits. Usual practice is to carry such gain or loss, if important, in the nonoperating section of the statement of income and expense.

Funds for Plant Replacement and Expansion

Unfortunately, a great deal of confusion has arisen among laymen about the distinction between a reserve and a fund. Some think that the creation of a depreciation reserve also establishes a fund to replace the property. Accountants know that a reserve may exist independent of a fund and that a fund can exist without a reserve. The depreciation reserve does not represent a fund of cash or other assets that have been set aside. It only expresses the usage of the asset. If the operation has been profitable, and if dividends have not been paid in excess of the net income after recognizing depreciation, then values of some sort are available to offset the charge for use of the plant and equipment.

Most companies do not establish funds for property expansion or replacement but use the general funds instead. However, such funds can be created, and some exponents believe that public utilities and wasting asset industries, such as mining, should establish such funds. Such funds are not necessarily to be measured by the depreciation reserve, because replacement costs may be quite different. The depreciation reserve is a measure of expired *past* value, not *future* requirements for replacement.

Plant and Equipment in Relation to Taxes

Many local communities and states levy real and personal property taxes or enforce payment of franchise taxes based on property values. Maintenance of adequate records can be a means of satisfying the taxing authorities on problems of valuation.

Plant and property values, through the resulting depreciation charges, are important from the federal income tax viewpoint. As mentioned previously, the depreciation allowance for tax purposes, if significantly different from depreciation for book purposes, can distort the profit before taxes and the tax charge. Where the estimate of useful life and the base for tax and book purposes are not greatly different, an effort should be made to bring the two in line. It may save the maintenance of a separate set of records. In any event, the burden of proof about the correctness of the depreciation claimed is placed on the taxpayer, who must keep the necessary records and other data to support the claim.

12

MANAGEMENT OF LIABILITIES

INTRODUCTION

It often has been said that the management, or planning and control, of the assets (excepting cash and temporary investments) of an enterprise rests largely in the hands of the operating executives but that management, or planning and control, of the liabilities and equity of the company is primarily the responsibility of the financial executives. In a certain sense this is true—up to a point—and the financial officers must exercise control over the liabilities of the entity to preserve its economic health.

The comments in this chapter relate to the practical or pragmatic considerations regarding liability planning and control, of which the controller must be intimately familiar. Remarks will relate to the traditional types of liabilities as well as new developments and concerns in this field of management.

LIABILITIES DEFINED

Although it is not the purpose of the chapter to deal at length with the accounting niceties regarding the recording of the liabilities of a company, the subject is defined for our purposes as:

> *Liabilities are the economic obligations of an enterprise that are recognized and measured in conformity with generally accepted accounting principles. Liabilities also include certain deferred credits that are not obligations (such as, for example, deferred credits from income tax allocations) but that are recognized and measured in conformity with generally accepted accounting principles.*

Liabilities are measured at amounts established in the exchanges involved, usually the amounts to be paid but sometimes at discounted rates.

OBJECTIVES OF LIABILITY MANAGEMENT

In the basic sense, the purpose of liability management is to assure that the enterprise has "cash adequacy"—the ability to meet cash requirements for any purpose significant to the short- or long-term financial health of the company. It is not merely to avoid insolvency or bankruptcy. From the standpoint of the controller, the more specific objectives of liability management might include:

- The recording and disclosure in accordance with generally accepted accounting principles of the financial obligations of the company.

316

- The reporting in proper form, as required by indentures or credit agreements, of the corporate liabilities.
- Through effective planning and control, the maintenance of a sound financial structure, including the proper relationship of debt to equity capital.
- Continuance of the ability to secure necessary borrowed funds in a timely manner and at a cost that is competitive.
- To institute and maintain controls that restrict commitments within well-defined limits so that they do not result ultimately in excessive and burdensome liabilities.
- To enable the company to be so well regarded in the financial marketplace that its common (and preferred) stock will command respect far into the future with an acceptable price-earnings ratio, and that the stock will reflect a gradual increase in earnings per share and consequent long-term appreciation for the benefit of the owners.
- To permit the company to maintain a prudent dividend policy.

All of these objectives of liability management are interrelated.

DIRECT LIABILITIES

In an attempt to categorize the types of liabilities and to indicate some of the matters to be considered by the controller, a brief commentary follows.

Current Liabilities

Generally, liabilities classified as current are those due to be paid within the operating cycle—that ordinarily is within a period of one year. The importance of the proper segregation of current liabilities from other liabilities rests in the role played by various financial ratios, such as the current ratio, when funds are borrowed.

By another related definition, current liabilities include those obligations whose liquidation reasonably is expected to require the use of existing current assets or the creation of new current liabilities. Included in current liabilities are:

- *Notes payable.* Represent the obligations of the company under legal instruments in which there exists an explicit promise to pay a specified amount at a specified time.
- *Accounts payable.* Accounts payable usually are largely trade accounts payable and represent the obligations of the firm to its suppliers. Since these liabilities are recorded at the time the title passes to the goods or the services are received, the financial officers should be satisfied that clean cutoffs on the obligations exist. This is especially true in those instances where the working capital or current ratio requirement is critical in a credit agreement or the company is nearing the limits specified.

  Additionally, credit balances in various asset accounts, such as accounts receivable, usually are reclassified to the accounts payable category—especially at year end—or when financial statements are published.

- *Accrued expenses.* When an obligation exists by reason of the benefits having been received but is not yet due and payable, it normally would be recorded as an accrued expense. Included would be such items as accruals for wages, salaries, commissions, rents, royalties, pension costs, and income and other taxes.
- *Accrued income taxes.* Special mention is made of this liability, since often it is composed of two segments. The normal tax due within a year would be recorded under current liabilities as "currently payable." However, using the principle of matching

costs with related revenues, yet recognizing that the tax laws permit the reporting of income in a different fiscal period than generally accepted accounting principles would either permit or require, there may be includable under current liabilities a "deferred" income tax obligation.

There are rather continuously numerous official releases by the Financial Accounting Standards Board (FASB), which provide new standards concerning income tax accounting. For example, in May 1992, the body issued Statement of Financial Accounting Standards No. 109—Accounting for Income Taxes. It supersedes FASB Statement No. 96, Accounting for Income Taxes and amends or supersedes a number of other accounting pronouncements. Statement No. 109 established financial accounting and reporting standards for the effects of income taxes that result from an enterprise's activities during the current and preceding years. It requires an asset and liability approach for financial accounting and reporting for income taxes. As the Standard says, "The objectives of accounting for income taxes are to recognize (a) the amount of taxes payable or refundable for the current year, and (b) deferred tax liabilities and assets for future tax consequences of events that have been recognized in an enterprise's financial statements or tax returns."

It is assumed the controller will keep abreast of tax reporting requirements and will see that the tax liability is properly recognized.

This distinction becomes important in calculating cash flows and when considering acceptable terms in indentures or credit agreements.

Long-Term Liabilities

Long-term liabilities, by definition, represent those obligations due in more than one year or those to be paid out of noncurrent assets. Only three limited comments need be made.

1. *Long-term leases.* If at its inception a lease meets one or more of the following criteria, it shall be classified as a capital lease by the lessee and placed on the balance sheet. Otherwise, it would be treated as an operating lease, with appropriate disclosure. The criteria for capitalization include:

   (a) The lease transfers ownership of the property to the lessee by the end of the lease term.

   (b) The lease contains a bargain purchase option.

   (c) The lease term is equal to 75% or more of the estimated economic life of the leased property (with certain exceptions).

   (d) The present value at the beginning of the lease term of the minimum lease payments—excluding certain costs—equals or exceeds 90% of the fair market value of the property over the related investment tax credit retained or expected to be used by the lessor.

   For the specific criteria and the exceptions, reference should be made to the literature of the American Institute of Certified Public Accountants (AICPA).

2. *Bonds.* Bonds are essentially long-term corporate notes issued under a formal legal procedure and secured either by the pledge of specific properties, or revenues, or the general credit of the issuer. Bonds differ from individual notes in that each represents a fractional interest of participation in a group contract, usually with a trustee acting as intermediary. The terms of the contract are set forth in the trust indenture.

3. *Other long-term obligations, etc.* Depending on circumstances, there may exist other obligations and like items that are classified either as long-term obligations or items

carried in the long-term section of the balance sheet above the shareholders' equity. These may include such items as:

○ Deferred income taxes

○ Deferred compensation

○ Accrued product warranty

○ Employees pension, indemnity, retirement, and related provision

○ Negative goodwill

○ Minority interests

The reader is referred to the various publications of the AICPA about the generally accepted principles that govern the recording of the item.

ILLUSTRATIVE PROVISIONS OF CREDIT AGREEMENTS

To be sure, within limits, indentures or credit agreements will be tailored to fit the desires of both the lender and the borrower. However, a great number of standard provisions apply to many loan agreements. Before further discussing the recording of the liabilities and, indeed, before considering the planning of indebtedness, it may be helpful to be aware of some of these usual provisions that relate to indebtedness limits and certain uses of cash. Excerpts from the note agreement for a ten-year private placement loan from an insurance company to a manufacturing concern include:

6A. *Current Ratio Requirement.* The Company covenants that it will not permit Consolidated Current Assets at any time to be less than an amount equal to 150% of Consolidated Current Liabilities.

6B. *Dividend Limitation.* The Company covenants that it will not pay or declare any dividend on any class of its stock or make any other distribution on account of any class of its stock, or redeem, purchase or otherwise acquire, directly or indirectly, any shares of its stock (all of the foregoing being herein called "Restricted Payments") except out of Consolidated Net Earnings Available For Restricted Payments; provided, however, that notwithstanding the foregoing limitations, the Company may make sinking fund and dividend payments on its outstanding preferred stock not in excess of $3,300,000 in the aggregate in any year, but provided further, that the amount of any such sinking fund payments and the amount of any such dividends paid or declared shall be included in any subsequent computation pursuant to this paragraph 6B. "Consolidated Net Earnings" shall mean consolidated gross revenues of the Company and its Subsidiaries less all operating and non-operating expenses of the Company and its Subsidiaries including all charges of a proper character (including current and deferred taxes on income, provision for taxes on unremitted foreign earnings which are included in gross revenues and current additions to reserves), but not including in gross revenues any gains (net of expenses and taxes applicable thereto) in excess of losses resulting from the sale, conversion or other disposition of capital assets (i.e., assets other than current assets), any gains resulting from the write-up of assets, any equity of the Company or any Subsidiary in the undistributed earnings of any corporation which is not a Subsidiary, any earnings of any corporation acquired by the Company or any Subsidiary through purchase, merger or consolidation or otherwise for any year prior to the year of acquisition, or any deferred credits representing the excess of the equity in any Subsidiary at the date of acquisition over the cost of the investment in such Subsidiary; all determined in accordance with generally accepted accounting principles including the making of appropriate deductions for minority interests in Subsidiaries. "Consolidated Net Earnings Available For Restricted Payments" shall mean an amount equal to (1) the sum of $10,000,000 plus 90% (or minus 100% in case of a deficit) of Consolidated Net Earnings for the period (taken as one accounting period) commencing on August 1, 20XX, and terminating at the end of the last fiscal quarter preceding the date of any proposed Restricted Payment, less (2) the sum of (a) the aggregate amount of all dividends and other distributions paid or declared by the Company on any class of its stock after July 31, 20XX, and (b) the excess of the aggregate amount expended, directly or indirectly, after July 31, 20XX, for the redemption, purchase or other acquisition of any shares of its stock, over the aggregate amount received after July 31, 20XX as the net cash proceeds of the sale of any shares of its stock. In the event that any shares of stock of the Company are issued upon conversion of convertible notes, bonds or debentures of the Company, the proceeds of the shares of stock so issued shall be deemed to be an amount equal to the principal amount of the obligations so converted. There shall not be included in Restricted Payments or in any computation of Consolidated Net Earnings Available For Restricted Payments: (x) dividends paid, or distributions made, in stock of the Company; or (y) exchanges of stock of one or more classes of the Company, except to the extent that cash or other value is involved in such exchange. The term "stock" as used in this paragraph 6B shall include warrants or options to purchase stock.

The company will not:

6C(2) *Debt*—Create, incur, assume, guarantee or in any way become liable for any Funded Debt in addition to the Funded Debt referred to in paragraph 8D, or create, incur, assume or suffer to exist any Current Debt, except

(i) Funded Debt of the Company or any Subsidiary provided that, after giving effect thereto and to the concurrent repayment of any other Funded Debt, Consolidated Net Tangible Assets shall be not less than an amount equal to (a) 250% of Consolidated Senior Funded Debt, and (b) 150% of Consolidated Funded Debt, and further provided that no Subsidiary shall create, incur, assume, guarantee or in any way become liable for any Funded Debt permitted by this clause (i) unless such Funded Debt shall be secured by a Lien on its property permitted by clauses (v), (vii) or (viii) of paragraph 6C(1), shall be of the type referred to in clause (iii) of paragraph 10G or shall constitute Funded Debt payable to the Company or another Subsidiary, and

(ii) Current Debt of the Company or any Subsidiary, provided that the aggregate Current Debt of the Company and its Subsidiaries permitted by this clause (ii) shall not be in excess of the Permitted Amount on any day after December 31, 20XX unless, during the fifteen months' period immediately preceding such day, the aggregate Current Debt of the Company and its Subsidiaries permitted by this clause (ii) shall not have been in excess of the Permitted Amount for at least 60 consecutive days, and further provided that no Subsidiary shall create, incur, assume or suffer to exist any Current Debt permitted by this clause (ii) unless such Current Debt shall be secured by a Lien on its property permitted by clauses (v), (vii) or (viii) of paragraph 6C(1) or shall constitute Current Debt payable to the Company or another Subsidiary:

6E. *Subordinated Debt.* The Company covenants that it will not (i) pay, prepay, redeem, purchase or otherwise acquire for value any Subordinated Debt except as required by the original provisions of the instruments evidencing Subordinated Debt or pursuant to which Subordinated Debt shall have been issued, (ii) amend the instruments evidencing Subordinated Debt or pursuant to which Subordinated Debt may have been issued in such manner as to terminate, impair or have adverse effect upon the subordination of the Subordinated Debt, or any part thereof, to the indebtedness evidenced by the Notes; or (iii) take or attempt to take any action whereby the subordination of the Subordinated Debt, or any part thereof, to the indebtedness evidenced by the Notes might be terminated, impaired or adversely affected. The term "Subordinated Debt" as used in this paragraph 6E shall mean any Funded Debt of the Company or any Subsidiary which does not constitute Senior Funded Debt.

Thus, it can be seen that overall debt constraints are included in this agreement and usually are a part of most credit agreements.

With respect to securing short-term credit, certain other types of restrictions may apply. Excerpts from a loan and credit agreement for short-term borrowing under a revolving line of credit between a manufacturer and a group of commercial banks contain clauses that, under specified conditions, do:

- Restrict certain payments (such as cash dividends or purchases of company stock).
- Restrict the sale or lease of assets.
- Require the maintenance of a given ratio of shareholders' equity to senior indebtedness and a minimum amount of shareholders' equity.
- Place restraints on specific contingent liabilities.
- Place limitations on acquisitions of other companies.
- Place limitations both on certain specific debts and on overall consolidated indebtedness.

The specific wording of some of the clauses relating to covenants or restrictions may be of interest:

> *Minimum Working Capital.* Maintain Consolidated Working Capital at a level whereby consolidated current assets are at least 175% of consolidated current liabilities of the Company and all Consolidated Subsidiaries and, in any event, of at least $200,000,000. In any calculation of Consolidated Working Capital, an amount equal to Covered Customer Advances shall be excluded from both consolidated current assets and consolidated current liabilities and deferred income taxes reported by the Company as a current liability in its consolidated balance sheet shall be excluded from consolidated current liabilities.

> *Negative Covenants.* So long as credit shall remain available to the Company hereunder and until the payment in full of all Notes outstanding hereunder and the performance of all other obligations of the Company hereunder, the Company will not, and will not permit any Consolidated Subsidiary to, without the prior written consent of Banks holding at least 66 2/3% in aggregate unpaid principal amount of the Notes, or, if no Notes are then outstanding, Banks having at least 66 2/3% of the aggregate commitments to make loans hereunder:

> *Restrictive P ayments.* Declare, pay or authorize any Restricted Payment if (a) any such Restricted Payment is not paid out of Consolidated Net Earnings Available For Restricted Payments and (b) at the time of, and immediately after, the making of any such Restricted Payment (or the declaration of any such dividend except a stock dividend) no Event of Default specified in § 8 and no event which with notice or lapse of time or both would become such an Event of Default has occurred and (c) the making of any such Restricted Payment would reduce Consolidated Tangible Shareholders' Equity below $225,000,000.

> *Sale, Lease, etc.* Sell, lease, assign, transfer or otherwise dispose of any of its assets, tangible and intangible (other than investments permitted by § 7B(7) and obsolete or worn-out property or real estate not used or useful in its business), whether now owned or hereafter acquired, excluding from the operation of this clause sales, leases, assignments, transfers and other dispositions (a) in the ordinary and normal operation of its business and for a full and adequate consideration, (b) between the Company and any Consolidated Subsidiary, and between Consolidated Subsidiaries and (c) by the Company not in the ordinary and normal operation of its

business provided the value on the Company's books of assets so transferred shall not exceed 10% of Consolidated Tangible Shareholders' Equity in the aggregate in any calendar year.

Maintenance of Shareholder's Equity. Permit the amount of Consolidated Tangible Shareholders' Equity at any time to be less than 100% of the then aggregate outstanding amount of Consolidated Senior Indebtedness or less than $225,000,000.

Contingent Liabilities. Assume, guarantee (which for purposes of this clause (4) shall include agreements to purchase or to provide funds for the payment of obligations of, to maintain the net worth or working capital or other financial test of, or otherwise become liable upon the obligations of, any person, firm or corporation) or endorse any obligation of any other person, firm or corporation (except the Company or a Consolidated Subsidiary, or any captive insurance subsidiary, as the case may be, as permitted by this clause (4)) or permit to exist any assumption, guarantee or endorsement, excluding from the operation of this clause, (a) assumptions, guaranties and endorsements in the ordinary and normal operation of its business as presently conducted, it being understood that performance guaranty bonds, bank guaranties for foreign work, advance payment bonds, direct guarantees for performance, or other surety bonds will be so considered; (b) guarantees by the Company or any Consolidated Subsidiary or direct obligations of the Company or any Consolidated Subsidiary for the payment of money, whether domestic or foreign, so long as an amount equal to the aggregate amount of such guaranteed obligations is deemed to be (without duplication). Indebtedness and/or Consolidated Senior Indebtedness, as the case may be, for purposes of §§ *7b(8)* and *7B(9)*; (c) guarantees of the Company or any Consolidated Subsidiary issued, or obligations assumed, in connection with acquisitions of assets permitted under § *7B(5)*, *provided* that obligations for borrowed money (whether guaranteed or assumed) shall be treated as provided in the next preceding clause (b); and (d) guaranties by the Company or any Consolidated Subsidiary of direct obligations of third parties for the payment of money, *provided* that if the then aggregate amount of such obligations shall exceed an amount equal to 15% of Consolidated Tangible Shareholders' Equity, the amount of such excess shall be deemed Consolidated Senior Indebtedness for purposes of this Agreement.

Acquisition of Assets. Acquire any assets of any other person through merger, consolidation or otherwise (including acquisition of capital stock of any other person if such acquisition is analogous in either purpose or effect to a consolidated or merger) except in the ordinary course of business, unless after giving effect to such acquisition (a) the Company shall be the surviving corporation, and (b) no Event of Default specified in § *8* or event which with notice or lapse of time or both would become such an Event of Default shall have occurred.

Other Debt. Incur or have outstanding any Indebtedness or become or be liable with respect to any Indebtedness or sell any obligations of the Company or any Consolidated Subsidiary, excluding from the operation of this covenant,

(a) the Notes:

(b) indebtedness, other than for borrowed money, incurred in the ordinary course of business of the Company or a Consolidated Subsidiary, *provided* such indebtedness is not prohibited under § *78B(4)* or *7B(5)*;

(c) liabilities in connection with capitalized leases;

(d) loans by the Company to Consolidated Subsidiaries, and loans by Consolidated Subsidiaries to the Company and other Consolidated Subsidiaries;

(e) indebtedness of the Company to Prudential, not exceeding $13,500,000, incurred pursuant to the Prudential Loan Agreement;

(f) commercial paper of the Company having a maturity of not more than nine months from its date, in amounts which in the aggregate do not exceed at any time outstanding the lesser of $75,000,000 or the sum of the unused Revolving Credit Commitments plus Bank lines of credit;

(g) existing indebtedness of Consolidated Subsidiaries not in excess of $2,075,000, *provided* that as said debt is paid or reduced it shall not be increased;

(h) a loan of X Company from a foreign bank in the amount of $2,075,000 (or the lira equivalent thereof), *provided* that as said debt is paid or reduced it shall not be increased;

(i) secured indebtedness permitted by § *7B(6)(g)* in an aggregate amount not to exceed the $100,000,000 original principal amount, *provided* that as said debt is paid or reduced it shall not be increased;

(j) other Consolidated Senior Indebtedness of the Company and Consolidated Subsidiaries which does not exceed $30,000,000 in the aggregate at any time, *provided* that the maturity of all such indebtedness in excess of an aggregate of $5,000,000 has been consented to in writing by Banks holding at least 66 2/3% in aggregate unpaid principal amount of the Notes, or, if no Notes are then outstanding, Banks having at least 66 2/3% of the aggregate commitments to make loans hereunder;

(k) borrowings from foreign sources in amounts not exceeding the equivalent of $50,000,000, *provided* the maturity and terms of all such indebtedness in excess of an aggregate of $5,000,000 has been consented to in writing by Banks holding at least 66 2/3% in aggregate unpaid principal amount of the Notes, or, if no Notes are then outstanding, Banks having at least 66 2/3% of the aggregate commitments to make loans hereunder;

(l) Subordinated Debt of the Company; and

(m) other Consolidated Senior Indebtedness of the Company (but not of any Consolidated Subsidiary), whether domestic or foreign, so long as after incurrence thereof (i) the then aggregate outstanding amount of Consolidated Senior Indebtedness of the Company and all Consolidated Subsidiaries would not exceed 100% of Consolidated Tangible Shareholders' Equity and (ii) neither the Company nor any Consolidated Subsidiary would be in default under this Agreement.

Limitation on Consolidated Indebtedness. Permit the Consolidated Indebtedness of the Company and all Consolidated Subsidiaries at any time to be more than 200% of Consolidated Tangible Shareholders' Equity.

In the day-to-day administration of loan agreements, it is obvious that the controller should be aware of the terms and should report the financial condition and financial data as required in the contract. Of equal or more importance, however, should be the controller's review of proposed financial actions to determine whether they would violate any present agreements and then to take appropriate action.

Aside from the reporting requirements, the controller should be aware of management's obligation not only to the shareholders, but also to the suppliers of debt capital. The indenture agreement may still be the best way of protecting the interests of the senior long-term lender. However, given some recent experiences wherein investment-grade bonds have been converted essentially into junk bonds in a very short period, the credit agreement may require more restrictive measures, taking into account the creativity of some lawyers, and the use of technical devices to circumvent some protective clauses. Many entities are now demanding the "poison put" provision discussed in the section on developments in the fixed income market.

PLANNING THE CURRENT LIABILITIES

Having discussed in a general way the different types of liabilities, it is now in order to review the planning process first for the current liabilities and later for long-term debt.

Planning of any specificity for current liabilities for most concerns relates to the annual business plan, for the next year or so, or to an even shorter time span. Basically, the short-term planning involves these three steps:

1. Determining, based on the operating requirements for each month and each month end, the level of each type of obligation expected (e.g., accounts payable, accrued expenses, accrued salaries and wages, accrued income taxes, notes payable, dividends payable).

2. Ascertaining from the cash forecast (see Chapter 8) whether any borrowings are necessary to meet the payment requirements, and incorporating this need and the payments into the plan.

3. Testing the consolidated plan at selected intervals, such as every reporting period or every quarter, to see if the terms of any or all credit agreements are being met—or if the indebtedness is within company norms or standards—and taking appropriate action if not (securing bank waivers, deferral of purchases, securing of special terms from suppliers, acceleration of cash receipts, etc.).

It may be observed that the level of most current liabilities, other than notes payable, will be the result of other operating segments of the annual plan. Thus, accounts payable will relate to purchases for inventory or obligations for current operating expenses; accrued salaries and wages will relate to the planned payrolls for the continuing operations, and so on. Any required short-term borrowings will derive from the cash planning.

In planning any element of current payables, it is practical to accumulate the segment based on the normal grouping of costs and expenses needed for each type of transaction. Thus, as reflected in Exhibit 12.1, the aggregate liability for purchases of raw materials and purchased parts (probably one entry in planning material purchases) is recorded for each month. Perhaps all other current purchases of an expense nature are journalized for each month. Any significant "other transaction" is recorded separately for the plan, just as would be done for the actual expense. Payments would be estimated based on an average lag time as described in Chapter 8.

The estimate of accrued salaries and wages is shown in Exhibit 12.2. The additions to the accrual would be in those groupings used to determine manufacturing costs (inventory) or other logical accumulations.

Based on the required borrowings and repayments as determined in the cash forecast, the plan for notes payable could be developed as in Exhibit 12.3.

The same procedure would be followed for each liability grouping deemed necessary and practical in the current liability planning cycle.

When all the current liabilities balances have been determined, they should be summarized as in Exhibit 12.4. As explained in the next section, the planned balances, as well as actual balances, should be measured against acceptable standards, as well as credit agreement requirements, and so on.

The above discussion of planning the current liabilities has been covered in the context of the annual business plan or any other short-term plan. The same principles would apply with respect to strategic planning or long-range planning (see Chapters 12 and 13), except that the time span usually can be by year and need not be by quarter or month. Moreover, the estimates may be arrived at on a ratio basis, and much less preciseness and detail usually are satisfactory.

THE ILLUSTRATIVE COMPANY
ACCOUNTS PAYABLE BUDGET
FOR THE PLAN YEAR ENDING DECEMBER 31, 20XX
(DOLLARS IN THOUSANDS)

Item	January	February	March	1st Quarter	Annual Total
Balance, beginning of month	$ 82,360	$88,530	$79,560	$ 82,360	$ 82,360
Add:					
Purchases—raw material	71,200	65,840	67,430	204,470	832,880
Purchases—capital assets	3,450	1,070	860	5,380	14,970
Manufacturing expenses	4,810	4,650	4,850	14,310	58,210
Marketing expenses	3,270	2,970	3,110	9,350	39,620
Research and development	1,920	1,840	1,870	5,630	24,940
Administrative expense	2,470	2,560	2,500	7,530	33,160
All other	80	40	100	220	860
Total additions	87,200	78,970	80,720	246,890	1,004,640
Deduct: Payments					
Raw material	69,800	72,010	65,840	207,650	840,120
Capital assets	520	3,450	1,070	5,040	13,810
Operating expenses	10,610	12,400	12,020	35,030	144,950
All others	100	80	40	220	860
Total deductions	81,030	87,940	78,970	247,940	999,740
Balance, end of month	$ 88,530	$ 79,560	$ 81,310	$ 81,310	$ 87,260

EXHIBIT 12.1   ACCOUNTS PAYABLE PLAN

STANDARDS TO MEASURE AND CONTROL CURRENT LIABILITIES

The planning task of the controller does not consist merely of determining what the level of current liabilities will be at stipulated times, based on operating plans or capital budgets or other financial plans. Additionally, these planned levels should be tested for acceptability. The standards by which such acceptability is judged should include (a) any legal requirements, such as those in bank lending agreements or in bond indentures and so forth; (b) those developed by the company (probably by the financial officers) as deemed prudent to avoid undue financial exposure; or (c) those acceptable to knowledgeable persons in the industry. Dun & Bradstreet, for example, periodically issues selected ratios on each industry, showing the median and upper and lower quartile for certain operating ratios and financial conditions. The company could measure itself against these industry ratios or against performance of selected competitors or against standards developed or used by commercial bankers, investment bankers, or financial analysts. If these tests reveal unacceptable conditions, then corrective action should be taken, as discussed in the next section.

THE ILLUSTRATIVE COMPANY
ACCRUED SALARIES AND WAGES BUDGET
FOR THE PLAN YEAR ENDING DECEMBER 31, 20XX
(DOLLARS IN THOUSANDS)

Item	January	February	March	1st Quarter	Annual Total
Balance, beginning of month	$ 26,310	$ 30,850	$ 34,710	$ 26,310	$ 26,310
Add: Gross payrolls					
Manufacturing	85,030	82,100	85,620	252,750	1,060,400
Marketing	31,810	30,720	31,940	94,470	375,100
Research and development	1,420	1,380	1,430	4,230	16,920
Administrative	20,640	20,600	20,650	61,890	247,560
Total additions	138,900	134,800	139,640	413,340	1,699,980
Deduct: Payments					
Salaries	41,800	42,300	42,300	126,400	506,600
Wages	92,560	88,640	107,710	288,910	1,155,640
Total payments	134,360	130,940	150,010	415,310	1,662,240
Balance, end of month	$ 30,850	$ 34,710	$ 24,340	$ 24,340	$ 37,740

EXHIBIT 12.2   ACCRUED SALARIES AND WAGES BUDGET

THE ILLUSTRATIVE COMPANY
NOTES PAYABLE BUDGET FOR THE PLAN YEAR
ENDING DECEMBER 31, 20XX
(DOLLARS IN THOUSANDS)

Month	Beginning Balance	Borrowings	Repayments	Ending Balance
January	$ —	$2,500	$ —	$2,500
February	2,500	—	—	2,500
March	2,500	2,500	—	5,000
April	5,000	—	—	5,000
May	5,000	—	1,000	4,000
June	4,000	—	500	3,500
July	3,500	—	500	3,000
August	3,000	—	1,000	2,000
September	2,000	—	—	2,000
October	2,000	—	1,000	1,000
November	1,000	—	—	1,000
December	1,000	—	1,000	—
Total	$ —	$ 5,000	$ 5,000	$ —

EXHIBIT 12.3   NOTES PAYABLE BORROWING PLAN

Some suggested ratios used to measure the acceptability of current liabilities include:

- Current ratio
- Quick ratio

- Minimum net working capital
- Current debt to net worth
- Current debt to inventory
- Number of days' payables on hand (accounts payable turnover)

Current Ratio

The current ratio is calculated by dividing the current assets by the current liabilities. It measures the protection the creditors have, even if the current assets prove to be less valuable than anticipated. Years ago, a ratio deemed satisfactory was 2 to 1. However, with the advent of the computer and improved receivables and inventory control, a ratio of between 1 to 1 and 2 to 1 is usually acceptable.

Quick Ratio

The quick ratio measures the relationship of the highly liquid assets—cash, temporary investments, and accounts receivable—to current liabilities. This ratio, also known as the liquidity ratio or acid test, is an indicator of what very liquid assets are available to meet the demands of the short-term creditors.

THE ILLUSTRATIVE COMPANY
SUMMARY OF CURRENT LIABILITIES PLAN
FOR THE PLAN YEAR ENDING DECEMBER 31, 20XX

| | Estimated Balance Current Year | Plan Year Ending 12/31/XX | | | |
| | | Quarter | | | |
Item		1	2	3	4
Notes payable	$ —	$ 5,000	$ 3,500	$ 2,000	$ —
Current maturities of long-term debt	2,500	—	—	—	2,500
Accounts payable	82,360	81,310	83,240	85,190	87,260
Dividends payable	870	910	910	910	910
Accrued salaries and wages	26,310	24,340	28,920	34,870	37,740
Accrued income taxes	1,450	1,500	1,500	1,500	1,500
Other accrued items	90	100	100	120	120
Total	$ 113,580	$ 113,160	$ 118,170	$ 124,590	$ 130,030
Selected Ratios					
Current ratio	2.0:1	2.0:1	2.1:1	2.1:1	2.2:1
Quick ratio	0.39:1	0.40:1	0.41:1	0.41:1	0.42:1
Net working capital	113,580	113,160	129,987	137,049	156,036
Current liabilities to net worth	0.25:1	0.25:1	0.26:1	0.27:1	0.28:1
Number of days purchases in payables	23.6	21.4	22.5	22.9	23.6

EXHIBIT 12.4   SUMMARY OF CURRENT LIABILITIES PLAN

Minimum Net Working Capital

This is an absolute amount—the difference between current assets and current liabilities. Some loan and credit agreements, including the one illustrated earlier, require a minimum amount of working capital at all times. The net amount indicates the extent to which the current assets could shrink and yet be sufficient to meet the current liabilities.

Current Debt to Net Worth

To the extent that assets are financed by the owners, there is more protection (more assets) for the creditors. A low current debt (or total debt) to net worth ratio is some measure of how the owners are supplying more relative funds.

Current Debt to Inventory

A high ratio of current debt as related to inventory would suggest that goods are purchased, processed, and sold without payments being made to suppliers. Depending on the relative ratio, as compared to the industry and trade practice, a high relationship would indicate inadequate financing.

Number of Days' Payables on Hand

The number of days' payables on hand is determined by dividing the accounts payable balance by the amount of purchases, and multiplying by the days in the period. For example, in Exhibit 12.1:

- The quarterly accounts payable balance planned is $81,310,000.
- Purchases for the period were planned at $246,890,000.
- Business days in the period are 65.

$$\text{Number of days payables on hand} = \$81,310,000 \div \$246,890,000$$
$$= .3293369 \times 65 \text{ days}$$
$$= 21.41 \text{ days}$$

Such a result should be checked against industry standards, if available.

CORRECTIVE ACTION

If the annual plan reflects an unsatisfactory condition regarding current liabilities, or if actual results are not acceptable, what action can be taken? The controller might examine these alternatives with the appropriate line executive:

- Possibility of reducing inventory levels through different purchasing terms, inventory handling methods, or inventory control, for example, just-in-time (JIT) inventories
- Reducing accounts receivable by granting special terms or cash discounts and the like
- Making special arrangements with suppliers to receive goods on consignment or special payment terms
- As a last resort, if the conditions appear temporary, asking the lenders to waive or relax the restrictive terms for a limited period

If the condition appears more permanent, perhaps additional equity capital or long-term debt may be desirable. Less ambitious business plans may be considered for a time: less capital expenditures, lower sales volume, and so forth.

If actual unsatisfactory conditions emerge, then some of these same planning alternatives may need to be reviewed.

RISKS OF TOO MUCH DEBT

The subject of long-term debt is closely related to the capital structure of the entity—meaning the combination of shareholders' equity and long-term debt that should be used to provide for the financing needs over the span of several years. In considering this subject, the goal of the financial executive should be to so arrange the financing that the owners of the business will receive the maximum economic benefit over the longer run, through the increase in the share price and constantly rising dividend income.

It can be demonstrated over a period of time, assuming normal profitability and the deductibility of interest expense for tax purposes, that prudent borrowing will increase the return to the shareholder. Given this potential of gain, there exists a powerful deterrent that discourages using long-term debt to the maximum of its availability. That deterrent is the risk associated with servicing the debt. For debts and debt service must be paid when due regardless of the financial condition of the company to avoid unwelcome restraints or, worse, the loss of the enterprise.

SOME BENEFITS FROM DEBT INCURRENCE

While the prudent financial executive should be aware of the risks of excessive debt, it is also necessary to recognize some of the advantages of a reasonable debt load. Here are a few:

- *Debt reduces tax payments.* Because most interest cost is income tax deductible, tax payments are lower. This assists in reducing the cost of capital used in the business.
- *Prudent borrowings can increase the return on capital to the owners.* If the earnings from this borrowed capital exceed the cost net of taxes, then the return to the shareholder is higher. (See section 32-14 on leverage.)
- *Debt imposes a discipline on management as to normal operations.* Investors know that too much cash can encourage wasteful spending practices. They tend to watch performance more carefully if sizable debt exists. Additionally, the management is more sensitive to the need for frugality to repay the debt. So more careful spending results.
- *Debt motivates managers and owners.* Lowering the equity base with borrowed funds probably makes it easier for the management group to acquire a significant stake.
- *Debt causes a more appropriate review of proposed capital expenditures and acquisitions.* Rigid repayment schedules probably cause a closer look at the economics of proposed expenditures as well as those units that don't produce sufficient earnings.

In summary, as one executive stated, "Debt is a just-in-time financial system."

SOURCES OF INFORMATION ON DEBT CAPACITY

For long-range financial planning, as well as judging the proposed terms or rating of contemplated new debt, what sources are available to secure guidance? In the final analysis, it must be management judgment that decides on acceptable limits for debt capacity. Some guidance in arriving at a decision may come from:

- *Institutional lenders or intermediaries.* Lenders, or commercial bankers, or investment bankers negotiate long-term loans at rather frequent intervals in contrast to the financial officer of an industrial enterprise. Consequently, they will be more familiar with the terms of recent agreements. Presumably, also, they are conservative and will tend to err in the conservative direction. They should be able to judge if proposed standards will be acceptable in the marketplace.

- *Action of competitors.* Ordinarily, the financial statements and loan agreements of comparable companies in the same industry are available. From such public information, individual companies and group norms can be obtained, together with ranges.

- *Analysis of past practice.* Finally, historical analysis of debt and income behavior in the particular company in times of adversity and normal conditions may provide some guide.

STANDARDS FOR DEBT CAPACITY

Conventionally, there are two types of standards by which to judge long-term debt capacity: a capitalization standard and an earnings coverage standard. In arriving at a debt policy for a particular company, each should be considered and interrelated. In working with internally generated data, the controller can make refinements ordinarily not possible with public data of other companies, thus guiding management about an acceptable relationship.

A widely used standard, often employed as a constraint in credit agreements, is the long-term debt-to-equity ratio. Thus long-term debt should not be more than, say, 25 percent of equity capital. It can also be expressed as a percent of total capitalization.

In using such a standard, several determinatives should be calculated, showing the impact, for example, of a 20 percent debt ratio versus a 25 percent ratio to judge the risk involved. Then, too, recognition must be given to the often wide variation between the principal of the debt and the annual debt service charge of interest and debt repayment. A loan may be paid off in 5 or 30 years. Whereas the ratio of debt to equity may be the same in each case in a given year, the debt service burden is substantially different. Conversely, whereas the debt ratio could improve dramatically with a shorter-term loan, the debt service drain remains the same until complete repayment.

The "earnings coverage standard" measures the total annual amount required for debt service to the net earnings available for servicing the debt. By relating the annual cash outflow for debt service (and perhaps other items) to the net earnings available for this purpose, it seeks to assure that even in times of adversity there are sufficient funds to meet the obligation. Obviously, the greater the probable change in cash flow, the higher the desired times-coverage ratio. The observed times coverage varies greatly by industry and by company. Typical well-financed companies may have a coverage of fifteen times or more.

In making analyses of the company, the controller can apply a great deal of sophistication in changing anticipated cash outflows to judge the impact. Thus it may be desirable to measure not only times coverage of net income to debt service but also other cash requirements that should not be disturbed, that is, dividends for shareholders, or certain research and development expenditures, or expected inventory build-up, or minimum capital expenditures. Each major cash outflow should be considered and reasonable sums provided even in times of adversity. An example of an analysis that might be made is shown in Exhibit 12.5. In this illustration, actual and planned cash sources and uses are satisfactory in the planning period.

THE AEROSPACE COMPANY

SOURCES AND USES OF CASH AND DEBT COVERAGE

(DOLLARS IN THOUSANDS)

	Actual			Planned			20X5 with Sales Decline	
	20XX	20X1	20X2	20X3	20X4	20X5	20%	30%
Sources of Cash								
Net income	$ 76,000	$ 82,000	$ 90,000	$ 93,000	$ 97,000	$ 100,000	$ 70,000	$ 50,000
Depreciation and amortization	42,000	45,000	47,000	48,000	51,000	52,000	52,000	52,000
Deferred income taxes	40,000	10,000	(40,000)	(10,000)	10,000	20,000	(20,000)	(20,000)
Total internal generation	158,000	137,000	97,000	131,000	158,000	172,000	102,000	82,000
Anticipated 20X5 debt offering	—	—	—	—	—	70,000	70,000	70,000
Loan and credit agreement—revolving	10,000	10,000	(20,000)	20,000	30,000	40,000	20,000	10,000
Common stockóunder options	1,000	1,000	1,500	2,000	2,000	1,000	—	—
Sale of fixed assets	4,000	—	—	3,000	—	—	—	—
Total sources	$ 173,000	$ 148,000	$ 78,500	$ 156,000	$ 190,000	$ 283,000	$ 192,000	$ 162,000

EXHIBIT 12.5 ANALYSIS OF CASH AVAILABILITY AND SELECTED DEBT COVERAGE

THE AEROSPACE COMPANY
SOURCES AND USES OF CASH AND DEBT COVERAGE
(DOLLARS IN THOUSANDS)

	Actual				Planned		20X5 with Sales Decline	
	20XX	20X1	20X2	20X3	20X4	20X5	20%	30%
Uses of Funds								
Accounts payable	10,000	5,000	1,000	—	5,000	20,000	10,000	5,000
Inventories	40,000	20,000	(20,000)	(10,000)	25,000	40,000	30,000	10,000
Accounts receivable	30,000	10,000	2,000	—	7,000	10,000	(20,000)	(30,000)
Income taxes (current)	50,000	31,000	37,000	41,000	43,000	44,600	44,600	44,600
Dividends	22,000	25,000	27,000	28,000	30,000	32,000	32,000	32,000
Capital expenditures	50,000	40,000	45,000	30,000	60,000	65,000	25,000	25,000
Debt repayment	4,000	4,000	5,000	7,500	7,500	7,500	7,500	7,500
Total uses	206,000	135,000	97,000	96,500	177,500	269,100	129,000	94,100
Increase (decrease) in cash	$ (33,000)	$ 13,000	$ (18,500)	$ 59,500	$ 12,500	$ 13,900	$ 63,000	$ 67,900
Other Data—Coverage								
Pretax income and interest/interest	7.6	7.9	8.6	8.8	9.1	7.2	5.3	4.1
Net income before interest/interest	4.5	4.7	5.1	5.3	5.4	4.3	3.3	2.7
Pretax income before rent and interest/ rent and interest	3.8	3.9	4.1	4.1	4.3	3.9	3.1	2.5
Long-term debt as percentage of capitalization	16	15	13	12	11	17		

EXHIBIT 12.5 ANALYSIS OF CASH AVAILABILITY AND SELECTED DEBT COVERAGE *(CONTINUED)*

The debt coverage ratios are very good. However, with a major drop in sales, even planned cutbacks in receivables, inventory, and capital expenditures result in coverage ratios that although adequate are substantially below the levels the financial management considers desirable in a cyclical type of business. The need for a new debt issue in 20X5 should be reexamined in terms of the probability or danger of a sales decline. However, a long-term debt has been continually declining from 16 percent of capitalization in 20XX to 11 percent in 20X4; and even with the planned $70 million new debt issue in 20X5 it reaches only 17 percent. Hence, the critical point in this example is earnings coverage, not capitalization.

The magnitude of the *probable* downturn in earnings and changes in various cash out-flows under such circumstances should be considered. A range of the *most probable* contraction in sales volume and, therefore, in net income should be determined and resulting times coverage determined.

In the final analysis, debt policy or appropriate capital structure can be determined only by an examination of the factors in the company and in the industry that influence the ability to repay debt. It is a matter of judgment and foresight regarding likely conditions, conservatively arrived at—and not mathematics.

BOND RATINGS

There exists a significant difference in interest cost, depending on the quality rating assigned to debt securities by the three rating agencies, and this is an important consideration in selecting aggregate debt limits. Standard and Poor's (S&P), Moody's Investor Service, and Fitch Investor's Service—the three debt rating agencies—assign ratings that characterize judgment about the quality or inherent risk in any given security. The rating will depend, among many other factors, on the debt coverage relationship.

The symbols Moody's uses for the highest four ratings may be summarized or characterized as:

1. **Aaa**. The best quality; smallest degree of investment risk and generally considered "gilt edge."
2. **Aa**. Judged to be of high quality by all standards.
3. **A**. Higher medium grade obligations, with some elements that may be present to suggest a susceptibility to impairment at some time in the future.
4. **Baa**. Lower medium grade. Lack outstanding investment characteristics and, in fact, have speculative characteristics as well.

The objective of many well-financed companies is to secure at least an Aa rating for its bonds.

Presentations to secure the bond ratings should be carefully prepared, because poor ratings are not easily overcome.

In determining a debt rating, the agencies need adequate financial data, such as:

- Consolidated balance sheets—perhaps five historical years and five projected years.
- Consolidated statements of income and retained earnings for five years historical and five years projected. Included would be dividends paid and per share data, including earnings, dividends, and book value.
- Consolidated statement of cash flows—again five historical years and five prospective years.
- Product group statements for historical and projected data regarding sales, operating margin, and margin rate.

The ratio analysis, including the coverage ratios, found helpful to the rating agencies is shown in Exhibit 12.6.

AEROSPACE CORPORATION
RATIO ANALYSIS

	Years Ended December 31				Projected Years Ended December 31				
	20XX	20X1	20X2	20X3	20X4	20X5	20X6	20X7	20X8	20X9
	Senior Total	Senior Total	Senior Total	Senior Total	Senior Total	Senior Total	Senior Total	Senior Total	Senior Total	Senior Total

Financial Ratios

Net current assets/long-term debt*

Net property/long-term debt

Net property and investments/long-term debt

Net tangible assets[†]/long-term debt

Long-term debt as percent of total capitalization

Coverage Ratios

Profit before rents, interest, income taxes, and non-cash charges/rents and interest

Profit before rents, interest, and income taxes/rents and interest

Profit before interest and income taxes/interest

Net income and interest/interest

Net income, rents, and interest/rents and interest

Long-term debt and capitalized rents[‡]/net income and noncash charges

EXHIBIT 12.6 RATIO ANALYSIS FOR USE BY RATING AGENCY

AEROSPACE CORPORATION
RATIO ANALYSIS

	Years Ended December 31						Projected Years Ended December 31				
	20XX	20X1	20X2	20X3	20X4	20X5	20X6	20X7	20X8	20X9
	Senior Total	Senior Total	Senior Total	Senior Total	Senior Total	Senior Total	Senior Total	Senior Total	Senior Total	Senior Total

Operating and Other Ratios

Current assets/current liabilities

Current assets/total assets

Net sales/net current assets

Net sales/net property

Pretax profit as percent of net sales

Net income as percent of net sales

Net income as percent of net worth

Accounts receivable as percent of sales

Inventory as percent of sales

---

* Long-term debt includes in all cases current maturities.

† Net tangible assets are defined as total assets less current liabilities, intangible assets, other deferred liabilities, plus current maturities of long-term debt.

‡ Annual rentals paid capitalized at ten times.

EXHIBIT 12.6 RATIO ANALYSIS FOR USE BY RATING AGENCY *(CONTINUED)*

LEVERAGE

In considering capital structure, the financial officers necessarily must recognize and study the impact of leverage. Essentially, leverage consists of financing an enterprise with senior obligations to increase the rate of return on the common equity. The action is known also as "trading on the equity."

An application of leverage is shown in Exhibit 12.7. Assume that the management has been earning, before income taxes, 37% on capitalization; that it believes it can continue to achieve this same return; and that the company can borrow at an 11% rate. If it borrows 20% of equity and continues the rate of return on assets, the earnings per share, with favorable leverage, increase from $5.00 to $5.70 and the return on equity rises from 19.98 to 22.79%.

However, if, under unfavorable leverage conditions, management were too optimistic and the earnings rate less than the bond interest rate, the results can be unsatisfactory—as illustrated in Exhibit 12.8. Here, the rate of return on capitalization was less than the bond interest rate.

From an investor standpoint, in good times, the leverage increases the earnings per share and the price of the stock. However, in adverse times, the reverse condition exists, and the stock of a leveraged company becomes less attractive.

CONTINGENCIES

To this point in this chapter, the discussion has been related to *direct* liabilities of the enterprise. However, the management of liabilities must extend to contingent liabilities, including proper accounting for the items and proper disclosure. Aside from the matters covered herein, the controller should recognize that contingent liabilities of certain types may be weighted by a lending institution in agreeing to amounts and terms and conditions in a proposed loan agreement.

ILLUSTRATION OF LEVERAGE UNDER FAVORABLE CONDITIONS		
	100% Common Stock	Common Stock, plus Bond Capitalization
Capitalization		
Bonds (11%)	$ —	$ 20,000,000
Common stock	100,000,000	100,000,000
Total	100,000,000	120,000,000
Number of common shares	4,000,000	4,000,000
Income		
Income before taxes and interest	$ 37,000,000	$ 44,400,000
Bond interest	—	2,200,000
Income before taxes	$ 37,000,000	$ 42,200,000
Income taxes (46%)	17,020,000	19,412,000
Net income for common	$ 19,980,000	$ 22,788,000
Return on equity	19.90%	22.79%
Earnings per common share	$ 5.00	$ 5.70
Dividend (40% payout)	$ 2.00	$ 2.28

EXHIBIT 12.7 FAVORABLE LEVERAGE

	100% Common Stock	Common Stock, plus Bond Capitalization
Capitalization		
Bonds (11%)	$ —	$ 20,000,000
Common stock	100,000,000	100,000,000
Total	100,000,000	120,000,000
Number of common shares	4,000,000	4,000,000
Income		
Income before interest and taxes	$ 10,000,000	$ 10,000,000
Bond interest	—	2,200,000
Income before taxes	10,000,000	7,800,000
Income taxes (46%)	4,600,000	3,588,000
Net income for common	$ 4,400,000	$ 4,212,000
Return on equity	4.4%	4.21%
Earnings per common share	$ 1.10	$ 1.05
Dividend (40% payout)	$ .44	$ .42

EXHIBIT 12.8   UNFAVORABLE LEVERAGE

Moreover, in planning for the direct liabilities of the enterprise, the controller may find it necessary to estimate the timing and amount of contingent liabilities that should be treated as direct debt on a probability basis.

Treatment of Long-Term Liabilities in the Annual Business Plan

Planning the long-term debt status for the coming year is one segment of the annual business plan. This phase of the business may be reported only as presented in the statement of financial position, with the beginning-of-the-year status and the end-of-the-year status indicated. However, if the items are numerous enough, or if the attention of the management and the board of directors should be directed to this matter, then the plan for long-term debt may be summarized and presented on an exhibit as in Exhibit 12.9. It should be noted that the proposed transactions are disclosed, as well as key ratios. In all published financial statements, the controller has the responsibility to properly value and properly disclose the significant long-term obligations in accordance with generally accepted accounting principles (GAAP). It is suggested that in most instances the same basis be used in the planning statements. Obligations and contingent obligations that are covered by footnote in the annual report to shareholders can be disclosed by oral or written commentary in reviewing the annual plan (or long-range plan) with management or the board of directors.

LONG-RANGE FINANCIAL PLAN

The strategic plans and long-range financial plans are much less detailed than the annual business plan. Accordingly, summarized data may be the only information formulated and provided to the management and the board of directors—unless, of course, they desire more detail, or if, because of great risks and the like, it is imperative these groups fully understand the debt status. In arriving at the planned indebtedness levels for the long-range plan, the

THE MAGRAUDY COMPANY
NO. 2 LONG-TERM DEBT
FOR PLAN YEAR ENDING DECEMBER 31, 20XX
(DOLLARS IN THOUSANDS)

Issue	Maturity Date	Interest Rate	Estimated Beginning Balance	New Indebtedness	Payments on Debt	Planned Ending Balance
Long-Term Debt						
Bank term loans	9/30/98	Floating Prime + 1 1/2%	$ 49,200	$ —	$ 4,200	$ 45,000
Loan from insurance company	12/31/99	14%	50,000	—	5,000	45,000
Proposed mortgage loan	6/30/03	13%	—	75,000	—	75,000
Other notes payable	12/31/94	10%–15%	5,850	2,000	2,850	5,000
Subordinated debentures	12/31/97	11%	35,000	—	4,000	31,000
Total			140,050	77,000	16,050	201,000
Other Long-Term Obligations						
Capital lease obligations			29,400	5,600	4,000	31,000
Accrued warranty costs			37,800	12,100	7,100	42,800
Other miscellaneous			2,760	—	760	2,000
Total			69,960	17,700	11,860	75,800
Total long-term obligations			$ 210,010	$ 94,700	$ 27,910	$ 276,800
Selected Ratios						
Long-term debt as percent of total capitalization			22			24
Debt to equity ratio			63			60
Times interest charges covered			12.2			9.6

EXHIBIT 12.9 SUMMARY OF PLANNED LONG-TERM DEBT

process is much as implied in Exhibit 12.5; that is, the plans are summarized year by year in sequence. If more capital is required to meet cash outflow or to correct an unsatisfactory current debt picture, then long-term capital is planned. If it appears the marketplace will accept indebtedness under suitable terms, then borrowings can be assumed. If the long-term debt percentage would be too high or if service coverage would be insufficient, then the sale of equity may be the route necessary. Again, the objective of the financial officers should be to maintain the company in such good financial health that, under most circumstances (good times or poor), it should be able to secure any needed capital under reasonably acceptable terms.

MANAGING LIABILITIES: SOME PRACTICAL STEPS

We have reviewed the objectives of liability management, planning the liabilities, and, among other things, provided some of the standards to measure the amount of current debt as well as long-term debt. While the concerns of the controller and other financial executives have been addressed, perhaps it will be helpful to summarize some of the desirable steps in properly managing liabilities. Because of the differing nature of the various types of liabilities, it is practical in the accounting, planning, and control activities to treat each group separately. Here, then, are some suggestions as to what the controller might do to assist in properly managing the liabilities:

- *Current Liabilities*
    - o *Plan* the liabilities by month or quarter or year as may be applicable (as in the annual business plan or longer-term strategic plan). This can be accomplished after the various assets levels (cash, receivables, inventories, plant, and equipment) are planned and when the operational plans (sales, manufacturing expenses, direct labor, direct material, selling expense, general and administrative) are completed.

        It is practical to group the current liabilities according to the categories to be identified in the Statement of Estimated Financial Position, such as accounts payable, accrued salaries and wages, accrued expenses, accrued income taxes, notes payable.

        The accounts payable plan or budget, when finalized, for the annual plan might appear as in Exhibit 12.10. The budget or plan for all current liabilities, by quarter, for the annual plan could be somewhat as in Exhibit 12.11. Note that certain pertinent ratios are shown.
    - o *Test* the plan for compliance with credit agreements or other internally developed standards such as current ratio, inventory turns, net working capital, and industry average or competitor performance. If necessary, modify the plan.
    - o *Analyze* each line item for ways to reduce the obligation, for example, use of JIT inventories to reduce accounts payable or notes payable. "What if" analyses of actions on other assets (terms of sale, etc.) or liabilities can be made to improve the status, if warranted. Take any appropriate action.
    - o *Monitor* the monthly or quarterly balances for any unfavorable developing trends, and take appropriate action.
    - o *Issue* the appropriate control or informational reports, such as to the supervisor of accounts payable, board of directors, or creditors. This might include updating the projected debt status to the year end.
    - o When appropriate, as in major developments, *revise* the financial plan.

THE NEW YORK COMPANY
ACCOUNTS PAYABLE BUDGET
FOR THE YEAR ENDING 12/31/XX
(DOLLARS IN MILLIONS)

Item	1st Quarter				Total	Year 20XX
	Jan.	Feb.	March			
Balance, beginning of month	$21,600	29,800	19,500		21,600	$ 21,600
Add:						
Purchases—raw materials and parts	14,300	12,400	13,600		40,300	149,800
Purchases—capital items	9,500	1,500	1,000		12,000	20,000
Subtotal	23,800	13,900	14,600		52,300	169,800
Expenses—						
Manufacturing	4,800	4,300	4,500		13,600	52,400
Selling	2,100	2,000	2,300		6,400	25,900
Research and development	1,200	1,400	1,500		4,100	15,000
General and administrative	1,900	1,900	1,900		5,700	22,800
All others	100	200	100		400	1,400
Total Additions	33,900	23,700	24,900		82,500	287,300
Deduct:						
Payments—Raw materials and purchased parts	13,600	14,400	12,900		40,900	161,700
—Capital items	1,500	9,500	1,500		12,500	20,000
—Operating expenses	10,600	10,100	11,200		31,900	124,200
Total deductions	25,700	34,000	25,600		85,300	305,900
Balance, end of month	$ 29,800	$ 19,500	$ 18,800		$ 18,800	$ 3,000

EXHIBIT 12.10 ACCOUNTS PAYABLE BUDGET

THE NEW YORK COMPANY
SUMMARY—CURRENT LIABILITY BUDGET
FOR THE PLAN YEAR ENDING 12/31/XX
(*DOLLARS IN MILLIONS*)

Item	Estimated Balance 12/31/XX	Plan Year Ending 12/31/XX			
		Quarter			
		1	2	3	4
Notes Payable—banks	$ 4,700	4,100	3,600	3,000	$ 2,000
Current Maturities— long-term debt	1,500	1,400	1,300	1,200	1,200
Accounts payable	21,600	18,800	17,400	10,600	3,000
Accrual salaries and wages	5,800	5,200	6,400	6,900	7,400
Accrual income taxes	1,400	2,300	2,500	2,500	1,500
Other accrued items	800	700	600	600	500
Total	$ 35,800	32,500	31,800	24,800	15,600
Selected ratios/balances					
Current ratio	1.9 to 1	2.2 to 1	2.4 to 1	2.4 to 1	2.5 to 1
Quick ratio	.50 to 1	.70 to 1	.70 to 1	.80 to 1	1.1 to 1
Net working capital	$ 68,020	71,500	76,320	59,520	$ 39,000

EXHIBIT 12.11 SUMMARY—CURRENT LIABILITY PLAN

- *Long-Term Liabilities*

  o *Plan* the long-term debt, by appropriate category, as in Exhibit 12.9, for the annual plan, or strategic plan, based on the commentary or factors reviewed in the chapter.

  o *Test* the plan, before finalizing, against credit agreement requirements, or standards for debt capacity, including that which might exist under the least favorable business conditions which are likely to prevail in the planning period. Adjust the plan, if required.

  o *Monitor* actual performance or condition periodically during the plan term for unfavorable developments, and take appropriate action.

  o *Report* on the financial condition and outlook to the appropriate interests (bankers, bondholders, board of directors, etc.).

- *As to All Indebtedness Items*

  o Review the accounting to ascertain that GAAP are followed, to the extent practical.

  o Periodically have the internal controls checked to assure the system is functioning properly.

  o Keep reasonably informed on the status and probable trend of the debt market, and the new debt instruments, both short and long term. If appropriate, this includes foreign markets. Such information may be gained from informal discussions with commercial bankers as well as investment bankers. Perusal of financial and business literature or periodicals also may be helpful.

Additionally, the controller and other financial executives should be sensitive as to the impact of new debt issues on the holders of existing debt.

By following these few commonsense practices, there should be no unpleasant surprises regarding the management of liabilities.

ACCOUNTING REPORTS ON LIABILITIES

Reports with respect to the status and management of liabilities will depend on the business needs. A limited number are necessary for monitoring the actual status and to disclose the results of short- and long-term planning. A suggested list includes:

- Usual monthly statement of financial condition perhaps by organization segment, comparing actual and planned status
- Monthly or quarterly comparison of actual liabilities with amounts, by detailed category, as compared with permitted amounts under credit agreements
- Planning reports comparing required indebtedness as compared to credit agreements and debt capacity
- Periodic analysis of special liabilities, whether actual or contingent:
  o Long-term leases
  o Unfunded pension plan liabilities
  o Exposures of various health care plan trusts and so forth
  o Foreign currency exposure
- Aging of payables
- Comparison of actual and budgeted obligations
- Detailed liability reports as required by credit agreements
- Periodic summaries of contingent liabilities and likely actual liability

The controller should prepare those reports for financial management, or general management, as appropriate, to guide the business, with suitable oral or written commentary.

INTERNAL CONTROLS

Internal control of liabilities runs the gamut from routine accounts payable and payroll disbursements to the periodic payment of notes payable under the various indenture terms and the like.

A fundamentally sound routine for the recording of liabilities is basic to a well-founded disbursements procedure. The essence of the problem is to make certain that no improper liabilities are placed in line for payment. Routines must be instituted to see that all liabilities are properly certified or approved by designated authority. The proper comparison of receiving reports, purchase orders, and invoices by those handling the detail disbursement procedure eliminates many duties by the officers; but the liabilities not covered by these channels must have the necessary review. The controller or treasurer, for example, must approve the payrolls before payment. The chief purchasing agent, or chief engineer, or treasurer, or some official must approve invoices for services, because no receiving report is issued. Certain special transactions may require the approval of the president. Again, invoices for such items should be checked against the voucher file for duplicate payments. In summary, the controller should consider the system of recording payables somewhat independently of the disbursements procedure to give added assurance that the necessary controls exist.

Moreover, if computers play a large part in processing liabilities, much acceptable software is available. However, the existence and extent of internal controls should be checked.

13

MANAGEMENT
OF SHAREHOLDERS' EQUITY

INTRODUCTION

Shareholders' equity is the interest of the shareholders, or owners, in the assets of a company, and at any time is the cumulative net result of past transactions affecting this segment of the balance sheet. This equity is created initially by the owner's investment in the entity, and may be increased from time to time by additional investments, as well as by net earnings. It is reduced by distributions of the equity to the owners (usually as dividends). Further, it may also decrease if the enterprise is unprofitable. When all liabilities are satisfied, the balance—the residual—belongs to the owners.

Basic accounting concepts govern the accounting for shareholders' equity as a whole, for each class of shareholder, and for the various segments of the equity interest, such as capital stock, contributed capital, or earned capital. This chapter does not deal with the accounting niceties regarding the ownership interest. It is assumed the controller is well grounded in such proper treatment, or will become so. The concerns relate to the shareholders' interest as a total and not any special accounting segments.

IMPORTANCE OF SHAREHOLDERS' EQUITY

As previously stated, capital structure is composed of all long-term obligations and shareholders' equity—in a sense, the "permanent" capital. Some would describe the capital structure of the enterprise as the cornerstone of financial policy. Such policy must be so planned that it will command respect from investors far into the future. But of the two basic elements, it is the shareholders' equity that is critical. This equity must provide a margin of safety to protect the senior obligations. Stated another way, in most instances, without the shareholders' equity, no senior obligations could be issued. It is for this reason, among others, that proper management of the equity is of paramount importance. In a sense, the controller, together with other members of financial management, must safeguard the long-term financial interests of not only the shareholders but also the providers of long-term credit, to say nothing of the sources of short-term capital such as commercial banks and suppliers. This is accomplished, in part, by properly planning and controlling the equity base of the enterprise.

ROLE OF THE CONTROLLER

Given the importance of shareholders' equity and the need to manage it prudently, what should be the role of the controller? In a general sense, as one of the principal financial officers of the corporation, the controller must properly account for the shareholders' equity, providing those analyses and recommending those actions that are consistent with enhancing shareholder value over the long term. The task would require attention to these specific actions:

- Properly accounting for the shareholders' equity in accordance with generally accepted accounting principles (GAAP). This includes the historical analysis of the source of the equity and the segregation of the cumulative equity by class of shareholder.
- Preparing the appropriate reports on the status and changes in shareholders' equity as required by agencies of the U.S. government (e.g., Securities and Exchange Commission), by management, and by credit agreements and other contracts.
- Making the necessary analyses to assist in planning the most appropriate source (debt or shareholders' equity) of new funds, and the timing and amount required of each.
- As appropriate, maintaining in proper and economical form the capital stock records of the individual shareholders, with the related meaningful analysis (by nature of owner—individual, institution, and so forth—by geographic area, by size of holding, etc.) or assuring that it is done. (In larger firms, a separate department or an outside service might perform these functions.)
- Periodically making the required analysis, reporting on, and making recommendations or observations on such matters as:
  - Dividend policy
  - Dividend reinvestment plans
  - Stock splits or dividends
  - Stock repurchase
  - Capital structure
  - Trend and outlook for earnings per share
  - Cost of capital for the company and industry
  - Tax legislation as it affects shareholders
  - Price action of the market price of the stock, and influences on it

Plainly, there is a grassland of financial subjects on which the controller can graze and in due course make useful suggestions.

Before a discussion of specifics about the planning phases regarding shareholders' equity, some interesting relationships should be understood:

- Rate of growth in equity as related to the return on equity (ROE)
- Growth in earnings per share as related to ROE
- Cost of capital
- Dividend payout ratio
- Relationship of long-term debt to equity

GROWTH OF EQUITY AS A SOURCE OF CAPITAL

As a company grows, it usually requires additional funds to finance working capital and plant and equipment, as well as for other purposes. Of course, it could issue additional shares of stock, but this might dilute earnings per share for a time or perhaps raise questions of control. Another alternative is to borrow long-term funds. Some managements may wish to do neither. As a result, the remaining source of long-term capital (excluding some assets sales, etc.) is the growth in retained earnings. But such a method is typically a slow way to gain additional capital. The rate of growth of equity is germane to establishing target rates of return on equity, selecting sources of capital, and monitoring dividend policy.

The annual growth in shareholders' equity from internal sources may be defined as the rate of return earned on such equity multiplied by the percentage of the earnings retained. It may be represented by this formula:

$$G = R(1 - P)$$

where

      G = annual percentage growth on shareholders equity

      R = annual net rate of return

      P = the payout ratio or share of earnings annually paid out as dividends

As an example, if a company can earn about 23% each year on its equity, and the payout ratio is 40%, then shareholders' equity will grow at 14% per year, calculated as:

$$\begin{aligned} G &= 0.23(1 - 0.40) \\ &= 0.23(0.60) \\ &= 0.14 \\ &= 14\% \end{aligned}$$

Under these circumstances, if the management thinks the company can grow in sales and earnings at about 30% per year, if additional funds will be needed at about this same rate, and if the dividend payout is to remain at 40%, then management will require some outside capital for the growth potential to be realized.

RETURN ON EQUITY AS RELATED TO GROWTH IN EARNINGS PER SHARE

Another facet of the shareholders' equity role is the relationship of the ROE to the rate of annual increase in earnings per share (EPS). This connection is often not understood even by some financial executives. Basically, the rate of return on shareholders' equity, when adjusted for the payout ratio, produces the rate of growth per year in EPS. It may be expressed in this formula:

Growth per year in EPS $=$ ROE $\times$ retention ratio

This relationship is illustrated in Exhibit 13.1. Thus, assuming a constant return on equity of 20% and a constant dividend payout ratio of 25%, the EPS growth rate is calculated by means of the same formula as for the growth of shareholders' equity:

$$\begin{aligned} G &= R(1 - P) \\ &= (0.20) \\ &= 0.20(0.75) \\ &= 0.15 \\ &= 15\% \end{aligned}$$

For illustrative purposes to management or the board of directors, these same factors can be translated into book value per share, earnings per share, and dividends per share, as shown in Exhibit 13.2. In such terms, explanations about the shareholders' interest often are more easily understood. It is to be noted in Exhibit 13.2 that, with a constant dividend payout ratio, the annual dividend rate of increase is the same as the annual growth rate in EPS.

THE ELECTRONIC COMPANY
RETURN ON EQUITY VS. EPS GROWTH
(DOLLARS IN THOUSANDS EXCEPT PER SHARE)

Year	Beginning Shareholders' Equity	Net Income	Dividends Paid	Ending Shareholders' Equity	Rate of Return on Beginning Equity	Dividend Payout (%)	EPS	Growth in EPS(%)
20X1	$ 250,000	$ 50,000	$ 12,500	$ 287,500	20%	25%	$ 5.00	—
20X2	287,500	57,500	14,375	330,625	20	25	5.75	15%
20X3	330,625	66,125	16,531	380,219	20	25	6.61	15
20X4	380,219	76,044	19,011	437,252	20	25	7.60	15
20X5	437,252	87,450	21,863	502,839	20	25	8.75	15
20X6	502,839	100,568	25,142	578,265	20	25	10.06	15
20X7	578,265	115,653	28,913	665,005	20	25	11.57	15

EXHIBIT 13.1 CONSTANT RETURN ON EQUITY VERSUS EPS GROWTH

GROWTH IN EARNINGS PER SHARE

Prudent financial planning will consider the impact of decisions on EPS. Management is concerned with the growth in EPS since one of its tasks is to enhance shareholder value. And continual increases in EPS each year will raise shareholder value through its recognition in a higher P/E ratio and usually a rising dividend payment. Moreover, the growth in EPS is one of the measures of management as viewed by the financial community, including financial analysts.

Given the importance of EPS, financial officers should bear in mind that the EPS will increase as a result of any one of these actions:

- The plow-back of some share of earnings, even as long as the rate of return on equity remains just constant—as illustrated by the calculations in Exhibits 13.1 through 13.2 . (A growth in EPS does not necessarily mean that the management is achieving a higher rate of return on equity.)
- An actual increase in the rate of return earned on shareholders' equity
- Repurchase of common shares as long as the rate of return on equity does not decrease
- Use of prudent borrowing—financial leverage (see Chapter 12)
- Acquisition of a company whose stock is selling at a lower P/E than the acquiring company
- Sale of shares of common stock above the book value of existing shares, assuming the ROE is maintained

Financial planning should keep all the alternatives in mind. But of all these actions, the one most likely sustainable and translatable into a healthy growth in EPS is a constant, or increasing, return on shareholders' equity.

			PER SHARE DATA				
			RETURN ON EQUITY VS. EPS GROWTH				
Year	1	2	3	4	5	6	7
Book value, beginning	$ 25.00	$ 28.75	$ 33.06	$ 38.02	$ 43.72	$ 50.28	$ 57.82
Earnings*	5.00	5.75	6.61	7.60	8.75	10.06	11.57
Dividends†	1.25	1.44	1.65	1.90	2.19	2.52	2.89
Retained earnings	3.75	4.31	4.96	5.70	6.56	7.54	8.68
Book value, ending	$ 28.75	$ 33.06	$ 38.02	$ 43.72	$ 50.28	$ 57.82	$ 66.50
Increase in EPS:							
Amount		$ .75	.86	.99	1.15	1.31	$ 1.51
Percent		15%	15	15	15	15	15%
Increase in dividends:							
Amount		$ .19	.21	.25	.29	.33	$ .37
Percent		15%	15	15	15	15	15%

* At 20% on beginning equity

† At 25% payout rate

EXHIBIT 13.2　PER SHARE—ROE VS. GROWTH RATE

COST OF CAPITAL

Investors are willing to place funds at risk in the expectation of recovering such capital and making a reasonable return. Some individuals or companies might prefer to invest in a practically risk-free security, such as U.S. government bonds; others will assume greater risks but expect a correspondingly higher rate of return. Cost of capital, then, may be defined as the rate of return that must be paid to investors to induce them to supply the necessary funds (through the particular instrument under discussion). Thus, the cost of a bond would be represented by the interest payments plus the recovery of the bond purchase price, perhaps plus some capital gains. The cost of common shares issued would be represented by the dividend paid plus the appreciation of the stock. Capital will flow to those markets where investors expect to receive a rate of return consistent with their assessment of the financial and other risks, and a rate that is competitive with alternative investments.

Knowledge of the cost of capital is important for two reasons:

- The financial manager must know what the cost of capital is and offer securities that provide a competitive rate, in order to be able to attract the required funds to the business.
- In making investment decisions, such as for plant and equipment, the financial manager must secure a return that is, on average, at least as high as the cost of capital. Otherwise, there is no reason to make an investment that yields only the cost or less. The manager is expected to gain something for the shareholder. Hence, the cost of capital theoretically sets the floor as the minimum rate of return before any investment should even be considered.

Prudent management of the shareholders' equity, then, involves:

- Attempting to finance the company so as to achieve the optimum capital structure, and, hence, a reasonable cost of capital
- Properly determining the cost of capital, and employing such knowledge in relevant investment decisions

COMPONENTS OF COST OF CAPITAL[1]

Before determining the amount of a company's cost of capital, it is necessary to determine its components. The following two sections describe in detail how to arrive at the cost of capital for these components. The weighted average calculation that brings together all the elements of the cost of capital is then described in the "Calculating the Weighted Cost of Capital" Section.

The first component of the cost of capital is debt. This is a company's commitment to return to a lender both the interest and principal on an initial or series of payments to the company by the lender. This can be short-term debt, which is typically paid back in full within one year, or long-term debt, which can be repaid over many years, with either continual principal repayments, large repayments at set intervals, or a large payment when the entire debt is due, which is called a *balloon* payment. All these forms of repayment can be combined in an infinite number of ways to arrive at a repayment plan that is uniquely structured to fit the needs of the individual corporation.

The second component of the cost of capital is preferred stock. This is a form of equity that is issued to stockholders and that carries a specific interest rate. The company is obligated to pay only the stated interest rate to shareholders at stated intervals, but not the initial

1. Reprinted with permission from pp. 270-278 of Steven M. Bragg, *Financial Analysis* (Wiley, Hoboken, NJ: 2000).

payment of funds to the company, which it may keep in perpetuity, unless it chooses to buy back the stock. There may also be conversion options, so that a shareholder can convert the preferred stock to common stock in some predetermined proportion. This type of stock is attractive to those companies that do not want to dilute earnings per share with additional common stock, and that also do not want to incur the burden of principal repayments. Though there is an obligation to pay shareholders the stated interest rate, it is usually possible to delay payment if the funds are not available, though the interest will accumulate and must be paid when cash is available.

The third and final component of the cost of capital is common stock. A company is not required to pay anything to its shareholders in exchange for the stock, which makes this the least risky form of funding available. Instead, shareholders rely on a combination of dividend payments, as authorized by the Board of Directors (and which are entirely at the option of the Board – authorization is not required by law), and appreciation in the value of the shares. However, since shareholders indirectly control the corporation through the Board of Directors, actions by management that depress the stock price or lead to a reduction in the dividend payment can lead to the firing of management by the Board of Directors. Also, since shareholders typically expect a high return on investment in exchange for their money, the actual cost of these funds is the highest of all the components of the cost of capital.

As will be discussed in the next two sections, the least expensive of the three forms of funding is debt, followed by preferred stock and common stock. The main reason for the differences between the costs of the three components is the impact of taxes on various kinds of interest payments. This is of particular concern when discussing debt, which is covered in the next section.

CALCULATING THE COST OF DEBT

This section covers the main factors to consider when calculating the cost of debt, and also notes how these factors must be incorporated into the final cost calculation. We also note how the net result of these calculations is a form of funding that is less expensive than the cost of equity, which is covered in the next section.

When calculating the cost of debt, it is important to remember that the interest expense is tax deductible. This means that the tax paid by the company is reduced by the tax rate multiplied by the interest expense. An example is shown in Exhibit 13.3, where we assume that $1,000,000 of debt has a basic interest rate of 9.5 percent, and the corporate tax rate is 35 percent.

The example clearly shows that the impact of taxes on the cost of debt significantly reduces the overall debt cost, thereby making this a most desirable form of funding.

$$\frac{(\text{Interest expense}) \times (1 - \text{tax rate})}{\text{Amount of debt}} = \text{Net after-tax interest expense}$$

Or,

$$\frac{\$95,000 \times (1 - .35)}{\$1,000,000} = \text{Net after-tax interest expense}$$

$$\frac{\$61,750}{\$1,000,000} = 6.175\%$$

EXHIBIT 13.3 CALCULATING THE INTEREST COST OF DEBT, NET OF TAXES

If a company is not currently turning a profit, and therefore not in a position to pay taxes, one may question whether or not the company should factor the impact of taxes into the interest calculation. The answer is still yes, because any net loss will carry forward to the next reporting period, when the company can offset future earnings against the accumulated loss to avoid paying taxes at that time. Thus, the reduction in interest costs caused by the tax deductibility of interest is still applicable even if a company is not currently in a position to pay income taxes.

Another issue is the cost of acquiring debt, and how this cost should be factored into the overall cost of debt calculation. When obtaining debt, either through a private placement or simply through a local bank, there are usually extra fees involved, which may include placement or brokerage fees, documentation fees, or the price of a bank audit. In the case of a private placement, the company may set a fixed percentage interest payment on the debt, but find that prospective borrowers will not purchase the debt instruments unless they can do so at a discount, thereby effectively increasing the interest rate they will earn on the debt. In both cases, the company is receiving less cash than initially expected, but must still pay out the same amount of interest expense. In effect, this raises the cost of the debt. To carry forward the example in Exhibits 13.3 through 13.4 , we assume that the interest payments are the same, but that brokerage fees were $25,000 and that the debt was sold at a 2% discount. The result is an increase in the actual interest rate.

When compared to the cost of equity that is discussed in the following section, it becomes apparent that debt is a much less expensive form of funding than equity. However, though it may be tempting to alter a company's capital structure to increase the proportion of debt, thereby reducing the overall cost of capital, there is a significant risk of being unable to make debt payments in the event of a reduction in cash flow, possibly resulting in bankruptcy.

CALCULATING THE COST OF EQUITY

This section shows how to calculate the cost of the two main forms of equity, which are preferred stock and common stock. These calculations, as well as those from the preceding section on the cost of debt, are then combined in the following section to determine the weighted cost of capital.

$$\frac{(\text{Interest expense}) \times (1 - \text{tax rate})}{(\text{Amount of debt}) - (\text{Fees}) - (\text{Discount on sale of debt})} = \text{Net after-tax interest expense}$$

Or,

$$\frac{\$95,000 \times (1 - .35)}{\$1,000,000} = \text{Net after-tax interest expense}$$

$$\frac{\$61,750}{\$955,000} = 6.466\%$$

Note: There can also be a premium on sale of debt instead of a discount, if investors are willing to pay extra for the interest rate offered. This usually occurs when the rate offered is higher than the current market rate, or if the risk of non-payment is so low that this is perceived as an extra benefit by investors.

EXHIBIT 13.4 CALCULATING THE INTEREST COST OF DEBT, NET OF TAXES, FEES, AND DISCOUNTS.

Preferred stock stands at a midway point between debt and common stock. It requires an interest payment to the holder of each share of preferred stock, but does not require repayment to the shareholder of the amount paid for each share. There are a few special cases where the terms underlying the issuance of a particular set of preferred shares will require an additional payment to shareholders if company earnings exceed a specified level, but this is a rare situation. Also, some preferred shares carry provisions that allow delayed interest payments to be cumulative, so that they must all be paid before dividends can be paid out to holders of common stock. The main feature shared by all kinds of preferred stock is that, under the tax laws, interest payments are treated as dividends instead of interest expense, which means that these payments are not tax deductible. This is a key issue, for it greatly increases the cost of funds for any company using this funding source. By way of comparison, if a company has a choice between issuing debt or preferred stock at the same rate, the difference in cost will be the tax savings on the debt. In the following example, a company issues $1,000,000 of debt and $1,000,000 of preferred stock, both at 9% interest rates, with an assumed 35% tax rate.

$$\text{Debt cost} = \text{Principal} \times (\text{Interest rate} \times (1 - \text{Tax rate}))$$
$$\text{Debt cost} = \$1,000,000 \times (9\% \times (1 - .35))$$
$$\$58,500 = \$1,000,000 \times (9\% \times .65)$$

If the same information is used to calculate the cost of payments using preferred stock, we have the following result:

$$\text{Preferred stock interest cost} = \text{Principal} \times \text{Interest rate}$$
$$\text{Preferred stock interest cost} = \$1,000,000 \times 9\%$$
$$\$90,000 = \$1,000,000 \times 9\%$$

The above example shows that the differential caused by the applicability of taxes to debt payments makes preferred stock a much more expensive alternative. This being the case, why does anyone use preferred stock? The main reason is that there is no requirement to repay the stockholder for the initial investment, whereas debt requires either a periodic or balloon payment of principal to eventually pay back the original amount. Companies can also eliminate the preferred stock interest payments if they include a convertibility feature into the stock agreement that allows for a conversion to common stock at some preset price point for the common stock. Thus, in cases where a company does not want to repay principal any time soon, but does not want to increase the amount of common shares outstanding, preferred stock provides a convenient, though expensive, alternative.

The most difficult cost of funding to calculate by far is common stock, because there is no preset payment from which to derive a cost. Instead, it appears to be free money, since investors hand over cash without any predetermined payment or even any expectation of having the company eventually pay them back for the stock. Unfortunately, the opposite is the case. Since holders of common stock have the most at risk (they are the last ones paid off in the event of bankruptcy), they are the ones who want the most in return. Any management team that ignores holders of its common stock and does nothing to give them a return on their investments will find that these people will either vote in a new board of directors that will find a new management team, or else they will sell off their shares at a loss to new investors, thereby driving down the value of the stock and opening up the company to the attentions of a corporate raider who will also remove the management team.

One way to determine the cost of common stock is to make a guess at the amount of future dividend payments to stockholders, and discount this stream of payments back into a net present value. The problem with this approach is that the amount of dividends paid out is problematic, since they are declared at the discretion of the board of directors. Also, there is no provision in this calculation for changes in the underlying value of the stock; for some companies that do not pay any dividends, this is the only way in which a stockholder will be compensated.

A better method is called the capital asset pricing model (CAPM). Without going into the very considerable theoretical detail behind this system, it essentially derives the cost of capital by determining the relative risk of holding the stock of a specific company as compared to a mix of all stocks in the market. This risk is composed of three elements. The first is the return that any investor can expect from a risk-free investment, which is usually defined as the return on a U.S. government security. The second element is the return from a set of securities considered to have an average level of risk. This can be the average return on a large "market basket" of stocks, such as the Standard & Poor's 500, the Dow Jones Industrials, or some other large cluster of stocks. The final element is a company's beta, which defines the amount by which a specific stock's returns vary from the returns of stocks with an average risk level. This information is provided by several of the major investment services, such as Value Line. A beta of 1.0 means that a specific stock is exactly as risky as the average stock, while a beta of 0.8 would represent a lower level of risk and a beta of 1.4 would be higher. When combined, this information yields the baseline return to be expected on any investment (the risk-free return), plus an added return that is based on the level of risk that an investor is assuming by purchasing a specific stock. This methodology is totally based on the assumption that the level of risk equates directly to the level of return, which a vast amount of additional research has determined to be a reasonably accurate way to determine the cost of equity capital. The main problem with this approach is that a company's beta will vary over time, since it may add or subtract subsidiaries that are more or less risky, resulting in an altered degree of risk. Because of the likelihood of change, one must regularly recompute the equity cost of capital to determine the most recent cost.

The calculation of the equity cost of capital using the CAPM methodology is relatively simple, once one has accumulated all the components of the equation. For example, if the risk-free cost of capital is 5%, the return on the Dow Jones Industrials is 12%, and ABC Company's beta is 1.5, the cost of equity for ABC Company would be:

Cost of equity capital = Risk-free return + Beta(Average stock return − Risk-free return)

Cost of equity capital = 5% + 1.5(12% − 5%)

Cost of equity capital = 5% + 1.5 × 7%

Cost of equity capital = 5% + 10.5%

Cost of equity capital = 15.5%

Though the example uses a rather high beta that increases the cost of the stock, it is evident that, far from being an inexpensive form of funding, common stock is actually the *most* expensive, given the size of returns that investors demand in exchange for putting their money at risk with a company. Accordingly, this form of funding should be used the most sparingly in order to keep the cost of capital at a lower level.

CALCULATING THE WEIGHTED COST OF CAPITAL

Now that we have derived the costs of debt, preferred stock, and common stock, it is time to assemble all three costs into a weighted cost of capital. This section is structured in an example format, showing the method by which the weighted cost of capital of the Canary Corporation is calculated. Following that, there is a short discussion of how the cost of capital can be used.

The chief financial officer of the Canary Corporation, Mr. Birdsong, is interested in determining the company's weighted cost of capital, to be used to ensure that projects have a sufficient return on investment, which will keep the company from going to seed. There are two debt offerings on the books. The first is $1,000,000 that was sold below par value, which garnered $980,000 in cash proceeds. The company must pay interest of 8.5% on this debt. The second is for $3,000,000 and was sold at par, but included legal fees of $25,000. The interest rate on this debt is 10%. There is also $2,500,000 of preferred stock on the books, which requires annual interest (or dividend) payments amounting to 9% of the amount contributed to the company by investors. Finally, there is $4,000,000 of common stock on the books. The risk-free rate of interest, as defined by the return on current U.S. government securities, is 6%, while the return expected from a typical market basket of related stocks is 12%. The company's beta is 1.2, and it currently pays income taxes at a marginal rate of 35%. What is the Canary Company's weighted cost of capital?

The method we will use is to separately compile the percentage cost of each form of funding, and then calculate the weighted cost of capital, based on the amount of funding and percentage cost of each of the above forms of funding. We begin with the first debt item, which was $1,000,000 of debt that was sold for $20,000 less than par value, at 8.5% debt. The marginal income tax rate is 35%. The calculation is as follows.

$$\text{Net after-tax interest percent} = \frac{((\text{Interest expense}) \times (1 - \text{Tax rate})) \times \text{Amount of debt}}{(\text{Amount of debt}) - (\text{Discount on sale of debt})}$$

$$\text{Net after-tax interest percent} = \frac{((8.5\%) \times (1 - .35)) \times \$1,000,000}{(\text{Amount of debt}) - (\text{Discount on sale of debt})}$$

$$\text{Net after-tax interest percent} = 5.638\%$$

We employ the same method for the second debt instrument, for which there is $3,000,000 of debt that was sold at par; $25,000 in legal fees were incurred to place the debt, which pays 10% interest. The marginal income tax rate remains at 35%. The calculation is as follows:

$$\text{Net after-tax interest percent} = \frac{((\text{Interest expense}) \times (1 - \text{Tax rate})) \times \text{Amount of debt}}{(\text{Amount of debt}) - (\text{Legal expenses})}$$

$$\text{Net after-tax interest percent} = \frac{((10\%) \times (1 - .35)) \times \$3,000,000}{(\$3,000,000) - (\$25,000)}$$

$$\text{Net after-tax interest percent} = 7.091\%$$

Having completed the interest expense for the two debt offerings, we move on to the cost of the preferred stock. As noted above, there is $2,500,000 of preferred stock on the books, with an interest rate of 9%. The marginal corporate income tax does not apply, since the interest payments are treated like dividends, and are not deductible. The calculation is the simplest of all, for the answer is 9%, since there is no income tax to confuse the issue.

To arrive at the cost of equity capital, we take from the example a return on risk-free securities of 6%, a return of 12% that is expected from a typical market basket of related stocks, and a beta of 1.2. We then plug this information into the following formula to arrive at the cost of equity capital:

Cost of equity capital = Risk-free return + Beta(Average stock return − Risk-free return)

Cost of equity capital = 6% + 1.2(12% − 6%)

Cost of equity capital = 13.2%

Now that we know the cost of each type of funding, we can construct a table such as the one shown in Exhibit 13.5 that lists the amount of each type of funding and its related cost, which we can quickly sum to arrive at a weighted cost of capital.

When combined into the weighted average calculation shown in Exhibit 13.5, we see that the weighted cost of capital is 9.75%. Though there is some considerably less expensive debt on the books, the majority of the funding is comprised of more expensive common and preferred stock, which drives up the overall cost of capital.

DIVIDEND POLICY

Dividend policy is a factor to be considered in the management of shareholders' equity in that:

- Cash dividends paid are the largest recurring charge against retained earnings for most U.S. corporations.
- The amount of dividends paid, which reduces the amount of equity remaining, will have an impact on the amount of long-term debt that can be prudently issued in view of the long-term debt to equity ratio that usually governs financing.
- Dividend payout is an influence on the reception of new stock issues.
- Dividend policy is an element in most loan and credit agreements—with restrictions on how much may be paid.

To Pay or Not to Pay Cash Dividends?

If a company has discontinued cash dividends, for whatever reason, or if a corporation has never paid a cash dividend, then most readers would appreciate the desirability of discussing whether cash dividends should be paid. However, even if cash dividends are now being disbursed, the question should be considered.

Some companies do not pay cash dividends on the basis that they can earn a higher rate of return on reinvested earnings than can a shareholder by directly investing in new purchases of stock. This may or may not be true. It should be recognized that one purpose of sound financial management is to maximize the return to the shareholder over the longer period. Therefore, this is the criterion: In the company involved, will it serve to increase

Type of Funding	Amount of Funding	Percentage Cost	Dollar Cost
Debt number 1	$980,000	5.638%	$55,252
Debt number 2	2,975,000	7.091%	210,957
Preferred stock	2,500,000	9.000%	225,000
Common stock	4,000,000	13.200%	528,000
Totals	$10,455,000	9.75%	$1,019,209

EXHIBIT 13.5 WEIGHTED COST OF CAPITAL CALCULATION

the long-term return to the shareholder by paying a dividend? This question is asked in the context that the return to the common shareholder consists of two parts: (1) the dividend and (2) the appreciation in the price of the security. The financial management of the firm should consider the type of investor attracted to the stock and the expectation of the investors. The examination of the actions of other companies and the opinion of knowledgeable investment bankers may be helpful. In general, the ability to invest all the earnings at an acceptable rate of return is not a convincing reason to pay no dividend. After all, a dividend is here and now, and future growth is more problematical. Probably, other than in the case of a highly speculative situation or a company in severe financial difficulty, some case dividend should be paid. This decision, however, is judgmental.

Dividend payments are determined by a number of influences, including:

- The need for additional capital for expansion or other reasons
- Cash flow of the enterprise
- Industry practice
- Shareholders' expectations

The amount to be paid may be calculated in one of two ways: (1) by the dividend payout ratio or (2) as a percentage of beginning net worth each year.

The most common practice is to measure dividends as a percentage of earnings. This payout ratio is determined as:

$$= \frac{\text{Annual dividends paid to common shareholders}}{\text{Annual earnings available for common shareholders (after preferred dividends)}}$$

In this example, the payout ratio of 25% is calculated in this fashion:

$$\text{Payout ratio} = \frac{\$12,500,000}{\$50,000,000}$$
$$= 0.25 = 25\%$$

Another way of calculating dividends, although less common than the payout method, is as a percentage of beginning net worth (book value attributable to common shares). The procedure is:

$$\text{Dividend payment ratio} = \frac{\begin{array}{c}\text{Annual dividends paid}\\ \text{to common shareholders}\end{array}}{\begin{array}{c}\text{Beginning common shareholder book}\\ \text{value (or retained earnings)}\end{array}}$$

$$= \frac{\$12,500,000}{\$156,250,000}$$
$$= 0.08 = 8\%$$

It has been suggested that a primary profit goal of an enterprise should be a specified rate of return on shareholders' equity. If this is accepted as a primary planning tool, then there is a certain logic that could justify using this same base (shareholders' equity) for the calculation of dividend payments—at least for internal planning purposes. Moreover, because earnings do fluctuate, there is an added stabilizing influence if dividends are based on book value. Also, as long as shareholders' equity is increasing and dividends are a constant rate of beginning net worth, then dividends would increase, the dividend payout ratio would drop, and the retention share of earnings would increase.

Dividend payment practices send a message to the financial community, and investors and analysts accept the pattern as an indication of future payments. Hence, when a dividend payment rate is set, a dividend reduction should be avoided if at all possible.

Dividend payment patterns may follow any one of several, such as:

- A constant or regular quarterly payment
- A constant pattern with regularly recurring increases—perhaps the same quarter each year
- A constant pattern with irregular increases
- A constant pattern with period extras so as to avoid committing to regular increases

In planning, any erratic pattern should be avoided.

LONG-TERM DEBT RATIOS

The subject of debt capacity is discussed in Chapter 12. However, the management of shareholders' equity must always keep debt relationships in mind when planning future financing, whether they be debt or equity.

There are two principal ratios used by rating agencies and the financial marketplace in judging the debt worthiness (or the value of equity) of an enterprise:

1. Ratio of long-term debt to equity.
2. Ratio of long-term debt to total capitalization.

The first ratio is calculated as:

$$\text{Long-term debt to equity} = \frac{\text{Long-term debt}}{\text{Shareholders equity}}$$

It compares the investment of the long-term creditors to that of the owners'. Generally, a ratio of greater than 1 is an indication of excessive debt. However, a company ratio should be compared to others in the industry (the leaders) or to industry averages, such as those published by Dun & Bradstreet, Inc.

The second ratio is calculated in this fashion:

$$\text{Long-term debt to total capitalization} = \frac{\text{Long-term debt}}{\text{Total capitalization (including long-term debts)}}$$

Again, a ratio of greater than 50%, as a rule of thumb, reflects excessive use of debt. Comparisons should be made with selected industry members (judged to be prudent business people) and industry averages.

OTHER TRANSACTIONS AFFECTING SHAREHOLDERS' EQUITY

In the management of shareholders' equity, any actions that are expected to impact this element of the financial statements should be reflected in the plans—the annual plan or the long-range plan, as may be appropriate. While earnings and dividends have been discussed, there are a host of other transactions that might be involved, including:

- Repurchase of common shares
- Conversion of preferred shares or convertible debentures
- Dividend reinvestment programs
- Exercise of stock options

- New issues of shares
- Special write-offs or adjustments

Before approving any such actions or agreements on such matters, the management should consider their impact on debt capacity, especially where debt ratios already are high.

LONG-TERM EQUITY PLANNING

For those entities with a practical financial planning system, the long-term planning sequence might be something like this:

- The company financial management has determined, or determines, what is an acceptable capital structure and gets the agreement of management and the board of directors.
- As a step in the long-range financial planning, the amount of funds required in excess of those available is determined by year, in an approximate amount.
- Based on the needs over several years, the desired capital structure, the relative cost of each segment of capital (debt or equity), the cost of each debt issue, and any constraints imposed by credit agreements, or the judgment of management, the long-term fund requirements are allocated between long-term debt and equity.
- For the annual business plan, any actions deemed necessary in the first year of the long-range plan are incorporated with the other usual annual transactions to form the equity budget for the year.

This is another way of saying that, ordinarily, the needs of additional equity capital are known some time in advance. They can be planned to take advantage of propitious market conditions, under generally acceptable terms, with the result that the cost of capital is usually competitive.

Normally, good planning will let management know well in advance the amount and timing of the requirements; it is not a sudden discovery. And the company continues to move toward its desired optimum capital structure.

Allocating Long-Term Funds between Debt and Equity

Now, let us provide some illustrations of these points. Assume that the company management has agreed with the recommendation of the chief financial officer (CFO), concurred in by the controller, and that the capital structure should be:

Segment	Preferred Structure	Minimally Acceptable Structure
Long-term debt	20.0%	25.0%
Shareholders' equity	80.0%	75.0%
Total	100.0%	100.0%

Moreover, at the end of the current year (20XX) the capital structure is expected to be (unacceptable):

Long-term debt	31.5%
Shareholders' equity	68.5%
Total	100.0%

THE JOHNSON COMPANY
FUND REQUIREMENTS
LONG-RANGE PLAN
(DOLLARS IN MILLIONS)

Item	Current Year (Estimated)	Plan Year					Total
		1	2	3	4	5	
Funds Required							
Working capital	$ 25	$ 30	$ 36	$ 42	$ 55	$ 30	$193
Long-term debt repayment	12	12	12	12	12	15	63
Fixed assets	15	14	40	50	15	40	159
Dividends	8	9	10	12	14	15	60
Total	$ 60	$ 65	$ 98	$116	$ 96	$100	$475
Internally Generated Funds							
Net income	$ 40	$ 45	$ 50	$ 60	$ 70	$ 75	$300
Depreciation	10	12	20	25	28	31	116
Total	$ 50	$ 57	$ 70	$ 85	$ 98	$106	$416
Funds required (excess)	$ 10	$ 8	$ 28	31	$ (2)	$ (6)	$ 59
Cumulative funds required (net)	$ 10	$ 8	$ 36	$ 67	$ 65	$ 59	

EXHIBIT 13.6   LONG-TERM FUND REQUIREMENTS

In the process of completing the strategic planning cycle and the related long-range financial plan, the required long-term funds, without designation as to type or source, are estimated to be $67 million in three years, as reflected in Exhibit 13.6, for a program of substantial growth. Furthermore, after a slight hesitation in plan years 4 and 5, management thinks the cycle is to repeat again.

Now, here, are some comments looking to the year-by-year review for allocation purposes between long-term debt and equity:

- *General.* Since the cost of equity capital is highest, and issuance of new equity tends to dilute earnings, equity capital should generally be used sparingly—only to maintain the borrowing base and to reach and remain at the desired capital structure.

- *Current year.* At the end of the current year, equity will provide only 68.5% of capital (Exhibit 13.7)—as compared to management's target of 80% and a minimally acceptable level of 75%. Obviously, the debt share of capitalization is too high.

- *Plan year 20X1.* Given the start of an acceleration in annual earnings, management decides to hold the dividend payout ratio to 20%, and to borrow the needed $8 million under the term loan agreement (interest rate of 15%). The equity share of capitalization, even so, will increase from 68.5% to 72%.

- *Plan year 20X2.* With $28 million in new funds required, the company decides, in view of the heavy investment in fixed assets and a lower borrowing rate available (12%), to issue a new mortgage bond. Some of the funds will be "taken down" or received this plan year and the balance in the next year. Despite the high level of borrowing, the equity share remains at 72%. The management decides it can "live with" such a level for a temporary period, given the high level of income.

- *Plan year 20X3.* The balance of the new mortgage bond proceeds covers the requirements with no reduction in the equity share of capitalization.

- *Plan year 20X4.* With the net income now at a level of $70 million, and a proposal by an insurance company to provide new funds through a new mortgage bond, management decides to (a) accept this new loan of $58 million and (b) pay off the more expensive term loan. Given the continued high level of earnings, equity capital at year end will provide 76% of the capitalization. This is within the minimally acceptable standard used by the company.

- *Plan year 20X5.* In this last year of the five-year long-range plan, management believes the growth cycle is ready to start again. Without going through the complete long-range planning cycle again, it asks the financial vice president to estimate fund requirements for two more years—the "contingency" years. This quick review discloses that another $50 million will be needed in 20X6, with *possibly* a limited amount required also in 20X7. Accordingly, to raise the equity capitalization to the desired 80% level (20X6 borrowings considered) and to provide the needed equity base for the 20X6 borrowings and expansion in future years, it plans for an issue of $50 million in equity funds.

THE JOHNSON COMPANY
ALLOCATION OF LONG-TERM FUNDS
BETWEEN DEBT AND EQUITY FOR THE PLAN
YEARS 20X1 THROUGH 20X5, AND CONTINGENCY YEARS 20X6 AND 20X7
(DOLLARS IN MILLIONS)

Year/Item	Beginning Balance	Net Income	Dividends	New Equity Offering	Ending Balance	Year-end Percentage of Capitalization
Shareholders' Equity						
Current year	$ 260	$ 40	$ 8	$ —	$ 292	68.5%
Plan years		20				
20X1	292	45	9	—	328	72.0
20X2	328	50	10	—	368	72.0
20X3	368	60	12	—	416	72.0
20X4	416	70	14	—	472	76.0
20X5	472	75	15	50	582	81.0
Contingency years						
20X6	582	80	16	—	646	80.0
20X7	646	85	17	—	714	83.0

	Beginning Balance	Debt Repayments	New Funds	Ending Balance	
Long-term debt					
Current year—estimate	$ 100	$ 10	$—	$ 90	
Term loan	46	2	—	44	
Mortgage bonds—present	146	12	—	134	31.5

EXHIBIT 13.7   LONG-TERM FUND ALLOCATION

	Beginning Balance	Debt Repayments	New Funds	Ending Balance	
Plan years					
20X1					
Term loan	90	10	8	88	
Mortgage bond—present	44	2	—	42	
	134	12	8	130	28.0
20X2					
Term loan	88	10	—	78	
Mortgage bond—present	42	2		40	
Mortgage bond—new	—	—	28	28	
	130	12	28	146	28.0
20X3					
Term loan	78	10	—	68	
Mortgage bond—present	40	2	—	38	
Mortgage bond—new	28		31	59	
	146	12	31	165	28.0
20X4					
Term loan	68	68		—	
Mortgage bond—present	38	2		36	
Mortgage bond—new	59	—	58	117	
	165	70	58	153	24.0
20X5					
Mortgage bond—present	36	13	—	23	
Mortgage bond—new	117	2	—	115	
	153	15		138	19.0
Contingency Years					
20X6					
Mortgage bond—present	23	13	—	10	
Mortgage bond—new	115	10	—	105	
Debenture—new			50	50	
	138	23	$50	165	20.0
20X7					
Mortgage bond—present	10	10		—	
Mortgage bond—new	105	10		95	
Debenture	50	—		50	
	$165	$20		$145	17.0

Note: The sum of the equity capitalization share at year end and that of long-term debt equals 100%.

EXHIBIT 13.7 LONG-TERM FUND ALLOCATION *(CONTINUED)*

The management and board of directors feel comfortable with the increased equity base both in the event of a downturn in business for a limited period, or should it need to borrow additional funds.

The summary of the planned debt reduction, new indebtedness to be incurred, shareholders' equity, and capitalization percentages is given in Exhibit 13.8. These planned capitalization changes also will be reflected in the statements of planned financial position for the years ended December 31, 20X1 through 20X5.

Other Suggestions in Managing the Capital Structure

The "Long-Term Equity Planning" Section provides guidance in allocating required funds annually between debt and equity. The disposition depends on the urgency of attaining a given preferred capital structure, or meeting debt indenture constraints, or other limitations. But managing the capital structure involves more than allocating the new capital needs between debt and equity. It also includes watching for signals that funding problems are slowly (or faster) developing, as well as providing safeguards against unwarranted action by the suppliers of funds.

A few of the steps that might be taken by financial management to avoid being caught off guard could include:

- *Be sensitive to those product lines which provide the highest return on capital as compared to those that consume or require relatively heavy amounts of capital, and produce a low rate of return.*

Thus, if a small share of the products requires, say, 70% of the new capital needs, and provides at least 70% of the return on capital, then the situation seems satisfactory. If, however, the products consuming 70% of the capital supply but a small return, then the matter requires careful monitoring. Perhaps a hurdle rate is needed by product line, or geographic area, or other factor. Then, careful estimates of requirements, by year, and expected return, by year, are made. Finally, actual performance then should be monitored to see if the expected increasing yields are forthcoming. Conservatism is required in predicting the capital requirements as well as the yield.

- *Continuously monitor the equity markets in an effort to judge when new equity should be acquired.*

    There are several stock market indicators to be followed which provide clues on the strength of the market, whether the market is overvalued, and whether new capital stock may be sold without diluting earnings. Included are:

    o The Standard & Poor's (S&P) 500 price earnings ratio, as well as the price/earnings ratio of the company stock.

    o The S&P 500 dividend yield and the yield of the company security.

    o Price-to-book ratio. Typically the price of a stock is considerably higher than its book value. One major reason is inflation, since book value understates the replacement cost of the underlying assets. Since about 1950, the S&P Industrials index has moved in a wide band defined in market bottoms as one times book value, and 2.5 times book value near market tops.

    So, this ratio may be a signal as to whether the market is overvalued. This price-to-book measure sometimes is less significant than others due to the influence of large stock buy-back programs, corporate restructuring, or merger frenzy.

    o The market breadth. Changes in the Dow Jones average versus the S&P 500 or the Nasdaq index.

The Johnson Company
Planned Changes in Capital Structure Plan
Years 20X1 Through 20X5
(DOLLARS IN MILLIONS)

Item	Interest Rate	Beginning Balance 1/1/X1		Increase (Decrease)					Ending Balance 12/31/X5	
		Amount	Percentage	20X1	20X2	20X3	20X4	20X5	Amount	Percentage
Long-Term Debt										
Term loan (existing)	15%	$ 90	⎰	$ (10) 8	$ (10)	$ (10)	$ (68)		$ —	—
Mortgage bond (existing)	14%	44	⎱	(2)	(2)	(2)	(2)	$(13)	23(a)	
Mortgage bond (new)	12%	—			28			(2)	26	
Mortgage bond (new)	11.5%	—				31	58		89	
Total		134	31.5%	(4)	16	19	(12)	(15)	138	19.0%
Shareholders' Equity										
Beginning balance		292							292	
Net income		—		45	50	60	70	75	300	
Dividends		—		(9)	(10)	(12)	(14)	(15)	(60)	
Net issue		—						50	50	
Subtotal		292	68.5%	36	40	48	56	110	582	81.0%
Total		$ 426	100.0%	$ 32	$ 56	$ 67	$ 44	$ 95	720	100.0%

Note: (a) To be paid off in 20X6—$13 million; 20X7—$10 million.

EXHIBIT 13.8 SUMMARY OF PLANNED CHANGES IN CAPITAL STRUCTURE

The relative trading volume. A high volume of, say, more than 200 million shares traded is said to be the sign of a strong market. Such factors, as well as the advice of investment bankers, may aid management in deciding on the approximate timing of a new stock issue.

- *Be careful in the search for the lowest cost sources of capital.*

  Not only must the cost be competitive, but the method and terms should be acceptable. Thus, in a private placement, perhaps the provisions should include a buy-back option to avoid the creation of a major voting block. Or maybe the acquisition of a cash-heavy source (existing cash balances and high cash flow) may be feasible.

- *Periodically check the cost of carrying current assets versus the return.*

  Must a switch be made from asset intensive activities to low-cost service type business?

- *Analyze existing investment in assets for sales candidates or improved utilization possibilities.*

  Strategic planning implies more than calculating the changes in each asset category each year, based on expected operations and existing turnover rates. It requires an analysis of turnover to see where improvements can be made (e.g., use of just-in-time [JIT] inventory methods) or idle assets, such as land which may be sold.

- *Relate predictable seasonal asset investment patterns, or cyclical ones, to incentives so as to reduce capital requirements.*

  Customers can be given special terms for early orders or early payment. Or, if an economic upturn is anticipated, this knowledge can be used to an advantage in inducing earlier-than-usual orders.

Proper strategic planning should look beyond operational expectations to wise asset usage (and prudent use of supplier credits).

SHORT-TERM PLAN FOR SHAREHOLDERS' EQUITY

In terms of management of shareholders' equity, the emphasis should be on planning—especially long-term planning so as to achieve the proper capital structure and use it as the basis for prudent borrowing. Additionally, the many other aspects already discussed need to be reviewed, and policies and practices developed or continued that will enhance the shareholders' value.

Having said this, the annual business plan for the next year or two should reflect all anticipated near-term actions that impinge on the equity section or on the financial statements. When completed, that section of the plan relating to shareholders' equity may be summarized as in Exhibit 13.9.

OTHER CONSIDERATIONS
Dividend Reinvestment Programs

A supplementary facet of dividend policy is the question of offering a dividend reinvestment plan to investors. Under such a plan, shareholders may invest their cash dividends in the common stock of the company—sometimes at market price, usually with no brokerage fee, and sometimes at a discount, that is, 5% of the market price. Many dividend investment marketing plans utilize shares purchased in the open market. Others permit the issue of original shares directly by the company.

Dividend investment plans have now been expanded to permit the purchase of additional shares over and above the dividend amount with cash payments—sometimes with a ceiling on such quarterly or annual purchases, say, of $5 million. Also, some companies permit the preferred shareholders or bond holders to purchase common shares with the quarterly or semiannual dividend or interest payments.

THE JONES COMPANY
STATEMENT OF PLANNED CHANGES IN SHAREHOLDERS' EQUITY
FOR THE PLAN YEAR 20XX
(DOLLARS IN THOUSANDS)

Month	Beginning Balance	Estimated Net Income	Dividend Payments	Purchase of Treasury Shares (a)	Estimated Dividend Reinvestments	Estimated Options Exercised	Ending Balance
January	$ 158,500	$ 2,650		$ 1,000			$ 160,150
February	160,150	2,410		1,000		$ 500	162,060
March	162,060	2,790	$ 1,720		$ 80		163,210
April	163,210	2,840					166,050
May	166,050	2,620		1,200		500	167,970
June	167,970	2,530	1,620		100		168,980
July	168,980	2,600		1,000			170,580
August	170,580	2,860				500	173,940
September	173,940	2,820	1,620		100		175,240
October	175,240	2,770		1,000			177,010
November	177,010	2,710				700	180,420
December	180,420	2,800	1,520		100		181,800
Total	$ 158,500	$ 32,400	$ 6,480	$ 5,200	$ 380	$ 2,200	$ 181,800

Note: (a) Board to be asked to authorize 130,000 shares at average price of $40 per share.

EXHIBIT 13.9 BUDGET FOR SHAREHOLDERS' EQUITY

Financial officers should consider such a practice. The costs of operating the program versus the probable level of participation (based on industry experience, etc.) should be weighed. Trustees who handle such plans for other corporations, competitors or otherwise, may be helpful sources of information.

Stock Dividends and Stock Splits

This chapter is not intended to be a treatise on the types of stocks that may be issued or their advantages or disadvantages, and the many related subjects. However, the controller should be aware of the accounting treatment of stock dividends as well as stock splits and the arguments for and against the issuance of such designated shares.

Basically, the New York Stock Exchange has ruled that the issuance of 25% or less of stock is a stock dividend and that the issuance of more than 25% is a stock split. Both are essentially paper transactions that do not change the total equity of the company but do increase the number of pieces or shares. However, depending on state law, the accounting treatment may differ. Thus a stock split may not change retained earnings; only the par or stated value is changed. A stock dividend may cause the paid-in-capital accounts and retained earnings to be modified (but not the *total* equity).

The controller should be aware of the pros and cons, the expense involved, and the procedure for issuance of dividends, or splits, or reverse splits.

Repurchase of Common Shares

Another subject to be considered by the financial management is the repurchase of common shares. Conceptually, a company is enfranchised to invest capital in the production of goods or services. Hence it should not knowingly invest in projects that will not provide a sufficiently high rate of return to adequately compensate the investors for the risk assumed. In other words, the enterprise should not invest simply because funds or capital are available. Business management should identify sufficiently profitable projects that are consistent with corporate strategy, determine the capital required, and make the investment. Hence shareholders might interpret the purchase of common stock as the lack of available investment opportunities. To some, the purchase of company stock is not an "investment" but a return of capital. It is "disfinancing."

Some legitimate reasons for the purchase of common stock are:

- Shares may be needed for stock options or employee stock purchase plans, but the management does not wish to increase the total shares outstanding.
- Shares are required in the exercise of outstanding warrants or for the conversion of outstanding convertibles, without issuing "new" shares.
- Shares are needed for a corporate acquisition.

Some guidelines to be heeded in considering a decision to repurchase shares are:

- If a company is excessively leveraged, it might do well to use cash to pay down existing long-term debt to reach the capital structure goal it envisages and not repurchase common shares.
- The management should examine its cash requirements for a reasonable time into the future, including fixed asset requirements, project financing (working capital) needs, and other investment options, before it concludes that excess cash is available and that the equity capital genuinely is in excess of the apparent long-term demands.

- The cash dividend policy should be examined to see that it helps increase the market price of the stock.
- Only after such a review, should the conclusion be reached to dispose of "excess equity" through the purchase of the company stock.

Given these conditions, timing may be important. Thus, if the market price of the stock is below book value, the purchase of shares in fact increases the book value of the remaining shares. It might be prudent to purchase shares below book value rather than at a price that dilutes the shareholders' equity.

Capital Stock Records

An administrative concern in the management of shareholders' equity relates to the maintenance of necessary capital stock records. In the larger companies, the stock ledgers and transfer records are kept by the transfer agent. The information relative to payment of dividends on outstanding shares, for example, is secured from this source. Quite often, the database is contained on computer files, and any number of sortings can produce relevant data regarding ownership:

- Geographic dispersion
- Nature of owners (individual, institution, etc.)
- History and timing of purchases
- Market price activity
- Volume of sales and the like

Under these circumstances, a ledger control account for each class of stock is all that is maintained by the company.

If a corporation conducts its own transfer department, then a separate account must be maintained for each stockholder regarding each class of stock. An illustrative simple form is shown in Exhibit 13.10. The ledger might contain:

- Name and address of holder with provision for address change
- Date of changes in holdings
- Certificate numbers issued and surrendered
- Number of shares in each transaction
- Total number of shares held

NAME AND ADDRESS COMMON			JOHN C. DOE 4161 MAXWELL ST. TOLEDO, OHIO 43612				
			Certificate No.		No. of Shares		
Old Balance	Date	Page	Dr.	Cr.	Dr.	Cr.	New Balance
	Dec. 12, 20XX	20		C 122		100	100
100	Jan. 16, 20X1	31		C 196		50	150
150	Nov. 17, 20X1	110	C 321		100		50

EXHIBIT 13.10 CAPITAL STOCK LEDGER SHEET

Optional information might include a record of dividend payments and the data mentioned above for the computer files.

The stock ledgers should be supported by registration and transfer records that give the details of each transaction. Transfer journals are not required in all states. In circumstances that justify it economically, computer applications may be desirable.

Finally, of course, sufficient records must be maintained to satisfy the reporting needs of the federal and state government—foreign holdings, large holdings, and so on.

The management, of course, has an interest in monitoring, perhaps monthly, large holdings and the changes therein. Such a review may provide signals about possible take-over attempts and the like. For this purpose, as well as soliciting proxies, the services of outside consultants, such as Georgeson & Co., that specialize in such matters, may be used.

INDEX